Roy C. Shelton

The Young Hölderlin

German Studies in America

Edited by Heinrich Meyer

No. 10

Roy C. Shelton

The Young Hölderlin

Herbert Lang & Co. Ltd.
Bern and Frankfurt/M.
1973

The Young Hölderlin

by

Roy C. Shelton

Herbert Lang & Co. Ltd.
Bern and Frankfurt/M.
1973

ISBN 3 261 00315 4

© Herbert Lang & Co. Ltd., Bern (Switzerland)
Peter Lang Ltd., Frankfurt/M. (West-Germany)
1973. All rights reserved.

Printed by Lang Druck Ltd., Liebefeld/Berne (Switzerland)

CONTENTS

A New Picture of Hölderlin
By Heinrich Meyer

A good many years ago, when Professor Shelton was my student, he chose as his seminar topic the Letters of Hölderlin. I suggested that he look into the strangely static formulae which the boy and young man Hölderlin used when writing to his family and even to his friends. For the lack of warmth and natural attachment to others seemed strange in a young man who would later become one of the greatest poets in the German language. Roy Shelton seemed eminently qualified for the investigation because he was a realistic American, outstanding intellectually, sensible, and attached to an equally sound and intelligent girl, and had not come under the influence of the George or Hellingrath mythology which seems to be the prerequisite of almost every German interpretation. The fact that Hölderlin was a boy, a student, a brother, a friend whom nobody would take for anything else but a boy, a student, a brother, a friend is lost to those who interpret him as if he had been from the outset a genius wrestling with the Gods. Shelton was not likely to mythologize about Gods, Genius and Fate, but promised to see what the facts were. The seminar paper turned out so informative that he simply had to develop it further till it grew into his dissertation. It was perhaps the best I have ever had the pleasure to direct, for it gave, as it seemed to me and the rest of the committee, the first true and non-fictional picture of Hölderlin as he appeared to others and to himself.

With this start it became almost inevitable that this new insight into the life should be applied toward an understanding of the poems as well. While the letters are not poetical, whatever wilful mythologizers may assert, and while they certainly were understood by the recipients in the same way as other letters they received, they nevertheless were the works of a writer or a poet and thus no doubt more than ordinary letters of average people. How can a poet-to-be help being something of a poet and a person who stylizes his life poetically long before he fully realizes his poetic capacities? Goethe, another lyric poet and in this respect similarly condemned to autistic verbalisation, analysed such experiences and interpreted them as "Anticipation". The poet anticipates in his imagination what he is going to be later. But how does this work when the young man is not only going to be a poet, but is loaded down with an hereditary weight that manifests itself so early, so steadily in autistic withdrawals, self-effacement, self-affirmation, and which showed all along those "Schübe" of which the psychiatrists used to write when they discussed the progressive manifestation of schizophrenia? The letters do, of course, show this process clearly enough. But what do the poems tell us?

It is here that Shelton has made one discovery after the other. Not being subject to the influence of *Germanisten,* critics, and mythologizers in the

German literary tradition, he was not inclined, let alone impelled, to evaluate anything in terms of Hölderlin's final achievement. He could read each poem as it stood and was meant at its time. It appears that nobody, really nobody, had seriously undertaken such a reading of Hölderlin's poems before Shelton. To be sure, there were those who were or meant to be objective, notably Böhm, who did not care much for the mythological Hölderlin, but they distorted the picture in another direction. Not being fully aware of Hölderlin's troubles all along, perhaps too dense, too healthy, too simple to understand so sensitive and abnormal a boy, they made everything seem rather average if not outright banal. The idea of the "Stiftlerphilosophie", for example, is a good indicator of this attempt to normalize Hölderlin and to overrate the companionship of the healthy gogetters Schelling and Hegel. At any rate, Shelton did not come under anyone's influence, he did not have any master to please, he could look at the sources and see what they would yield. This he has done.

The result is the first Hölderlin biography that is free from modern conceptualizations and back-interpretations. It is a biography of the young boy and man in terms of all the sources. Shelton has no axe to grind, he does not depend on the opinion of other Hölderlin students, he is free and wants to remain free from all bias. It does not matter to him whether Hölderlin was inclined one way or another, whether he was sick or well, whether he wrote prose or verse, whether he was miserable or happy. Those who "care about" such matters run the risk of identifying themselves with Hölderlin, of "feeling themselves into" him and thereby making themselves over into what they imagine Hölderlin to have been. The outcome is the Georgian or Hellingrathian projection of a seer and poet who cannot be seen as he was, but only as he wanted to be. But such poetifications overlook the simple fact that Hölderlin suffered from schizophrenia and that the outbreak of madness is not a matter of a moment, but the result of a life-time of suffering and even self-inflicted hurt for which a genetic capacity was given from the beginning.

Shelton accepts reality and tells us what he found. This is what I would call the ideal biography. It is not a false and weak distortion like the pitiable book of Michel which strikes many as a truly Hölderlinian work, but a true, a real biography. Shelton analysed every word and paid no attention to secondary sources. He has read hundreds of books and papers, but what he used was in the end only the works of Hölderlin himself and the other primary sources, letters by Hölderlin and other documents by his contemporaries. Thus he cites Vietor's edition of the Diotima letters, the edition of Beissner and Beck, and, for the parts not yet published there, the Hellingrath volume in question. He also cites Goethe, Schiller, Schubart and the others whom Hölderlin read and imitated. There is no arguing with those who want to have "their" Hölderlin, be it the presently fashionable "Revolutionary" or any other partial presentation. They need not be contraverted anyhow. These fashions are in the habit of changing very quickly when the propagandists have made their rounds among the universities that pay for visiting lecturers. Shelton does not offer "his" Hölderlin to oppose previous interpretations. He simply offers the one and only Hölderlin whom the facts, *all* the facts taken together, reveal to us. I am happy to have this distinguished book in our series, and I am confident that it will revolutionize Hölderlin studies. At any rate, nobody can overlook it in the future if he wants to know *what* Hölderlin was.

The form of the book is entirely dependent on the sources. Since all sources had to be used impartially, the amount of material must determine what can be analysed. On the other hand, not all issues are obvious. Many have to be found through careful analysis of Hölderlin's readings and writings and thus presuppose already to some extent the insight which the biographer obtains gradually into the whole person. This necessitates frequent looking ahead and going back again in time.

It will be interesting to see what the true scholars in the field, those who have worked with the sources and who know all the material and therefore can also assay the gaps in our knowledge without feeling the urge to fill them with fancies, in other words those whose opinion matters, especially Beck and Beissner, will say to this book. To me who am not a Hölderlin expert it has opened up many new prospects. The supercilious masters of "immanente Interpretation", that outdated remainder from the long past days of the New Criticism which, like so much else that had its day elsewhere, became rejuvenated in Germany when Germany began to discover what had happened elsewhere during the years of Hitler and World War II, these hindsight experts will probably continue to declare for a while longer that only the works matter. Yet, those who want to understand the works of Hölderlin will have to know his life. Else such foolishness as that of Heidegger will be the outcome.

Needless to say, facts cannot possibly damage a work, and no fact that entered into Hölderlin's life and work can deprecate the poetical powers he attained. These remain astonishing even, yes, even the more so, when one realizes that behind them stood this shrinking sufferer who tried not to hurt others and yet had to do just this in order to become the poet *he knew he had to be.* As few have looked into the poems of the young Hölderlin, I would call their attention to just one single fact that needs further investigation, perhaps a study along linguistic and philological lines: How was it possible for the young imitator of Schubart and then of Klopstock, whose imitations sound somewhat awkward and naively childish, next to adopt with almost parodistic assurance the meters, rhythms, weighted rhymes and the very diction of Schiller's rhetoric, and then come forth with that tone of his own which we recognize immediately as truly and solely Hölderlin's? The Hölderlinian quality, the minor key, the drooping elegiac sadness, the hopelessness and the sense of fated inevitability, that quality which everyone can hear immediately when he looks at "Trennen wollten wir uns . . . .", is so distinct from the boyish imitations and the touching attempt to conform to Schillerian diction when, at heart, Hölderlin could not help knowing that he was a truer poet than his temporary idol and guide Schiller, that one wonders whether the emerging realization of his own failure in life, the gradual awakening to the discovery of his failures as a person, was not itself a spur for his poetry and the source and substance as well as the form of his emerging great poems.

Shelton gives enough suggestions and shows the connection between life and work sufficiently to enable others to continue where he has left off. His study will surely help many to see the real Hölderlin, not a figment such as Hölderlin himself may have made out of his life, to hold on to when life became insufferable. Not to confuse such deviation from normal behavior with poetry as such is the first essential of objective investigation. Roy Shelton never confused facts with fictions and therefore could give the Facts which explain the Fictions.

Do you know that I am now forced to
celebrate the anniversary of my own
sensations, the anniversary of that
which was so precious to me, but
which never really was?

Dostoyevsky,
White Nights

INTRODUCTION

The following is a study of Friedrich Hölderlin's life up to his mysterious
departure from Jena in June 1795. It was undertaken in the belief that much
new could be learned through an objective study of the existing biographical
documents. Hölderlin scholarship to date, with its traditional emphasis on the
formalistic aspects of the late poems, the "historical significance" of Hölderlin's
philosophic contributions in *Hyperion, Empedokles,* and the fragmentary essays,
and the relationship of his works to twentieth-century schools of thought, has
not yet fully investigated two areas of inquiry which are fundamental to all the
rest.

The first of these two questions, formulated most simply, is: Who was
Friedrich Hölderlin? It is strange that, despite the many thousands of pages
devoted to Hölderlin since he was "discovered" by Norbert von Hellingrath in
1910, we have as yet no reliable understanding of the man himself. His
personality, the way in which he perceived and reacted to his environment, and
the influence of his perceptions on his poetry are areas of study and concern
which have been all too often papered-over by clichés. This is partially because
most of the work on Hölderlin has been carried on in the twentieth century,
which has shown more interest in speculatively surmised "meaning" than in
objective fact. More important, however, the whole mythological quality of
Hölderlin studies, deriving from Hellingrath and Bettina von Arnim before him,
has supplied us with a whole warehouse of cheap clichés, such as "poet-
prophet," that quasi-religious type who is supposed to have been commissioned
by "the gods" to deliver a message to man in poems so dense that only
professors of German literature can understand them. So reverent an attitude
precludes objective or disinterested evaluation and thus leads to a subjective
appreciation of both the poems and the life of the poet. Wilhelm Michel's *Das
Leben Friedrich Hölderlins* is a good example of the resulting pseudo-biography
in which everything is seen as necessarily leading up to the late poems. The
poems are the last word, the absolute truth; and the poet's life is nothing more
than the message of the poems, the message from "the gods," objectified in the
mundane stuff of earthly existence.

The second relatively unexplored area is found in the years of Hölderlin's life prior to 1795. This omission, of course, follows naturally from the above-mentioned preoccupation with the late poems. For, if they alone are important enough to merit close study, then one is justified in passing over the school years with a few summary remarks about how unoriginal Hölderlin's poetry was then and how, nevertheless, either this or that individual image would become important in later years. The problem is that those very years of unoriginal poetry were the formative years of the man; to ignore or slight Hölderlin's youth is to pass up the opportunity of watching him grow into the late Hölderlin by solidifying his perceptions of reality through contacts with other people and ideas.

This study is a frank attempt to reach an understanding of Hölderlin's development in human terms. We proceed from the belief that an artist's work is largely determined by his perception and interpretation of reality as he experiences it. We shall, therefore, investigate primarily his estimation of his own place among his fellow men so that we may trace the development of all the longings, dreams, loves, hates, resentments, aversions, and fears that found expression both in the way he lived and in the way he wrote poetry. Central to our study will be observations of the way in which he synthesized his experience and his reactions to it into a self-image; for when one is dealing with a lyric poet, the image of self, the quality of the poet's self-awareness, is of critical importance. But, since he lived before he wrote poetry and formed his ideas about himself through his contacts with other people, we shall conduct much of our investigation in distinctly non-literary terms. We shall concentrate on his relationships with his family members and friends, teachers and acquaintances, sweethearts and boyhood heroes. We shall, in a word, try to discern how he saw himself and how he perceived human life in reality, before he transformed his perceptions into the idealized images and the oblique language of his poetry.

When we discuss his poems we shall treat them as documents in the development of his personality. This will not, of course, tell us anything about the artistic merit of his work; but it will tell us why he wrote his poetry in the first place, why he so desperately wanted to be a poet, and what inner needs his poetry fulfilled. Most important of all, we may be able to discover by what internalization process he transformed those personal feelings, which had their origins in real life, into art. If we succeed in that, then we shall have gone a long way toward answering the question: Why did this man write this particular poetry? And that is — or should be — the goal of all biographers of literary figures.

In keeping with my aim of objectivity, I have quoted almost exclusively from original sources. The most important reservoir of material is the Stuttgart Edition of Hölderlin's *Sämtliche Werke* under the editorship of Friedrich

Beissner, particularly volumes VI and VII of letters and documents, edited by Adolph Beck. Volume VII, which contains almost all of the original documents pertaining to the period treated in this book, appeared after my work was well underway. While a few sections had to be rewritten, the new and more detailed information contained in the latest volume by Beck both strengthened my conclusions and made reliance on older, less reliable, editions no longer necessary.

This is not a study of Hölderlin scholarship, but a study of the young Hölderlin — a subject about which previous works have had little to say. I have, consequently, devoted the notes at the end of the book almost solely to citations from original sources. I have made exceptions only in those few cases where specific passages in secondary literature are commented on.

Finally, since much had to be reproduced *verbatim,* overcoming the language barrier was a major problem. Quotations in prose appear in English in the text. The notes will direct the German-reader to the original. The poems were more troublesome. They appear only in German. I originally intended to supply a prose approximation of each poem in the notes. But what resulted was always unsatisfactory and too often misleading. The meaning of the discussions, however, depends on the reader's ability to read German only in a few chapters; and, since there, as much depends on the tone as on the meaning, translations would not help much.

This book is possible only because Friedrich Beissner, Adolph Beck and their co-workers have provided in the *Stuttgarter Ausgabe* not just a critical edition but perhaps a more reliable and complete repository of data about Hölderlin's life and work than exists for any other German author. I should also like to express my sincere appreciation to the Faculty Research Committee of Middle Tennessee State University for the generous grant which has made the publication of this work possible.

In a more personal vein, I wish to express my appreciation to Professor Heinrich Meyer of Vanderbilt University for his interest in me personally and in the progress of this book. Much of whatever value this book has is due to his understanding criticism of both the dissertation from which the present work grew and of the manuscript itself. Its shortcomings, however, are mine.

Murfreesboro, Tennessee   Roy Shelton

1.

FAMILY AND CHILDHOOD

In 1799 Hölderlin looked back over his life and tried to discover why, at age twenty-nine, he felt himself slipping into an ever deepening depression — a forerunner of the long night of insanity in which he would spend more than half of his life. From Homburg, where he had been living with Isaac von Sinclair since he had left the Gontard house in Frankfurt, he wrote his mother: "It was not you, dearest Mother, who gave me this inclination toward melancholy, from which I now, of course, cannot quite free myself. I see fairly clearly over my entire life, almost all the way back into my earliest childhood, and know quite well when my spirit began to bend this way. You will hardly believe it, but I remember all too well. When my second father died, whose love is still so unforgettable to me; when, with inconceivable anguish, I was made to feel like an orphan and had to look each day upon your sorrow — then my soul fell prey to this seriousness, which, of course, with the passing years, could only increase."[1]

Johann Christian Friedrich Hölderlin was born on 20 March 1770 in Lauffen, a small Swabian village on the Neckar River. His father, Heinrich Friedrich Hölderlin, was a *Klosterhofmeister,* a minor official representing the Consistory seated in Stuttgart who was entrusted with the financial management of the lands surrounding a former Benedictine nunnery dating from the tenth century. Thirty-four year old Heinrich Hölderlin lived in one of the small secondary buildings with his twenty-two year old bride Johanna, née Haym. In 1770 the house in which Hölderlin was born was one of the few structures in the complex that were still serviceable; the rest had fallen into disrepair during the centuries of disuse since the Duchy of Württemberg had gone Protestant.

---

[1] 180.31ff.

The following principles have been adopted for citing references in the works referred to most frequently.

Citations from Hölderlin's works are from *Sämtliche Werke*(Große Stuttgarter Ausgabe), edited by Friedrich Beissner. (8 vols.; Stuttgart: W. Kohlhammer Verlag, 1944ff.). This edition is indicated only by a volume number followed by a part number (if applicable) and the page number.

"Hellingrath Edition" refers to *Hölderlin. Sämtliche Werke,* edited by Norbert von Hellingrath and continued by Ludwig Pigenot and Friedrich Seebass (6 vols.; Berlin: Propyläen Verlag, 1913—1923).

For Hölderlin's letters Volume VI of the Beissner Edition was used exclusively. Citations are indicated through the letter number and line number separated by a period.

Both Heinrich's and Johanna's families consisted chiefly of churchmen. Heinrich's father, Friedrich Jakob Hölderlin (1703–1762), had also been *Klosterhofmeister* in Lauffen. His grandfather, Hans Conrad (1672–1719), had been a Church administrator. His great-grandfather Alexander (1637–1705) had been a pastor at Grüntal. At least two earlier Hölderlins had served as *Bürgermeister* in Nürtingen. Johanna's line shows the same professional affiliation.[2] Both the Hölderlins and the Hayms were related several times over to other clerical families. It was from these families that almost all of the poets and intellectual leaders of the next century would spring – along with a tendency toward mental disorders.[3] The Hölderlins had married into the Hun family three times within the last hundred years before the poet's birth. Mental disorders were not uncommon, particularly in the male line. As late as 1909 a student descended from one branch of the family was admitted to the clinic at Tübingen because he was suffering from a disorder closely resembling Hölderlin's.[4] On Johanna's side there was a tendency toward depression and melancholy. Johanna herself inherited more than her share of these characteristics.

Hölderlin never knew his real father, for Heinrich died when Fritz, as Hölderlin's parents called him, was two years old.[5] Six weeks later Johanna bore a daughter whom she named Heinrike, perhaps in honor of her dead husband. In 1799 Hölderlin thanked his mother for her assurances about his father's character. "What a good and noble man!" he wrote. "Believe me, I have often thought of how cheerful he always was and how I would like to be like him."[6] But this may have been mostly conjecture, prompted by bits of conversation among older family members that he overheard. Mingled with that may have been the half-remembered, half-imagined figure of the smiling father bending over the cradle or watching the first faltering steps of his first-born.

The only father that Hölderlin ever knew was *Bürgermeister* Gok of Nürtingen, a friend of Heinrich Hölderlin, whom Johanna married in 1774. When Hölderlin was four years old Gok moved his new family onto a small piece of

---

2 VII, I, p. 263. Hölderlin's maternal great-grandmother, Johanna Judith Sutor, was a descendant of Regina Bardili-Burckhardt, to whom many Swabian poets and thinkers were related.

3 See Wilhelm Lange, *Hölderlin. Eine Pathographie* (Stuttgart, 1909) and Ernst Kretschmer, *The Psychology of Men of Genius* (New York, 1931). In 1787 Johann Friedrich Blum, the future son-in-law of Hölderlin's father's sister, referred in his diary to his fiancee's "inherently gloomy spirit – her unabating stubornness and the . . . inhereted melancholy – which cost the lives of her grandparents and parents on both sides, and which has killed all her close relatives" (VII, I, p. 268).

4 Wilhelm Böhm, *Hölderlin* (Halle, 1928–1930), Vol. II, p. 673.

5 The cause of death was a stroke, which, like mental disorders, appears frequently in the family history (VII, I, p. 267).

6 180.29ff.

land that he had recently inherited.[7] The next five years were the happiest of Hölderlin's entire life. In October 1776 Johanna gave birth to Karl Gok, the only member of the family circle who would outlive his half-brother. The sister, who was called Rike by the family, married young and was widowed before she was thirty, thus following in her mother's footsteps. Later she too sank into a condition of extreme melancholy.[8]

When he later longed for relief from tension and yet felt that he too was slipping into a period of depression, Hölderlin thought of his childhood, which meant to him a time of carefree innocence and sinless irresponsibility that he could never recapture. In his poetry he would relate childhood to his vision of the "Verjüngung" (revitalization) of the whole world. He also wrote specifically of his own childhood as that care-free time of his life before he had fallen prey to the storms of self-doubt, timidity, self-pity at the thought that he alone suffered because he was denied normal social intercourse, and shame because he repeatedly disappointed those he loved. In 1797, as he sat at the feet of Susette Gontard, he wrote:

> In jüngern Tagen war ich des Morgens froh,
>> Des Abends weint' ich; jezt, da ich älter bin,
>>> Beginn ich zweifelnd meinen Tag, doch
>>> Heilig und heiter ist mir sein Ende.[9]

His childhood paradise lasted only five years. The stepfather he had loved so dearly died in 1779. He came to believe later that Gok's death had a profound effect on his developing temperament and expressed that belief in his poetry long before he admitted it to his mother. As early as 1786 he wrote:

> Ach als einst in unsre stille Hütte
> Furchtbarer! herab dein Todesengel kam,
> Und den jammernden, den flehenden aus ihrer Mitte
> Ewigteurer Vater! dich uns nahm;
> Als am schröklich stillen Sterbebette
> Meine Mutter sinnlos in dem Staube lag —
> Wehe! noch erblik ich sie, die Jammerstätte,
> Ewig schwebt vor mir der schwarze Sterbetag — [10]

When he visited the grave of the poet Thill in 1789 and wrote the poem "An Thill's Grab," he identified the dead poet and the graveside setting with the loss of his stepfather.

---

[7] Karl Gok indicated in his *Lebensabriß* that "concern for the education of her children" moved Johanna to marry Gok (VII, I, p. 673).
[8] VI, 2, p. 516.
[9] I,I, p. 246 (lines 1—4).
[10] I, I, p. 15 (lines 25—32).

Als ich ein schwacher stammelnder Knabe noch,
  O Vater! lieber Seeliger! dich verlohr,
    Da fühlt' ichs nicht, was du mir warst, doch
    Mißte dich bald der verlaßne Waise.[11]

It was not only Gok's death that remained forever locked in his memory, but also the effect of the sad event on his mother. In his poetry, just as in the letter quoted at the beginning of this chapter, the image of her in her hour of grief returned to haunt him again and again. If she was really as demonstrative of her grief as he portrayed her in his poem, the sight of her may well have terrified the children. The two younger children may have looked to their big brother Fritz for consolation. Throughout his life he demonstrated a deep concern for the well-being of his brother and sister, which was pathetic because it was ineffectual.[12] Most important, he was probably the only one of the children who really understood what was happening. Even then, when he was only nine years old, he may have wanted to reach out and console his mother but found that he was powerless to do so.

This is the earliest recognizably biographical image that appears in his poetry. He would mark the death of his "second father" as a great turning point in his life, as the point at which his self-doubt and sense of isolation from others began to plague him. He had had to watch the sad business from a distance; he had felt that he had a proper role to play but did not know how. He never would.

A normal boy would have outgrown the trauma. That Hölderlin did not was perhaps partly because Johanna seems never to have gotten over her grief either. She was now thirty-one years old and had three children to care for. Within eight years she had lost two husbands and a child that had been born one year after Hölderlin. We know from her letters that she was a pious woman who took her responsibilities to her children seriously. But she was morose. Only once would

---

11   I, 1, p. 83 (lines 5—8).

12   Throughout the years dealt with in this book, Hölderlin took a lively interest in Karl and tried to influence his intellectual development. In November 1790, when he learned that Karl was experiencing difficulties in composition, he suggested that they exchange essays (37.24ff.). In the single essay that Hölderlin sent Karl (which seems to have gone unanswered) he used the opportunity to show off his scholarship and the degree to which he had mastered scholarly language (38.12ff.). In August 1793 he began giving Karl advice about what he should be reading (No. 62). One month later he wrote the famous letter introducing Karl to his notion of philosophic friendship for the sake of "mankind" (No. 65). Throughout his stay in Waltershausen and particularly after his move to Jena, Hölderlin used his letters to Karl to introduce him to Fichte's philosophy (which he was not always careful separate from his own thoughts) (80.26ff. and Nos. 86 and 97). In the letters to both Karl and Rike, Hölderlin showed little interest in their real life other than through mere stereotype expressions of concern for their well-being. In this sense his letters to his brother and sister are strange in that they could well have been written to relatively close friends. Even the letters to Karl show interest only in the boy's *future* life.

her eldest son ever refer to her as cheerful.[13] Most of the time he tried to suppress any information that might have upset her or caused her worry. She was the prototype of the "good woman," the preacher's daughter who went through life with shoulders squared and jaws set, as if she were carrying a cross. She drew her strength from her religion and found justification for her retiring, yet stern, nature in the precepts of Pietism, which demanded relentless self-examination and prostration before the deity as the price of salvation. She admonished her children to "dulden," remain submissive, accept their lot, and endure whatever God meted out to them.[14]

In Hölderlin, who, as Charlotte von Kalb and Schiller recognized, needed to stop thinking about himself so much and examining his every thought and mood,[15] the immediate influence of his mother, who constantly directed his thoughts inward upon himself and later admonished him in tone, if not in words, to return to the religion of his fathers and to the profession for which God had intended him, could only wreak spiritual havoc.

There was never any doubt about his future. As the son of a churchman he could attend the theological seminary in Tübingen free of charge. He went to the *Lateinschule* in Nürtingen and was instructed there by the Precepter Kraz and the *Diakonus,* Nathaneal Köstlin. He was a good student. It was easy to teach him to appreciate the world of ideas and books and the value of knowledge. All these would stand him in good stead in his appointed profession.

The first poem that has been preserved dates from the year 1784. It is a

---

13   Even that reference is indirect. He wrote on 10 July 1797 that she should occupy her mind with reading because otherwise her mind would "make work and worry for itself due to its natural vivacity" (141.26ff.).

14   The tragedy which arose from the simple woman's inability to understand her son make life easier for him can be seen in her letters to Sinclair and to Hölderlin in 1804 and 1805. On 27 August 1804, although Hölderlin was in no way responsible for his actions by then, she wrote to Sinclair: "Dear Hölderlin is still keeping me waiting for a letter from him, which I can hardly explain to myself, since he took leave of me with such tender sentiments and promised to write me soon" (Hellingrath Edition, VI, pp. 367ff.). She could not help her son. Lacking understanding of his condition, she inadvertantly reverted to the kind of admonishments that she had always used in her well-intentioned, but misguided efforts to get him to pull himself together. On 29 October 1805 she wrote to him: "I entreat you particularly not to neglect your duties to our dear God and Father in heaven. We can achieve no greater joy on earth than standing in the grace of God. We will strive for this with all seriousness so that we will be together there where there will be no separation any more" (*Ibid.,* p. 372).

15   In January 1795 Charlotte von Kalb was particularly anxious for Hölderlin to find acceptance in Jena. She wrote Schiller: "You and Fichte attract him" (VI, 2, p. 714) and tried to convince Frau Gok to make it possible for him to stay in Jena rather than having to take another job as *Hofmeister* (VI, 2, p. 715).

Schiller wrote Goethe on 30 June 1797: "His [Hölderlin's] situation is hazardous, since such characters are so hard to reach." He continued: "I would not give him up if only I know how it might be possible to get him out of his own society and make him susceptible to a beneficial and lasting influence from without."

fourteen-year-old's poem of thanks to his teachers as he prepared to leave the *Lateinschule.* He referred to his studies as "the joyous path" *(die frohe Bahn).* He wished his teachers glory and honor. Already he seems to have been developing an exaggerated respect for learned men. He saw in his studies the promise of a fulfilling life, which, at that early age, he still considered perfectly compatible with service to the Pietist God. This appreciation of knowledge and of the rewards that education promised would stay with him. But, within a few years, his ideas about what education should be and what he should set as the proper goals of his study would be radically altered.[16] Now, however, he seemed perfectly contented with the idea of studying in the Church schools and becoming a minister. In the poem "An M.G.," which dates from about the same time, he was already practicing fire-and-brimstone sermons.

Only one motif, in his poem of thanks to his teachers, suggests the later Hölderlin, and that only as a prelude.

> Froh eilt der Wanderer, durch dunkle Wälder,
> Durch Wüsten, die von Hize glühn,
> Erblikt er nur von fern des Lands beglükte Felder,
> Wo Ruh' und Friede blühn.[17]

This image would also reappear, but it too would undergo a dramatic change. Here the hardships that beset the wanderer struggling toward his goal of peace and security are the same that plague any young man setting out into life. There is no indication that the goal is not entry into the profession that his mother, stepfather, and probably his real father had planned for him. Later the image of the wanderer would be used to symbolize something quite different. For he would find in the next few years that the hardships along his path were greater than those which plagued his friends and classmates; and he would soon discover that his goal was not at all compatible with his mother's plans for his life. His goal would soon become other-worldly, mythological, idealistic, unreal.[18]

But, in a deeper sense, the goal would remain the same. He already knew intuitively that "Ruh und Friede" (peace and quiet) were the things that he longed for most of all — the yearned-for goal of all his strivings. He may, of course, have only been repeating the words he had heard in church or at school. Later he would express his longing for peace with a frantic intensity — and mean it.

---

16 Hölderlin tried to leave school in the spring of 1787 and again near the end of 1789. Already in April 1789 he had admitted at least indirectly to his mother that he was determined to become a poet when he told her of his visit to Schubart (26.19ff.). In June 1791 he admitted that he no longer considered marriage and "a peaceful parsonage" a real possibility (45.14ff.).

17 I, 1, p. 11 (lines 5—8).

18 See the discussion of his letter to Karl Gok in the late summer 1793 at the beginning of Chapter 11.

Froh kehrt der Schiffer heim an den stillen Strom
Von fernen Inseln, wo er geerndtet hat;
    Wohl möcht' auch ich zur Heimath wieder;
      Aber was hab' ich, wie Laid, geerndtet? —

Ihr holden Ufer, die ihr mich auferzogt,
    Stillt ihr der Liebe Laiden? ach! gebt ihr mir,
      Ihr Wälder meiner Kindheit, wann ich
        Komme, die Ruhe noch Einmal wieder? [19]

Up until his fourteenth year, while he could still play in the forests and along the banks of the Neckar with his half-brother Karl, he looked forward to school and never doubted that personal fulfillment would come when he achieved his professional goal. The wanderer existed only in his mind, as a poetic decoration or as the kind of self-glorification to which all imaginative boys are inclined. That he might someday be a wanderer himself, excluded from the rewards of real life, would never have occurred to him then. Both feet seemed firmly planted in life. He knew who he was and where he was going. He accepted it all as a matter of course.

Then, in the autumn of 1784, he took the two-hour walk to Denkendorf. There in the *Niedere Klosterschule* he began the semi-monastic life of a student, which would last for the next nine years. During those years something went wrong.

---

[19] I, 1, p. 252 (lines 1—8).

2

DENKENDORF AND MAULBRONN: FIRST REFLECTIONS

"Since I have returned to Nürtingen, several observations have made me wonder how it is possible to reconcile cleverness in one's behavior, sociability, and religion. I have never seemed to be able to do it; I always vacillated back and forth. Sometimes I had good impulses, which probably resulted from my natural sensitivity and which were therefore all the more transitory. It is true, I would think, now I am an upright Christian, everything was at peace within me, and particularly nature would, in such moments (for this peace seldom lasted much longer than that), make an extraordinarily vivid impression on my heart; but I could not endure having anyone around me, always wanted to be alone, and seemed, as it were, to despise mankind; and the slightest difficulty would drive me to despair, and then I became all the more frivolous. If I tried to be clever, then my heart became spiteful, and the slightest insult seemed to convince it of how very evil men were, how very devilish, how much one had to be wary of them, and how one had to avoid the slightest intimacy with them; if, on the other hand, I tried to counteract this misanthropy, then I found that I was taking pains to please men but not God. You see, my dear Helper, in this way I vacillated back and forth always, and whatever I did overshot the mark of moderation."[1]

Hölderlin was almost sixteen years old and had been at the *Niedere Klosterschule* in Denkendorf for fifteen months when he wrote the first letter that has been preserved of his correspondence to Nathanael Köstlin, the *Diakonus* — the "Helper" — of the congregation at Nürtingen and one of the teachers to whom he had written the poem of thanks more than a year before. The letter is significant because it gives evidence that, at age sixteen, Hölderlin was already suffering from ambivalent social attitudes, which fluctuated between normal need for companionship and hypersensitive, suspicious, slightly condescending attitudes toward others.

The Cloister School at Denkendorf was situated in a town of 1000 people. It was directed by the Prelate Erbe, a man of seventy who exercised rigid control over school curriculum and discipline.[2] The daily routine of the school

---

[1] 1.8ff.

[2] Rudolf Magenau wrote about life in the school, in which he enrolled in 1782: "How frightened I was when, for the first time, I heard the slipping of the bolt which held us imprisoned from morning until night, with the exception of one hour in the day. How frightened I was when I first heard the voice of the Prelate threatening us with expulsion and terrible incarceration! What a feeling welled up in me when I saw this same man eavesdropping with pricked-up ears at my comrades' room! Avarice — often carried to the basest extremes, underhandedness, and shamelessness were the chief traits of his

resembled that of a monastic order. From five o'clock in the morning until eight in the evening activities were rigidly prescribed. Fifty-nine and one-half hours each week were set aside for instruction and study. Only one-third of that time was actually spent in class; the rest was supposed to be used for study and meditation. This emphasis on meditation and self-appraisal was characteristic of the Pietism of the Duchy. It demanded that the student, at age fourteen, lay aside all childishness and adopt the sorrowful, self-deprecating piety that was felt to be proper for a clergyman. The student's activities were thus designed to suppress all the frivolity and playfulness that we now recognize as requisite to healthy development. Only two hours each day – one each after the midday and evening meals – were left free for recreation. On application, one might receive permission to take a one-hour walk each week. But even the little free time that the student was allowed was of little use to him. Play was forbidden. One was supposed to be thoughtful, serious, reflective, and pious; that meant that one was expected to spend one's free time walking about and discussing serious topics with classmates. Rough play was strictly forbidden. Joking, laughing – even smiling – were frowned upon.[3]

Such unnatural restrictions on normal boyhood activity would radically affect the growth of a normal boy. For Hölderlin it could only be disastrous because he found it impossible to take part in all the minor revolts through which unusually restricted boys relieve tension.[4] It has become almost a cliché to trace Schiller's development back to his experiences in the *Karlsschule* and to point out that *Die Räuber* might never have been written had Schiller not been tyrannized by Karl Eugen personally. Schiller's first drama was not only important in the development of the German drama; it was also a vehicle of escape for Schiller and his classmates. It was an experience in comradeship. The students could do nothing to combat overtly the oppression of the Duke and his hand-picked teachers; and so they gathered secretly after hours and took vicarious pleasure in listening to the rantings of Karl Moor in praise of Brutus, the classical assassin of tyranny. Much of what was rumored to be conspiratorial activities in the theological seminary in Tübingen during Hölderlin's time was probably no more serious than other minor revolts in which generations of students had indulged.[5] Karl Eugen took it seriously only because he was

character. ... To pounce upon the young collection of his pupils with the zeal of Hildebrand* was his greatest joy. To keep them in continual, slavish awe his foremost amusement. Often he suddenly broke into a cell and scolded and bellowed without knowing what he wanted to scold and bellow about. If he found anyone playing chess or dominoes, then one could obtain forgiveness and pardon only with a page-long *Carmine deprecatorio*" (VII, 1, pp. 332). *Beck notes that "Hildebrand" refers to Pope Gregory VII, the opponent of Heinrich IV *(Ibid.).*

3 Wilhelm Michel, *Das Leben Friedrich Hölderlins* (Bremen, 1949), pp. 17ff.

4 Beck remarks that Hölderlin received punishment only rarely in Denkendorf and then only for mild infractions (VII, 1, p. 332).

5 VII, 1, p. 450.

infected by the wave of panic that swept like a plague over the nobility throughout Europe in the wake of the French Revolution. The revolts of German youth remained most often a rebellion on paper. The revolutionary fervor of Schelling and Hegel were sublimated in their philosophizing after they emerged from the schools and entered into real life; their philosophies soon became accepted parts of the curriculum at state schools in Prussia and elsewhere.

But, if the revolutionary fervor of the students in the Duchy had no immediate political influence, such sentiments provided a safety valve for the release of tension. Boys who were united in their resentment could make insulting remarks about the Duke or the school authorities and feel like revolutionaries. They were oppressed, but they took heart and were able, through commiseration, to weather those trying years.

Hölderlin was different. He knew it before his sixteenth birthday. In his first letter to Köstlin the boy put his finger squarely on the personal weakness that would plague him all his life, which made it impossible for him to find relief from the pressures of school through sharing his resentments and hardships with his fellow sufferers. It was not only that he felt oppressed by the school authorities, from whom he had probably expected the same tender treatment that he had received from Köstlin back in the *Lateinschule*. He was also cut off from the other students. He wanted to be a good Christian and took seriously his duties both to his Church and to his God. But his single-minded adherence to the Christian's code of behavior isolated him from his friends. Why should it have been so? Were the other boys not Christians also? Were they not also the future officers of God's Church in the Duchy? Was he really among such miserable sinners that normal relationships with the other students and service to God were incompatible?

Hölderlin seems to have thought so, for he referred to his classmates in words that a preacher might have used to characterize the blackest sinner: "evil," "devilish"; "one must be wary of them ... one had to avoid the slightest intimacy with them."[6] When he tried to act otherwise, he found that he was pleasing men but not God. He promised that he would make a new start, but he betrayed his real feelings in the last part of the letter. He wrote: "And just today I looked back upon my behavior toward God and men up to now, and I have made a decision to become a Christian and not a vacillating dreamer, pleasant to men, without adopting their truly sinful habits."[7]

This letter is the first record of his self-awareness. It was an awareness of being miserable and yet painfully different from all the other miserable boys. He was not the good boy he would have liked to be; and yet he could not solve his

[6] 1.23ff.
[7] 1.29ff.

dilemma by being like the others because his sensitivity told him that they were coarse, callous, sinful. And so he could not endure having others around him; he wanted to be alone.

In the same month, November 1785, he wrote the poem "Die Nacht," which begins:

> Seyd gegrüßt, ihr zufluchtsvolle Schatten,
> Ihr Fluren, die ihr einsam um mich ruht;
> Du stiller Mond, du hörst, nicht wie Verläumder lauren,
> Mein Herz, entzükt von deinem Perlenglanz.
>
> Aus der Welt, wo tolle Thoren spotten,
> Um leere Schattenbilder sich bemühn,
> Flieht der zu euch, der nicht das schimmernde Getümmel,
> Der eitlen Welt, nein! nur die Tugend liebt.[8]

At about the same time he wrote the poem "An M.B." The initials have traditionally been interpreted to mean "Mein Bilfinger," which would mean that the poem was written to one of his classmates. Recently it has become clear that the poem may not have been intended for Bilfinger at all.[9] He could have written it to his half-brother Karl. Particularly the lines

> O lächle fröhlich unschuldsvolle Freuden,
> Ja, muntrer Knabe, freue dich,
> Und unbekümmert, gleich dem Lamm auf Frühlings-Haiden,
> Entwikeln deine Kräfte sich[10]

sound as if he intended the poem for someone younger than he, perhaps someone not yet subjected to the hardships of school life. This impression is supported by the last four stanzas.

> Nicht Sorgen und kein Heer von Leidenschafften
> Strömt über deine Seele hin;
> Du sahst noch nicht, wie tolle Thoren neidisch gafften,
> Wann sie die Tugend sehen blühn.
>
> Dich sucht noch nicht des kühnen Lästrers Zunge:
> Erst lobt sie, doch ihr Schlangengifft
> Verwandelt bald das Lob, das sie so glänzend sunge
> In Tadel, welcher tödtlich trifft.

---

8 I, 1, p. 3 (lines 1—8).
9 I, 2, p. 5.
10 I, 1, p. 5 (lines 1—4).

Du glaubst mir nicht, daß diese schöne Erde
So viele unzufriedne trägt,
Daß nicht der Welt, der dich der Schöpfer gab, Beschwerde,
Nur eigner Kummer Seufzen regt.

So folge ihr, du edle gute Seele,
Wohin dich nur die Tugend treibt,
Sprich; Welt! kein leerer Schatten ists, das ich mir wähle,
Nur Weisheit, die mir ewig bleibt.[11]

It may well be that he was writing to his brother who not only had, as yet, no knowledge of school life and its hardships, but also had not yet entered into the troubled period of puberty nor encountered the "army of passions" which would soon "pour over thy soul." The tone of the poem anticipates the letters which, in later years, Hölderlin would write to Karl; for in them he would also be quite free with advice about how Karl should live his life and would often adopt a learned tone in an effort to display his knowledge of life and learning.[12]

Yet still, whoever may have been in his mind when he wrote. "An M.B," there is an unmistakable thematic unity in the poem and the letter to his old teacher. With the awakening of his self-awareness, with his first reflections about himself and the world round about him, he found that he was alone in a world that he perceived to be distinctly hostile. He reacted in two ways: He reached out for consolation and companionship; and he began to verbalize his plight in poems. It does not matter that he expressed his thoughts in the language of the theology student, for such a vocabulary came naturally to a young man who still thought that he would one day become a preacher. It matters only that the sentiments expressed in the poem were the same ones that he expressed to Köstlin. He was compelled to give expression to his thoughts to another — and to himself.

In December 1785 he wrote his mother that he was busy with schoolwork, had plans for poems that he had to — and wanted to — write,[13] and was looking forward to seeing his family at Christmas. He had no money and was afraid he would not be able to afford gifts for Karl and Rike. We gain some initial insight into the relationship between mother and son when we read his request that she

---

[11] I, 1, p. 5 (lines 5—20).
[12] Passages which appear to me to have been calculated to impress Karl prior to Hölderlin's departure from Frankfurt include: 62.6ff.; 86.7ff.; 97.13ff.; 116.28ff.; 119.5ff.; 121.16ff.; 131.33ff.; and 133.13ff. I have not extended this list to include passages from letters written after Hölderlin's departure from Frankfurt because of the change in tone which his correspondence with Karl underwent, beginning before his departure. During the latter part of his sojourn at the Gontard house, his letters began to assume that intense, almost morbid quality of utter seriousness that characterize all of his letters from that point on.
[13] 2.2ff.

buy the gifts for him and deduct the amount from his inheritance.[14] He did not
mention that crisis of a month before, although it had been intense enough to
wring from him a plea for help to his teacher and two, as far as we know,
unprecedentedly personal poems, which differed drastically from the kind of
poetry he would normally have written in order to meet an assignment. His
hesitancy to reveal his doubts to his mother stands in marked contrast to the
letter to Köstlin, which he had begun with the words: "Your continuing
kindness and love for me and, in addition, your wise Christian life have
awakened in me such love and respect for you that, to speak quite openly, I can
look upon you only as my father."[15] He closed the letter with the words: "Be
my leader, my father, my friend."[16] We shall see that he was painfully aware
that he was a half-orphan and that the lack of a father's influence made it
difficult for him to relate to other men without circumscribing the relationship
with poetic embellishments. Even now we can see that important elements
needed for normal development were missing. He was correct when he said that
it was difficult for him to enjoy uninhibitedly the companionship of other boys.
He also could not be sure that his mother would understand his feelings.

Ten months later, in October 1786, he completed his studies at Denkendorf.
He ranked sixth in a class of twenty-nine.[17] From Denkendorf he would go on to
the more advanced *Klosterschule* at Maulbronn, and from there on to the *Stift*
(theological seminary) at Tübingen.

In 1558 the Cistercian monastery in Maulbronn had been converted into an
evangelical *Klosterschule*. When Hölderlin enrolled at age sixteen, he found life
less rigid than at Denkendorf. Here too only about nineteen hours each week
were devoted to instruction with much time left for individual study.
Restrictions on the students' activities were far less severe. Visits to town and
hikes in the countryside were permitted rather liberally. Students could visit and
form friendships within the better families of the town and visit the homes of
preachers in the surrounding villages. On the other hand, the student was rarely
left to his own devices. The "professor" who was on duty for the week was
constantly walking about through the rooms during the hours allotted to
individual study. The student's life was, by modern standards, still rather strictly
regulated. Even so, school discipline was much less severe and the opportunities
for social contacts far greater than they had been at Denkendorf. This fact is of
some importance; for, as we shall see, Hölderlin's letters from Maulbronn show
the same attitudes and the same spirit of isolation that we have seen in the letter

14   2.14ff.
15   1.3ff.
16   1.36ff.
17   VII, 1, p. 315.

to Köstlin. His inability to feel at ease with other students and to relate to them satisfactorily continued and, if anything, increased.[18]

There are wide variations in both the form and the contents of the letters from Maulbronn. How he wrote and what tone he adopted depended largely on the identity of the recipient. To his mother he wrote matter-of-factly; personal feelings either were not mentioned or were presented carefully. This type of calculation in his prose is almost completely lacking in the letters to Immanuel Nast, the nephew of both the Director and one of the *Famuli* at Maulbronn.[19] He did not live in Maulbronn but was a secretary at the *Rathaus* in Leonberg. He stands at the beginning of a long line of best friends to whom, throughout most of his life, Hölderlin would write letters of apparently unbridled self-expression. The letters to Nast are written in an irregular style in which the interjectory phrase plays a dominant role. So hastily, so feverishly were they composed that the sentence structure was fragmentary and the punctuation unsystematic. We shall investigate these letters in the next chapter to see what they reveal about the relationship between the two boys. Here we concentrate on Hölderlin's attitudes toward his classmates and the social world in general.

His first letter to Nast, which was probably written in January 1787, makes it all too clear that his ambivalent attitudes towards himself and others, which we noticed in the letter to Köstlin, were not passing fancies. He wrote: "It annoys me that my old moodiness still descends upon me."[20] A few weeks later he wrote: "You should not be surprised that with me everything is so garbled, so contradictory – I mean that I have a trait from my boyhood years, a part of my former heart – and that is still the dearest to me – it was a waxlike tenderness, and that is the reason why I, in certain moods, can weep over anything – but this part of my heart has been so badly mishandled while I have been in the Cloister – even the good, carefree Bilfinger can scold me for talking like a dreamer – and thus I also have the beginnings of a certain coarseness – so that I often get into a rage – rail out at my brother, without knowing why – when scarcely the appearance of an insult is there."[21] "My heart – it is so evil – I once had a better one – but they have taken it away from me."[22]

The idea that he had conflicting traits, tenderness and brutality, was a more

18 Magenau, who condemned Denkendorf for the narrow-mindedness of the administrators, thought that the administrators in Maulbronn, particularly the Prelate, were "all too liberal." The school offered "an open road" to dissipation, which resulted in "a great inclination to drink." The townspeople, according to Magenau, wanted the students' business, and so the student's money "overcame all obstacles," so that "nightly excursions had become the rule" and the "worst crimes" were ignored. In Maulbronn "many youths had found a grave for virtue" (VII, 1, p. 366).

19 VI, 2, pp. 492f.

20 3.10f.

21 4.8ff.

22 4.20ff.

candid expression of the dilemma of sociability versus godliness with which he had confronted Köstlin. But now something else becomes clear. He really saw himself as the victim, the true Christian who was being martyred by the cruel people with whom he lived. "They" were responsible for the coarseness that he was discovering within himself and of which he felt ashamed. His consciousness of being different had now gone one step further. He was better than others and he was suffering because of his goodness.

In January he wrote of his friend Bilfinger in the castigating tone of the school authorities, who had taught him that joy was sinful. "Bilfinger is probably my friend — but he is too happy to look out for me ... he is always happy — I am always hanging my head. ... I can tell you that I am the only one — who, except by name, knows not one girl, not one scribe — or anyone belonging to the social world of Maulbronn."[23] Then he expanded the indictment: "When Efferenn, Bilfinger, etc. — want to amuse themselves at a recital, they leave an empty place rather than call Hölderlin."[24]

In February he wrote in an even more despairing tone: "... why should I allow them to force my best intentions into the stockade and interpret my most innocent actions as crimes — oh that there are such evil men among my comrades, such miserable characters — if friendship did not make me good once in a while — then I should wish that I were anywhere else but in the company of men."[25] At times his lamentations sound almost like monologues, as if he were writing for himself and had forgotten Nast altogether. "If I could just once write something cheerful. But have patience! It will come — I hope — or — or — have I not borne enough? Did I not already as a boy experience things that would wring sighs from a grown man? And has it been better for me as a youth? And this is supposed to be the time when we have it best of all! My God! am I alone like this? Everyone happier than I? And what have I done? "[26]

It is unfortunate that only the letters to Nast have survived of all the letters that he must have written to his friends during this period of his life. It might be revealing to compare his self-appraisal and untempered outbursts in the letters to Nast to his letters to Bilfinger and Märklin. It would be particularly interesting to know whether he wrote similarly intimate letters to Bilfinger, whom he repeatedly accused of insensitivity when he was writing Nast.[27] Not because such letters to Bilfinger would indicate that Hölderlin was two-faced, but because it might be easier then to determine how much of his pathos was *Dichtung* and

23 4.25ff.
24 4.33ff.
25 5.6ff.
26 5.19ff.
27 Hölderlin was full of praise for Bilfinger in November 1787, when he told Nast how Bilfinger had renounced his interest in Luise, thus leaving the field open for Hölderlin's timid courting: "he renounced her voluntarily — for he had not spoken with her at all — and so our friendship came about" (15.94f.).

how much *Wahrheit*. The relation between the two boys was actually largely verbal. They seem to have met during the Christmas vacation, just a few weeks before Hölderlin suddenly began pouring out his heart to his new friend. Enthusiasm for literature seems to have been the only interest they had in common. Emotions about which Hölderlin had only read permeated his attitudes and often determined his reactions to real experience. Most important, his idea of Nast as the "friend of the poet" resulted from his reading. Without letters to other friends it is difficult to say where reality ended and literature began. The themes about which he wrote were sometimes grotesque. The above passage about everyone being happier than he was prompted by a toothache, which, in his young mind, was no less tragic than unrequited love and ostracisim from the company of his classmates. With unashamed seriousness he wrote about everything that happened to him, however trivial, as long as it was unfortunate and thus reenforced the poetic misery that, as he imagined, he suffered.

His adolescent lack of discretion about what subjects were really worthy of tragical interpretation vanished from his letters in later years. It is strange that this weakness persisted when he tried to construct a plot for a novel or a drama; for in both *Hyperion* and *Empedokles* he did not show much discretion in his treatment of external reality. He could not. Only the spiritual state of his protagonist was of any real importance.[28] The sensitivity, which seems so exaggerated in his early letters, is closely related to his creative process; even in his late poems the external event that sent his spirit soaring was, viewed objectively, often relatively inconsequential. His reactions to external stimuli were disproportionate to their importance. Later he suppressed the obvious childishness of his early letters, but there are indications that true maturation was lacking. A normal boy would not have reviewed the tragedy of his life merely because his tooth hurt. Similarly, a normal man would not have tried three times to construct a tragedy with almost no external action. But then, on the other hand, a normal man would not have looked out on a pond in which two swans were swimming side by side and then write the lines:

Mit gelben Birnen hänget
Und voll mit wilden Rosen
Das Land in den See,
Ihr holden Schwäne,
Und trunken von Küssen
Tunkt ihr das Haupt
Ins heilignüchterne Wasser.

28 Eduard Mörike first noted that weakness in a letter to Johannes Mährlen, dated 21 May 1832: "Finally the whole thing has the appearance of nothing but a touching caricature, nothing but individual, incomparably true and beautiful lyrics, timidly transferred onto a plot" (Eduard Mörike, *Briefe,* [Stuttgart, 1959], p. 328).

Weh mir, wo nehm' ich, wenn
Es Winter ist, die Blumen, und wo
Den Sonnenschein,
Und Schatten der Erde?
Die Mauern stehn
Sprachlos und kalt, im Winde
Klirren die Fahnen.[29]

"Die Mauern stehn sprachlos und kalt." Then too the walls of the school
stood as speechless and cold as the stockades into which his fellows forced his
"best intentions." And yet, for all his suffering, he did not mention his problems
to his mother until he had decided to break through those walls and quit school.
During the spring of 1787 he mustered up his courage. In the Easter vacation he
went home and asked his mother to let him leave the school. She must have been
surprised and hurt, for, after he had returned to Maulbronn for the resumption
of classes in April, he wrote her: "You may believe me now — that, except in the
quite extraordinary case in which my fortune would obviously be improved, the
thought of deserting my class will never enter my head. I see now that one can
be more useful to the world, that one can be happier, as a village preacher than if
one were — God knows what else."[30]

This was the first of only two letters to his mother which have been preserved
from his first year at Maulbronn. He repented of his wish to leave his profession,
but then, at the end of the letter, he wrote: "My hair is now in perfect order. I
have it in rolls again. And why? For your sake! For I am not interested in
pleasing anyone here."[31]

Then in late May or early June he wrote: "I again have a good deal of work
on my back, and work in which one's mental powers are severely put to task — I
mention only in passing that Bilfinger's coffee and my sugar are used up and that
I have often yearned for a breakfast — when I have gotten up early — and while I
have been suffering from these steady and severe headaches — and recently I
forced myself, with a terribly empty stomach, to eat some soup which your
hungriest laborer would not want to eat . . . ."[32] This passage is followed by the
apologetic: "You will laugh at this long-winded request [for coffee], but it was
only so that you might get some idea of what a cross we must bear in the
Cloister."[33] Then he launched into a detailed description of the frivolity of the
other students and the tyranny of the school administrators. He concluded:
"But so it goes in the world. I am learning, praise God! to adjust to it more and

29   II, 1, p. 117 (lines 1–14).
30   9.2ff.
31   9.18ff.
32   10.2ff.
33   10.13ff.

more. I can assure you, dear Mamma, that I, who have been the most discontent of people, am no longer one of the malcontents."[34]

Three years later he would write to her from Tübingen: "It is quite indescribable how much pressure the *Stipendium* is under";[35] and "– I can assure you that I would pass my days joyfully and would be content with my fate if only you, with your sadness, did not cause me so many dismal hours."[36] The latter passage also followed an apology for causing her concern. These few letters to his mother from 1787 anticipate, therefore, a curiously strained tone which runs through every letter he ever wrote her. He was excessively sensitive to her displeasure; his reactions to her moods were extreme, which would explain why he either avoided writing her altogether or, when that was no longer possible, kept his letters noncommittal, suppressing, as far as possible, any hint of his discontent. He seems to have tried consciously to avoid saying anything that she, as a good Christian mother, would have regarded as exaggerated, silly, or sinful. Only when circumstances made it necessary for him to let her know what he was thinking and seek her approval did he really try to communicate with her.[37] Often he met stubborn, practical resistance and the lack of understanding from her that he had feared all along. These he learned to expect, and in the ensuing years he came to dread them, which made frank communication even more difficult. Hence his repeated failures to let her know that things were not going well for him until he had decided to act on his own. Now, in 1787, he tried to tell her that he needed to get out of the oppressive school atmosphere; later he would tell her almost nothing of his problems until he had either actually lost his job or resigned. We, who can look back over all his letters with a foreknowledge of what happened in Waltershausen and Jena, Frankfurt and Homburg, can observe in each of these cases how he grew more agitated from month to month and how he tried, through hints and allusions, to prepare her for his next move, on the one hand, and yet avoid upsetting her, on the other. But his hints were often so subtle, he was always so careful not to commit himself prematurely and thus give her a chance to interfere with his plans, that his behavior probably seemed to her to be a series of impetuosities, consistent only in that they all served as excuses for not meeting his professional duties and his responsibilities

---

34   10.34ff.
35   33.7ff.
36   26.6ff.
37   This is particularly striking in his utter silence about his troubles with Fritz von Kalb until December, 1794, when he was sure that he would have to leave the employ of the von Kalbs (91.39ff.), although he had told Neuffer of his troubles as early as October (88.43ff.). On 22 May 1795 he gave her no reason to suspect that he was weighing alternatives (101.22ff.). Even in Frankfurt, although he mentioned that he might find it necessary to leave as early as November 1797 (148.44ff.), when he did leave, it came as a complete surprise to his mother, whom he informed from Homburg of his "long prepared move" (165.4ff.).

to his family, and irresponsible in that he was steadily eating away at his inheritance without making any visible progress toward establishing himself professionally so that he would be able to live a normal life and support a wife and family.

Hölderlin knew his mother and was well aware that he could expect no understanding from her for his ideas about how he was more sensitive than others and how he needed to protect himself from hurt. To Nast he might glorify himself through playing the social outcast; but when he wrote his mother he felt it necessary to assume a quite different role. To her he tried to appear as the poor student who was clenching his teeth in a manful effort to do his duty and satisfy her, even if that meant living on the verge of starvation. Slaving away, constantly suffering from mental and physical exhaustion, enduring splitting headaches, forcing himself to eat the unpalatable food that his tormentors provided him, and forced by his mother's insistence to submit to the tyranny of school administrators and to try to adjust to the sinful life of his fellow students! Interesting is the way in which he juxtaposed his comments about how sinful the other students were and his assurances that he was learning to adjust, as if he was trying to suggest that she, through her lack of understanding, was forcing him to compromise with sin and yield to temptations that he alone had hitherto overcome.

Much has been written about what a loving son Hölderlin was and how he willingly sacrificed himself for love of Mother even though that meant submitting for long years to the torturous routine of school life. All that is, in one sense, true in fact – but not in intent. He did not willingly sacrifice himself, nor did he suffer in silence. He reminded her repeatedly that his school years were a burden and that he was bearing a cross for her sake. He let her know through a thousand turns of speech that his lot would have been a happier one if only she had not tortured him with her admonitions, but that, because of her, he had been spiritually crushed. This probably made her suffer almost as much as he suffered. He complied with her wishes; but he let her know how great was his sacrifice. Both were part of his attitude toward her. Obedience and resentment, love and fear – first one and then the other predominated. Neither was ever completely absent. He signed his letters "Obediently" or "Your obedient son," even when he was trying to thwart her.

To Mother he claimed that he was learning to adjust. But, shortly thereafter, he wrote Nast: "Here I cannot hold out! No, truly! I must leave – I have decided firmly either to write my mother tomorrow – so that she will take me out of the Cloister, or to ask the Prelate for several months sick-leave, because I have spit blood several times. You see, my friend, I am slowly sinking. Be consoled!!! Just do not grieve for me!!!"[38]

[38] 11.24ff.

He did not write his mother, nor did he request leave so that he might go home and argue his case once more. He had learned during the Easter vacation that he would not accomplish his aim through a direct confrontation with Mother. These threats to Nast merely show that his claims that he was learning to adjust were calculated to avoid another argument or more admonitions to "dulden." They anticipate what would happen two years later, when, in the late autumn of 1789, he would again decide that he could, under no circumstances, endure school life any longer and, strengthened by day-dreams in which he had convinced himself of his heroic nature, would obtain sick-leave and plead his case once more to Mother. That time, however, he would suggest an alternative profession, thus taking advantage of the proviso he had made more than two years before, when he had promised never to consider leaving his profession unless something better turned up.

In March 1801, when he was already on the brink of insanity, Hölderlin wrote Christian Landauer from Hauptwyl: "Oh! You know already, you see into my soul when I say to you that it overwhelms me even more mightily than before − just this − that I have a heart in me and know not why, can communicate with no one here, can reveal myself to absolutely no one here."[39]

From Tübingen, after he had been released from the psychiatric clinic as incurably insane, while he was living under the care of the carpenter Zimmer, he wrote a number of letters to his mother up to her death in 1828, of which the following may serve as an example:

"Most Honerable Mother!
I write you once again. Please be good enough to receive this letter as you have received all my letters and remember me with kindness. I devotedly commend to you what is within me and call myself

Your most devoted son
Hölderlin"[40]

Here we come very close to Hölderlin's most essential weakness, which previous Hölderlin biographers have not seen because no one has yet evaluated the biographical data to see how Hölderlin related to his fellow students, his friends and his family, when he was not − or *should* not have been − writing poetry. The answer to that question seems to be that, from the beginning, he related to others very poorly and, as time went on, less and less. The notion that Hölderlin was *only* a poet is, in a bizarre sense, true. For he could not relate to others frankly, openly, without poetic embellishments, without mythologically restructuring the simplest human relationships, without conjuring up "the god in us" as a symbol of real communication, which seemed precious, god-like, to him

39 230.6ff.
40 No. 281.

only because real communication was so difficult for him. We see in his early letters that real communication was stifled from the very beginning. When he was called upon to deal with a real, unpoetic individual he found only coarseness, sinfulness, and danger. He grew embarassed, withdrew into himself, and wrote letters to others, whom, because they were not around him, he could recast in the mold of an imagined worthy recipient of his innermost thoughts. When he wrote letters, he wrote Literature.

Nevertheless, that does not justify our treating them as literature. If we do so we will miss the self-protective aspect of his poetic posing. When he wrote Nast, and later Neuffer, he could say some rather profound things because he was writing as a poet. But when he wrote his mother or Schiller, neither of whom looked upon him as a poetic genius, he found it difficult to express himself. Why? Because he was at his best when he could retreat behind the poetic formula, the stock expression, or the stereotyped response. When he was forced to come to grips with reality, he lost his balance. His letters to Schiller were alternately groveling or pitifully pretentious. To his mother he wrote more and more in a series of say-nothing formulae and claimed that he could not be more explicit because he was "in a hurry."[41] The letters to her after 1806 are but an extension to absurd proportions of the reticence that he had already displayed to her as a student.

A similar narrowness will be noted in his poetry, which revolves around a very limited number of themes, all of which share the same characteristic: They are pure form, pure formulae; they are aspects of real life, but frozen, idolized, robbed of the breath of life. In his poetic works he sharply distinguished between those people with whom he could communicate and those with whom he could not. He classified his acquaintances in a similar way. Each person with whom he came into contact in life, as well as each character in his works, was either one of the select group of people who understood the poet — or was banished to the realm of the prosaic.

How completely, even in these early years, he was spiritually isolated from others, we shall discover in the next chapter, in which we shall examine the letters to Immanuel and Luise Nast, to whom he *seemed* to communicate his most secret thoughts. We shall see that his apparent frankness resulted from his being able to play the role of the poet and transform the prosaic reality of relatively casual relationships into the stuff of poetic dreams, which he then tried to live out in his life.

---

[41] The frequency of Hölderlin's claims that haste forced him to write less than she expected is symptomatic of this tendency to avoid communicating with her and shows how early his reticence toward her was established. In the years covered by this book, the formula occurs in more than one-third of his letters to her: 2.2ff.; 9.23; 17.13f.; 18.39; 23.29f.; 26.27; 34.34f.; 55.35; 73.29ff.; 79.31ff.; 82.47; 85.43ff.; and 96.2ff.

But we shall remember that these were real people, not characters in a novel or drama. And, if we keep in mind that the people to whom he wrote his most intimate letters were young men and women of the same background as he who went on to live normal lives without letting the highly egocentric, excessively idealized literature of that time, by which they all were affected to some extent or other, interfere with the way in which they lived in society, then we shall be able to perceive the abnormality of being *only* a poet and of seeking out people whom one does not know and to whom one has only the responsibility of charming or torturing them with soulful phrases and exaggerated poses.

3

"LOVE AND FRIENDSHIP": IMMANUEL AND LUISE NAST

In the foregoing pages we have seen how Hölderlin's isolation from his schoolmates and his conviction that he was more holy, more sensitive, and a more devout servant of God than his fellow students can be seen as early as November 1785 in his first letter to Köstlin. It has become a cliché to appeal to the genius' need to suffer in order to accomplish his historic mission. In that way it has been possible to explain why the living Hölderlin never measured up to the "poet-prophet" stereotype that, for so long, was superimposed over the reality of his life.[1] This appreciation permeated the Hölderlin revival in the early years of this century despite the objections of psychologists, who were either ridiculed or ignored.[2]

No one *needs* to suffer, and certainly not for the sake of poems that one may write at some time in the future. There is, of course, definite cause and effect between the man's life and the poet's work; but one cannot seriously maintain that poems, written *after* the suffering has begun, should be regarded as the cause of the suffering. The poems, the novels, or the plays that one writes may affect one's life, but not *before* they are written and only in very concrete ways. If Hölderlin had not written the fragmentary version of *Hyperion,* which Charlotte von Kalb urged Schiller to publish, he would never have had the

---

[1] An example of how the myth has been used to excuse Hölderlin's inability to adapt to real-life demands is found in Alessandro Pellegrini's *Friedrich Hölderlin: Sein Bild in der Forschung* (Berlin, 1965), when Pellegrini summarizes the myth-oriented treatment of Hölderlin's life in the passage: "We know today that alienation from reality was the necessary path for the poet in order for him to push beyond individual subjectivity to an experience of universal significance as he became conscious of a fantasy world to which he assigned objective worth — a world which, through his poems, became truth and life" (p. 14).

[2] Heinrich Lange comments on the fate of his earlier book: *Hölderlin. Eine Pathographie* in *Genie, Irrsinn und Ruhm* (3rd edition, Munich, 1942), which he wrote under the pseudonym, Wilhelm Lange Eichbaum: "These very (psychiatrically cool, rational) judgments concerning the *Nachtgesänge* were noted as *progress* by the *most important* of the Germanisten. . . . The generally hated psychiatrist cannot really ask for more.

"But soon afterwards there appeared the young Hellingrath, who naturally had never learned anything about psychiatry, and praised just these rather confused, archaically dream-like, even formally disintergrating poems as the highest prophecies. Even the old, highly gifted theologian Noack turned against such minds: 'thoughtless phrase-mongers twaddle about Hölderlin's divine madness . . . .'

"So the author's judgments were certainly not 'value judgments from a limited sense of values' (Jaspers, p. 84), but rather from the sense of values of the sciences of psychiatry and *Germanistik* and also of the majority of all healthy laymen. 'Limited' is, of course, only Hellingrath's sense of values, who has experienced the psychotic as mr-tr [the particular and uncanny], as noumenal" (p. 322).

opportunity of working with Schiller during the first half of 1795. He would have been forced to find another job as soon as he resigned as Fritz von Kalb's tutor in January 1795, and he might then have already been employed when the position in the Gontard house became available later that same year. He might then have never met Susette Gontard and might never have remained stubbornly with Sinclair in Homburg, living off the balance of his already seriously depleted inheritance and refusing to give up his notion of founding a literary journal, while he was slipping letters through the hedge to Susette. He might then never have written the poems that, a century later, earned him a place in literary history alongside Goethe and Schiller. It is not *what* he wrote that determined his life (as Hellingrath suggests when he uses the contents of the late poems to explain the earlier years), and certainly not before the poems were written. That he had to write something; that he was compelled by something within him to devote himself so single-mindedly to his verses; that his attitudes during his earliest years reappear in poems written years later — all these are obviously related facts. But they are meaningfully related only in the sense that both the development of his poetry and the course of his life express his developing personality.

In this sense it is fallacious to search through his life for a single traumatic shock or a series of specific events compelling him to write as he did. In the search for determinants, the individual actions, the events, the crises, and the conflicts are not in themselves crucial. They are rather symptomatic. When we said above that Hölderlin's life might have been different if he had not been able to attract Schiller's attention and delay the inevitable search for a new job as a *Hofmeister* until the Gontards were looking for an educator for their son, we meant only that he would have ended up somewhere else among other people. But it is problematic whether the kind of life he led from then on would have been very different. We must not suppose that he might have found a woman more attainable than Susette, with whom he might have settled down and passed his life while writing poetry more along the lines of Mörike, whose self-protective mechanism was more reliable than Hölderlin's. For there is reason to suspect that his behavior would not have been substantially different. He would still have had the same perceptions, the same feelings, and the same needs that were denied fulfillment. A biography in which everything is represented as the result of events external to the subject (therefore accidental) would be as erroneous as Hellingrath's mythological explanations. And it would be fallacious for the same reason: One satisfies oneself when one has found a number of external phenomena (either events or poetry) which one then assumes to have been "causes." But, in proceeding in this way, one assumes no inner compulsion in accordance with which Hölderlin actually helped shape and direct his own life. Both the life and the works are looked upon as the results of sheer accident. Biography then degenerates into an idle wringing of hands. If only he had not encountered all the conflicts; if only he had not had to cope with a boy who masturbated; if only Schiller had been more understanding or had dropped dead before he read the *Thalia-fragment;* if only Hölderlin had fallen in love with another woman; if only Gontard had not been so unreasonable as to object to his wife's spending all her time with the *Hofmeister;* if only everyone asked had agreed to contribute to Hölderlin's journal — if only — if only — if only!

The purpose of this excursion is to point out that there is no reason to believe that Hölderlin's life would have been substantially different, that he would have remained mentally intact on into old age, or that he would have written poems that were less intense, less tortured, less idealistic, less Hölderlin, even if all the particulars of his life had not been as they were. He was not, after all, really so victimized by life. Much of his torment sprang from internal, not from external, causes. Masturbation, it is true, was considered far more serious in those days; but the incident with Fritz did not make nervous wrecks of Charlotte von Kalb or her husband as it made of Hölderlin. Schiller was not really so unreasonable in expecting Hölderlin to write in a certain way if he hoped to be published in journals that Schiller was editing. Nor was Gontard really so unreasonable in dismissing his employee (if he really dismissed him at all). For, if he looked upon Hölderlin as normal, then he was quite justified in regarding the unusually close relationship between his wife and the *Hofmeister* as a threat to his family; if, on the other hand, he felt that Hölderlin was incapable of threatening his marriage, then he was equally justified in concluding that Hölderlin was abnormal and in no condition to educate a young boy. One should not forget that there is good reason to suspect that Hölderlin was dismissed from a similar position as *Hofmeister* a few years later in Switzerland because of his abnormal behavior.[3]

The tragic course of his life was due not to a series of unfortunate coincidences but to his inability to adjust even to relatively peaceful surroundings. That, coupled with his massive persecution complex, caused him to invent problems where there were none, to exaggerate the seriousness of real difficulties, to cling to his isolation, and to glorify himself as a martyr. If he had simply been more sensitive than others, then he would have seen things which others could not see — but not things that consisted of sheer fantasy! If he had really had such unerring insight into human life as has been assumed ("the god within us"),[4] then he would not have constantly misinterpreted the attitudes

---

[3]   Lothar Kempter, *Hölderlin in Hauptwyl* (St. Gallen, 1946) pp. 59f.

[4]   Cf.: "It was Hölderlin's experience that between two people who are genuinely attuned to each other an essence of life [*Lebenswesenheit*] of a definite, almost plastic character is formed; this is part of the natural pantheism in Hölderlin's character. The concentrations of life [*Lebensverdichtungen*], as they occur in a particular time (moment, *kairos*), in a particular place, between particular people, are to him something divine which has assumed form [*etwas Gestalthaft-Göttliches*] against the background of the obliterations of life (which he knows with equal clarity). This [divine something that has assumed form] he honors as the God of the time" (Michel, p. 103).

and intentions of others toward him. In his helpless timidity he awakened affection and sympathy in a number of people. Charlotte von Kalb gave him three months' unearned wages when he quit his job as her son's tutor.[5] Schiller wrote Goethe as late as 1797 that he hated to give Hölderlin up for good, even though Hölderlin had left Jena without a word, leaving Schiller with the task of filling the space in *Die Horen* reserved for Hölderlin's translations as best he could.[6] Sinclair seems to have paid Hölderlin's salary out of his own pocket, after he had obtained for his friend the appointment as librarian in Homburg.[7]

That Hölderlin did see himself as a martyr despite so many kindnesses does not indicate ingratitude so much as a peculiar sort of insensitivity. He accepted all the help he received from others as his due while he remained unshaken in his conviction that he was the victim of general persecution. Moreover, he did not reciprocate kindnesses except verbally. When his mother was forced to sell her house because of financial difficulties while her son was working in Frankfurt, he offered only verbal consolation, even though he was living frugally and saving his money.[8] Neither in his personal life nor in his works is there much to suggest that his appreciation of others as real individuals was even normally acute. In his works this resulted in such characters as Hyperion, Diotima, and Empedokles, who were both unreal and unimaginable. His oversensitivity to the attitudes of others toward him was complemented, quite understandably, by a blind spot in his perceptions: He failed to consider the needs of others and never seems to have understood that more was required of a "friend" or of an "obedient son" than mere verbal professions of appreciation and understanding.

When Goethe decided to take up *Faust* once more, in the 1790's, after a lapse of some twenty years, he was filled with nostalgia for a lost time. That time past appeared as "hovering forms." He wrote in the dedication to *Faust I:*

> Gleich einer alten, halbverklungnen Sage
> Kommt erste Lieb' und Freundschaft mit herauf;
> Der Schmerz wird neu, es wiederholt die Klage
> Des Lebens labyrinthisch irren Lauf
> Und nennt die Guten, die, um schöne Stunden
> Von Glück getäuscht, von mir hinweggeschwunden.

---

5 92.76ff.
6 See note 15 to Chapter 1.
7 Sinclair's "Promemoria" to the Landgrave Friedrich Ludwig, dated 7 July 1804 (Hellingrath Edition, VI, p. 364).
8 He wrote on 10 July 1797: "I would advise you to occupy your mind with reading along with your other work, because otherwise it [your mind] will make work and worry for itself due to its natural vivacity. Or, if you don't want to do that, Dearest Mother! then write me right long letters? I will repay you in proportion, and that would also, perhaps, turn your mind in a cheerful direction (141.29ff.).

When Goethe tried to recapture the tone-feeling of *Urfaust* the images of his youth came automatically: "first Love and Friendship." When Hölderlin celebrated his homecoming something quite different happened.

> Froh kehrt der Schiffer heim an den stillen Strom
>   Von fernen Inseln, wo er geerndtet hat;
>   Wohl möcht' auch ich zur Heimath wieder;
>   Aber was hab' ich, wie Laid, geerndtet? —
>
> Ihr holden Ufer, die ihr mich auferzogt,
>   Stillt ihr der Liebe Laiden? ach! gebt ihr mir,
>   Ihr Wälder meiner Kindheit, wann ich
>   Komme, die Ruhe noch Einmal wieder? [9]

These images are characteristic of many of the late poems.[10] The poet stands alone in nature. The surrounding landscape produces a mood, which the poet then generalizes and endows with symbolic significance. But where were his own hovering forms of "first love and friendship"? Where are all the loves about whom he had written from Maulbronn to Homburg? Where all the friends? Somehow they had vanished. One might object that it is unfair to judge Hölderlin's and Goethe's poetry according to standards that apply only to Goethe. That objection would be valid if we were intent on evaluating the two in an attempt to conclude which was the greater poet. As a descriptive statement, however, it is revealing that this is about the closest Hölderlin ever came to writing poetry about the real course of his life. There is *no* work in which he looked back on his youth and celebrated *real* memories of the joys and sorrows of time past.

At about the same time that Goethe wrote the dedication to *Faust I*, he was reflecting on his life. He promised to visit Lotte in Wetzlar und burned many old letters, including those from his old friend Merck, who had recently died. Much of Goethe's poetry is strikingly reflective — a trait that has made possible the flood of poorly conceived biographical works on Goethe in which the old game of finding in his life the prototypes for the characters he created, with little regard for the process by which he internalized his experience, has been played out to infinity. Hölderlin's poetry is not reflective but projective. He did not experience relationships in the social realm and then internalize and poeticize them, as did Goethe. For the starting point of Hölderlin's poetry was often something he had read. His reading supplied him with the modes of thought by which, driven by insecurity, he embellished reality, making a fairy-tale of his childhood and a tragedy of his life. Experience supplied him only with the

---

[9] See note 19 to Chapter 1.
[10] Cf.: "Heidelberg" (II, 1, pp. 14f.); "Der Neckar" (II, 1, pp. 17f.); "Rückkehr in die Heimath" (II, 1, p. 29); "Der Gefesselte Strom" (II, 1, p. 67); and "Ganymed" (II, 1, p. 68).

personalities that more or less corresponded to the poetic figures about whom he had read and with whom he felt most at ease. Onto these real people he projected the full, preconceived images, so that the individual friend or beloved was subjected to all sorts of revisions and tortured, often unconvincing, transfigurations. The image in his mind, the ideal friend or "love," always existed in his fantasy before he found the suitable recipient of the image in life. This was true of Diotima. It was also true of his attitude toward Schiller, the composite of the father-teacher fixation, which we first saw in the letter to Köstlin.

In this light the letters to Immanuel and Luise Nast, which have hitherto been discussed very superficially by Hölderlin's biographers, become very important and must be investigated in some detail. In his relationships with his first friend and first love we see Hölderlin, for the first time, projecting his wish-dreams onto other people; and from these letters we get some indication why this habit was to help produce such a tragic life and such intense poetry. These early letters are decidedly adolescent. There is nothing particularly abnormal about a young man, particularly one who finds himself in an oppressive school, seeking and finding a friend or sweetheart onto whom he projects all his unrealistic notions about what love and friendship, neither of which he has really experienced, should be. Nor is there anything abnormal about seeking fulfillment in a relationship with a young friend or sweetheart whom one does not really know. In the letters to Immanuel and Luise Nast we shall discover not so much abnormality as rather a trait that would later assume abnormal prominence. As we shall see, abnormality would begin when the adolescent patterns of these years continued into his adult years and became substitutes for normal human relationships — stereotyped feelings that he used to shield himself against reality because he preferred his self-created world of dreams to real life.

"I left you and I was quite at peace — I felt so good in my nostalgia of farewell — and even now, when I think back to how we became friends at the first glance — how we lived together so closely and so happily, then I am glad that I had you for these few days."[11] "It is wonderful that you have such a sensitivity for nature — I have always flattered myself that our hearts beat in unison — but now I believe it for certain."[12] These lines were written by Hölderlin to Immanuel Nast less than six weeks after they had met for the first time. They mark the beginning of a long correspondence of impassioned letters in which Hölderlin would pour out his heart to his new friend. The correspondence revolves around a limited number of themes: Nast is seen as the

---

11 3.2ff.
12 4.4ff.

only true friend of the poor, mistreated boy at the *Klosterschule;* Luise Nast is
the boy's passionate love; literature is the strongest single interest that the
friends have in common.

One learns little about Nast from Hölderlin's letters. He was important almost
solely as the spiritual opposite of Hölderlin's classmates, the only friend with
whom the unfortunate student could share his true feelings. At the beginning of
the correspondence Hölderlin usually played the wounded hero who had
already, despite his youth, been badly wounded in his battle against the
unfeeling world. "You must not imagine that you will find a copy of your own
heart in me; no! My friend! You must not be surprised that everything about me
appears so stunted — so contradictory."[13] "I once had a better [heart] — but
they have taken it from me."[14] "Oh, Brother! Brother! I am such a weak
character, but I admit it to no one but you — and it is true, is it not, that you
have sympathy for me, rather than laugh at my having shed tears upon receiving
your letter."[15] (He had received the letter at mealtime, and Bilfinger, who was
sitting nearby, had laughed at him for weeping.) "You see, Brother! I am not
ashamed to tell you of my weaknesses, and that excuses me a little — with you —
but otherwise — oh, that this letter does not get into other hands — into the
hands of those who are the enemies of men — for they would say — he is a
fool!!!"[16]

This polarity, which was invariably set up by Hölderlin to distinguish Nast
from his classmates, was at least partially invented. It was written for the
impression on Nast, from whom he sought approval for his sentiments,
understanding for his unhappiness, and a reciprocation of his feelings. To some
degree he was playing a role, competing with his favorite authors in producing
pathetic situations. But that was not all. He was not only playing a role. For the
consistency with which he kept up the martyr's tone would suggest a deep need
for a friend and confidant with whom he could share his real concerns. There are
indications that he was afraid that Nast might turn out to be no different from
all the others; he was careful to suggest that he himself knew that others,
perhaps even Nast, might look upon his pathos, his complaints about all sorts of
woes from ostracism to toothaches, as childish. He was as candid as he dared be.
But he was not always secure in his belief that his candidness would be received
by Nast as a true friend should respond to such honesty. Often he tried to
prompt his friend to the proper reaction. "You will think that I am a fool; yet I
do not know whether it is self-love or — or — such thoughts comfort me."[17]
". . . if you were like the others around me — oh, I will be silent — Forgive me

13   4.6ff.
14   4.20f.
15   11.12ff.
16   13.43ff.
17   3.27ff.

this time, Dear; you hardly know me — and know me already as the type of person who reproaches the One who, in infinite wisdom, directs our destinies."[18] When he was trying to convince Nast to visit him, he wrote: "You say you *want* to come; oh, then promise me, my Friend — I know for certain that you will grant me a few happy hours — But you are a man, and a man is moved only by promises. You know how many wishes go unfulfilled, and how much it hurts! And is this one also to go unfulfilled? "[19]

Much in the letters to Nast is exaggerated and could not, even in that day, have been taken seriously. The letters to Luise are more convincing, even though we shall find in them as well a strong admixture of themes and emotions which were borrowed from his reading and a conception of love that would have been unthinkable without the influence of Schiller's early plays. Friendship between Hölderlin and Nast was based on the ideals, interests, and enthusiasms that they shared. Nast thought once of getting away from it all and joining the troops leaving Württemberg for the Cape of Good Hope; Hölderlin immediately assured his friend that he would follow him.[20] Mostly their enthusiasms were poetic, because the poets were the heroes of the youth of that time. There are many references to poetry in Hölderlin's letters to his friend. In the very first letter Hölderlin wrote that he intended to learn the music that Zumsteeg had composed for Karl Moor's song in the fourth act of *Die Räuber* "in honor of Schiller."[21] "Ah, how many times I have pressed his hands in my thoughts when he has his Amalia pour out her yearnings for Karl. — !"[22]

In February he reacted violently when Nast recommended that he read Wieland's poem, "Der Neue Amadis." "You ask me how I like your Amadis — I say — not at all. And why? ? — Not because Wieland is not my favorite anyway, nor because I had rather read a fairy-tale uninterrupted by satire, but — and I say this in all modesty — because things appear in it that are not to be read by sensitive people like — unfortunately — me!!! Oh Brother! Do you say that I have only half read it? I thank God that my fantasy is still unspotted and that the poet who would make an innocent blush disgusts me! Be honest with me my Friend, does it not do your heart more good when you read the great singer of the *Messiah?* or our Schubart's stormy Ahasveros? or the fiery Schiller? Convince yourself through his *Fiesko* and *Kabale und Liebe* — in the latter one finds a good girl — think of me when Luise stands there with her gaze directed, unprejudiced, into eternity. See if I am not right. When I recall that passage I always think: If I were to lose such a girl, if I were once again such a lout as I generally am in my unhappy hours, then I would read the passage again and

18 5.29ff.
19 7.18ff.
20 3.6ff.
21 3.23f.
22 3.25ff.

again, and there I would find enough fresh air. I see already that you are laughing at me; you are thinking: Before one mouths about losing, one must first — have? ? — ? "[23]

Then in September he wrote: "Something new! Something beautifully, refreshingly new! I have Ossian, the bard without equal, Homer's great competitor, I have in my hand. You must read him, Friend. Your valley will become the valley of Kona, your Engelberg a mountain of Morven — Such a sweet, nostalgic feeling will come over you — you must read him — I cannot declaim. He will accompany me to Nürtingen in the vacation, and there I will read him until I half know him by heart.

"I do not know whether I will be able to visit you in the vacation. At least I will not be able to on the way there. I cannot write anything — the good, blind Ossian spins around in my head."[24]

> Ach Freunde! welcher Winkel der Erde kan
>   Mich deken, daß ich ewig in Nacht gehüllt
>   Dort weine? Ich erreich' ihn nie den
>   Weltenumeilenden Flug der Großen.[25]

In that same year Hölderlin wrote the poem "Mein Vorsaz," which was the first in which he gave expression to his poetic ambitions. He did not mean that he merely hoped to write good poems. He was speaking rather of a dedication of his life and, perhaps still unconsciously, of a renunciation of his mother's plans for his life. He saw in the poet a kindred spirit, the social outcast who suffered much as he himself was suffering, because he was superior to others, holier, and more sensitive. The poet, like Hölderlin, was more precious than the common run of men. Hölderlin was sincere in his professions of love for Nast. But to him friendship was already something other than the everyday relationship between close acquaintances. These invariably brought hurt and suffering. Friendship he conceived as something Klopstockian — belonging to a higher realm, beyond suffering and sin. "Mein Vorsaz" begins:

> O Freunde! Freunde! die ihr so treu mich liebt!
>   Was trübet meine einsame Blike so?
>   Was zwingt mein armes Herz in diese
>   Wolkenumnachtete Todtenstille?
>
> Ich fliehe euren zärtlichen Händedruk,
>   Den seelenvollen, seeligen Bruderkuß.
>   O zürnt mir nicht, daß ich ihn fliehe!
>   Schaut mir in's Innerste! Prüft und richtet! —[26]

[23] 6.15ff.
[24] 12.1ff.
[25] I, 1, p. 28 (lines 13—16).
[26] I, 1, p. 28 (lines 4—11).

Friendship then, as he conceived it in his poetry and as he practiced it, did not produce completely candid self-revelation to the friend. He was seldom really candid; more often he revealed all the reasons why he *could not* tell his friends everything. When he addressed his friends in the poem "Mein Vorsaz" he really expressed only the extent of his loneliness. In reality he revealed even that much only to Nast. True candor remained beyond him. His need to protect himself against all unwanted intrusions from without choked off the impulse to true self-revelation. Often he produced an intense and detailed analysis of himself for several lines only to veer sharply aside and begin talking about Nast, whose reaction he tried to anticipate and, at times, forestall. "I can already see that you are laughing at me,"[27] he wrote; and "you may think that I am a fool."[28]

Had he read Klopstock's small essay "Concerning Friendship"? There is good reason to assume that he had. Klopstock was one of his favorite poets and certainly the poet whose work he imitated most often. He had recommended Klopstock to Nast as a substitute for Wieland. When he finally confessed to his friend that he was in love with Luise Nast, he proclaimed: "How I then felt so undeniably that love and friendship are men's greatest happiness on earth,"[29] which may be an echo of Klopstock's words: "Friendship and love are two plants from the same root. The plant has only a few more blossoms.

"When I say that friendship . . . is *the second great happiness* that we may enjoy, not only in this world but in the world to come, then I have said just about everything that can be said about it; but how few there are who do not consider this merely a mirage. And yet I will, as it were, speak a little of this mirage."[30] Klopstock went on to say that each friend must entrust everything about himself to the other. "My friend often does not wait for me to discover his shortcomings but rather tells me about them beforehand."[31]

It would be easy to deduce, as Michel has done, from the exaggerated quality of many of the letters that Hölderlin was largely insincere and that he was interested solely in Luise, which would mean that Immanuel would have been nothing more than a convenient tool for establishing contact with the family.[32] This view, while containing some little truth, does not do justice to the complicated needs of the young man that defined his relationship to Immanuel. His torment, his resentments, and his dreams of a life better than the one holding him captive needed to be shared. He needed confirmation of his feelings.

27 6.33f.
28 3.27.
29 15.14f.
30 Friedrich Gottlieb Klopstock, *Ausgewählte Werke* (Munich: Carl Hanser Verlag, n.d.), pp. 936f.
31 *Ibid.,* p. 937.
32 ". . . no doubt Hölderlin cultivated this friendship with the young secretary chiefly for the sake of his Immanuel's pretty cousin" (Michel, p. 25).

He moved eclectically through the worlds of both men and books. Just as he rejected Wieland in favor of authors whose works reflected his own sentiments, so also did he shun contact with classmates who did not understand him in favor of the one friend who proved to be a receptive audience for his exercises in self-pity, his self-accusations, and his indictments of his classmates. He found in Nast the friend for whom he had been searching since he had written Köstlin and had asked his former teacher to be his "father." He found in Immanuel the friend that he had been promised by Klopstock, the friend as dear as any sweetheart, with whom he might share all those feelings that needed sharing. However lacking in candor individual passages in the letters to Nast may have been, the compulsion to express himself to a friend, which caused him to seek out and embrace Nast, was just as genuine as his need to reveal himself in poetry.

The marked tendency to self-analysis, which dictated much of the subject-matter of both the poems of that time and the letters to Nast, was only partially the result of his life-long training in that strain of Pietistic Christianity that demanded merciless self-examination and the ruthless unmasking and stamping out of all imperfections that separated the sinner from his God. This tradition served, no doubt, as a catalyst through providing a justification and suggesting appropriate motifs for self-analysis. The impetus, however, came from within. Hölderlin, as we have said before, was a poet by his very nature. But, in a way, that is a deceptive statement. When we say that, we are concentrating on the historical role of the man, and that tends to obfuscate what he really felt as an adolescent and make it difficult to understand why he acted as he did. It is more nearly correct to say that he felt compelled to communicate everything he discovered in his endless Odyssey into his own spirit and that this need was one of the major determinants of both his life and his poetry. In both he displayed an astounding preoccupation with himself and his own cares, often at the exclusion of much that makes life rich, meaningful, or even bearable.

Friendship, as he conceived and tried to practice it, was inseparable from his poetry. He followed Klopstock in his attempt to reveal himself completely to his chosen confidant, and this often gave his utterances the appearance of ruthless honesty. He admitted, for example, that he felt unworthy of Nast's love, that he knew his heart to be "evil," and that he was often unfair in his estimation of others and of their intentions toward him. And yet, as in his poetry, he succeeded in turning faults into virtues and examples of his unfairness toward others into proofs of his moral superiority. His heart was evil because "they" had taken a better heart from him. Here one encounters that characteristic turn of thought that prevails in so much of his late poetry: The poet suffers because of his own weakness, which would not matter if the world were but a little more understanding and appreciative of his goodness. And so, when he followed Klopstock's admonition to candor, it was not only in order to be worthy of the chosen one's friendship but also to glorify himself in an acceptable form. He did not want help so much as he wanted confirmation. He did not want merely to hear his friend say that his shortcomings did not matter, but rather that they were holy faults because they proved him superior to all the ignorant and insensitive louts who were oppressing him.

All that was too much to expect in reality. No wonder he was constantly disappointed! He wrote to Nast: "No one likes me here — now I am starting to seek friendship with children — but that is, of course, very unsatisfying."[33]

Seven years later he would again seek ideal friendship in a child, when he tried to convince himself that Fritz von Kalb, the nine-year-old boy whom everyone else knew to be of limited intelligence, was ready for true friendship with his tutor and that tutor and student might at once begin strolling arm in arm down the road to Kantian *Vernunft*. In 1787 recourse to the company of children was only "unsatisfying"; in 1794 it would be disastrous.

He searched so desperately for friendship and found real friendship so disappointing largely because the friendships that he succeeded in establishing were anemic relationships based on idealistic preconceptions about what a true friend should be rather than on a realistic appreciation of his friend. His lack of true candor, his inability to reveal himself without circumscribing all his confessions with poetic embellishments, made it difficult for him to find friends among his classmates. Only with Ludwig Neuffer and Rudolf Magenau in Tübingen and with Isaac von Sinclair and Christian Landauer later was he able to find even temporary fulfillment in relationships with young men with whom he was in contact every day. Neuffer and Magenau, however, were members of the *Dichterbund* and were infected with the same poetic virus as Hölderlin at the time of their closest friendship; Sinclair showed an almost exaggerated respect for Hölderlin's learning and character in the initial stages of their friendship[34] and was very careful, in later years, to help Hölderlin in such a way that he never knew that he was living off Sinclair's charity. These three men — Neuffer, Magenau, and Sinclair — were the only exceptions to the rule stated above; otherwise Hölderlin's closest relationships seem to have been with men with whom he could communicate through letters alone.

"Ich fliehe euren zärtlichen Händedruk," he wrote in "Mein Vorsaz." When he was surrounded by his classmates in Denkendorf he sought a friend and consoler in Köstlin, whom he only saw during his short visits to his home town. In his Maulbronn years he found Nast, who did not even live in town, and chose him above all classmates. From 1791 to 1793, while he was living with Hegel and Schelling, he wrote in his letters to Neuffer that he existed only through memories of the *Bund*. Only after he had been separated from Hegel for a number of years did he begin to glorify his old roommate as a friend. In each

---

33 4.23
34 See Sinclair's letter to Franz Wilhelm Jung (Hellingrath Edition, VI, p. 243).

instance perfect friendship seems to have been a relationship that existed primarily on a verbal plane; his perfect friends were mostly men whom he could imagine as the type of friend he wanted — men who seemed to approve of everything he did and who saw in him the man he wanted to be.

This aspect of his life is also related to his poetry. For both his poetic vision of life and his conception of friendship, which was one of the most important constituents of his vision, were the product of his fantasy and his reading. He wrote to Nast: "Another hour dreamed away. I was even with you — I can do that best of all in my lazy evening hours — when I am alone in darkness."[35] In October 1787, when he had returned from his vacation, he wrote: "I have much to say to you, Brother! But my head is again so confused, so many different things are once more in my heart. Where I have just been in the vacation, I found unfulfilled wishes and imperfect joys — I do not know whether it is imagination or reality — what I see I enjoy only half-heartedly — everything is so empty for me — and I often reproach myself that I no longer have a warm, heartfelt sympathy for the fate of my brothers, as I once did! Alas, Brother, tell me, dearest Brother, am I this way alone? the eternal, eternal victim of whims!"[36]

"I do not know whether it is imagination or reality." In retrospect we know that it was reality. He had begun a process of withdrawal into his world of dreams that would continue into his adult life. This letter was written during the initial stage of that process. From this point on his letters would, in one sense, be more important than oral communication. We do not say that merely because we have access only to his letters and not to his spoken words. It is known that he made a weak face-to-face impression on Goethe and Schiller and that he was very shy and withdrawn when he met people in flesh.[37] Only in his letters did he, in this period at least, ever attain even the semi-revelation of self that we have characterized above. Even this much candor he produced only in letters to Immanuel and Luise Nast, with whom he could share his dreams of uncompromising idealism.

[35] 5.2ff.

[36] 13.4ff.

[37] Schiller's first impression of Hölderlin is recorded in his letter to Charlotte von Kalb of 10 October 1793 (VII, 1, pp. 468f.). Shortly after he had arrived with Fritz in Jena in November 1794, Hölderlin probably made a particularly bad impression on Goethe. One day, when he visited Schiller, he was so taken by his hero that he did not catch the name of the rather reticent stranger to whom Schiller introduced him. Only later that day did he overhear a conversation in which it was mentioned that Goethe had been at Schiller's house (89.52ff.). Although Goethe seems not to have held that *faux pas* against Hölderlin, he never succeeded in making much of an impression on Goethe, who wrote Schiller on 23 August 1797: "Hölderlin was at my place yesterday; he looks somewhat depressed and sickly, but he is really likeable and honest with modesty, in fact, even with timidity. He went into various matters in a way that betrayed your influence; a number of main ideas he has assimilated quite well, so that he could easily pick up a number of them again. I advised him particularly to make small poems and to choose for each a human interest theme."

Thus the seemingly unrestrained outpouring of sentiment in his letters to Neuffer is in no way incongruent with that famous letter to his brother Karl in which he admitted that he had lost interest in individuals and had decided to devote himself to the good of mankind. He meant it literally. For, from 1787 on, he seems to have been less and less interested in individuals as individuals. More and more the stereotypes of the "sweetheart of the Poet" or "the Poet's friend" came to influence decisively both his perception of life and his poetic expression of it. The personal letter to a half-real, half-imagined friend or "sweetheart" gradually became acts of compensation for all the gestures of real friendship and love that he could not make in life. This would be obvious in his strange attitude toward Schiller, to whom he would excuse his flight from Jena with the complaint: "Your nearness oppressed me."[38] But there soon followed a stream of letters in which he, ever more desperately, tried to salvage his relationship with Schiller and restructure it along the lines of his preconceptions about friendship. ("Say one word to me, and you will see how I am changed."[39]) From a safe distance only did he find it possible to assert himself against the older man's overwhelming personality. But his self-assertion and subsequent rebellion against his mentor were *only* poetic, only verbal; they are found in his poems and, to some slight extent, in his letters — but never in his actions.

The same psychological process of self-protection was at work in his "love-life" as well. Even as early as 1787, in his adolescent love affair with Luise Nast, he anticipated his later postulation of all-healing love, which would be personified in Susette Gontard in life, in Diotima in his novel and poems. He noticed Luise soon after he arrived in Maulbronn. For months he was afraid to approach her. It was, as he wrote Nast, Luise's brother who finally brought the boy and girl together. For months Hölderlin was tortured by the suspicion that his friend Bilfinger might also be interested in her. There was not much to the romance in reality. They went for weeks on end without seeing each other. He probably knew Luise no better than he knew her cousin Immanuel. But that mattered little to Hölderlin, in whose imagination she became everything that the sweetheart and wife of a great poet should be. It was not Luise herself, the simple, relatively unimaginative daughter of the *Verwalter,* that mattered. In Hölderlin's dreams, played out for hours on end late at night between the protective walls of the *Klosterschule,* only "love" mattered — only the wish-dreams of personal grandeur, passionate romance, and the reconciliation of the champion and outcast with the world through the power of love.

Here too, as was true of his relationship to Immanuel, his isolation dictated his perceptions and his categories of thought. Friendship made isolation

38 102.9ff.
39 129.39f.

endurable. Love offered the hope of eventual reconciliation with the world from which he had been cruelly expelled. All this has a familiar ring to anyone possessing even the most superficial knowledge of the literature of the time. Hölderlin had written Nast that he had often dreamed of shaking Schiller's hand for letting Amalia yearn so dramatically for Karl Moor. The words of which he must have been thinking read:

> He sails on stormy seas — Amalia's love sails with him — he wanders through the virgin sands of the desert — Amalia's love makes a green carpet burst forth from the burning sands beneath him, and the wild weeds blossom — the noon sun singes his bare head, the northern snows shrivel the soles of his feet, hailstones rain down upon his temples, and Amalia's love rocks him to sleep amidst the storm. Seas and mountains and horizons separate the lovers — but their souls transcend the dusty dungeon and meet in a paradise of love.[40]

How easy it must have been for Hölderlin, whose imagination sufficed to convince him that Klopstock's true friend might really be found in a boy of his age even though he lived among classmates who seemed to be living refutations of such a thesis, to put Amalia's words in the mouth of a girl whom he did not know. If he could cling to his belief that such an ideal friend might be found when he lived surrounded by boys, how much more unrealistic must have been his ideas about what he never had anything to do with — girls! How much he must have yearned for a woman like Amalia!

In the autumn of 1787 Hölderlin won Luise and they exchanged rings. He wrote two stormy letters to Immanual Nast. In the first he hinted broadly at the news, but refrained from giving a complete account of the courtship because he had promised Luise that he would let her break the happy news to her cousin. "Oh, friend," he wrote, "you will learn from a dear mouth the source of all my joy, all my sorrows, all my lamentations — you will be able to understand then — the enigmatic moods in which I have often written you. If you could see into my heart just now, Brother, how everything seems so quiet, so peaceful, so contented, you would be happy yourself — and tell your own sweetheart how I now never grumble at Him Who gives me my destiny, Who, so good, so wise, divides out happy and mournful days — Oh, I was such a fool — I believed often, when men hated me, when I was persecuted through scorn — when everything conspired to rob me of a single longed-for hour — that God did not love me — believed — that He was angry at love!!!"[41] Shortly thereafter he wrote: "God in Heaven! I never want to go back to those days — Brother! Brother! days in which doubt rose in my mind about the Master of my destiny — about which I cannot tell you. He has forgiven me for them — the All-Merciful One — I have

---

[40] *Die Räuber*, Act IV, Scene 4.
[41] 14.5ff.

recanted with many a tear, many a nightly prayer. — Others soon noted the sorrow in my soul — and in the entire *Klosterschule* I was regarded as dangerously melancholy. Luise heard of it, and her sorrow matched my own. Sleep fled me at night — and all energy by day —— mostly I throttled my feelings — when I wrote you — then I thought — you would perhaps laugh at me — so far did I go in my distrust of everyone."[42]

All of his troubles he thus interpreted as the results of his unhappy love-life. Now he would change completely. He would no longer be the sullen, morose, distrusting outcast. Love for Luise would reconcile him with the world from which he had been estranged. This passage was not merely an unconsidered outburst of enthusiasm, committed to paper unthinkingly in a moment of overflowing joy. The all-healing power of love, love for Urania, the all-reconciling life-force, love as a means by which he might reenter the world of men, love as the source of the champion's strength — these ideas would return over and over again both in his feelings for real women and in his poetry. From Tübingen he would write to Luise Nast two years later: "Luise — what will I have in you — you will cheer me up in the dismal hours, you will make sweet the burdens that I must bear, you will reconcile me with the world whenever I am insulted."[43] He might as well have written that she, like Amalia, would make the desert of his barren life sprout forth a green and luxuriant carpet or that her love would rock him to sleep in the midst of the storm.

When he wrote these words he was in earnest. He probably really believed that in a future life with her in a small cottage in some Swabian village, where he would be the spiritual leader of God's flock, he would find reconciliation with the world of men. He seldom dissembled knowingly. Even the half-truths he told his mother from time to time were largely the products of self-deception, of that curious process of self-delusion by which he managed to reduce the most complex problems to the simplest, most unrealistic terms. As we shall encounter so often in the following pages, he communicated most eloquently when he had succeeded in deluding himself to such an extent that he believed firmly in his self-constructed world of dreams. When he had solved a problem conceptually through working out a verbal solution, he relapsed into self-protective silence.

Immediately following the eruption of passion when he announced his engagement to Luise Nast, he became a less passionate letter-writer than he had been. His letters to Nast became distant, factual. Never again in his letters to Nast did he ascend to the heights of eloquence that he had so often scaled during the early months of 1787.

Shortly before he left Maulbronn to begin his stay of five years at Tübingen, he wrote the poem "An Luise Nast," which begins:

[42] 15.108ff.
[43] 30.17ff.

Laß sie drohen die Stürme, die Leiden
Laß trennen — der Trennung Jahre
Sie trennen uns nicht!
Sie trennen uns nicht!
Denn mein bist du! Und über das Grab hinaus
Soll sie dauern die unzertrennbare Liebe.[44]

Here we catch our first glimpse of the chronology of Hölderlin's creative process. We know that he had read Schiller's *Räuber* by January 1787 because he shows knowledge of the play in his first letter to Nast. Months of shyness and reticence followed, during which he came to love passionately the simple little girl, who, to him, had soon become anything but plain and simple. To Hölderlin Luise had soon become the living embodiment of all the wonderful and virtuous traits that a heroine should exemplify. Both the reality and the fantasy that went into his perception of Luise were carefully, although unconsciously, measured out so as to produce an imagined lover who could supply all the approval, consolation, and encouragement he needed. She became to him the great source of strength in his battle with the world; she represented the instrument of future reconciliation between the poet and the world that mocked him. This image of her appeared first in the letters to Immanuel, then in the letters to her, and finally in the poetry. His perceptions were, in the end, realized in the poems; but they had little to do with life.

Hölderlin's "first love and friendship" would not last in fact. Even his passion for Luise proved to be very fragile very soon. Every one of their letters indicates that Hölderlin was suffering from moods of deep depression.[45] Luise was not enough to effect the reconciliation that he expected, although he would not see that until 1790, when he broke the engagement. Nast would also disappear from his life. There is no indication that he made any effort to keep up the correspondence with Nast after he left Maulbronn.[46] Other loves and friends would replace the cousins. But the types — the unreal Immanuel and Luise of the letters and poems — would remain. Those relationships envisioned on a plane above life, those substitutes for real social contacts, which he denied himself, would be elaborated endlessly. The imagined true friend would be sought in Neuffer, Schiller, and Sinclair. The image of the perfect woman he would

---

44 I, 1, p. 64 (lines 1—6).
45 The only exception to this is the first of his preserved letters to her. And yet, even then he seems to have been preparing her for his moodiness when he wrote: "If I only might remain as content as I am now. But — I love you in all moods — my situation is, after all, not the worst" (22.24ff.).
46 On 17 April 1789 Nast wrote his friend in the school: "I don't know whether I should be angry with you or whether I should ask you not to be angry with me. For it is almost unforgiveable that we were like marmots the whole winter; but I forgive you and you [forgive] me too, don't you? " (VII, 1, p. 17).

transfer from Luise to Elise Lebret and Susette Gontard. Susette would become
the potential reconciler that Luise had been.

> Komm und besänftige mir, die du einst Elemente versöhntest,
>   Wonne der himmlischen Muse das Chaos der Zeit,
> Ordne den tobenden Kampf mit Friedenstönen des Himmels
>   Bis in der sterblichen Brust sich das entzweite vereint,
> Bis der Menschen alte Natur die ruhige große,
>   Aus der gährenden Zeit, mächtig und heiter sich hebt.[47]

From Maulbronn on, the formulae would be elaborated and made more
cosmic in their implications, more fulfilling for him. They never really changed
after that. Luise and Immanuel Nast never seem to have occurred to him when
he wrote his later poems — certainly not in the way that Goethe's "first love and
friendship" occurred to him. For Goethe's old friends and sweethearts existed in
his mind as memories. Hölderlin had no need for such memories; for Luise and
Immanuel Nast had been swallowed up by their successors. When Hölderlin
wrote "Heimkehr" in later years, there was no reason for him to remember his
own "hovering forms." All his memories were exhausted in the formulae; all
were "realized" in his poems and in his dream-world, both of which he
constantly revised. Here in his tendency to reduce the phenomena of life to
clichés, which he constantly updated, we find the origin of that philosophic
strain in his work in which his thought shows resemblance to Hegel's historic
thought. For Hegel's assertion that all western thought was realized ("aufgeho-
ben") in his own system is echoed by Hölderlin, not only in the poems in which
he traced the development of the idea of freedom from the cradles of civilization
to his own time, but implicitly in his way of perceiving reality, in his habit of
never letting his poems become obsolete and foreign to him, and in his stunted
development, which resulted in his settling on the most adolescent clichés and
elaborating them for the rest of his life.

---

[47] I, 1, p. 231 (lines 1—6).

4.

THE EARLIEST POEMS: 1785–1788

In the late spring of 1800, Hölderlin returned home to Nürtingen for the first time in more than four years. He had not seen his mother since December 1795. For almost three years he had lived at the Gontard house in Frankfurt. Then, after his peculiar relationship to his employer's wife had made life there unbearable for him, he had lived in Homburg with his friend Isaac von Sinclair for more than a year. There he had tried to start a literary journal and establish, once and for all, his financial independence from his mother. In both undertakings he had failed. None of the literary figures whom he had asked for contributions had agreed to help him. Schiller had even advised him to give up the whole idea.[1] Gradually he had used up all the savings that he had accumulated while he had been living in Frankfurt. In the end he had to return home in much the same way as in 1795 — hat in hand, a failure who could not support himself and who was again forced to borrow, as he had done so often before, from the inheritance that his mother still controlled, although he was, by then, thirty years old.[2]

He spent only a few days in Nürtingen. From there he traveled on to Stuttgart, where he spent the summer at the home of Christian Landauer.[3] He supported himself as best he could by tutoring young men in philosophy and Greek. But this proved to be financially unsound as well. Later Landauer wrote Hölderlin's mother that he was returning her son's rent for that summer, but warned her not to tell her son, who would, as Landauer correctly supposed, have been ashamed at having lived off the charity of a friend.[4]

Emotionally Hölderlin was near the end. He may have half known it himself, for in his letters, in his poems, in everything he wrote at that time, a tone of sorrowful resignation had set in. He had become the prophet, mourning that he would not live to see the golden age of poetic truth that he had been predicting for so long, and of which he saw himself as the forerunner. Everything he wrote was assuming that unearthly quality of higher vision which is possible only when one has suffered much and is now looking beyond everyday cares. Now he was convinced that his own cares were of little consequence because his individual

[1] VI, 2, p. 976.
[2] Frau Gok's accounts are reprinted in full in VII, 1, pp. 281–293.
[3] Christian Landauer was a businessman in Stuttgart who ran a family fabric shop with his brothers, Christoph Friedrich and Ludwig, but who was interested in art and culture. Hölderlin made his acquaintance no later than the fall of 1795. His treatment of the already ailing Hölderlin was more than understanding (VI, 2, pp. 1024ff.).
[4] Hellingrath Edition, VI, pp. 344ff.

fate was swallowed up by — realized in — the fate of the German nation.

It was during that summer of 1800 in Stuttgart that he wrote many of his most moving poems. When he could not support himself, when he found himself in the midst of an intense personal crisis with which he could not come to grips, he succeeded in transforming his personal concerns into symbols of timeless significance and in representing the realization of his unrealistic dreams and the solution to his inner conflicts as the dawn of a new era for his own people, as well as for all mankind. He also thought of Diotima and wrote:

> Wohl! ich wußt' es zuvor. Seit der gewurzelte,
>   Allentzweiende Haß Götter und Menschen trennt,
>   Muß, mit Blut sie zu sühnen,
>   Muß der Liebenden Herz vergehn.
>
> Laß mich schweigen! o laß nimmer von nun an mich
>   Dieses Tödtliche sehn, daß ich im Frieden doch
>   Hin ins Einsame ziehe,
>   Und noch unser der Abschied sei!
>
> Reich die Schaale mir selbst, daß ich des rettenden
>   Heilgen Giftes genug, daß ich des Lethetranks
>   Mit dir trinke, daß alles
>   Haß und Liebe vergessen sei.[5]

As with all of Hölderlin's late poems, one must have read each poem and each letter repeatedly before one can hope to penetrate the symbolism. None of the later poems stands alone. Subtle allusions run from one poem to an earlier one and, when he revised the earlier one, as he so often did, back again, so that none can be fully explicated individually. This peculiarity of Hölderlin's collected works dooms the aesthetic or formalistic approach from the outset. If one is to come to an understanding of what the individual images were probably supposed to signify, then one must be fully acquainted with Hölderlin's vision both inside and out, because the vision is self-contained. The world of the late poems is complete within itself; the allusions, those connecting links which, in earlier years, had related the symbols to a given piece of reality had long since fallen away. The structure of the poet's mind no longer had anything to do with the mental habits of the naive interpreter. The image bears only the most general resemblance to the experience that originally set the internalization process in motion.

It is this quality of almost complete generality that has made it possible for twentieth century critics to read almost anything into Hölderlin's late poems, so that we are now asked alternately to believe that Hölderlin was a sort of

---

[5] II, 1, p. 24 (lines 13—24).

Baudelaire-related, purely aesthetic phenomenon (Pellegrini), an Existentialist (Heidegger), a forerunner of Nietzsche (Hellingrath, Pigenot), and an early National Socialist (Alfred Rosenberg, Kurt Hildebrandt).[6] Such free-wheeling interpretation "works," but only in the sense that anyone can construct an arbitrary hierarchy of meanings parallelling the symbols. Unfortunately, all such interpretations, even the most diametrically opposed, work equally well. Whether an opinion gains currency or not is thus determined not so much by whether the critic has really understood Hölderlin – or even made much of an effort – but merely by how compelling is his prose.

What *Hölderlin* meant can only be learned if one follows the development of his thought from the very beginning, is careful to observe when and under what conditions basic themes first appeared, and then, of course, tries to determine why and how they were internalized in order to reappear again as generalized symbols.

By the time he wrote the poem "Stuttgart," for example, the creative process had become automatic. The sight of Stuttgart after a summer shower was enough to set off a whole series of habitually related symbols in his mind. And yet, *why* the symbols fell so readily into place, *why* they were employed to represent particular feelings and attitudes cannot be seen in the poem. The poem itself appears to have resulted from a sudden, unannounced inspiration. In reality, the images that appear in the late poems had been developing from a relatively small number of personal fixations for a number of years.

The common denominator of all Hölderlin's works is his exclusiveness, his autism, his painful awareness that he is separated from others by an immense gulf and by the fascination that his abnormality exerted upon him. In this curious way he used the epistolary form in *Hyperion* so that he might become the old Hyperion, who was writing the letters to Bellarmin, and thus interpret, rather than merely recount, the experiences of his youth. But this is only the most obvious example of how he maintained the gulf between himself and the objects of his art. This technique, which Paul Böckmann has called "Distanz-erhaltung,"[7] is most obvious in *Hyperion* because, in the course of an extended prose narrative, it could only make for confusion. But *Hyperion* is by no means unique in this regard. *Empedokles* is just as indirect. In all the versions the real action has already taken place when the curtain first goes up. There remains only for the characters to deliver symbolic monologues and then for the protagonist to draw his extreme conclusion – and leap into the volcano.

It was in his lyrics that Hölderlin came into his own. In them he succeeded in

---

6   The most thorough summary of Hölderlin scholarship until the most recent years can be found in Alessandro Pellegrini's *Friedrich Hölderlin. Sein Bild in der Forschung* (Berlin: Walter De Gruyter and Co., 1965).

7   Paul Böckmann, *Hölderlin und seine Götter* (Munich, 1935), pp. 191ff.

masking his indirectness and habitual procrastination. His poems often seem almost brutally direct. But, even in his apparent simplicity, there is something deeply enigmatic. His most straight-forward declarations invariably prompt the question: To what does this relate? What is he — so simply — talking about?

Why the enigma? Simply because he created the illusion of simplicity and directness whenever he confronted his ideal, his fantasm. It was to the fantasm that he spoke. The piece of reality that had once stood behind the fantasm was now missing altogether. Only the symbol remained. He spoke to the symbol alone; for the symbol, the verbally constructed dream-world, had absorbed his attention for so many years that he now perceived it as concrete reality. Now he was able to dispense with real experience altogether.

This can be an effective literary device. George built his entire career on such enigmatic poetry and, along with his disciples, claimed Hölderlin as his own. He was wrong. George and Hölderlin are worlds apart. For Hölderlin obscurity was no literary device. Much of his most obscure poetry was simple and direct — to him! Reality, experience, and relations to other people on the normal social plane were inaccessible to him. Unable to communicate with people, he created an elaborate, comfortable code through which he could talk to himself.

He was cut off from real experience quite early in life. Experience in the social dimension and the resulting need to perceive life as it was had little opportunity to correct his progressively fantastic ideas about what living was all about. Too sensitive, too easily hurt, he cut himself off from even the limited social contacts that were available to the student in the theological schools. As we have seen from his letters, he was perfectly aware of what he was doing. But he had no choice. In his later poetry there is much to suggest that the tone of sorrowful resignation resulted from his long and intimate association with loneliness. "Wohl! ich wußt' es zuvor," he wrote in "Der Abschied." When he wrote about himself he was, more often than not, ruthlessly honest. "I knew it before." He meant just that. And then: "Everything is still the same." This is the characteristic attitude toward reality which condemned him as a novelist. For there could be little suspense generated when, in the second letter to Bellarmin, before *any* of the story of what had gone on before had been told, he wrote:

"My work on earth is finished. I set about my work with great will-power, have bled over it, and have made the world not one penny richer.

"Lonely and without fame I return and wander through my Fatherland, which, like a garden of death, stretches all about; and perhaps there awaits me the dagger of the hunter, who looks on us Greeks as a delicacy, like a beast of the forest."[8]

But what is still the same? That the "lover's heart" must perish because of "all-divisive hate." "All-divisive" — separation, isolation, alienation, the gulf

---

[8] III, p. 8.

separating him from other people and his dreams from all hope of realization. For him there is no hope of consolation, no solution to his dilemma, save in spiritual death, which he represents through the cup of poison. That he drinks willingly, even asking for it, "so that all things, hate and love, may be forgotten." Why love also? Because, as we shall see in the following pages, love for the ideal woman, love for Diotima, was part of the dream-world that he invented for compensation – the dream-world that, in the end, could not sustain him. His ideal of perfect love for the perfect woman did not result *in* his loneliness but *from* it. It could never have been realized in life; it did not have its roots in life. This all began many years before he ever saw Susette Gontard. When he broke his engagement to Luise Nast in 1790, he wrote her: "And I would think that my love is not for this world."[9] He was right. His love was the outgrowth of his torment – of his hatred for the world in which he was unable to live and find fulfillment.

All this is said in order to indicate what was to come more than a decade later. We learn through this excursion into the future that his final mental breakdown was not the result of an accident, as was believed for so long. We know now that catatonic schizophrenia is not caused by a sunstroke.[10] Nor will an unhappy life produce so classic a case as Hölderlin's unless the personality has, inherent within it, one fatal weakness from the beginning: an inability to face situations in adult life to which normal people adjust everyday. The usual course of the disorder can be read in the professional literature of psychology: Behind a retiring exterior, frustrations and resentments gradually mount up; unable to attack his impaired social relationships directly, the victim withdraws and ultimately develops an inverted value system for comparing his own worth to the worth of others and often judges himself to be of extraordinary worth, so much so that everyone else appears to be jealous of his superiority because they are incapable of understanding what he grasps without effort; finally come the delusions of persecution. In direct ratio to the growing feelings of inadequacy, the delusions of grandeur assume progressively absurd proportions. "I am the lord of the world!" "I am the King of France!" Similar, perfectly serious assertions of institutionalized schizophrenics fill the pages of professional literature.

(Hölderlin, at the very beginning of his correspondence, saw himself as the only true Christian among all his classmates!)

There is no more difficult mental disorder to treat than advanced catatonic schizophrenia. In the advanced stages the victim lives completely within his self-contained world of delusion. Even the trained psychiatrist penetrates into this twilight region only rarely. From outside, from the realm of normality in which socially determined modes of thought prevail, it is inaccessible – as much so as Hölderlin's late poetry.

[9] 31.45.
[10] See the autopsy report in Hellingrath Edition, VI, pp. 468f.

"I am the only true Christian!" That was the still unconscious conviction that we discovered at the bottom of his first letter, to his former teacher Köstlin. He admitted then that he often took offence when there was no real justification, but he seems to have looked upon that as nothing more than a tendency toward minor errors in judgment. It seems never to have occurred to him that his whole estimation of others' intentions might be in error. He wanted to repair his disrupted relations with his classmates "without adopting their truly sinful habits."

That was the beginning of his correspondence. The poem "Die Nacht" was the first of many that he wrote during his first four years at the Cloister Schools.

Seyd gegrüßt, ihr zufluchtsvolle Schatten,
Ihr Fluren, die ihr einsam um mich ruht;
Du stiller Mond, du hörst, nicht wie Verläumder lauren,
Mein Herz, entzükt von deinem Perlenglanz.

Aus der Welt, wo tolle Thoren spotten,
Um leere Schattenbilder sich bemühn,
Flieht der zu euch, der nicht das schimmernde Getümmel,
Der eitlen Welt, nein! nur die Tugend liebt.

Nur bei dir empfindt auch hier die Seele;
Wie göttlich sie dereinst wird seyn,
Die Freude, deren falschem Schein so viele Altäre
So viele Opfer hier gewiedmet sind.

Weit hinauf, weit über euch, ihr Sterne,
Geht sie entzükt mit heilgem Seraphsflug;
Sieht über euch herab mit göttlich heilgem Blike,
Auf ihre Erd, da wo sie schlummernd ruht . . .

Goldner Schlaf, nur dessen Herz zufrieden
Wohlthätger Tugend wahre Freude kennt,
Nur der fühlt dich. — . Hier stellst du dürfftig schwache Arme
Die seine Hülfe suchen vor ihn hin.

Schnell fühlt er des armen Bruders Leiden;
Der arme weint, er weinet auch mit ihm;
Schon Trost genug! Doch spricht er, gab Gott seine Gaben
Nur mir? nein auch für andre lebe ich. — .

Nicht von Stolz, noch Eitelkeit getrieben,
Kleidt er den nakten dann, und sättigt den,
Dem blasse Hungersnoth sein schwach Gerippe zählet;
Und himmlisch wird sein fühlend Herz entzükt.

> So ruht er, allein des Lasters Sclaven
> Quält des Gewissens bange Donnerstimm,
> Und Todesangst wälzt sie auf ihren weichen Lagern
> Wo Wollust selber sich die Ruthe hält.[11]

The sentiments we found in his earliest letters filled the poems of the same period. Here he fled into nature not because of any great love for nature but because he sought its "shadows full of refuge." He greeted the moon as a friend because the moon listened to him "not as slanderers eavesdrop." He fled expressly "from out the world where raging fools do mock." Nature then appealed to him because it was the very opposite of "the world's glittering tumult." In communion with nature he anticipated the joys that one day ("dereinst") would be. Others, however, sought only its "false seeming" here on earth.

This was the beginning of his nature poetry and reveals already the place of nature in his perception. It represented seclusion and escape before anything else.[12] In it he found release from tension and peace — all those things that he needed so much. Because he found them in the loneliness of natural beauty he had written Nast that he preferred loneliness to the company of the other boys at school.

And yet, his feeling of his own superiority had already prompted him to imagine himself as the savior of others. He was sensitive to other people in their suffering and wept with them. That was not enough. His religion taught him that God had not given him talents to be hidden; he was obligated to live for others as well as for himself. As the poem moves on, he becomes something other than the poor sufferer who had fled the company of men in the opening stanzas. He entered the world of men as comforter and savior — almost as a Christ figure.

The image of himself as the good Samaritan, the consoler of the oppressed, would bear abundant fruit in later poems. Within a few years that image would have developed into the role of educator of his people. It is to this office that Diotima appoints Hyperion at the end of the first volume of the novel, when she says: "Thou shalt become the educator of our people, thou shalt become a great man, as I hope."[13]

In Hölderlin's life the same image would appear in more and more pathetic forms. When he learned that Ludwig Neuffer's betrothed was dying of tuberculosis he wrote a letter in which, instead of effectively consoling his

---

[11] I, 1, pp. 3f.
[12] That his original love for nature was grounded in his need for seclusion made him susceptible to Schiller's treatment of nature in "Die Künstler." But, because Hölderlin's feeling for nature was more genuine than Schiller's, he never shared Schiller's theme that nature in the modern world was dead. For Hölderlin love of nature remained a way of reestablishing contact with the gods. See Chapter 9.
[13] III, p. 89.

friend, he fell back on the same day-dream consolations that worked for him; this resulted in the gruesome passage: "I shall not leave you. I will call out to you without ceasing, and I would say it if I had just come from your corpse and hers: Pain can hurl me to the ground, but it cannot overcome me as long as I *will.*

"Let her go on ahead, if it should be so, along the infinite path to fulfillment! You will hurry after her, even if you remain here for several years yet. Pain will give wings to your spirit, you will keep pace with her, you two will be one, as you are, and whatever is joined together will find itself once again."[14]

Already in 1785 something was terribly wrong. But wrong with whom? With him? Or with everyone else? Again one sees the dilemma in both his letters and his poems. He felt, for example, that he had to stay in school in order to please his mother, even if that meant compromising his standards in an effort to get along with boys who were sinful. He was destined to suffer. If he stayed in school he would have to live in self-imposed isolation to avoid sin; if he were true to himself and ran away, then he would have betrayed his mother's love.

Fate! The agonizing fate of being duty-bound to live in a world he felt to be evil. In that same month of November 1785 he wrote the poem "Der Unzufriedne":

> Schiksaal! unglüksvolle Leiden
> Heist du Sterblichen die Freuden,
> Die die steile Laufbahn hat,
> Grausam rauben. Bange Thränen
> Die sich nach der Bahre sehnen,
> Zu erzwingen ist dein Rath.[15]

The Christian conception of sin appears frequently in the earliest poems as a general category under which he understood everything that he found unpleasant in himself and others. Of himself he wrote:

> Viel, viel sind meiner Tage
> Durch Sünd entweiht gesunken hinab
> O, großer Richter frage
> Nicht wie, o lasse ihr Grab
> Erbarmende Vergessenheit
> Laß, Vater der Barmherzigkeit
> Das Blut des Sohns es deken.[16]

---

14 87.35ff.
15 I, 1, p. 6 (lines 1–6).
16 I, 1, p. 8 (lines 1–7).

And of the sinfulness of others he wrote:

> Banger Schauer faßt die trübe Seele,
> Wenn sie jene Thorenfreuden sieht,
> Welt, Verführung, manches Guten Hölle,
> Flieht vor mir, auf ewig immer flieht![17]

These are, in part, the traditional sentiments of the theology student, of the young, would-be preacher practicing admonitions to an imaginary congregation. In part he was merely practicing the art of self-examination and the recanting of sins required of him by his religion. But it was also the seed from which burst forth the sublime, terrifying blossoms of his greatest poetry, through which run the suspicion that he may also have been deserted by the divinity. "I thought God did not love me," he wrote Nast in October 1787. Thirteen years later he wrote:

> Aber Freund! wir kommen zu spät. Zwar leben die Götter,
>   Aber über dem Haupt droben in anderer Welt.
> Endlos wirken sie da und scheinens wenig zu achten,
>   Ob wir leben, so sehr schonen die Himmlischen uns.[18]

These lines, when read with a foreknowledge of what he had suffered in life, are the expression of ultimate despair. But it is a despair that sounds almost placid. Only the poetic images remain; vanished are the experiences that had lain behind them — experiences so painful that these compensatory images had to be developed so that he might be able to come to terms with his suffering. The lines are a general, obliquely expressed statement about the relationship between the poet and his time. Here we encounter again the strange way Hölderlin internalized his anxiety. As his anxiety increased; as his feeling of guilt, which resulted from his repeated failure to gain the respect of family and friends through the life he had chosen for himself, ate away at his self-confidence; as he came to feel himself more and more the victim, trapped in a hostile world from which there was no escape — then he fled more and more into his poetry. But, even more than that, he came to demand more and more from the artificial world of dreams that he had created. He demanded real fulfillment from unreal dreams, and he was inevitably disappointed. The old question of who was responsible for his plight, which had worried him in his school days, had become academic. We see this when we watch him writing "Der Abschied," quoted in the first part of this chapter. Resentment, which had been so evident in the first version of the poem in the formulation "all-divisive hate,"[19] disappeared from

---

[17] I, 1, p. 13 (lines 13–18).
[18] II, 1, p. 93 (lines 109–112).
[19] II, 1, p. 24 (line 14).

the second version. It was replaced by "the deep-rooted deformity, fear"[20] — an emotion more in keeping with the image of the suffering poet.

Hence the apparent paradox, the deep schism between his life and poetry that has led — or misled — so many to regard Hölderlin as some sort of superman who succeeded in overcoming his torment. As he grew older and became more and more inextricably entangled in the subtle, yet ultimately destructive coils of his progressively more complicated relationships with others, he began to come into his own as an artist. The more he lost his self-control, the more control he demonstrated in his poetry.

That is the appearance. To accept the appearance at face value, however, would be to make nonsense of the biographical fact that he was, after all, overwhelmed in his struggle with reality. The truth is that he did not overcome his problems but merely reinterpreted them, internalized them, and refused steadfastly to take real action. This was a fine solution for lyric poetry, in which everyday reality need be conceded only a bare minimum of integrity. When he wrote his poems he could do anything he wished with his life and make whatever he wanted of his experiences. Reality did not resist the most far-fetched interpretation, because it was reduced to words with which the poet could do anything he wanted. That he did, in fact, deny everyday reality to such an extent both in his life and in his poetry indicates that his perception of reality was impaired by his overwhelming need to refuse to recognize problems that demanded real solutions.

In life, however, such a solution was disastrous. He concentrated exclusively on the dream-world that he had made for himself, not only when he wrote poetry but also when he went about the everyday business of looking for a job, gaining the support of those whose help was an absolute necessity for anyone hoping to establish a literary career, and getting along with his employers. Thus it was that, even as he tottered on the very brink of insanity, he was able to write his most powerful verses.

In these early years, when his self-awareness was just taking form, his resentments and feelings of inadequacy appeared more openly than they did later. He wrote in the poem "An M.B.":

> Dich sucht noch nicht des kühnen Lästrers Zunge:
> Erst lobt sie, doch ihr Schlangengifft
> Verwandelt bald das Lob, das sie so glänzend sunge
> In Tadel, welcher tödtlich trifft.[21]

In the poem "Das Menschliche Leben" he developed a similar line of thought as if he were writing a sermon.

---

20 II, 1, p. 26 (lines 13f.).
21 I, 1, p. 5 (lines 9–12).

Menschen, Menschen! was ist euer Leben,
Eure Welt, die tränenvolle Welt,
Dieser Schauplaz, kann er Freuden geben,
Wo sich Trauern nicht dazu gesellt?
O! die Schatten, welche euch umschweben,
Die sind euer Freudenleben.[22]

The disappearance of overt resentment in later years did not mean that he no longer felt it. His letter to Rike in which he told how much he resented Frankfurt society because the gentry always made him feel like "the fifth wheel on a cart" should be enough to dispel any such notion.[23] Resentment had merely been detached from reality and internalized. Concealed, seldom expressed directly, it became an important determinant in the mythology of the lonely poet and his ideas about the place of the poet in the modern world.

The mistreatment that he suffered during his school years was to become the *necessary* alienation of the poet-prophet, which was prescribed by destiny. The question of where the guilt lay, of who was to be held accountable, which he had answered ambivalently in his letters, were also unanswered in the later works. Why? Because the question of guilt became more or less academic when the gods began to play an important role in his thought. When the poet became the servant of the gods; when he came to regard himself as ordained by the divinity to deliver a message to his people; when the gift of prophecy had set him apart from all others, who could not hear the words of divinity or appreciate the message that the poet brought – then no one could be at fault.

This did not mean that Hölderlin was any less alienated than before; nor did the underlying feeling of guilt, the suspicion that his aloofness was somehow sinful and that he, as he had indicated in "Die Nacht," was really obligated to search for reconciliation with others, cease tormenting him. His misgivings about how well he had justified his aloofness can still be seen in "An die Deutschen," which he wrote in 1800.

Spottet nimmer des Kindes, wenn noch das alberne
    Auf dem Rosse von Holz herrlich und viel sich dünkt,
        O ihr Guten! auch wir sind
            Thatenarm und Gedankenvoll!

Aber kommt, wie der Stral aus dem Gewölke kommt,
    Aus den Gedanken vieleicht, geistig und reif die That?
        Folgt die Frucht, wie des Haines
            Dunklem Blatte, der stillen Schrift?

---

22   I, 1, p. 13 (lines 1–6).
23   148.77ff.

Und das Schweigen im Volk, ist es die Feier schon
  Vor dem Fest? die Furcht, welche den Gott ansagt?
    O dann nimmt mich, ihr Lieben!
      Daß ich büße die Lästerung.[24]

The poet — and here we speak of the *real* Hölderlin — was no less isolated from others than he had been before. But the need to blame, the need to sin against others through uttering blasphemies, as he had done in the poems of the earlier years, had all been overcome. The tragedy was no longer anyone's fault. It was fate — the destiny of the poet.

That same mythology, which included the promise of a Golden Age, served another function as well. It relieved him of all responsibility of seeking reconciliation with others, because, according to the mythology, reconciliation between the poet and the common herd was impossible at that point in history. He longed for such a reconciliation ("O dann nimmt mich, ihr Lieben!") and hoped that the unresponsiveness of others to his message was merely the "Feier vor dem Fest." For that would have meant that the Golden Age was much closer than he dared hope.

But what he was really saying was this: If only I were wrong; if mankind would hurry up and change and become demigods like me; if only they were able to get along with me on my own terms. Underlying this and many other of the late poems is the poet's conviction that he could not be reconciled with the Germans of his day unless they became the new Greeks, the worthy recipients of his friendship.[25]

Both the isolated genius and the common herd were then the victims of seemingly immutable historical laws. They happened to be so unfortunate as to live in one of those periods in which the universe was divided sharply into mutually exclusive spheres. On the one hand there was the divine (poetic) order; on the other there was the earthly (social) order. Neither had anything to do with the other. Common men had been deserted by the gods. They were the fortunate ones, because they were not aware of their spiritual poverty. Only the poet suffered consciously. He alone knew the awful truth that all was not as it should be and that human life was infinitely poorer in spirit than it had been in ages past and would be sometime in the future. Only he who was cursed with the power of prophecy knew the terrible truth of which Hölderlin sang in "Brod und Wein":

---

24 II, 1, p. 9 (lines 1–12).
25 See "Gesang des Deutschen (II, 1, pp. 3ff.) and "An die Deutschen (II, 1, pp. 9ff.).

Nemlich, als vor einiger Zeit, uns dünket sie lange,
   Aufwärts stiegen sie all, welche das Leben beglükt,
Als der Vater gewandt sein Angesicht von den Menschen,
   Und das Trauern mit Recht über der Erde begann,
Als erschienen zu lezt ein stiller Genius, himmlisch
   Tröstend, welcher des Tags Ende verkündet' und schwand,
Ließ zum Zeichen, daß er einst da gewesen und wieder
   Käme, der himmlische Chor einige Gaben zurük,
Derer menschlich, wie sonst, wir uns zu freuen vermöchten,
   Denn zur Freude, mit Geist, wurde das Größre zu groß
Unter den Menschen und noch, noch fehlen die Starken zu höchsten
   Freuden, aber es lebt stille noch einiger Dank.[26]

According to this vision the poets, those few who still partook of the gifts left
behind by the heavenly chorus, belong to both realms. Their mission was to
serve as mouthpieces for the vanished deities — a mission that condemned them
to partial separation from both gods and men.

Nicht, was wohl sonst des Menschen Geschik und Sorg'
   Im Hause und unter offenem Himmel ist,
     Wenn edler, denn das Wild, der Mann sich
      Wehret und nährt! denn es gilt ein anders

Zu Sorg' und Dienst den Dichtenden anvertraut!
   Der Höchste, der ists, dem wir geeignet sind,
     Daß näher, immerneu besungen
      Ihn die befreundete Brust vernehme.[27]

Armed with this view of things, the poet was in a position to effect a
thorough transevaluation of his own experience. Men could not understand him
because the divine spark had died out within them. They could not understand
that he who had heard the divine voices was justified in forsaking normal life.
They looked upon the poet as a malcontent, a dreamer, a good-for-nothing. The
poet, of course, could be blamed least of all. Isolation was not merely his
inescapable destiny — it was his duty! His complaints were then not really born
of hatred and resentment; they rather reflected the deepest love and concern for
his fellow men. That he constantly rebuked others for their insensitivity; that he
condemned his brothers for their narrowness and sinfulness; that he wrote at the
end of his novel that he had not found a single human being *(Mensch)* among the
Germans — all these merely marked him as the educator of his people whose task
it was to prepare them for that future time at which they would again live

---

26 II, 1, p. 94 (lines 125–136).
27 II, 1, p. 46 (lines 9–16).

together with the gods in harmony. *All* men would then live in harmony with the gods — and with the poet. Diotima, whose beauty had hitherto been perceived by the poet alone, would take her place in the common *Volksmythologie* alongside the gods and heroes.[28]

If this leaping from decade to decade is confusing, it is necessary to demonstrate that the late Hölderlin of Hellingrath is an invention. This should be obvious to anyone who has read the Hellingrath line of interpretation, which, because of a number of influences in German intellectual life at the beginning of this century too complicated to be discussed here, accepted the "prophecy" of the late poems as really prophetic. It is uncanny that so many writers have taken everything Hölderlin wrote at face value. He was always *right*. He became a prophet, just because he said he had become a prophet. Then he proceeded to interpret human life and the history of humankind *correctly!*

But he was not a prophet. German history and the history of mankind, which Hölderlin, in a letter to his brother in 1800, claimed to be on the very threshold of the new and glorious age he had been prophesying,[29] has *never* culminated in anything dimly approximating Hölderlin's vision. The most essential ingredient, undisturbed harmony, has never come about and never will.[30] It will not do to say that he meant it all "symbolically." His letter to his brother in 1800 makes it very clear that he meant it seriously.

If one is content to ignore objective fact and cling to the unsubstantiated notion that Hölderlin was a prophet, then one has entered into the area of mythology or religion, where this study, or any "study," will be of no value. If one, on the other hand, wants an answer to the objective question: What impelled Hölderlin to his *wrong* ideas about life, which he felt so strongly that he posited them as a vision from on high? — then one must look at the man himself.

So far we have seen some indication that the binding tie between the clumsily constructed poems and the feverishly scribbled letters of the theology student in the 1780's and the powerful hymns of the late Hölderlin is to be found in his autistic view of himself. The late Hölderlin was simply the theology student who had suffered longer. In the years between "Die Nacht" and "Brod und Wein," his personal weakness determined his actions more and more. His mania to overcome his problem assumed psychotic proportions. His inverted appreciation of himself and others and of their attitudes toward him became pronouncedly paranoid. In order to integrate his experiences into a meaningful whole so that he might be able to explain to himself why his life had to be as it was, he was forced to adopt ever more unrealistic categories. These categories, which Kant

28   I, 1, p. 242 (lines 6—8).
29   222.25ff.
30   And yet Alfred Rosenberg claimed Hölderlin for the Nazi movement in *Mythus des 20. Jahrhunderts* (Munich, 1937), pp. 425—439).

might have called his regulative ideas, eventually became his mythology. At bottom, it was only a rationalization. "Das Reich Gottes," as Hölderlin envisioned it, was nothing more or less than the wish-dream of a future time in which everyone would live in harmony with the divinity, and thus with Hölderlin. This explanation is, of course, less poetic, less complimentary to Hölderlin than others that have been offered. Yet it alone explains why Hölderlin would have been compelled to misread history so grossly that, in the letter to Karl Gok in 1800, a passing armistice, one of many during those troubled years, was proclaimed as a sure sign that the new day was dawning. Reduced to its most prosaic terms, Hölderlin's dream was of an age in which he would be able to establish meaningful relationships with everyone, because everyone would be just like him!

It all began with the theology student. In 1803 the theology student who had written poems like any other young man, who had dreamed of preaching fire-and-brimstone sermons, peeped for one last time from behind the veil, behind which he would soon disappear forever, and wrote:

> Johannes. Christus. Diesen möcht'
> Ich singen, gleich dem Herkules, oder
> Der Insel, welche vestgehalten und gerettet, erfrischend
> Die benachbarte, mit kühlen Meerwassern aus der Wüste
> Der Fluth, der weiten, Peleus. Das geht aber
> Nicht. Anders ist ein Schicksal. Wundervoller.
> Reicher zu singen.[31]

The lack of formal similarity between the aesthetic masterpieces of later years and the early, largely imitative, poetry explains why no one seems to have recognized that the exclusiveness of the poet was anticipated in the "only Christian" fiction of the early poems and the "I alone am sensitive" attitude in the letters to Nast. The common denominator of his works had little to do with style; it is found in his attitude toward others.

The growth of his poetry is thus the story of how the motifs and his handling of them flowed from his isolation. If he had not found it well-nigh impossible to get along with his fellow students, then he would never have written his former teacher that he could not seem to control his attitudes, and there would never have been a conflict. If he had ever been able to relax and accept others and himself as they and he were, then he would never have been compelled to try to escape from school. If he had ever really been able to assert himself successfully, then he would have been able to strike out on his own, leave school, and forsake everything, as Schiller had done; he would not have had to stay in school and escape in fancy instead of in fact. Both aspects of his personality taken together

---

[31] II, 1, p. 181 (lines 151—157).

explain why he developed the idea of becoming a poet as a solution to his problems.

This insight, gained from his letters, holds true for the early poetry also. For he was not only convinced that he was being unjustly persecuted, but also that he was unable to do anything about it. He could not attack his problems directly; thus he attacked them indirectly. His reading and the fantasy life he found in the literature of the day suggested how this might be done. It is therefore not surprising that he imitated what he read.

It has become a cliché to say that his earliest poems were imitations of Schubart and Klopstock and also to refer to them as "Pietistic." But one cannot dispense with these early works by relegating them to the relatively uninformative category of Pietism. No one feels obligated to write his personal poetry in the language of a preacher unless he has found in works written in such language thoughts that correspond to what he feels called upon to say. His early poems are not merely Pietism in verse any more than his poems from 1790 to 1796 are "merely" copies of Schiller. A young man does not, after all, copy an author's style simply because he has decided to write poems and happens to find a volume of the model's works lying open on the desk. It is more instructive to set aside the term "Pietism" and examine these earliest, admittedly imitative, poems in an effort to find out *why* Hölderlin was moved to write in the same manner as Schubart and Klopstock in the first place.

Schubart was, at that time, a prisoner in the Hohenasperg dungeon. He was the convenient symbol of the victim. In and out of jail all his life for his unrelenting integrity as a journalist, he must have seemed a kindred spirit to Hölderlin, who felt himself the prisoner of the school authorities. In 1785 and 1786 Schubart's collected poems were being published. We know that Hölderlin had access to some of Schubart's works because he suggested that Nast read "Ahasveros" instead of Wieland's satires. This poem, a free adaptation of the Eternal Jew theme, had appeared in the volume of poems published in 1785.[32] In that same volume there appeared a number of poems in the tone of the long-suffering martyr, which would have appealed to Hölderlin and which seem to have directly inspired his earliest poems.

Schubart, for example, had written in his "Morgenlied":

> Wenn mich es martert, daß die Welt
> So schimplich mich verwarf,
> Und wenn mir eine Thrän' entfällt,
> Weil ich nicht reden darf.

---

32 "Ahasveros" in C.F.D. Schubart, *Des Patrioten Gesammente Schriften und Schicksale,* (Stuttgart, 1839) IV, pp. 65—69.

> Nicht reden darf mit einem Freund,
> Nicht scherzen mit dem Kind,
> Soll schweigen, wie ein Menschenfeind,
> Wenn Brüder um mich sind.[33]

And in "Abendlied" he had written:

> Von Menschen, die mich haßen;
> Von Freuden selbst verlaßen,
> In öder Einsamkeit . . .[34]

All these sentiments are directly reflected in Hölderlin's early poems and letters. "Menschenfeind" (enemy of men), forsaken by friends, loneliness — all these can be seen in "Die Nacht." But he was not merely copying Schubart, but was at work adapting what he read into vehicles of his own feelings. Schubart had written in "Anders Morgenlied":

> Christen leben sich nicht selber,
> Leben sie, sie leben Gott![35]

Hölderlin, the only Christian in the school, as he thought, was already living for God. His problem was in learning to live in peace and harmony with others. Thus he took Schubart's lines, shifted the emphasis, and came out with

>   gab Gott seine Gaben
> Nur mir? nein auch für andre lebe ich.[36]

He needed comfort and support from others. At age fifteen he felt cheated out of life. He sought reasons and justifications for his suffering. He must have had some such thoughts in mind when he read Schubart's "Anderes Morgenlied," which reads:

>   Ach! Nun bitt' ich für die Meinen,
> Ferne sind sie, Gott, von mir!
> Heißer Dank, vermischt mit Weinen,
> Steigt im Morgenlied zu dir;
> Band' und Elend traf nur mich,
> Und nicht sie, wie preis ich dich!

---

33 *Ibid.,* III, p. 38.
34 *Ibid.,* p. 46.
35 *Ibid.,* p. 44.
36 I, 1, p. 3 (lines 23f.).

Sieh in ihren weißen Locken
Meine treue Mutter steh'n.
Und von langem Weinen trocken,
Ihre Augen zu dir fleh'n;
Säusle jenes Lebens Ruh'
Gott! ihr einst im Tode zu.

Meine Gattin! ach nun fließen
Bitt're Tränen in mein Lied,
Siehst du sie zu deinen Füßen,
Wie sie, für mich betend, kniet,
Misch' in ihrer Liebe Pein
Hohe Christenhoffnung ein!

Meine Kinder, ewig preisen,
Ewig preisen will ich dich,
Denn du sorgtest für die Waisen,
Vater! mehr als väterlich;
Lenkt sie deiner Gnade Zug,
O! so sind sie reich genug!

Meinen Freunden gib die Freuden,
Die du mir genommen hast,
Gern will ich alleine leiden,
Tragen meines Elends Last;
Fällt nur mein verscherztes Glück
Auf den Freund von mir zurück![37]

How this poem must have gripped the young Hölderlin! He must have seen in it a poetic mirror of his own predicament. For he also saw himself as a martyr. He also suffered for the sake of his family and interceded with God for their happiness. These feelings open what is, perhaps, the most revealing of his poems from Denkendorf: "Die Meinige." It is characteristic that he actually intensified the importance of the sufferer to the point that he compared himself to Christ.

Ich will betten für die lieben Meinen
Wie dein großer Sohn für seine Jünger bat –
O auch Er, er konnte Menschentränen weinen,
Wann er bettend für die Menschen vor dich trat –[38]

Hölderlin followed Schubart's example when he wrote "Die Meinige" in devoting individual passages to each member of his family and calling down God's blessing upon them. It was in this role of intercessor that he first wrote of

37 Schubart, III, pp. 42f.
38 I, 1, p. 15 (lines 5–8).

his feelings for his family. Almost automatically his mind riveted on the death of his step-father Gok. If, in later years, he always thought of his mother as mournful and cajoled her to cheer up and not submit completely to her innate capacity for sadness, that may well have been the result of her life-long attitude, which impressed upon him the fact that she was a poor widow who had been cheated of life. When he first wrote of his mother in his poetry, it was in connection with his stepfather's death. He wrote:

Ach als einst in unsre stille Hütte
Furchtbarer! herab dein Todesengel kam,
Und den jammernden, den flehenden aus ihrer Mitte
Ewigteurer Vater! dich uns nahm;
Als am schröklich stillen Sterbebette
Meine Mutter sinnlos in dem Staube lag –
Wehe! noch erblik ich sie, die Jammerstätte,
Ewig schwebt vor mir der schwarze Sterbetag –

Ach! da warf ich mich zur Mutter nieder,
Heiserschluchzend blikte ich an ihr hinauf;
Plözlich bebt' ein heilger Schauer durch des Knaben Glieder,
Kindlich sprach ich – *Lasten legt er auf,*
Aber o! er hilft ja auch, der gute –
Hilft ja auch der gute, liebevolle Gott ––
Amen! amen! noch erkenn ichs! deine Ruthe
Schläget väterlich! du hilfst in aller Noth!

O! so hilf, so hilf in trüben Tagen,
Guter, wie du bisher noch geholfen hast,
Vater! liebevoller Vater! hilf, o hilf ihr tragen
Meiner Mutter – jede Lebenslast.
Daß allein sie sorgt die Elternsorgen!
Einsam jede Schritte ihres Sohnes wägt!
Für die Kinder jeden Abend, jeden Morgen –
Ach! und oft ein Tränenopfer vor dich legt!

Daß sie in so manchen trüben Stunden
Über Witwenquäler in der Stille weint!
Und dann wieder aufgerissen bluten alle Wunden,
Jede Traurerinnerung sich vereint!
Daß sie aus den schwarzen Leichenzügen
Oft so schmerzlich hin nach seinem Grabe sieht!
Da zu sein wünscht, wo die Tränen all' versiegen,
Wo uns jede Sorge, jede Klage flieht.

O so hilf, so hilf in trüben Tagen
Guter! wie du bisher noch geholfen hast!
Vater! liebevoller Vater! hilf, o hilf ihr tragen,
Sieh! sie weinet! — jede Lebenslast.
Lohn' ihr einst am großen Weltenmorgen
All' die Sanftmuth, all die treue Sorglichkeit,
All' die Kümmernisse, all die Muttersorgen,
All' die Tränenopfer ihrer Einsamkeit.

Lohn' ihr noch in diesem Erdenleben
Alles, alles, was die Teure für uns that.
O! ich weiß es froh, du kanst, du wirst es geben
Wirst dereinst erfüllen, was ich bat.
Laß sie einst mit himmlisch hellem Blike
Wann um sie die Tochter — Söhne — Enkel stehn, —
Himmelan die Hände faltend, groß zurüke
Auf der Jahre schöne Stralenreihe sehn.

Wann sie dann entflammt im Dankgebette
Mit uns in den Silberloken vor dir kniet,
Und ein Engelschar herunter auf die heilge Stätte
Mit Entzüken in dem Auge sieht;
Gott! wie soll dich dann mein Lied erheben!
Halleluja! Halleluja! jauchz' ich dann;
Stürm aus meiner Harfe jubelnd Leben;
Heil dem grosen Geber! ruf ich himmelan.[39]

There are not many poems in which Hölderlin wrote of his mother. Here we see why it was to be so. There can be no doubt that the tender sentiments and the pity he expressed for the woman, who had already lost two husbands so early in life, was genuine. In this, perhaps the most realistic poem he ever wrote, Hölderlin played neither the martyr nor the hero. He was simply the little boy who loved his mother and who had suffered a long time because he had been forced to stand by and watch her suffer without being able to help. The thought of her had come to mean sadness, mourning, funeral processions to the old graveyard, where he noticed that she always caste a mournful glance toward the grave of her departed husband.

This was reality. His impotence, his inability to console her and fill her life with happiness, so that she might, with the passing of time, forget that she too was one of life's victims, are themes which were not his favorites. That he wrote about them at all would indicate that they were genuine.

[39] I, 1, pp. 15f. (lines 25–80).

And they were too painful. He looked to the future for her happiness and recognized that, if it was to come at all, it must come with her surrounded by her children and grandchildren.

Could he provide that happiness? The poem was a prayer. First, he asked for help in making her happy. But soon he was asking God to perform the miracle Himself.

In the section devoted to his sister Rike, there was already much that anticipated the "love" motif of later years. Of her he wrote:

> Wie sie in das Herz des Kämpfers Frieden
> Tränen in des bangen Dulders Auge giebt –
> Wie dann keine Stürme mehr das stille Herz ermüden,
> Keine Klage mehr die Seele trübt.
> Wenn sie frei einher geht im Getümmel,
> Ihr vor keinem Spötter, keinem Hasser graut,
> Wie ihr Auge, helleschimmernd, wie dein Himmel,
> Schrökend dem Verführer in das Auge schaut.
>
> Aber Gott! daß unter Frühlingskränzen
> Oft das feine Laster seinen Stachel birgt –
> Daß so oft die Schlange unter heitern Jugendtänzen
> Wirbelt, und so schnell die Unschuld würgt – !
> Schwester! Schwester! reine gute Seele!
> Gottes Engel walte immer über dir!
> Häng' dich nicht an diese Schlangenhöhle,
> Unsers Bleibens ist – Gott seis gedankt! nicht hier.[40]

Just as revealing is the way he anticipated his later ideas about friendship in the lines dealing with Karl, to whom he felt especially close all his life.

> Guter Carl! – in jenen schönen Tagen
> Saß ich einst mit dir am Nekkarstrand,
> Fröhlich sahen wir die Welle an das Ufer schlagen,
> Leiteten uns Bächlein durch den Sand.
> Endlich sah ich auf. Im Abendschimmer
> Stand der Strom. Ein heiliges Gefühl
> Bebte mir durchs Herz; und plözlich scherzt' ich nimmer,
> Plözlich stand ich ernster auf vom Knabenspiel.

---

[40] I, 1, p. 18 (lines 97–112).

Bebend lispelt' ich: wir wollen betten!
Schüchtern knieten wir in dem Gebüsche hin.
Einfalt, Unschuld wars, was unsre Knabenherzen redten —
Lieber Gott! die Stunde war so schön.
Wie der leise Laut dich Abba! nannte!
Wie die Knaben sich umarmten! himmelwärts
Ihre Hände strekten! wie es brandte —
Im Gelübde, *oft zu betten* — beeder Herz![41]

Here we see quite clearly that Schubart provided only the original impetus to write a certain type of poetry. As Hölderlin wrote the poem, however, the motif of prayer for one's loved ones took on a uniquely intense quality which had somehow been lacking in Schubart's verse. Schubart's prayer had been related specifically to his imprisonment and amounted to a song of thanksgiving to a merciful God who had visited His wrath on the poet alone while sparing the poet's family and friends. Hölderlin's poem was not limited to a particular situation. For him, life itself was the misfortune. His spiritual existence itself was in jeopardy.

The idea of self-sacrifice he also handled differently. For Schubart this was the heart of the poem; it had grown out of his willingness to suffer in the place of others. Hölderlin only began with the reference to his own Christ-like role; then the poem became something else. The undefined disaster of living in this sinful world burst out of the original motif of self-sacrifice. The calamity was too great for his sacrifice to matter much. Life was, at bottom, a tear-filled, sorrowful business.

This leads us to the basic difference between Schubart's and Hölderlin's poems, which began from similar perceptions. Schubart expressed thanks only for the goodness that he had received — even through being arrested and thrown into prison. Hölderlin, on the other hand, prayed for relief, prayed for all things good. Dissatisfied with his own fate and that of his family, half-orphaned, suffering from the unrelenting sadness of his mother — he sought heaven on earth. He prayed that his mother might be happier, that his sister might be supported in her struggle to maintain her virginal purity, and for a return to that most beautiful moment of friendship in God that he had enjoyed on the banks of the Neckar with Karl. Freedom from despair, purity, the brotherhood of prayer and piety — these motifs give us an approximate idea of what Hölderlin saw as perfection in life.

It is not surprising that they were all somehow related to childhood. He wanted to cancel out the effects of his stepfather's death on the family and restrain the growth of his brother and sister toward maturity. All this would

---

41 I, 1, p. 19 (lines 121–136).

indicate quite clearly his own fear of growing on into adulthood. For at the basis of the poem lay a deep longing for a bygone time of love and security, innocence and play, which had once been his to enjoy.[42]

In the course of life families fall apart. The old ties loosen. Parents die; brothers and sisters go out and live their own lives. The family into which one is born gradually disintegrates. Normally it is replaced by the family which one establishes when one marries and has children. But Hölderlin would never be able to establish a family, and so the pain he experienced with each loosening tie to his childhood never was soothed.

Did he know this at that time? Probably not. Are we then not, perhaps, overinterpreting? Is it not possible that we are reading certain thoughts into Hölderlin's works that in reality never occurred to him and that he never intended to express? Is it not possible that Böhm, Michel, Böckmann, and Hellingrath were wise in passing over those early years in, at most, a few pages, because they simply *have nothing to do with* the Hölderlin of later years? Should we not merely accept the advice implicit in Hellingrath's words: "I *can not* tell you of the content of these youthful years – of the bloom of his life – for they do not yet manifest themselves in his work; the poems of that time say nothing to us"?[43]

But what is the alternative? According to Hellingrath's still widely accepted view, the Poet – the only Hölderlin that should interest us – was born only through his love for Diotima.[44] All other influences which may have led either to his growth as a poet or to his eventual collapse are held to be insignificant. "According to an inner law," wrote Hellingrath, "this bloom had to break. It is of little importance to search for all external forces which contributed to that."[45] For, to Hellingrath, the world of the late Hölderlin was possible only after Susette Gontard (or Diotima, for Hellingrath, significantly, makes no distinction between the woman and the mythological figure) had fulfilled her own mission, which was supposedly this: "giving being to Hölderlin's world *(der Welt Hölderlins Dasein zu geben)*."[46]

---

[42] The theme of yearning for childhood as a lost time occurs most obviously in "Die Stille" (I, 1, pp. 42ff.), "An die Ehre" (I, 1, p. 94), "Einst und Jetzt" (I, 1, pp. 95f.), "Die Weisheit des Traurers" (I, 1, pp. 9ff.). The theme falls away during the period of the Tübingen Hymns, but soon returns again in "An die Natur" (I, 1, pp. 191ff.), which serves as a prelude to the renewed celebration of childhood during Hölderlin's stay at Frankfurt, beginning with "An die Unerkannte" (I, 1, pp. 197ff.).

[43] Norbert von Hellingrath, "Hölderlin's Wahnsinn" in *Hölderlin-Vermächtnis* (Munich, 1947) pp. 52ff.

[44] Hellingrath proclaims: "Now world had to flow into world, and in flowing together, awaken to being [*Dasein*]. The awakening to being of the world, in Hölderlin's language, the 'arising of a common sphere,' and thus of a 'common divinity' – that was what actually took place" (*Ibid.*, p. 155).

[45] *Ibid.*, p. 153.

[46] *Ibid.*, p. 156.

Now, one must seriously ask what Hellingrath meant by that, at best, nebulous formulation. There are only two possibilities. Either he meant that she brought about the *factual* realization of Hölderlin's world or that she made possible the *poetic* realization of the dream. The former is patently absurd. Hölderlin's poetic vision became fact neither in his lifetime nor in Hellingrath's time. Obviously then, he must have meant that Diotima's love made possible the creation of the late poems, that is to say, that his love for her opened up to him the vision which he then expressed in poems.

Hellingrath writes of Hölderlin's farewell from Frankfurt and Susette Gontard: "Then they were separated by the perception that a continuation of their love would not be as worthy as a complete break *(ein ganzes Ende);* they were separated by their consciousness that the actual essence had been fulfilled: giving being to Hölderlin's world."[47]

This is, of course, factually inaccurate in the first place. There was no "complete break" *(ganzes Ende),* as Hellingrath suggests. The liason was dragged out for months and years, while they met secretly in the garden and swapped letters through the hedge. It ended only in 1800, when Hölderlin realized that he would never bring out a journal and would have to return to Swabia. Nor is there any basis for Hellingrath's consoling assumption that there was a mutual "consciousness" *(Bewusstsein)* that Susette had served her purpose. On the contrary, there is every reason to assume just the opposite! In the draft of a letter which Hölderlin evidently intended to enclose in the second volume of *Hyperion* and send to Susette, he apologized that the work was not as good as it might have been *if he had been able to sit at her feet long enough to become a real artist!*[48]

Much of this information was not available to Hellingrath. But then, we do not seek to impugn his motives, but simply to measure his understanding of Hölderlin against the available biographical data, many of which make his views untenable. The false biographical understanding upon which Hellingrath based many of his notions led him to the following idea about what happened to Hölderlin after the break with Diotima: "A great reconciliation begins. With both hands he seizes his holy torment, objectifies it *(stellt es aus sich heraus),* kneels before it as before the grace of the gods, which mercifully bends his all too light being back toward the earth."[49]

Behind the over-zealous rhetoric and pronouncedly religious imagery of the above passage there lurks a hint of true understanding about what Hölderlin was doing when he wrote poetry. He did celebrate his own torment, objectify it in his poems, and worship it as a sign that he was a chosen mouthpiece of the gods.

---

47 *Ibid.*
48 "Had I been able to develop into an artist gradually at your feet, I believe I would have become one rapidly. . . ." (198.7ff.).
49 Hellingrath, p. 157.

But all this had little to do with Susette Gontard except insofar as she had been the last woman whom Hölderlin identified with the "perfect love" image, which he had already developed long before in his imagination and in his poetry. For he had *always* written of the love who would reconcile him with the world. Hellingrath's word "reconciliation" *(Versöhnung)* makes sense. And yet the assertion that, in the later years, a real reconciliation actually took place through his being somehow brought back to earth through the weight of his sorrow — all that is sheer poetry. If it were true, then Hölderlin's progressive loss of touch with reality from that point on would make no sense at all.

The poetic world, which became the domain in which he lived spiritually after he lost Susette and which Hellingrath dates from 1797 on, can already be discerned in the poems from Denkendorf and Maulbronn. As early as 1787 he was lamenting his alienation and creating an ideal, understanding female to hear his complaints and sympathize with him.

In 1786, for example, he wrote the poem "An Stella," which begins:

> Du gute Stella! wähnest du mich beglükt.
>> Wann ich im Thale still und verlassen, und
>> Von dir vergessen wandle, wann in
>>> Flüchtigen Freuden dein Leben hinhüpft?
>
> Schon oft, wenn meine Brüder, die Glückliche
>> So harmlos schliefen, blikt ich hinauf, und fragt
>> Im Geist, ob ich glüklich seie —
>>> Bin ich ein glüklicher Jüngling, Stella? [50]

Already he turned to his imaginary love so that he might give voice to the fears and misgivings which no one else would understand.

> Doch giebt es Wünsche, denen der Spötter höhnt —
>> O Stella! du nicht! höhne dem Armen nicht! —
>> Giebt unerfülte Wünsche — Tugend,
>>> Hehre Gefährtin! du kennst die Wünsche.
>
> Ach laß mich weinen! — nein! ich will heiter sein!
>> Ist ja ein Ort, wo nimmer gewünscht wird, wo
>> Der Sterbliche sein Schiksaal preiset, —
>>> Dort ist es, wo ich dich wiedersehe. [51]

In the summer of 1787, while he was tortured with his life at Maulbronn after he had tried to convince his mother that she should let him quit school and while he was suffering from the pangs of half-real unrequited love for Luise Nast, he wrote the poem "Klagen," which begins:

[50] I, 1, p. 21 (lines 1–8).
[51] I, 1, p. 21 (lines 13–20).

Stella! ach! wir leiden viel! wann nur das Grab —
  Komme! komme kühles Grab! nimm uns beide!
    Siehe Stellas Tränen, komme
      Kühles ruhiges Grab.

O ihr Menschen! o so gerne wollt' ich euch
  Alle lieben, warm und treu! o ihr Menschen
    Sehet diese Stella haßt ihr'
      Gott vergebe es euch![52]

This poem occupies a unique position in Hölderlin's works. Nowhere else, not even in the famous passage near the end of *Hyperion*, did he allow his resentment to appear so stark and unveiled. Here he plots sweet revenge. In the fifth and sixth stanzas, Hölderlin — the only Christian — allowed himself to dream of how, at the Last Judgment, he would inform on the others, before he succumbs to guilt at such decidedly unchristian thoughts and exhibits Christ-like forgiveness.

Stella! weinen werd' ich bis ans Grab um dich
  Weinen, Stella, du um mich — weinen! aber
    Am Gerichtstag will ichs sagen
      Vorm versammelten Erdkreis:

Diese sinds, die Stella quälten — aber nein!
  Gott im Himmel! nein! vergieb diesen Quälern
    Laß mich sterben — oder tragen
      Diese Leiden — mein Gott.[53]

This poem does not seem to be an imitation of anything he had read. Here he adopted the same attitude that he had displayed in the letter to his mother after she would not allow him to quit school. Association with others and the unrelenting pain which such association caused him made him evil. Was this his way of adjusting to life among men, as he had written in the letter? Perhaps so. For mixing in the affairs of the world seems to have meant to him a loss of holiness. The inference we drew from the letter is now substantiated by a poem written at about the same time. But even here he shielded his true feelings. Just as he had seen all his sinfulness as the result of his mother's insistence that he stay in school, so now it is explained as a reaction of righteous indignation against the sinners who were tormenting his beloved.

Here we see also the beginning of another characteristic guilt reaction: He transferred the role of the martyr to someone else, whom he then felt called upon to defend. This was not merely a poetic device but a complicated

---

52 I, 1, p. 26 (lines 1—8).
53 I, 1, p. 26 (lines 17—24).

compensatory twist in his thought processes which relieved him of guilt feelings. Here too the poem substantiates what we already observed in the letters. He wrote to Immanuel Nast in January 1787: "You see, my friend, it is not self-love or exaggerated sensitivity which made me so indignant — someone else [Luise], whose welfare is more important to me than my own, was insulted."[54]

This aspect of his written remains, by which the letters and poems demonstrate the same thought-patterns, pertains also to the themes about which he had read. What he read he tried out in letters to Nast at about the same time that the same thoughts were initially appearing in his poems. "Love" and "Friendship" he adopted as symbols through which he might be able to integrate his experiences. Ultimately they became substitutions for real social contacts. The people who, in his mind at least, more or less fit the models then became citizens of his dream-world.

These individuals, the partners in those ethereal relationships of "Love" and "Friendship," were already seen as the confidants of the poet. In 1787 the image of himself as the poet made its appearance. In the poem "Mein Vorsaz," the most famous of the pre-Tübingen poems and the only one of this period which has hitherto received much individual attention at all, he gave rather mature expression to his resolution to become a great poet. This poem is so important, the thoughts reveal so fully how early the ingredients which ultimately went into the later, more famous, poems germinated, that it deserves to be reproduced here in its entirety.

> O Freunde! Freunde! die ihr so treu mich liebt!
> Was trübet meine einsame Blike so?
> Was zwingt mein armes Herz in diese
> Wolkenumnachtete Todtenstille?
>
> Ich fliehe euren zärtlichen Händedruk,
> Den seelenvollen, seeligen Bruderkuß.
> O zürnt mir nicht, daß ich ihn fliehe!
> Schaut mir in's Innerste! Prüft und richtet! —
>
> Ists heißer Durst nach Männervollkommenheit?
> Ists leises Geizen um Hekatombenlohn?
> Ists schwacher Schwung nach Pindars Flug? ists
> Kämpfendes Streben nach Klopstoksgröße?
>
> Ach Freunde? welcher Winkel der Erde kan
> Mich deken, daß ich ewig in Nacht gehüllt
> Dort weine? Ich erreich' ihn nie den
> Weltenumeilenden Flug der Großen.

[54] 5.12ff.

Doch nein! hinan den herrlichen Ehrenpfad!
  Hinan! hinan! im glühenden kühnen Traum
    Sie zu erreichen; muß ich einst auch
    Sterbend noch stammeln; vergeßt mich, Kinder![55]

"Mein Vorsaz," the only poem of the period which the biographers have felt worthy of any individual discussion at all, is also the most misunderstood. Michel, for example, sums up his understanding of the poem in one sentence: "The ode from the Maulbronn period 'Mein Vorsaz' proclaims, of course, at the beginning, the joy of friendship . . . ., but, in the development [of the theme], it merely expresses the thought that he will only regard himself as a qualified (berechtigter) recipient of his friendship when he has succeeded in 'Pindar's flight' or (in attaining) Klopstock's greatness."[56]

This amounts to a misreading of the poem which, in turn, obscures its significance in Hölderlin's poetic development. Hölderlin never gives any indication that he sought friendship after he had scaled the heights. This interpretation actually inverts the relationship which Hölderlin saw between friendship and poetic development. Friendship was seen almost as the prerequisite of poetic success. He was fond of the quotation from Goethe's Iphigenie: "Lust und Liebe sind die Fittige zu großen Taten."[57] This was what he meant when he later quoted the passage from Herder's Tithon und Aurora to Neuffer: "Often a friend will be such a genius [inspiration]."[58] Again and again these ideas return in his poetry and in his letters: "Love" and "Friendship" alone sustain him in life and drive him on to perfect his art. They form the basis of the mythological view of the mankind which was to be. His poems were often meant for his friend or his sweetheart. And in the lines from "Brod und Wein" which were reproduced earlier, he began his lament about the impossibility of attaining the poetic greatness of past ages by addressing his friends: "Freunde, wir kommen zu spät."

Michel's mistake seems to result from his taking Hölderlin's farewell to his friend at face value. As we keep noticing he was never really open and candid with anyone, even with his closest friends. He felt that he was different from them, although he had enough in common with them for communication to be possible. But he felt he was somehow apart, that he had been set apart from all others by some force over which he had no control. But he did not leave his friends; nor did he feel that he should leave them until he had become a great poet. This relationship with his friends he saw as a fluctuating process by which

---

[55] I, 1, p. 28.
[56] Michel, p. 43.
[57] The quotation appears first in Hölderlin's entry in Hegel's Stammbuch (VII, 1., p. 349) and then in a letter to Karl on 2 June 1796 (121.3). On 28 November 1791 he varied the quotation to read "Liebe und Freundschaft" (47.26f.).
[58] 83.40.

he first fled into solitude to wrestle with his poetry, and then, after he had done battle, he returned to his friends for comradeship and spiritual renewal. He did not wish to renounce friendship here, but to structure it according to the model which he was developing in his mind.

The model he got from Klopstock.

The author of the *Messias* and so many poems in Greek metrics was, not only for Hölderlin but for his entire generation, the embodiment of the pure poet, the divinely inspired prophet who stood apart from all others. Hölderlin had pointed to Klopstock and Schubart as alternative reading when he had tried to convince Nast not to waste his time on Wieland. Years later, when he was passing what remained of his life at the carpenter Zimmer's home in Tübingen, he was often heard reciting aloud Klopstock's odes.

Preference for Klopstock above all others was a normal evaluation in the 1780's. Schubart, as late as 1790, published an essay in E.F. Posselt's *Archiv für ältere, vordeutsche Geschichte, Staatsklugheit und Erdkunde* entitled "Kritische Skala der vorzüglichsten deutschen Dichter", in which he reduced the attributes of the ideal poet to a finite number of categories. To these categories he assigned a numerical value of, at most, twenty, and, on the basis of his scale, proceeded to rate the leading German poets of the time. Klopstock led all others in a list which included Wieland, Bürger, Uz, Gessner, Lessing, Gerstenberg, Ramler, Goethe, Denis, Gleim, Schiller, and both Stolbergs. Schubart comments on his findings as follows: "Klopstock's poetic genius is unmistakable; it blows into one's face like a flame with every word. He possesses elevation of spirit, depth of feeling, fullness of tone, power of speech, as does no one else. The wellsprings of his feelings run inexhaustible." He goes on to say: "Klopstock is, by far, our leading poet and will remain so for a long time to come, since our nation is becoming less and less receptive to true poetic feelings."[59]

All this sounds somewhat strange to us, to whom Klopstock sounds stilted, unnatural, and, at times, almost unreadable. But our ears have grown accustomed to Hölderlin, and we have grown up with Goethe. To many of us even Schiller sounds old-fashioned.

In the late eighteenth century it was different. No one would have guessed then that professors would one day single out 1797 as the high-point of modern German literature. Great poetry was often thought of as the business of the last generation. Hölderlin confessed later that he was reduced to tears at the idea that with the death of Wieland great German literature might have come to an end.[60] He left no doubt that he felt Neuffer's Homer translation to be a daring enterprise because his friend was, in effect, crossing swords with Voss.[61] Voss'

---

59   Schubart, VI, p. 137.
60   89.32ff.
61   93.95ff.

Luise was so popular that Goethe's *Hermann und Dorothea* was initially received as a poor imitation. The *Xenien* show quite clearly that Goethe and Schiller felt that they had no chance of establishing themselves as dictators of taste until they had cut down to size a number of opponents, many of whom are scarcely known today. Few, if any, suspected that, in the judgment of later generations, the writers of the 90's would stand head and shoulders over all that had gone before.

It is thus not surprising that when Hölderlin began to appropriate themes from his reading and use them in his own poetry, he turned primarily to Klopstock. But there were also compelling personal grounds for his preference. With Hölderlin one is always, even in these earliest years, dealing with a lyrical genius. Others were copying Klopstock's poems because it was the thing to do. This entered, to some extent at least, into Hölderlin's efforts as well. But there was an intensity in his imitations and there were slight variations of themes which would suggest that his imitations were not merely imitations. He never discarded the Klopstockian themes as his art matured. He rather elaborated them, because in them he had found fitting symbolic representations for his own perceptions. It was not merely the tone and form of Klopstock's poetry which flooded into his own in the late 1780's. The formal aspects, which have been stressed so much in Hölderlin studies, may have been, at least in the early stages, relatively unimportant. He did, after all, take Schiller as his formal model after 1790. But the themes he had found in Klopstock formed, from these years on, basic ingredients in his thought. Several of these were later elaborated so that they contributed much to the birth of his mythology.

Most obviously, the cult of friendship — that "Friendship" of uninhibited embraces and kisses given and received by young men — he found in Klopstock. We do not know precisely when he first read Klopstock's *Gelehrtenrepublik,* just as we were unable, in the last chapter, to say whether he had read Klopstock's essay "Über die Freundschaft." *When* he read these particular works is, however, incidental. For we know that he was already enthusiastic about Klopstock's poetry, from which he could have gotten the essentials of Klopstock's Friendship theme.

In the poem "Auf einer Haide Geschrieben," one of his first nature poems, Hölderlin wrote:

> — Und ihr, ihr edlere, kommet!
> Edle Greise und Männer, und edle Jünglinge, kommet!
> Laßt uns Hütten baun — des ächten germanischen Mannsins
> Und der Freundschaft Hütten auf meiner einsamen Haide.[62]

And also in "Die Teck":

---

[62] I, 1, p. 30 (lines 30–33).

Hütten der Freundschaft, der Seegen des Herrn sei über euch allen!
Aber indessen hat mein hehres Riesengebirge
Sein gepriesenes Haupt in nächtliche Nebel verhüllet,
Und ich kehre zurük in die Hütten der biederen Freundschaft.[63]

The images of "der Freundschaft Hütten" and the turn of phrase "echter germanischer Mannsinn" bear the unmistakable mark of Klopstock, as does his use of the comparative ("edlere") for sake of the meter. More important, however, is the fact that even his conception of friendship between individuals seems to have been taken directly from Klopstock. The latter had written in the last stanza of his poem "An Herr Schmidten" (1747):

Ich sah dich still an, und nur Uranien
Allein bemerket, dir aber unbemerkt,
    Weissagend, in prophet'schem Geiste,
      Segnet ich, Schmidt, dich zum heilgen Dichter.[64]

But Hölderlin was not Klopstock. He was his pupil for a time, but he was never enslaved. His nature, his preoccupation with himself and with his own problems precluded slavish imitation of his favorite poet. If he took over themes, tone, and mood; if he seized the idea that friendship and love were ideal relationships open to the poet alone; if he wrote in Klopstockian meters and spoke Klopstockian language — then this was because he found in Klopstock's works ways of expressing what he already felt, but could not yet express independently. He needed a guide. But the way in which he would go was already clear from the imitations. Klopstock often *played* the role of the lonely poet. Hölderlin felt it far more deeply than his predecessor and *lived* it.

This can be seen most clearly in the poem "Am Tage der Freundschaftsfeier," which he seems to have written *before* he transferred to Tübingen. The time is important because it demonstrates that, when he later wrote like Schiller, he was still trying out new ways of expressing something which he had felt compelled to say for years. In this poem the *Dichterbund* and his Schillerian hymns were anticipated. But, now at least, he did not take Schiller's "An die Freude" as his model but Klopstock's "Auf meine Freunde."

This is clear in the opening lines. Klopstock's poem had begun:

Wie Hebe kühn, und jugendlich ungestüm,
Wie mit dem goldnen Köcher Latonens Sohn,
    Unsterblich, sing' ich meine Freunde,
      Feiernd in mächtigen Dithyramben.

---

[63] I, 1, p. 57 (lines 85–88).
[64] Klopstock, p. 11.

Willst du Strophen werden, o Lied, oder
Ununterwürfig Pindars Gesängen gleich,
   Gleich Zeus' erhabnen trunknen Sohne,
     Frei aus der schaffenden Seele taumeln? [65]

This conversation with the song itself related to the choice of verse forms. The alternatives were the Pindaric dithyrambic form, which he had used earlier, or the more restrained rhymed songs of praise, which had abounded in the Baroque era. Klopstock compromised. Hölderlin, on the other hand, wrote "Am Tage der Freundschaftsfeier" in a loose style, an arbitrary arrangement of lines of irregular length, for which there was no model. Like Klopstock, however, he opens with a justification for the form:

   Ihr Freunde! mein Wunsch ist Helden zu singen,
Meiner Harfe erster Laut,
Glaubt es, ihr Freunde!
Durchschleich' ich schon so stille mein Tal,
Flammt schon mein Auge nicht feuriger,
Meiner Harfe erster Laut
War Kriegergeschrei und Schlachtengetümmel. [66]

This apology for his song, which assumes the form of an excuse that it was the first sound from his harp, is characteristic for Hölderlin at this time, who was not yet sure of himself. He had written in "Mein Vorsaz":

   Ich erreich' ihn nie den
Weltenumeilenden Flug der Großen. [67]

He also follows Klopstock's lead in announcing the purpose of his song. He may have felt unable to match Klopstock's more measured verses and thus took refuge in a less demanding form. But there is a discrepancy more basic than the formal one. Klopstock developed a long poem in praise of his friends. His control of his subject matter is complemented by his self-assurance when he says:

   Die deutsche Nachwelt, wann sie der Barden Lied –
Wir sind die Barden – künftigen Schlachten singt,
   Die wird dein Lied hoch im Getöse
     Eiserner Kriege gewaltig sein. [68]

---

65 *Ibid.*, p. 12.
66 I, 1, p. 58 (lines 1–7).
67 I, 1, p. 28 (lines 15f.).
68 Klopstock, p. 4.

For Hölderlin the controlled tone was not suitable. It was the other motif, the idea of the embattled son of the next generation of Germans, that struck a responsive chord. We will see the image of the embattled champion, returning from the field of strife to rest in the arms of his friends or those of his love, in the poems from the first year at Tübingen. It was this image which Hölderlin, the lonely theology student at odds with the world and needing desperately to believe that he was playing some role of significance, found so attractive. If he could not be the cavalier poet sitting in the banquet hall and singing the praises of his friends, then he would be the warrior returning from a deadly struggle to sing to his friends the warrior's song of combat. The uncontrolled flow of irregular lines was a suitable mode of expression for the catalogue of sorrows and list of horrors through which the poet, while displaying certain Ossian qualities, established his credentials as Klopstock's warring posterity:

> Ich sah, Brüder! ich sah
> Im Schlachtengetümmel das Roß
> Auf röchelnden Leichnamen stolpern,
> Und zuken am sprudelnden Rumpf
> Den grausen gespaltenen Schädel,
> Und blizen und treffen das rauchende Schwerd,
> Und dampfen und schmettern die Donnergeschüze,
> Und Reuter hin auf Lanzen gebeugt
> Mit grimmiger Miene Reuter sich stürzen
> Und unbeweglich, wie eherne Mauren
> Mit furchtbarer Stille
> Und Todverhöhnender Ruhe
> Den Reutern entgegen sich streken die Lanzen.
>
> Ich sah, Brüder! ich sah
> Des kriegrischen Suezias eiserne Söhne
> Geschlagen von Pultawas wütender Schlacht.
> Kein wehe! sprachen die Krieger,
> Von den blutiggebißnen Lippen
> Ertönte kein Lebewohl –
> Verstummet standen sie da
> In wilder Verzweiflung da
> Und blikten es an das rauchende Schwerd,
> Und schwangen es höher das rauchende Schwerd
> Und zielten – und zielten –
> Und stießen es sich bitterlächelnd
> In die wilde braußende Brust.[69]

---

[69] I, 1, p. 58 (lines 21–33).

Only now that he had sung of himself did he introduce the friends whom he
had invited to hear his song:

> Willkommen, du! —
> Und du! — Willkommen!
> Wir drei sinds?
> Nun! so schließet die Halle.
> Ihr staunt, mit Rosen bestreut
> Die Tische zu sehen, und Weirauch
> Am Fenster dampfend,
> Und meine Laren —
> Den Schatten meiner Stella,
> Und Klopstoks Bild und Wielands, —
> Mit Blumen umhängt zu sehen.[70]

The direct reference to Klopstock is, by now, unnecessary to establish that
"An meine Freunde" was uppermost in Hölderlin's mind and served as a model
for "Am Tage der Freundschaftsfeier." More revealing than the similarities are the
differences. Klopstock was never the poet that Hölderlin was. Much of
Hölderlin's superiority is to be found in Schubart's "depth of feeling" category,
in which, in the eyes of the eighteenth century, Klopstock excelled. "An meine
Freunde" is a very long and a very diffused poem. Klopstock paraded before the
drunken poet's eyes the shades of departed ones with whom he felt spiritual
kinship. Much of what he said was connected only in the sense that the people
he praised were poets, and mostly German poets. Amidst the abundance of
erudition and name-dropping, however, occur a number of motifs which
Hölderlin emphasized in his own poem.

Before he began the recital of specific poets, Klopstock wrote of the true
friend in general:

> Des spott' ich, der es unbegeistert,
>   Richterisch und philosophisch höret.

> Den segne, Lied! ihn segne mit festlichen
> Entgegengehenden hohen Begrüßungen,
>   Der dort an dieses Tempels Schwellen
>   Göttlich, mit Reben umlaubt, hereintritt.[71]

And he wrote of Rabener:

> Haßer der Torheit, aber auch Menschenfreund,
> Allzeit gerechter Rabner! dein heller Blick,
>   Dein lächelnd Antlitz ist nur Freunden,
>   Freunden der Tugend, und deinen Freunden

---

[70] I, 1, p. 59 (lines 43–53).
[71] Klopstock, p. 13.

Stets liebenswürdig. Aber dem Tor bist du
Stets furchtbar. Lach' ihn ohne Barmherzigkeit
    Tot. Laß kein unterwürfig Lachen,
        Freund, dich im strafenden Zorne stören.

Stolz und demütig ist der Tor lächerlich.
Sei unbekümmert, wüchs auch der Narren Zahl
    Stets; wenn zu ganzen Völkerschaften
        Auch Philosophen die Welt bedeckten:

Wenn du nur einen jedes Jahrhundert nährst,
Und weisern Völkerschaften ihn zugesellst;
    Wohl dir! wir wollen deine Siege,
        Die wir prophetisch sehn, feierlich singen.[72]

Near the end of the poem he introduced the notion that the poets of whom he sang were living in a poetically barren age and that he must, therefore, pin his hopes on some future time.

Komm, goldne Zeit! Komm, die du die Sterblichen
Selten besuchest, komm! laß dich, Schöpferin!
    Laß, bestes Kind der Ewigkeiten,
        Dich über uns mit verklärtem Flügel!

            . . . .

Aus allen goldnen Altern begleiten dich,
Natur, die großen Dichter des Altertums,
    Die großen neuern Dichter. Segnend
        Seh ich ihr heilig Geschlecht hervorgehn![73]

The exclusive association of poet-friends who had in common the dream of a better world which could not be understood by the "philosophers" or "fools"; the contempt for all things prosaic; the right of the poet to play Rabener and judge his fellow man in a holy rage and yet, at the same time, be considered the "friend of men" — these were the themes that struck Hölderlin and which he subsequently adapted to his own ends. For Klopstock such themes were more or less confined to literature. Direct references to the poet's singular position among men account for a relatively few lines in the entire poem. Klopstock's exclusiveness was something learned, the acquired superiority of the educated man or the patrician attitude of an in-group. He exuded confidence. He said expressly that true beauty would prevail even if the pedants increased into multitudes, as long as poets like Rabener found at least one follower each

---

72 *Ibid.*, p. 15.
73 *Ibid.*, p. 21.

century. Throughout "An meine Freunde" Klopstock had been feeding his and his friends' egos. The tone was not really very solemn. He playfully had addressed his song, asked what meters it would like to choose for itself, and dallied at the banquet table with his sweetheart.

For Hölderlin, the opposite of the rough-and-tumble sportsman Klopstock who was always respected and admired by his friends and associates, these themes, which their inventor did not take very seriously, made sense out of painful experiences at school and provided the structures for his compensatory day-dreams. Hölderlin also was shoring up his ego – but desperately. He made of Klopstock's embattled warrior the poet of his feast. His battle was real; he adopted the role which Klopstock suggested in order to justify his preference for loneliness and poetry to companionship. Part of this might be said of Klopstock also. But Klopstock's tone was one of self-confidence. Hölderlin seemed unable to convince himself. His tone is as shrill as it had been when he wrote Köstlin or Nast and apologized for complaining so much. *His* first song was not the measured tune of the poet at all but the rough lament of the war hero, in which the "shout of war and den of battle" *(Kriegergeschrei und Schlachtengetümmel)* predominate.

Klopstock's feast was a timeless, unending affair; he celebrated his friendship with the others as a permanent condition of his life. Hölderlin presented the celebration of friendship as something quite extraordinary. Klopstock's culturally determined exclusiveness became something personal when Hölderlin adopted the motif. He admitted only two unnamed friends to the hall before closing the door. Even within the banquet hall no one could forget that a hostile world was waiting outside and threatening destruction. The eternal battle between poetic friendship and the prosaic and unfeeling world was reproduced symbolically within the hall. On the wall hung two pictures: the beloved Klopstock and the hated Wieland! Klopstock's banquet in "An meine Freunde" was, moreover, a sumptuous affair. The true friends were celebrated as they entered ("mit Reben umlaubt"). Hölderlin's three-man banquet was a make-shift meal which took place between battles.

> Ich wolt' in meiner Halle Chöre versammeln
> Von singenden rosichten Mädchen
> Und kränzetragenden blühenden Knaben,
> Und euch empfangen mit Saitenspiel,
> Und Flötenklang, und Hörnern, und Hoboën.
>
> Doch – schwur ich nicht, ihr Freunde
> Am Mahle bei unsers Fürsten Fest,
> Nur Einen Tag mit Saitenspiel

Und Flötenklang, und Hörnern und Hoboën,
Mit Chören von singenden rosichten Mädchen
Und kränzetragenden blühenden Knaben
Nur Einen Tag zu feiren? [74]

The friends remained unnamed, shadowy figures to whom the song is addressed. He recalls only in passing the day on which they sealed their *Bund;* for he sings, as he had foretold at the beginning, not of friends but of heroes. And the real hero is Hölderlin, who now laments his unhappy fate of having to live in such a time and in the midst of such people.

Ihr hörtet so oft mich sprechen,
Wie lang' es mir werde
Bei diesem Geschlechte zu wohnen,
Ihr sahet den Lebensmüden
In den Stunden seiner Klage so oft.

Da stürmt' ich hinaus in den Sturm
Da sah' ich aus der vorüberjagenden Wolke
Die Helden der eisernen Tage herunterschau'n.
Da rief' ich den Nahmen der Helden
In des hohlen Felsen finstres Geklüft,
Und siehe! der Helden Nahmen
Rief ernster mir zurük
Des hohlen Felsen finstres Geklüft. [75]

He reaches the depths of despair when he says:

O Brüder! Brüder!
Da weinte der Schwärmer blutige Tränen,
Auf die Disteln des Turmes,
Daß er vieleicht noch lange
Verweilen müsse unter diesem Geschlechte,
Da sah' er all' die Schande
Der weichlichen Teutonssöhne,
Und fluchte dem verderblichen Ausland,
Und fluchte den verdorbnen Affen des Auslands,
Und weinte blutige Tränen,
Daß er vieleicht noch lange
Verweilen müsse unter diesem Geschlechte. [76]

---

[74] I, 1, pp. 59f. (lines 54–65).
[75] I, 1, pp. 60f. (lines 86–98).
[76] I, 1, pp. 61f. (lines 117–128).

Then, finally, he returns to the characteristic, escapist concept of friendship:

Jezt wohn' ich gerne
Unter diesem Geschlechte,
Jezt werde der Thoren
Immer mehr! immer mehr!
Ich habe eure Herzen.[77]

"Am Tage der Freundschaftsfeier" is, of course, an adolescent imitation. Whatever is original, including the shift of emphasis toward exaggerated tragedy and loneliness, is about what one might expect from a gifted boy who was imitating his favorite poet. All young men play the martyr at one time or another. That is no more unusual than for a sixteen year old boy to write letters to his friend in which he cries on his shoulder. It is, however, unusual that Hölderlin carried the same adolescent themes on into his adult years. The celebration of friendship before the decisive battle appears in *Hyperion*, which was written by a man of twenty-six.[78] The idea that he *could not* write whatever poetry he wanted to write because of the world in which he lived and the age in which he was unfortunate enough to be born, returned again in 1795 in a letter to Schiller. "I feel only too often," he wrote, "that I am no extraordinary person. I freeze and congeal in the winter that surrounds me. So forged of iron is my heaven; and I am so made of stone."[79]

When he planned to publish the journal *Iduna* and saw his plans collapse, he wrote to Susette Gontard: "The famous ones, whose participation was to serve as my shield, have left me in the lurch. And why shouldn't they? Everyone who makes his name in the world seems to detract from them; then they are no longer the only idols . . . ."[80]

The young Hölderlin, it would seem, was no more adolescent than the Hölderlin of later years. For his defensive posture toward others continued. In the Cloister Schools he saw the other students as sinful because they either did not recognize his superiority or were jealous of him. He plotted to take his revenge upon them at the Last Judgment. Later he felt that he was being plotted against by the famous authors because they were afraid that he would surpass them.

He wrote this letter, in which he attacked, by implication, Goethe, Schiller, Schelling, and all others who were not inclined or willing to contribute to his journal, to Susette Gontard, his Diotima. She was the only one to whom he could reveal his true thoughts. His relation to Schiller had been strained for a number of years. Hegel was still in Frankfurt, but Hölderlin had lost contact

77 I, 1, p. 62 (lines 137—141).
78 III, pp. 105ff.
79 104.28ff.
80 195.28ff.

with Schelling. Neuffer, the *Bundesbruder* of the Tübingen years who had been privy to many of his secret thoughts, received little news from his old friend now. His brother had never really measured up to the ideal image of the friend, although Hölderlin had tried to make him over in that image.

Susette alone was left. In this sense Hellingrath was right: She was the last one who seems to have been able to reach him. To her he did objectify his sorrow and celebrate it. But there was no real reconciliation; this letter is filled with bitterness. In a draft of a letter near the end of June 1799, he wrote her: "Each day I must call up once more the vanished deity. When I think of how great men in great times reached out around themselves like a great fire and kindled everything wood and leaden into flames, which ascended with them to heaven – and then when I think of myself and of how I often, like a flickering lamp, wander about, forced to beg for a drop of oil in order to burn for yet a little while – then a wondrous trembling runs through every part of my body, and softly I pronounce that terror-filled word: the living dead."[81]

Later he wrote her: "It is indeed worth all the tears we have shed in these years that we should not have the joy which we might give each other; but we must cry out to the heavens when we think that we may both have to perish along with our greatest strengths because we do not have each other."[82]

In the poem given earlier he had asked her to pass him the hemlock cup!

There was no reconciliation. The dream of a better world, the dream of a perfect love with Diotima, was never realized. His last letters to Susette are filled with the deepest despair. She was already ill. A few years later he would return, half-deranged, from southern France to find a letter from Sinclair waiting for him in Nürtingen. Susette had died. This was not the beautiful end of the dream which Hellingrath tried to transform ino reality through his eloquence. This was separation, pain, suffering, death, and madness.

Why did it all come out that way? Because, as we indicated earlier, the dream was unrealizable. It lacked all substance. The love that filled him was a verbal love. It had begun as words, and it ended as poetry. If Hellingrath's mythology is not fact, it is at least a literary tradition of which Hölderlin was quite well aware because he helped invent it. If Susette did not reconcile him with the world, he had believed for many years that she would do so. From the beginning, in poems and letters to Luise Nast, the beloved was seen as the great reconciler and was thus to share in his glory through reflecting the spiritual light which he cast over the world. She was to transform him.

None of this was new. It too had been developed by Klopstock, who had already introduced into German literature the mythological image of the beloved whose goodness and purity elevated the innocent youth above others.

In the poem "Die Verwandlung" he had written:

81 182.1ff.
82 198.12ff.

Als ich unter den Menschen noch war, da war ich ein Jüngling,
    Weiblich und zart von Gefühl,
Ganz zur Empfindung der Liebe geschaffen. So zärtlich und fühlend
    War kein Sterblicher mehr.
Also sah ich ein göttliches Mädchen; so zärtlich und fühlend
    War keine Sterbliche mehr.
Aber ein unerbittliches Schicksal, ein eisernes Schicksal
    Gab mir ein hartes Gesetz,
Ewig zu schweigen, und einsam zu weinen. So zärtlich und elend
    War kein Sterblicher mehr.[83]

Hölderlin's realtionship to Luise Nast must have been somewhat similar to
this. Shy, reticent, not knowing how to act, it was months before he got up his
courage to approach her. When they were engaged, he wrote Immanuel Nast:
"Oh, you do not know her completely, Brother — I saw her in society — saw her
without being noticed by her other playmates — oh, how different she is with
me!"[84] Now, his own "hard law" *(hartes Gesetz)* to be silent had been abolished.
He had already spoken of it often. For he constantly lamented to Nast the fact
that he could not reveal to his dearest friend the thing that was in his heart. This
was also Klopstock's theme. Then, when he finally wrote Nast candidly of his
feelings for Luise, he echoed the idea that she was completely different when
they were alone, which he may have found in Klopstock's lines:

So geht De-ahna daher: Nun bleibt sie voll heimlicher Wollust,
    Daß sie dein Herz besitzt, und vor Entzückungen, stehn.
Also bleibt ein besungenes Mädchen (ein göttlicher Dichter
    Brachte sie der Nachwelt, und den Unsterblichen zu),
Darum bleibt sie auf einmal entzückt, tiefsinnig, und lächelnd,
    Unter der Versammlung ihrer Gespielinnen stehn;
Auf die Unsterblichkeit stolz, wenn ihre Schönheit dahin ist,
    Hat sie doch den Nachruhm, ihre Gespielinnen nichts.[85]

To Klopstock the little girl was different from all her playmates because the
poet had sung her praises and had thereby made her immortal. She was
remembered by posterity because of her association with the poet. All this bore
fruit in Hölderlin's imagination. Years later the same idea was voiced by Diotima
at the end of the first volume of *Hyperion,* when she confirms her lover as the
educator of the Greek people. "Thou shalt be the educator of our people; thou
shalt be a great man, I hope. And when I embrace thee then, I shall dream that I
were a part of this magnificent man; then will I rejoice as if thou hadst given me

[83] Klopstock, p. 49.
[84] 15.149ff.
[85] Klopstock, p. 26.

a part of thy immortality, as Pollux did to Castor. Oh, I will be a proud maiden, Hyperion!"[86]

His poetic conception of "Love" was closely associated with his notions of "Friendship." Yet there was a difference. The "Friend" supported the poet and helped prepare him for the hard struggle. The Beloved, on the other hand, contributed to the rejuvenation of the world and shared the glory of the poet. For "Love" was, by definition, eternal and was to last beyond all hardship and all separation, including death.

In "Stella" Hölderlin had hoped for an early death for both him and his Beloved. For, in the afterlife, they would have their reward.

Klopstock had written in "Fanny":

> Dann wird ein Tag sein, den werd ich auferstehn!
> Dann wird ein Tag sein, den wirst du auferstehn!
> Dann trennt kein Schicksal mehr die Seelen,
> Die du einander, Natur, bestimmtest.[87]

When Hölderlin was about to transfer to the seminary in Tübingen and thus begin the several years of separation from Luise, he wrote "An Luise Nast," which begins:

> Laß sie drohen die Stürme, die Leiden
> Laß trennen — der Trennung Jahre
> Sie trennen uns nicht!
> Sie trennen uns nicht!
> Denn mein bist du! Und über das Grab hinaus
> Soll sie dauren die unzertrennbare Liebe.[88]

Already he had strengthened Klopstock's theme. Twelve years later, when he wrote "Der Abschied," the theme of the reunion of the lovers in death returned.

> Hingehn will ich. Vieleicht seh' ich in langer Zeit
> Diotima! dich hier. Aber verblutet ist
> Dann das Wünschen und friedlich
> Gleich den Seeligen, fremd sind wir.
>
> Und ein ruhig Gespräch führet uns auf und ab.
> Sinnend, zögernd, doch izt faßt die Vergessenen
> Hier die Stelle des Abschieds,
> Es erwarmet ein Herz in uns,

---

86 III, p. 89.
87 Klopstock, p. 40.
88 I, 1, p. 64 (lines 1–6).

Staunend seh' ich dich an. Stimmen und süßen Sang,
  Wie aus voriger Zeit hör' ich und Saitenspiel,
    Und befreiet, in Lüfte
      Fliegt in Flammen der Geist uns auf.[89]

The latter is great poetry, of course, while the former is largely imitative
verse-making. But the images, the concepts, the pronouncedly escapist manner in
which he circumscribed love and represented the place of the Beloved in the
poet's life remained the same. These did not change. He grew as a poet, at least
in the sense that he learned to write poetry rather than mere verses. But *what* he
said remained relatively constant. And his attitude toward life itself, which made
such an unearthly concept of love necessary in the first place, grew more
eccentric as the years passed. Always the Beloved existed only for him and might
be sacrificed for his sake. She was his alone ("Denn mein bist du!") and, like
him, was misunderstood by others. From the beginning to the end his Beloved
was no lover in the normal sense but a mother-like woman, a consoler, a verbally
manufactured inspiration for a purely verbal vision.

And it all began before he ever saw or heard of Susette Gontard. Under her
influence the "Love" fixation grew and even supplanted "Friendship" to a
degree. But the nature of the fixation had been determined in the earliest school
years.

No one seems to have recognized this. No one seems to have noticed that the
lines, written in 1788:

Dort am schattichten Hain wandelt Amalia.
  Seegne, seegne mein Lied, kränze die Harfe mir,
    Denn sie nannte den Nahmen,
      Den, du weists, des Getümmels Ohr

Nicht zu kennen verdient. Stille, der Tugend nur
  Und der Freundschaft bekannt, wandelt die Gute dort.
    Liebes Mädchen, es trübe
      Nie dein himmlisches Auge sich.[90]

anticipated the lines written ten years later:

Komm und besänftige mir, die du einst Elemente versöhntest
  Wonne der himmlischen Muse das Chaos der Zeit[91]

as well as:

Du schweigst und duldest, und sie versteh'n dich nicht.[92]

89 II, 1, p. 25 (lines 25–36).
90 I, 1, p. 23 (lines 9–16).
91 I, 1, p. 231 (lines 1ff.).
92 I, 1, p. 242 (line 1).

For we know from his letters that he regretted, most of all, that he had not been allowed to sit at Diotima's feet and become a poet, that she too was to have brought order into his poetry, blessed his song, and placed wreathes upon his harp. Here again his autism and self-protectiveness dictated his choice and employment of themes. The others did not deserve to hear what he had to say and could not appreciate her beauty. She belonged to him alone – and was superior only through her association with him. When he wrote in Frankfurt: "Thou who reconciled the elements," this was but a restatement of the passage in a letter to Luise Nast: "You will reconcile me with the world when I am insulted."

Hölderlin would have denied that his poetic life began with Susette Gontard, as Hellingrath would have it. He gave ample testimony himself that "Love" had always meant the same things to him and that Susette had merely corresponded to the image of the Beloved that he had already developed. When he fell in love with Susette, he wrote the poem "Diotima" still in Schillerian meters. For Schiller he rewrote the poem twice. But through all the rewritings he preserved at least the spirit of the statement of his foreknowledge of her existence and of the role that she would play in his life which appears in the earliest version:

> Da ich noch in Kinderträumen
> Friedlich wie der blaue Tag,
> Unter meines Gartens Bäumen
> Auf der warmen Erde lag,
> Da mein erst Gefühl sich regte,
> Da zum erstenmale sich
> Göttliches in mir bewegte,
> Säuselte dein Geist um mich.
>
> Ach und da mein schöner Friede
> Wie ein Saitenspiel, zerriß,
> Da von Haß und Liebe müde
> Mich mein guter Geist verließ,
> Kamst du, wie vom Himmel nieder
> Und es gab mein einzig Glük
> Meines Sinnes Wohllaut wieder
> Mir ein Traum von dir zurük.[93]

Here we approach the true nature of love in Hölderlin's life and poetry. It hovered around him in his childhood. It was reconciliation in the most profound sense, because it was intimately connected with the innocence and purity of childhood to which he longed to return. It was a solution for disharmony and

---

93 I, 1, p. 213 (lines 39–48).

discord and, as such, was the only alternative left open to the adult for whom the childhood innocence was no longer accessible.

This is borne out by the fact that love became particularly important to him twice in his life: during the lonely school years when he felt rejected and mistreated by his classmates and in 1796, after he had spent several months of self-imposed exile in Nürtingen following his flight from Jena. He seems to have been particularly susceptible to romantic flights of fantasy whenever his relations to others were seriously impaired. Shortly before he admitted to Immanuel Nast that he loved Luise, he had written: "No one likes me here."[94] A few months before he met Susette, he had written Schiller: "I was always tempted to see you [in Jena], and always saw you only to feel that I could be nothing to you."[95]

Rejection, receptivity to love, and love as a refuge were all forms of internalization of experience. There is good reason to believe that they increased as his resentments grew.

On 24 July 1796 Hölderlin sent a letter to Schiller which included the revised version of the poem "Diotima," which he had undertaken at Schiller's request. Seldom in the history of art has an artist so completely revised a work, against his better judgment, at the insistence of a friend. On the other hand, he sent along also the poem "An die Klugen Rathgeber" in which he took his revenge on his mentor.

> Ich sollte nicht im Lebensfelde ringen,
> So lang mein Herz nach höchster Schöne strebt,
> Ich soll mein Schwanenlied am Grabe singen,
> Wo ihr so gern lebendig uns begräbt?
> O! schonet mein und laßt das rege Streben,
> Bis seine Fluth in's fernste Meer sich stürzt,
> Laßt immerhin, ihr Ärzte, laßt mich leben,
> So lang die Parze nicht die Bahn verkürzt.[96]

Hatred, resentment, and indignation do not generate great poetry. A mere misanthrope would never be a Hölderlin. He would be too callous, his resentment too obvious, his indignation always too ugly.

Nevertheless, at the basis of Hölderlin's poetry — of his need to write poetry — lay an autistically dicated self-protectiveness against a world he resented. For, if a mere misanthrope could not have written "Im Winde klirren die Fahnen," neither could it have been written by a well-adjusted man who lived in harmony with others.

---

94 4.23.
95 102.12ff.
96 I, 1, p. 223 (lines 1–8).

If this sounds somewhat paradoxical, it should. Hölderlin's psyche was an extremely complex organ which eventually foundered on the great dilemma he was never able to resolve: How was he to survive in a world he could not accept, when he found it impossible to reject men completely and really become a misanthrope?

He was an incorrigible procrastinator. Unable to endure normal human contact, he was just as unable to throw everything over, strike out on his own, and really distance himself from others. He dreamed of being a nameless wanderer without any ties; he wrote a novel in which the protagonist ended as the hermit he himself should have become. But he could never quite bring himself to do it. His need for love and respect was so great that he always had to give it one more try, transpose the fantastic notions of "Love" and "Friendship" onto another – and experience disappointment all over again.

So he fled into a verbal world, into books, and into the poems and plays of Schiller, Schubart, and Klopstock. This he chose as his place of solitude.

This rather lengthy exploration into the first poems of the young Hölderlin has grown far beyond a mere commentary on them alone; it has been necessary in order to demonstrate that they really do relate to something which we are wont to call "the real Hölderlin." Through repeated references to the poems and events of later years we have been able to uncover connections and growth patterns which have hitherto gone unnoticed. We have demonstrated a unity in theme and thought pattern between the earliest poetic efforts and the later masterpieces.

Something else has come to light also. *Because* the important themes and thought patterns were developed in the 80's and not in the 90's, Hölderlin was excessively dependent on other poets for his imagery. This dependency was in turn perpetuated by his exclusiveness, which prevented experience from maturing his perceptions and broadening his poetic range. We are quite aware, of course, that this implies that he was, in one sense, a derivative poet. Others have seen this differently. Previously, Hölderlin the schoolboy has been seen as merely an imitator, while the later Hölderlin was seen as something completely new. Common sense would make one suspect that such a view is untenable. The striking unity in themes and imagery in his earliest works and those of later years now show that such a fiction is, at best, unnecessary.

The young Hölderlin was not merely an imitator of Klopstock or anyone else, any more than Goethe's first published poems are "merely" Rococo. If one thinks so, then one does not understand the importance of mimicry. Hölderlin did not imitate Klopstock and Schubart simply because he had nothing better to do, but because he found in their works modes of expression which were or seemed to be suited to his own perceptions. Even in the earliest works the themes and images assumed a new intensity under his hands. They were transformed from traditional verse-making formulae into motifs of genuine, living alienation. Love, friendship, nature, prayer, martyrdom — all assumed a unified structure under his hands when he grouped them all under the general tone-feeling of autistically determined isolation. To him they ceased to be literature and became truth — the truth he lived.

This opens a new range of appreciation of Hölderlin and his works. I must confess that I have never liked the Hölderlin who emerges from the theories of the aestheticians, because he seemed to be terribly obscure, or from the notions of the mythologists, because he seemed to be talking about things which were terribly relevant but non-existent. Approached aesthetically or mythologically, no amount of rhetoric can save Hölderlin from the charge of a lack of originality. He seems often to have said what others had said and almost in the way they had said those things.

But he said them better. He was not an aesthete. The origins of his themes are important only in so far as the obvious borrowings demonstrate that one has to look for his uniqueness somewhere else than in the mere concepts which he appropriated. The tone, the intensity, the seriousness of his works must eventually be traced back to his attempt to *live* what he wrote, which distinguishes him from all others who only wrote about it. *We* see that he was writing mythology. *Hölderlin* saw himself seriously constructing an alternative to life as he perceived it, real life, his own life, the life he felt to be such a waste. That the fantasies cannot be taken seriously by us (however much we *pretend* to believe it all as we sit in our book-lined studies) does not matter. He took them seriously because they were his last resort. Only because he took them seriously, only because he needed them to be real, was he able to probe his psyche and reveal the deeper dreams, the ideals, the archetypal ideals which are never brought into the realm of consciousness by most of us.

Finally, all of this makes untenable any talk of the pre-ordained poet. The need to be a poet came first. One might indeed speculate that, had he lived at another time, he might never have written poetry at all. Is it not possible that he turned to poetry only because the alternative forms for the expression of deep concern were so limited? How much was he dependent on the fact that the whole of Germany was expressing itself on paper? If he had lived in France, would he have been a revolutionary instead? If he had lived in the twentieth century, would he have been too deeply involved in student revolts to sit for hours and carefully write and rewrite a few lines of verse? For there is certainly a curious similarity between the way he seized upon clichés which were in the air at the time and the way in which modern malcontents seek to revitalize the world by reinterpreting old political clichés.

However, that may be, Hölderlin lived in Swabia, attended the theological schools, and was drawn to poetry. His expression was verbal and his solutions symbolic. When he was sixteen or seventeen he made his choice: He would strive for the laurel wreath. And in 1788 he expressed his determination to compete in the poetic lists in the poem "Der Lorbeer."

> Nein! ich wolte nichts auf dieser Erden!
> Dulden all' der Welt Verfolgungen
> Jedes Drangsaal, jegliche Beschwerden,
> All des Neiders bittre Schmähungen ––[97]

The poem ends:

> Aber still! Die goldne Bubenträume
> Hört in ihrer Nacht die Zukunft nicht –
> Schon so manche Früchte schöner Keime
> Logen grausam mir ins Angesicht.[98]

---

[97] I, 1, p. 36 (lines 21–24).
[98] I, 1, p. 37 (lines 37–40).

5

THE TÜBINGER *STIFT*

The theological seminary at Tübingen is the traditional center of Swabian intellectual life. Founded on the site of a former Augustinian monastery at the command of Herzog Ulrich in 1547, the *Stift* was charged with the education of the young men who would become not only the spiritual leaders of the Duchy but the educators of the next generation as well. These young men were the sons of a distinct intellectual aristocracy. In the records of the institution the same family names appear for generation after generation.[1] This is perhaps the clearest indication that the sudden eruption of poetic and philosophic genius among former *Stiftler* at the end of the eighteenth century was as much the result of genetics as of education and training. The close in-breeding of a rather small number of families, all descended from men who had been selected by the educational system with its centuries-old emphasis on the humanistic skills of linguistic ability and adeptness to abstract reasoning, all continuing in the families' professional traditions and constantly intermarrying, goes a long way toward explaining why a theological seminary located in an area of Germany which lacked many of the advantages enjoyed by the established centers of culture and learning of the time began producing, and has continued to produce, a long line of distinguished poets and thinkers. Kepler, Schelling, Hölderlin, Hegel, Kerner, Uhland, Mörike, Schwab, Vischer, and Goes are but a few of the illustrious alumni of the *Stift,* most of whom can claim lineage from some branch of the clerical family tree.

This preponderance of distinguished alumni cannot be explained through any supposed excellence of instruction, least of all during the last years of the eighteenth century when Hölderlin, Hegel and Schelling were in attendance. For these years marked one of the lowest points in the school's history. Martin Leube, who has chronicled the fortunes of the *Stift,* has also noted this paradox of relatively poor education being offered at the very time at which some of the most promising students, who would later make reputations for themselves as poets and philosophers, were in attendance. Leube remarks that "the emergence of a great number of important men in the last third of the [eighteenth] century is really such a riddle, even more so when one considers that the Karlsschule must have been taking the best human material away from the religious institution; after all, such men as Schiller and Curvier escaped the *Stift* by way of the new school."[2]

---

[1] See the list of *Stiftler* in the appendix to Martin Leube's *Die Geschichte des Tübinger Stifts. 1770—1950* (Stuttgart, 1954). pp. 692ff.

[2] *Ibid.,* pp. 6f.

Competition with the Karlsschule should not, however, be exaggerated. Before the new school was opened in 1770, the decline of the *Stift* was already evident. By 1750 Georg Bernard Bilfinger, President of the Church Council of Württemberg, had recommended that the *Stift* be done away with as an independent institution altogether and only Herzog Ulrich's original decree of 1536, which stipulated that three sons of needy Stuttgart families should begin their education at the state's expense each year, be left in effect. Other reform proposals, even though less extreme than Bilfinger's, had met with no success.[3]

At the heart of all the school's problems lay its subservience to the state church. The precautions taken by the Herzog and his Church Council to insure the dogmatic purity of the clerical youth were often unnecessarily restrictive and, not infrequently, oppressive.[4] Gradually this conservative, provincial, narrow-minded suspiciousness of all opinions that smelled ever so slightly of heterodoxy came into conflict with the praiseworthy tradition of academic freedom, which had always been more or less respected. For all of Hölderlin's and his generation's complaints of oppression, academic freedom, at least in its narrow definition, seems never to have been infringed upon. Schnurrer, the Director of the *Stift* at that time and a scholar in his own right, was particularly zealous in safeguarding the student's right to read whatever they might want to read – a right which extended even the works of Voltaire and Rousseau.[5] There was no list *librorum prohibitorum.* The students read quite openly the works of Schiller, even though less than a decade before he had had to flee the Duchy in order to see his *Räuber* staged, which had been banned as subversive by Karl Eugen.

The result of this conflict was a constant morale problem among the students. Through the works of the *Sturm und Drang* authors, as well as Rousseau and Wieland, they were exposed to new and, for Swabia, quite radical ideas about innate human dignity, the uncorrupted innocence of Rousseau's natural man, the unfettered titanism of the *Sturm and Drang Genie,* and the derring-do of Schiller's revolutionary heroes. All these ideas had a tremendous impact on boys who were forced to accept a semi-monastic way of life. Many accepted them as enthusiastically as the *Jugendbewegung* would accept the pronouncements of Nietzsche and Stefan George a century later. The man who, relying on his own instinct, made his own rules and dared to oppose the dictates of tradition was

---

[3] *Ibid.,* pp. 40f.

[4] On 29 February 1792 Ernst Gottlieb Bengel, who had graduated with Neuffer and who served until 1799 as *Repetent* and would in 1812 become *zweiter Superattendent* of the *Stift,* indicated in a letter to Neuffer that the students knew what to expect from the planned reform. "The *Stipendiaten* . . . are presently more afraid than ever because of the imminent reform; they do not want to let it be known, however, but rather assert *hautement* that they will put a different complexion on things through their protests" (VII, 1,. p. 428).

[5] VII, 1, p. 407.

the hero of the day. As is so often the case with young men just awakened intellectually and suddenly exposed to new ideas which are doubly compelling because they are so irreverent, the ideas were often taken for reality or, at least, for a goal which might be fully realized if one but pursued it single-mindedly enough and sacrificed oneself for one's convictions. These new ideas, which meant in reality a rejection of the entire fundamentalist value structure in which they had been indoctrinated in the Cloister Schools, were accepted just as whole-heartedly as the old forms were condemned.

But when they laid their books aside, they could not help but be impressed by the startling contrast between the world of beauty and fulfillment about which they read and the real life they led in Tübingen. The strictly regulated life at the *Stift*, which tradition prescribed and the churchmen were intent on preserving, was no doubt depressing enough in its own right. The *Stiftler* enjoyed no privacy at all. The spying of the *Repetenten* and the *Famuli* was notorious and undermined the rapport between the students and the *Repetenten* — whose legitimate function was to help direct the studies of younger students. Unfortunately, Karl Eugen confirmed that the *Repetenten* were to be held largely responsible for maintaining discipline when he set about preparing his reform in 1791.[6] The students had more free time than they had enjoyed in the Cloister Schools. But the restrictions against excursions, sleigh-riding, dancing, smoking, and other activities meant that they had more freedom in theory only. And yet, although these were on the books, Schnurrer let the students break them quite readily; he admitted during the investigation of the *Stift* in the late 1790's that he never enforced the stricter rules on students whom he knew and had come to trust.[7] Discipline must then have seemed more a matter of whim than of principle, whenever the rules were rigidly enforced. The very laxity of discipline and the haphazardness of its enforcement probably undermined all respect for the school authorities, particularly when the most popular books of the day were questioning all restrictions. Hence the morale problem was such a festering sore that the seminary became notorious during Hölderlin's time as a veritable hot-bed of revolutionary conspiracy. Karl Eugen visited the *Stift* several times in vain efforts to determine if there was really anything to persistent rumors that a republican club was active among the *Stiftler*.[8]

Moreover, the physical condition of the school was scandalous and was probably the Herzog's original concern, which then grew into the sweeping reforms of 1791. In his summary of recommendations of 1787, Karl Eugen was already paying special attention to the attitudes and behavior of the students themselves. He noted "rejection of good hard work, superficial knowledge from

---

6 Leube, pp. 54ff.
7 *Ibid.*, pp. 11ff.
8 VII, 1, pp. 443ff.

periodicals, contempt for theology, a tendency to show off heterodoxical opinions without having first considered them critically .... frivolousness and high living, contempt for the laws ... false ideas about freedom, a lack of practical knowledge about life, a lack of sympathy for the clergy, and a desire not to be what they are and should be."[9] He went on to remark: "A theologian forced into his profession is a reflection on the state; poor education at home and in the lower schools gives the Herzog cause to remark out of his duty as the father of his land that the schoolmasters in the Duchy stand in need of improvement; moreover, the all-too late appointment of theologians should be alleviated by a reduction of the number to be absorbed; finally, it is our sad experience that many of our weak subjects come from the Lower Cloister Schools, for which reason basic reforms should be undertaken with regard to them."[10]

These words, written one year before Hölderlin's enrollment, show a good deal of insight into the general conditions of the school and the nature and temperament of the student body. The same observations appeared, often with only minor changes in the wording, in the final version of the Reform Proclamation of 1791.[11] But the Herzog and his advisors had mistaken the symptoms for the disease. When the reforms had been carried out, buildings renovated, school discipline regularized and changes made in the curriculum, the real problem — the traditional restraints on natural development and the students' consequent lack of pride in the school and in their profession — had been left untouched. Karl Eugen and the Church Council, naturally suspicious of new ideas which seemed at odds with the concept of an autocratic state confirmed by divine authority and the fundamentalist precepts of the Church, had simply moved toward stricter enforcement of school discipline, as if the only thing wrong with the old regulations had been the manner in which they had been enforced. The proposals for liberalizing discipline, which had, in fact, been tabled during the five years of consultation, had been, for the most part, ignored.[12] Even such extraneous practices as the orderly marches of the *Stiftler* to church services on Sunday morning — an event particularly dreaded by the students because they were the targets for ridicule by the other boys in town as they marched along in their long black robes — were continued at the express command of Karl Eugen. That the entire concept of the *Stiftler* as a semi-monk might well be out of date and could very well aggravate the already rebellious temper of the students, seems never to have occurred to the reformers. The result was then a reform from above which, in many ways, merely fanned the flames of resentment and rebelliousness spreading from the bottom up.

9   Leube, p. 52.
10   *Ibid.*, p. 53
11   *Ibid.*, pp. 54ff.
12   *Ibid.*

The appearance of a relatively large number of outstanding poets and philosophers among the alumni of a second-rate school is understandable. It was not, however, the result of hereditary factors alone; nor was it a phenomenon that simply took place in spite of the school. Throughout the works of the two great *Stiftler*, Hölderlin and Hegel, one encounters that famous and often exaggerated spititual kinship between the two men which, in fact, had its roots in a common reaction against their student experiences and some degree of cooperation in drawing up alternatives. The building blocks of their at once philosophic and poetic dreams were formed by the new ideas which were in the air — however clandestinely — at the *Stift*. The zeal with which they devoted themselves to their ideals was no more unique than their starting points were original. What Hölderlin and Hegel accomplished differed from the intellectual play of the other students in quality, but not in kind. They continued to nurture and shape their ideas for years after they left Tübingen, while lesser men, for whom the heroic posturing of the student was no longer necessary when they no longer felt the pressure of school life, simply discarded their ideals when they attained their freedom. That these two did continue along the paths upon which they had set out as boys may or may not be a sign of genius. Without it, however, genius would never have ripened and brought forth its fruits. The fact is that neither of them ever escaped the youthful enthusiasm for Rousseau, Schiller, Kant, and the Greeks, nor from their partisan condemnation of the old learning which enslaved rather than liberated the mind and deadened rather than quickened the fantasy. However much they developed their thought or poetry from the rudimentary beginnings of the Tübingen days; however fundamentally they revised the form of their visions, as Hegel matured and as Hölderlin's maturation went awry — the *Stiftler* was always lurking just below the surface. For in Tübingen the psychological preoccupations which would last a lifetime were given definite shape.[13]

At bottom, the appearance of Hölderlin, Hegel, and Schelling from the ranks of the *Stiftler* seems to have resulted from three highly talented Swabian youths, all of whom sprang from the clerical families, being subjected to the semi-monastic life of the *Stiftler* at a time during which the books to which they were naturally drawn by reason of their inherited sensitivity to and interest in humanistic themes were proclaiming the possibility of a better life and admonishing man to cast off the old and worn-out values and strike out on a new road.

The life of the *Stiftler* was, of course, abnormal in itself. The ill-advised asceticism of the theological schools would have profoundly affected the development of any young man with normal sensitivities. The *Stiftler* was, in

13 "By my third year in Tübingen, it was finished. The rest was superficial..." (152.93f.).

fact, looked upon as somewhat odd. Not only the boys in town, who ridiculed them on the way to church, felt this way. Johann Friedrich Flatt, under whom Hölderlin studied Kantian philosophy, remarked in 1795: "In Tübingen one does nothing but make new professors. If one could only make the students better! But these, and particularly the *Stipendiaten,* are mostly a rather queer lot."[14]

In Tübingen the *Stift* still stands — complete with locked doors, mimeographed lists of the week's *Repententen,* and halls resounding with the hymns which were sung in Hölderlin's day. Outside, past the Philosopher's Fountain, down one of the temperamentally wandering streets which angle elusively through the *Altstadt* towards the River Neckar, stands the old house which once belonged to the carpenter Zimmer. In 1804 one of the "queer lot" returned to Tübingen. From 1806 on, in this house, he lived out the last thirty-seven years of his life, the hopeless victim of insanity.

[14] Leube, p. 18.

6

HÖLDERLIN'S FIRST YEAR IN THE *TÜBINGER STIFT*

Hölderlin enrolled in the theological seminary in October 1788. In the autumn of 1793 he completed his formal education and put behind him the student's life which he had led, more and more unwillingly, for nine long years. Outwardly he progressed normally through the prescribed levels of the curriculum. On 3 December 1788, less than three months after his enrollment, he passed the required examinations in languages, history, logic, arithmetic, and geometry, and received his baccalaureate.[1] During the next two years he studied in the philosophical faculty and heard lectures in logic, metaphysics, natural law, general practical philosophy, history, Greek, Hebrew, mathematics, and theoretical and experimental physics. In September 1790 he became a *Magister,* after submitting two "specimina" to the philosophical faculty. These first attempts to come to grips with philosophic and aesthetic issues on a disinterested academic plane were entitled: "Parallele zwischen Salomons Sprüchwörtern und Hesiods Werken und Tagen" and "Die Geschichte der schönen Künste unter den Griechen."[2] For the next three years he studied theology. Then, in the fall of 1793, he received his "Zeugnis" from the *Stift* which included the remark:

> Studia theologica multo cum successu tractavit.
> orationem sacram recte elaboratam decenter recitavit.
>   Philologiae, imprimis Graeciae, et philosophiae,
> imprimis Kantianae, et litterarum elegantorum assiduus
> cultor.[3]

Inwardly, however, something was taking place which was quite at odds with the accepted aim of his studies. Inwardly he was undergoing a continuing and violent reaction to all the oppression and cruelty, both real and imagined, which school and the prospect of serving the Church for the rest of his life had come to mean to him. As we know he had already, in the comparatively peaceful environment of the Cloister School, shown a marked sensitivity to his surroundings and a need to avoid all tension and stress by creating his own make-believe world of dreams, to which only those few people, like Immanuel and Luise Nast, who pitied him and seemed to accept the heroic self-image which he had developed, gained admittance. For Hölderlin the turmoil of life in the *Stift* could only be catastrophic.

---

[1] VII, 1, pp. 382f.
[2] IV, 1, pp. 176ff. and 189ff.
[3] VII, 1, p. 479.

First, the oppression from which, as he was convinced, he was constantly suffering was now felt by the other students as well. Hölderlin may well have taken part when the freedom tree was planted and may have heard Schelling insult the Herzog when he was interrogated.[4] In any case, he was no longer merely a poor misfit, unable to adjust to the accepted order of things. He gradually came to see himself as a revolutionary united with others who were also bent on the destruction of the older order and who, like him, drew consolation from the example of France.[5] If he could not feel at one with the other students socially, at least he could share in their beliefs. During his first year in Tübingen this spiritual fellowship brought about renewed self-confidence. His ideas about himself, his future life, and, perhaps most significant of all for his further development, his responsibilities to his family and its professional traditions gradually changed.

Secondly, his revolt was no longer essentially negative. He discovered a set of alternate beliefs and ideals. For the most part these were extensions of those ideas which had already captivated him at Maulbronn. But now he saw clearly that he was not alone and imagined that much of the road that he was to travel had been chartered by Plato, Kant, and Schiller. Because the intensely idealistic notions of justice, freedom, humanity, and spiritual beauty were now shared with young men such as Ludwig Neuffer and Rudolf Magenau, they took on a reality for him which they had never had when he had been day-dreaming and had known that he was day-dreaming. The morality of the superior Christian, which he had reserved for himself almost exclusively during the earlier years, now became the posture of intense dedication to mankind, and this he shared with others.

Finally, in the writings of the intellectuals he found still another type of comradeship. Men whom he did not know and who had no idea of his existence were thinking the same thoughts, verbally formulating what he only felt, eloquently objecting to the practices and conditions which he himself found objectionable, and living lives which pointed to alternatives to the clergy. All this represented to him the hope of contributing to the well-being of his fellow men without forever sacrificing himself and his genius in the service of a doctrine in which he could no longer believe without serious reservation and to which he could not enthusiastically commit himself and his life. The motifs which we saw in his first poem of thanks to his teachers, his hopes for fulfillment and fame through pursuits of the intellect, were still major elements in all his dreaming

---

[4] Ephorus Schnurrer heard the rumor that a freedom-tree had been planted and passed the word on to Karl Eugen on August 1793 that the rumor that such an event had taken place in his presence was a fabrication (VII, 1, p. 444). Schwab reported the planting of the tree and Hölderlin's presence on the occasion as fact (VII, 1, p. 448).

[5] See Philipp Refues' remarks on the effect of the French Revolution on the *Stiftler* (VII, 1, p. 452).

and planning. But the particulars and the way in which he imagined himself attaining fulfillment had changed drastically. No longer could he be content with the provincial image of the learned man, the servant of God going about visiting the sick and blessing babies. His horizons broadened during that first year in Tübingen. He began to see his eventual sphere of activity as encompassing the entire nation and, ultimately, all mankind.

Inwardly then, although he did not know it then and would not for several years, he was preparing himself for the role of the wandering, homeless prophet. As a matter of course he thought of the prophet as a poet who would bring salvation to a benighted humanity through the power of his word. By 1793, when he bade farewell to the *Stift,* a life in the church as one of its servants would no longer be a real possibility.[6] It would have come to mean the same as spiritual death and the wanton betrayal of his genius and his mission.

". . . if you only could have seen me, how I shed tears of the most heartfelt joy at this new indication of your so inexpressably sweet love, how I felt, at that moment, so deeply what I possess in you, how once more my days pass in tranquility and joy. Oh my darling! even in our separation your love is happiness, even in this yearning for your sweet heart there is ecstasy. For each moment tells me that you yearn for me just as much, that these few years are just as long for you as they are for me."[7]

"How lucky I am! How much luckier I would be if, wrapped in your arms, I could pour out at your feet all the ecstasy that fills my heart. It is a joy for me to think of how I used to wait so patiently and yet so full of longing at that place [of ours] until I saw my precious at her window, and how the thought thrilled me that you had eyes for nothing in the world save for your Hölderlin, and that I now dwell in your heart . . ."[8]

Hölderlin wrote these words to Luise in January 1789. He had been away from her for at least four months. He had written before. Probably in December he had written her a letter which, although it has not survived, seems from her reply to have been written in tones of deep depression. She wrote back: "You are right. Your dear letter caused me much grief. For nights on end I was unable to sleep."[9] It may have been that his loneliness in the new school, the strange surroundings, which may have been frightening for him at first, and the pressure of the examinations for his baccalaureate had been enough to throw him into one of his fits of depression. His words, whatever they were, troubled Luise.

---

6 The thought that he might be forced to become a vicar plagued him throughout his life. In his last letter to Schiller, for example, on 2 June 1801, he wrote: ". . . unless something intervenes I shall be forced to go in a few weeks to a country preacher as his vicar" (232.33f.).
7 25.1ff.
8 25.19ff.
9 VII, 1, pp. 8ff.

They probably hurt her also, because she, no doubt, missed him as much as he missed her. But that was precisely what he wanted to hear. He wanted reassurance that she still longed for him and would wait for him until he had earned his degree and could think about marrying her and starting a family. Even now, as he told her how much she meant to him and tried to soothe her, he found it impossible to surpress the cry of the martyr. "Oh Luise," he wrote, "is it never possible to be near you anywhere, with good people around? "[10]

He was changing during his first few months at Tübingen, but those changes which he was undergoing are not directly accessible to us, because all but two letters from that period have been lost. The first, the letter to Luise Nast, reveals the same attitudes which he had exhibited at Maulbronn. So also does the letter to his mother from April 1789. He had gone to Stuttgart with Neuffer during the Easter vacation, where he had met two of the leading lights of Swabian literature. Neuffer had connections with both Schubart, who had but recently completed his prison term, and Gotthold Friedrich Stäudlin (1758–1796), the editor of the *Swabian Almanach,* and had introduced his new friend to the two men.[11] The letter to his mother begins with an apology for upsetting her. "It hurts me terribly, dear Mamma! that I must see you so sad and downcast – and particularly over me and my behavior. As far as the past is concerned, I beg you for forgiveness a thousand times. Yesterday, when I went to God's table, I asked Him for forgiveness."[12]

Here again he was the submissive son, willing to comply with her wishes and admit his past misbehavior. We do not know what his mother's objection was, but we can be relatively certain that Hölderlin's contrition was merely a formality. For he then wrote: "As far as my present situation is concerned, I can assure you that I would pass my days quite happy and contented with my fate if only your sadness did not cause me so many dark hours. I beg you, as lovingly as I can, I implore you by your duty as a mother and a Christian, which you conscienciously fill – even to the point of all too great sadness – to cheer up, enjoy the beauty of spring, rejoice in the beautiful green which God has given back to our fields and trees."[13]

In later years Hölderlin would speak of the "Altklugheit" of his Tübinger years.[14] Here he avoided saying that he was really happy and contented. He merely passed the blame for his unhappiness on to her. The thought that he

---

[10]   25.37ff.

[11]   Neuffer's letter to Stäudlin is lost. In a fragment of a letter to Hölderlin, written from 20 to 24 March 1789, he wrote to his friend that he had represented him as "full of enthusiasm for poetry, given to the serious, the sublime and the visionary, and unsympathetic to the frivolous, and a deadly enemy of the epigram. Greek literature is his hobby" (VII, 1, p. 12).

[12]   26.1ff.

[13]   26.6ff.

[14]   45.10 and 22.

would be happy "if only you . . ." and particularly the reference to the student's life as "my fate" [Schiksal] betray his real feelings. And yet, in the midst of his apology, he struck a new note of confidence as he deftly altered the line of thought and directed attention to her failings, thus putting her on the defensive because of her over-zealousness in admonishing him to behave properly. This new confidence may have come in part from his still detectable elation at having met Schubart and Stäudlin, which soon bubbled over and interrupted the curious apology which was really no apology at all. "You have probably heard," he wrote, "that I was in Schubart's house and that he received me with friendliness and fatherly gentleness."[15]

He even spoke openly of his intention of becoming a poet. "He [Schubart] asked me about my parents and wanted to know if they could support me in meeting the expenses of a poet — and when I answered yes, he told me that I should thank God as humbly as I could for that, and I was quite touched by it. Ah, it would be such a joy to be the friend of such a man. I spent the entire afternoon at his home."[16]

His interest in writing poetry was probably not alarming for his mother, for it had not yet emerged as a threat to his prospective career as a clergyman. But the contrast between his elation and enthusiasm for his new acquaintances in Stuttgart and his feelings about his "fate" could hardly have escaped her. Was this the first sign of that rebelliousness which, seven months later, would erupt in a series of uncontrollable outbursts aimed at the *Stift,* his mother, and finally at the fiancée who had promised to wait for him? Were there other letters which might have suggested a gradual polarization of the clergy and the poetic life in his mind? We do not know. If there were others, they have not survived.

One thing is evident: His search for others to blame and his willingness to lash out in accusations, half-veiled and always of short duration, against those people who should have meant the most to him had not changed. He must have been very miserable, for now he dared to suggest to his mother that he blamed her and thus ran the risk of upsetting her and bringing a new flood of pious recriminations down on his head. One must suspect that he needed to make just as miserable as he was himself all those whom he felt to be responsible for his misery, whether that meant his mother or Luise.[17] He may also have been unconsciously preparing the way for his attempted escape in November.

All this is speculation, based on a few remaining bits of information from that time. Yet, what is known of his attitudes toward others would suggest that he was transferring his submissiveness and affection to some degree from his mother and Luise to men like Schubart and Stäudlin and to the few friends in the *Stift*

---

15 26.17f.
16 26.19ff.
17 See Hölderlin's farewell letter to Luise Nast (No. 31).

who shared his enthusiasms and objections to the existing order of things. From men of reputation such as Schubart, everyday kindness, even the observation of the host's duty toward visitors in his home, were received by Hölderlin as manna from heaven, much as he later would wait breathlessly for "one kind word" from Schiller.[18]

The friendship of those who understood him and accepted him for what he saw himself to be was a constant need. The dear friend he found during the early months in Tübingen was Christian Ludwig Neuffer (1768–1839), the son of a secretary in the Church Council in Stuttgart. Neuffer was two years older than Hölderlin and adopted his younger friend's enthusiasms for philosophy and literature. With Rudolf Magenau, Hölderlin and Neuffer would found the *Dichterbund* in 1790, which they modelled after Klopstock's *Gelehrtenrepublik*. Neuffer, in contrast to Hölderlin, accepted his own "fate" in the form of an appointment to a vicarage in Stuttgart when he left the *Stift* in 1791. He published journals in later years and seems to have had little difficulty in reconciling his professional life and his literary interests. This man, so different from Hölderlin in many respects, shared Hölderlin's experiences more directly than anyone else in the years that followed. He seems to have been the only person to whom Hölderlin confessed in writing his love for Susette Gontard. Only Sinclair seems to have similarly enjoyed Hölderlin's confidence for any comparable length of time.

The friendship with Neuffer must have been cemented very early. In March 1789 Neuffer wrote a poem to celebrate his younger friend's nineteenth birthday. The poem is not a particularly genial production. It is nonetheless striking that the same self-conception which we have observed in the letters which Hölderlin wrote at Maulbronn and the same demand for a friend as a savior, a rock to which one might cling, find expression in Neuffer's poem.

> Meinem lieben Hölderlin
> zu seinem Geburtstage d. 28. März 1789

Sorglos und einsam gehet oft ein Pilgrim,
  Ahndet keine Gefar, auf schwüler Reise,
    Sehnet sich in kühlende Schattengänge
      Mosiger Eichen.

Gleitet vom Pfad dann, irret tiefer immer
  In den düsteren Wald, wo tausend Stege
    Durcheinander kreuzen, und in verborgene
      Klüfte sich senken.

---

[18] 129.39 (Cf. 124.13ff.).

Nächtlicher wird sein Weg und dornenvoller,
  Kalte Schauer umfangen ihn; zurükbebt
    Er mit jedem Schritte. Wo soll er hingehn?
      Ringsum kein Ausweg!

Schrekliche Nacht entschwebt auf breitem Fittig
  Izt vom Himmel herab, und weht Entsezen
    In die tiefverödeten Felsenschlünde,
      Die ihn umschliessen.

Otterngezüchte zischen um ihn, Wölfe
  Heulen fürchterlich durch die öde Stille,
    Und aus schwarzen hangenden Wolken fahren
      Zakige Blize.

Sterne und Mond verlöschen "Ha! verschworen
  Hat die ganze Natur sich meinem Elend!
    Furchtbar hallts der schroffige Felsenabgrund,
      Furchtbar der Wald es.

Wütig ergreift Verzweiflung ihn, empöret
  Tausend Todesgestalten seinem Geiste . . .
    Aber, o der Wonne! ein Stralenwölkchen,
      Schwebet hernieder.

Aus dem Gewölke schlüpft ein Engel Gottes
  Reicht dem Zitternden traulich seine Rechte,
    Leitet ihn auf sonnige Frühlingsauen
      Aus den Geklüften.

Mir, o Theurer! warst du dieser Engel,
  Als zur Freundschaft du mir die Rechte botest —
    Nimm dafür den heisesten Dank an diesem
      Festlichen Tage!   Neuffer.[19]

One perceives, of course, the tremendous gulf which separated the two friends in terms of talent. As poets they were beings of different orders. There is no comparing the poetry of the two young men. But, in life, the ability to verbalize one's perceptions is not always crucial. In life, in seeking companions, the identity of interests alone is often sufficient. Hölderlin would never have written this poem. He would never have squandered this reservoir of heart-felt themes without producing something more than a mere poem of thanks for the companionship of a friend on the friend's birthday. His own poems to friends were quite different. The attachment to the individual was used as a springboard

---

[19] VII, 1, pp. 193ff.

from which he then leaped into the world of myth and meaning, that is, back into his dream world, much in the same way he later used natural phenomena as bearers of meanings which actually had their origins in his mind. The whole idea of the poet in the midst of a hostile world he always reserved for poems in which the readers attention was not divided, in which everything could relate to his own precarious situation. Other figures tend to become a reflection of himself and seldom maintain the autonomy which Hölderlin himself enjoyed in this poem by Neuffer. Here Hölderlin brings salvation to Neuffer. In Hölderlin's own poetic vision the friend only supports him, makes real life bearable, or helps him gain access to the realm of the divine where only Hölderlin is actually at home. Finally Hölderlin would never have represented nature as enemy. He was always careful to reserve this function for other human beings or make it quite clear that barren wastes and the like were thoughtless men's work.[20] The tulmultuous fury which Neuffer generates here leads to nothing that would justify all the commotion. All the demonic forces of the cosmos have been called forth to invade the poet's world in a sort of Wagnerian prelude to "Happy Birthday to You."

But all the poetic fallacies of Neuffer's poem count for little against the singular spiritual kinship of the two young men. All the feelings of personal inadequacy, all the self-delusion through which the student, chafing at the many bonds which enslaved him, suddenly transformed reality into a cosmological celebration of his own dilemma and his salvation through the divine gift of friendship — these are the very themes of Hölderlin's own poetry. These are, in fact, the sentiments which had dominated his letters from Maulbronn and which would return in the letters from Tübingen after Neuffer and Magenau left the *Stift* in 1791. They also lie at the heart of the early poetry — and one is tempted to say, of all his poetry.

The childish quality of Hölderlin's poetic perception has been noted by others, but usually as something to be applauded, as something super-poetic, as somehow connected with the German mystique of childhood. What we mean here is probably best described by the word adolescent. The childhood about which Hölderlin wrote was never a reality. The "golden days of childhood" and the fuss he made about becoming a man were the adolescent's solutions to the difficulty of growing up.[21] This is, for the critic, easy to miss. The power of his words, the eloquence of his speech, the resonance of his thunder often compell the reader to accept his vision despite the advice of his better judgment. But the adolescent rantings of the letters and the sentiments which lie behind the poems

---

[20] The reconcilitation of nature and man would be the task which Diotima would lay on Hyperion: "There will be only *one* beauty and nature and men will be *united* in *one* all-embracing divinity" (III, p. 90).

[21] See 86.2ff.: 88.68; and 76.53.

are the same. In the clumsiness of Neuffer's verse the adolescence of the motifs, which were Hölderlin's own, becomes obvious. The psychological role of friendship: salvation from a world which *seems* hostile because the poet looks upon it as such, escapes in Neuffer's poem the obfuscation of which Hölderlin was capable. This may, in part, be true not simply because Hölderlin was much more talented than Neuffer but also because to Hölderlin these ideas were never merely cultural themes as they were for Neuffer, who never allowed his enthusiasm for poetry or his aesthetic opposition to the narrow-minded realm of theology to impair his ability to fit into the world. For Hölderlin these adolescent ideas corresponded to a deep-seated personal need; for adolescence was then, and would be from then on, his permanent stage of emotional development.

If Neuffer, for whom poetry would remain an avocation, felt so intensely the need for a fellow sufferer, how much more must the incomparably more sensitive Hölderlin have suffered! How much more would he have to seek salvation from his dilemma in the supernatural realms of poetically conceived love and friendship!

Just how oppressive he felt his life in the seminary to be before he, Neuffer, and Magenau established the *Dichterbund* can be seen in his actions during the tumultuous fall and winter of 1789–1790, when Hölderlin, the mild-mannered boy who consistently received good marks in conduct,[22] suddenly exploded in a fit of rebellion.

On 5 November Karl Eugen visited the *Stift* and publicly demanded stricter adherence to school discipline.[23] The *Protokollbuch,* in which the *Ephorus* recorded cases requiring disciplicary action, contains the following entry for 20 November, five days after the Herzog's visit:

> On Tuesday last, the tenth of this month, the *Mägdleinprovisor* brought the following complaint to me, the *Ephorus,* toward evening. He said that he had been walking down the Münzgaße when a student came alongside him, having run up to him from the opposite side of the street in front of the New Building, and knocked his hat from his head with the words: 'Don't you know that you are obliged to remove your hat for a *Stipendiat?* ' He, the complainant, declared to the *Stipendiat* his intention of reporting the incident to the *Ephorus.* The *Stipendiat* replied that that was exactly what he should do and that he would go along with him. So they both proceeded through the Burschhof toward the *Ephorat's* house. Below the house, however, the *Stipendiat* left him and proceeded alone to the Cloister Gate.

---

22 In Denkendorf Hölderlin always received either "polit" or "gut" in "Sitten" (VII, 1, pp. 320ff.). In Maulbronn he received "gut", "recht gut," and "fein" (VII, 1, pp. 357ff.).
23 VII, 1, pp. 404f.

He, the *Provisor,* inquired of someone beneath the gate as to the identity of the student and received the answer: he was Candidate Hölderlin. Since he was, after all, employed at a public school, it was important for him to obtain satisfaction. I, the *Ephorus,* had the Candidate Hölderlin appear before me after the evening meal was finished. He did not deny the affair and simply appealed to the fact that the *Provisor* had not removed his hat for a *Stipendiat.* In general, however, the *Stipendiat* appeared to be proper and moderate while making his excuses. Incarceration for six hours for the infraction, etc. The *Provisor* should, however, be admonished by Herr Doktor Märklin not to neglect to show politeness to the students in the future.[24]

Hölderlin's apparently calm and polite acceptance of his punishment was deceptive. The cauldron within him had come to a boil and would spill over again. Within two weeks he wrote his mother, asking her to apply for sick leave for him, so that he might visit her in Nürtingen. His excuse was that he had an injured foot, and he was not using it merely to escape from the *Stift* for a few weeks. He intended to confront his mother once and for all with his conviction that he could not endure one more day in the seminary.

Only the last page of his letter to his mother has been preserved. He wrote: "You see, dearest Mamma, my physical and mental condition is aggravated in these surroundings; you can conclude for yourself that the unrelenting vexation, the restrictions, the unhealthy air, and the bad food are weakening me physically sooner than would be the case in freer surroundings. You know my temperament, which cannot be denied simply because it *is* my temperament anymore than it can endure mistreatment, oppression, and scorn."[25]

There is little new in this letter. He had been more or less convinced for several years that he was being victimized and could only be miserable as long as he was in school. But up to now he had admitted it only to Nast and, we may assume, Neuffer. Whenever he had written his mother he had been more restrained. He hinted at his dissatisfaction, portrayed the hardships of school life, and contented himself with hints and allusions to his real feelings. Now he suddenly dropped all pretense. There was no more apologizing for being a bad Christian or for his failure to appreciate the advantages of his educational opportunities. He asserts boldly that he is simply not suited for school life and cannot change the way he is. This is his "temperament," and thus there was nothing to do with sin.

He confronted his mother with facts and cast aside the old role of the penitent son who was trying as hard as he could to adjust. He no longer admitted the possibility that he was being unreasonable or acting impulsively. The *Stift* and its administrators were unreasonable. He thus implied that his mother and Luise Nast were asking too much if they expected him to continue in the school, which could mean nothing but continued suffering. He had now shifted all blame from himself, thus continuing the practice of casting all responsibility onto someone else which had first appeared in the letter to his mother in April 1789. Moreover, he had found an identifiable enemy in the school authorities who had recently dared to imprison him, even though he had been guilty of nothing more serious than insisting that the *Mägdleinprovisor* show him the respect which was due him.[26]

Did he imagine himself to be another Schubart, who had spent twenty years in prison because he had refused to yield to the tyranny of Karl Eugen — the same Karl Eugen who, five days before Hölderlin's assault on the dignity of the *Provisor,* had demanded greater servility from the students? Did he already see himself as the reformer who, through demanding the respect due him individually, was striking a symbolic blow for the rights of all oppressed students? The vocabulary which he used in the letter to his mother suggests that these ideas played some role in his thinking. In a letter to Neuffer, who had been away from school when Hölderlin had been incarcerated, the idea of justice became the dominant theme. "I would have written you from Tübingen," he wrote, "but the vexation, the chicanery, and the *injustices* which I had to endure made me even indifferent to friendship. In fact, dear friend, my fate is beginning to take on the aspects of a real adventure. If only nothing had happened except that I hurt my foot the day before you arrived [in Tübingen] and had to leave without seeing you! If only you had been in Tübingen all this would not have happened."[27]

His persecution fixation is somewhat tiring. It is repeated with infinite variations from his years at Maulbronn to his last attempt to establish himself as an author in Homburg, when he would write Susette Gontard that the men of reputations feared his poetic genius and were trying to protect themselves against competition by destroying his career.[28] Behind most of what he did and wrote lay a massive persecution complex. At first he apologized for it, felt guilty about it, pleaded for help from his teacher and his friends, sought a "love" to reconcile him with the world, and, in general, recognized that the difficulty lay within himself. The first year at Tübingen changed all that. Others suffered as he, and they could not all be wrong — not the entire generation which was longing for deliverance.

---

26 The vaguely rebellious sentiments in which Hölderlin shared led to the Herzog's receiving a flood of rumors about democratic sentiments among the students. See Karl Eugen's and Schnurrer's exchange of letters about the rumors (VII, 1, pp. 404ff.).

27 28.2ff.

28 195.31ff.

Now, in the autumn in 1789, he clothed his dilemma in the attractive robes of social significance for the first time. Justice and the concepts of ideal right and wrong had emerged into his consciousness and justified his feelings of superiority to his tormentors. He was the champion of the rights of students — the champion of mankind's rights — and could not behave differently because, as he now convinced himself, all his feelings of hostility, which he had first taken as an indication of his sinfulness, had turned out to be justified, legal, legitimate, and the only way in which a sensitive man of conscience could react.

Here one sees the first manifestation of his boundless concern for humanity, his later insistence on subordinating his own happiness to the task of reforming the world for the sake of future generations. The peculiar form of humanitarianism, which he would go on to celebrate in *Hyperion* and *Empedokles,* was emerging directly from his own problems and providing the mechanism of escape from his feelings of inadequacy and guilt. From now on his own cares, his own internal crisis, would be projected onto the whole of mankind,[29] so that he would always be able to convince himself that he was acting out of a concern for his fellow men, when, in reality, he was the slave of inner compulsions over which he had no control. It was this self-delusion which enabled him to write his brother almost four years later that he was not interested in individuals any more and was going to devote his life to the service of mankind, while leaving unanswered such questions as how he was planning to earn his living. By then the questions that should have concerned him primarily at that point in his life, and the questions which concerned his family more and more, did not seem important enough to him to deserve an answer.

---

[29] See No. 65 and the discussion of the *Hyperion* fragments in Chapter 12.

7

THE EARLY POEMS FROM TÜBINGEN

Hölderlin's interpreters have discussed the poems that he wrote during his first year in Tübingen at best quite summarily and sometimes not at all. That is understandable. Seen as poetry alone, as poetry apart from life, they would not appear to be worth much discussion, for they are aesthetically inferior to almost everything he wrote from 1790 on. He was still groping for themes and forcing everything he tried into the meters that he had learned from Klopstock, Schubart, and Matthison. He had not yet discovered that Schiller's poetry could be just as important to his own verse as the themes of Schiller's early plays were to his day-dreams, and he had, therefore, not yet appropriated his compatriot's meters and diction. Even in the poems in which he loosed his poison darts at the Church, he still wrote of the coming of the Antichrist and berated mankind for its sinfulness.[1] He felt allegiance to the spirit, if not to the practice, of his fathers' religion and celebrated in two poems the heroics of the Protestant hero, Gustav Adolf.[2] The vision of ancient Greece, which would grow so important in the later years, had not yet risen to a position of prominence in his mind. It is true that in the poem "Männerjubel" he took his images from Pindar; and in "Die Vollendung" he turned a phrase that suggests at least a very superficial, perhaps even second-hand, knowledge of Winkelmann's view of antiquity ("Voll hoher Einfalt/Einfältig still und groß").[3] But these are overshadowed by themes from Swabian history in the poems "Kepler" and "An Thill's Grab."

All of these poems were written in the early months of his first year at Tübingen and show only a random selection of themes and images. Much, almost all in fact, is second-hand; little came from his experience. Only in the latter part of 1789, perhaps during the weeks in which he tried to escape from the *Stift* for good, did he drop intellectual pretense and devote his talents to personal lyric in the poems "Zornige Sehnsucht," "An die Ruhe," "An die Ehre," "Einst und Jezt," "Die Weisheit des Traurers," and "Selbstquälerei."

The chronological sequence in which the poems were written yields new insight into his development. During the early months he fumbled with purely intellectual themes and wrote poems that, viewed aesthetically, are among his poorest. These poems are never quite convincing, because, however much he worried his subject, he never quite succeeded in coming to grips with it. In

---

[1] The language of the preacher is particularly striking in "Die Bücher der Zeiten" (I, 1, pp. 69ff.) and the two poems about Gustav Adolf (I, 1, pp. 85ff.).

[2] "Gustav Adolf" is preserved in full (I, 1, pp. 85ff.); of the other poem only the end is extant (I, 1, pp. 88f.).

[3] I, 1, p. 75 (lines 21f.).

"Männerjubel" he started with Pindar's "Horen" and then dropped them after the first three stanzas in order to launch into an impassioned defense of man's freedom against the forces of oppression. In "Bücher der Zeiten" he spent almost one hundred lines in depicting the gory details of the age of the Antichrist and then, unable, as yet, to break out of the fundamentalist tradition, recounted the traditional mythology of the Second Coming, which he did not really find very convincing himself. In "Gustav Adolf" he devoted twenty-six lines to an exhortation of the people to fall down in reverence on the sacred spot of land where Adolf was murdered, a scant fifteen lines to Adolf's deeds, and the remainder of the poem, some fifty-odd lines, to the worthlessness of the world and the common man's inability to appreciate the great hero. But, as the months rolled by, he pushed the historical themes more and more into the background and sang more resonantly and in fuller voice of his own feelings.

Throughout that first year in Tübingen, as his agitation and resentment increased, he became more and more absorbed in his misery. Gradually the intellectual veneer fell away from his verse. First the historical themes disappeared in the poem "Vollendung," in which he expressed his doubts that the spiritual peace that his fathers had found through their religion even in the face of death would ever be his. Then he began to blend historical fact with his own feelings. Thill, a minor Swabian poet, was identified with the living Hölderlin standing by his grave. Finally, near the end of that year, he dropped all the images that he had borrowed from others, stepped forth boldly and cried:

> Ich duld' es nimmer! ewig und ewig so
>   Die Knabenschritte, wie ein Gekerkerter
>   Die kurzen vorgemeßnen Schritte
>   Täglich zu wandeln, ich duld es nimmer!
>
> Ists Menschenloß — ists meines? ich trag es nicht
>   Mich reizt der Lorber, — Ruhe beglükt mich nicht.[4]

This thematic progression from his enrollment in the *Stift* in the autumn of 1788 up to the crisis of the late autumn and early winter of 1789—90 provides a microcosmic review of his development as a poet in general. For his life consisted of a series of withdrawals which affected his artistic growth. When he failed to escape from the *Stift,* as we shall see, he withdrew into the pseudo-fellowship of the *Dichterbund* and suddenly began producing his first great poems — poems in which real people play almost no role whatsoever but vanish before the powerful, yet abstract, ideals that he drew from within himself. This period of withdrawal lasted about three years. When he went to Waltershausen and Jena his production dwindled. Only the several fragments of

---

4 I, 1, p. 90 (lines 1—6).

Hyperion and a handful of poems were produced during those months. In the six months that he spent with Schiller in Jena he worked on *Hyperion* exclusively, but could not finish it. Only after he had again taken recourse to flight from his responsibilities and from those who made demands on him, first from Jena and then from Nürtingen, first from Schiller and then from Mother, did he again experience another surge of creativity. In the dream-world of Diotima he finished the first volume of *Hyperion*. During those same months his verse underwent a thorough metamorphosis in both form and expression, for it was then that he finally freed himself once and for all from Schiller's influence on his poetry, if not from the older man's influence on him personally.

These great surges of creativity always came when he fled life and its cares, narrowing his sphere of activities to his poetry alone and thus limiting his mental activity to self-analysis. As a result, his poetry became ever more internal until those poems that originated near the end of his creative life were completely personal, sheer self-expression, with no real attempt to portray or come to grips with the world with which he was so rapidly losing contact.

When we consider the themes of Hölderlin's poetry in general, we discover something else. Themes and thoughts that he found in his readings alone and which had nothing to do with the cares that constantly concerned him only confused him. He was not able to treat a theme simply because it appealed to him aesthetically, as could Goethe. He was only able to make something out of thoughts and themes which lent themselves to his own very self-centered concerns. For this reason the intensity of his poetry is balanced by an extreme narrowness. His great poems are not the richest in detail but are rather the most paltry. He could no more think like a philosopher and develop a theme conceptually than he could marry and accept a normal life. He seems to have been almost incapable of objective thought, as we shall discover when we discuss the Tübingen Hymns. Only that which he could internalize and use to mirror what he already felt, could he master.

Now his poetry was to revolve more and more exclusively around one theme: the abyss that yawned all about him and separated him from others. The growth of his poetry was thus, to a great extent, a narrowing in on this single theme and a gradual accumulation of images to express his own reaction to his plight, through which he sought to overcome it symbolically and regain access to the world of men. The unrelenting tension, the constant agitation at being unable to accept normal responsibilities in life, provided the intensity that makes his verse unique.

The same image of the embattled champion that we have seen developing from his experiences and his compensatory day-dreaming through his years of loneliness at Maulbronn, is the binding tie, the thread that runs throughout all the early poems from Tübingen. As he cast about for themes he was in fact testing each image to see if it would bear the heroic message that he felt compelled to preach.

In "Männerjubel" he dropped the classical imagery after three stanzas and began recounting the heroic struggle of man against the forces of oppression. Now, as in later years, he emphasized the masculinity of the hero,[5] perhaps thereby compensating for his own faltering manliness which had been stunted due to the influence of his mother. His repeated emphasis on "becoming a man" was to him a considerable undertaking, and he set forth all sorts of humanistic qualities as prerequisites for accomplishing the task. On the other hand, he never allowed himself to be forced to demonstrate his own masculinity. When all the bombast is set aside, one discovers that Hölderlin often wrote of the humanistic qualities, of which there was so much talk at that time, as prerequisites for manliness, thereby emasculating his oppressors and, by implication, asserting his own superior manhood. In "Männerjubel" we can see this process at work. Hölderlin changed Pindar's designation of the "Horen" from "Justice," "Order," and "Peace," to "Justice," "Order," and "Love of Fatherland," which he had found in Klopstock, who had used the themes in connection with his society of patriotic "Friends." Freedom concerned Hölderlin most of all:

> wir sind der Erhabnen Söhne.

> Es glimmt in uns ein Funke der Göttlichen;
> Und diesen Funken soll aus der Männerbrust
> Der Hölle Macht uns nicht entreißen!
> Hört es, Despotengerichte, hört es![6]

He then proceeded to describe the forces against which the hero had to defend his divinity: "Despotenflüche";[7] "Und dräute tausendarmigter Pöbel, uns / zu würgen"; "tausendzüngige Pfaffenwut / Mit Bann den Neuerern."[8]

Similarly, in the poem "Bücher der Zeiten," Hölderlin identified the despot as the culprit who would unleash an age of misery upon the world, a blood-bath in which the pious and the sinful would alike be consumed. From despotism all evil would flow as mankind tumbled from one level of depravity to the next. After the armies of the despot had laid waste to the great edifices of civilization, all human relations would be perverted:

---

[5] The quality of masculinity is emphasized in a particularly adolescent way in the *Hyperion* fragments, in which the hero plays the same role of impetuous, stormy spirit that Hölderlin had played in his letters to Luise Nast (See Chapter 12). The first scene of the earliest extant *Empedokles* fragment opens with a conversation between Pathea and Delia, both of whom seem to have something of a crush on Empedokles (IV, 1, pp. 3ff.).

[6] I, 1, p. 67 (lines 20—24).

[7] I, 1, p. 68 (line 34).

[8] I, 1, p. 68 (lines 37—39).

Da steht geschrieben
   Vatermord! Brudermord!
   Säuglinge blaugewürgt!
   Greulich! Greulich!
   Um ein Linsengericht
   Därmzerfressendes Gift
   Dem guten, sicheren Freund gemischt. — .
   Hohlaugigte Krüppel
   Ihrer Onansschande
   Teuflische Opfer. — .
   Kannibalen
   Von Menschenbraten gemästet —
   Nagend an Menschengebein,
   Aus Menschenschädel saufend
   Rauchendes Menschenblut.
   Wütendes Schmerzgeschrei
   Der Geschlachteten über dem
   Bauchzerschlizenden Messer.
   Des Feindes Jauchzen
   Über dem Wohlgeruch,
   Welcher warm dampft
   Aus dem Eingeweid. — .[9]

The language is once more that of the fire-and-brimstone preacher admonishing his congregation to turn away from sin. The solution to man's dilemma is traditionally Christian. Christ comes and all is well.

   Jammerst du jezt noch, Frommer?
   Unter der Menschheit Druk? [10]

"Der Menschheit Druk" — the burden of life within real life is the burden of the hero. Hölderlin celebrated Gustav Adolf as the "Bruder des Schwachen," "der gnadenlächelnde Sieger," "Erwäger des Rechts," "Feind des Eroberers," "Hasser des Stolzen," "Schützer des Frommen," "Trockner der Märtyrerstränen," and, significantly, "Steurer der Pfaffenwut."[11] But Adolf fell victim to the world that he was trying to serve.

   Doch wehe! unter den Treuen
   Lauscht' ein Verräter;
   Er dachte — der Verräter — den Höllengedanken,
   Und — Gustav — sank.

[9] I, 1, p. 70 (lines 45—66).
[10] I, 1, p. 73 (lines 47f.).
[11] I, 1, p. 87 (lines 65—72).

Ha! Verräter! Verräter!
Daß in der Todesstunde dein Weib dich verdamme,
Und wehe! über dich rufen deine Söhne,
Und deine Enkel die That ins Ohr dir heulen,
Bis deine Blike erstarren im Grauen des Meuchelmords,
Und deine Seele flieht vor den Schreken der Ewigkeit.[12]

Within the real world, within real life with its give and take, its fine balance between freedom and responsibility, the hero is always victimized. Others are seen as opposed to the heroic figure and, in that light, are judged "traitors." The conflict between the hero and the world is thus made absolute as the struggle between freedom and necessity; normal responsibility to the inhabitants of the prosaic, unheroic world about him, the need to conform — all these are "despotism." It does not really matter how he characterized the despotism and oppression that closed in on the hero, although it is significant that he managed to designate the clergy, the political despot, and the mob as the particular culprits, since the narrowness of school theologians, the sinfulness of the "mob" of fellow students, and political oppression were the very problems which caused him concern. What is important here is that the abyss between the hero and the prosaic world was complete. There could be only unrelenting hostility between the spheres of the poetically heroic and the real.

This goes to the heart of Hölderlin's curious conception of heroism. The element which produces the hero is loneliness. The essence of heroism is to be found in the individual's steadfast refusal to compromise with life or with others. The hero's life is one of tension — unrelenting tension. He is, therefore, a victim, a martyr. This hero-martyr type appears in Hölderlin's novel as the Greek youth Hyperion who nurtured in his breast almost archetypal memories of his fatherland's past glory and thus suffered a hellish torment in the eighteenth century world from which the glory of the past has vanished.[13] It appears again in the *Empedokles* fragments as the philosopher-prophet who is slowly ripped apart by a love of mythological god-like men, which makes it impossible for him to find companionship among men who are no longer gods or among gods who no longer have anything to do with men.[14] These themes were already in evidence in the earliest poems from Tübingen. He selected his images at random; but, in retrospect, we can see the image of the hero-martyr already developing. The images he chose were not always up to the task he assigned them. Kepler and Gustav Adolf were chosen ill-advisedly. But now he had discovered that the genius, the heroic individual, belonged to a unique world of common men and everyday events.

---

[12] I, 1, p. 86 (lines 43—52).
[13] See Hyperion's discourse on Ancient Greece (III, pp. 76ff.).
[14] This can be seen in Empedokles's first speech in the earliest version of the drama (IV, 1, pp. 14ff.) which defines his situation for all the fragments.

Hence the combination hero-martyr. In life the hero was really no hero at all. In real life he could only be the martyr. The only glory for him in life was that of the passive sufferer who endured the persecutions meted out to him by inferior men for the sake of fulfillment in another realm. In "Männerjubel" the "Mann" suffered without complaint and without repaying his oppressors in kind. He resisted all attempts to extinguish the spark of divinity within him — *passively*. Victory was seen simply as not *yielding* in his conviction that he was the offspring of the *Horen*.

> Was überwiegt die Wonne, der Herrlichen,
>   Der Töchter Gottes würdiger Sohn zu sein?
>   Den Stolz, in ihrem Heiligtum zu
>   Wandeln, zu dulden um ihretwillen? [15]

When the despots, the mob, and the priests threaten them

es lachen

Ihrer die Söhne der Töchter Gottes.[16]

And when they are threatened with torture and death, when they find that they are the guests of cannibals,

sie dulden gern,

> Verlachen eure Blutgerüste,
>   Folgen den Vätern zu Schwerd und Folter.[17]

Torture, persecution, betrayal, mockery, martyrdom — these were the rewards of the hero in the real world. He had to seek fulfillment somewhere else. Only when isolated from others could he be heroic. Hölderlin never relinquished the hope of an eventual consummation of life on earth in terms of traditional Christian eschatology. And when he wrote of the Second Coming in "Bücher der Zeiten," he was not above enjoying in anticipation his final revenge:

> Und, Spötter, spottest du
> In tanzenden Freuden
> Noch des furchtbarn Richtstuhls? [18]

Just as Hölderlin fled from real people and all intercourse with his "sinful" fellows, so did he envision fulfillment for his hero anywhere but in the world of men. In another realm, among comrades worthy of sharing in his cause, the martyred outcast became hero.

---

[15] I, 1, p. 68 (lines 29—32).
[16] I, 1, p. 68 (lines 39f.).
[17] I, 1, p. 68 (lines 46—48).
[18] I, 1, pp. 73f. (lines 149—151).

The *Wirtembergisches Repertorium* had published in 1782 an article by Johann Jakob Azel, entitled: "Schreiben über einen Versuch in Grabmälern nebst Proben." Included was an illustration of a gravestone for the Swabian astronomer and natural scientist Johannes Kepler (1571—1630), whose work in dioptrics had contributed substantially to the perfection of the telescope, and whose laws of planetary motion had served as a foundation upon which Sir Isaac Newton erected his own edifice of cosmological motions. In this design Newton is seen receiving the torch from Kepler. The inscription by Schiller reads: FORTVNA MAIOR/ NEVTONI/ PER SIDERA DVCTOR.[19]

It was perhaps Schiller's authorship of the inscription which first attracted Hölderlin's attention. The result was the poem "Kepler," in which Hölderlin represents his compatriot as the genial hero of the intellectual world. To reach Kepler's side the poet has to leave the world and ascend into the upper spheres of the cosmos ("die Gefilde des Uranus").[20] The way to the heroic regions is lonely and daring ("einsam und gewagt"),[21] for "the course demands an iron tread *(eheren Tritt heischet die Bahn)*." The poet must muster his courage.

> Wandle mit Kraft, wie der Held, einher!
> Erhebe die Miene![22]

When he has arrived he sees the spirit of Newton bow his head before the grave of his forerunner and hears him say:

> "Du begannst, Suevias Sohn! wo es dem Blik
>
> Aller Jahrtausende schwindelte;
> Und ha! ich vollende, was du begannst,
> Denn voran leuchtetest du, Herrlicher!
> Im Labyrinth, Stralen beschwurst du in die Nacht.
>
> Möge verzehren des Lebens Mark
> Die Flamm' in der Brust — ich ereile dich,
> Ich vollends! denn sie ist groß, ernst und groß,
> Deine Bahn, höhnet des Golds, lohnet sich selbst."[23]

Here the hero is among his equals. He is now appreciated. He passes the torch of knowledge to one who is his equal and who will surpass him. History is seen as a cycle of generations of heroes — each inching forward and, at the end, passing — willingly — the torch to the younger follower. Here Hölderlin anticipated the demands which he would later make of Schiller, who, to

---

[19] I, 2, pp. 383f.
[20] I, 1, p. 81 (line 2).
[21] I, 1, p. 81 (lines 3f.).
[22] I, 1, p. 81 (lines 5f.).
[23] I, 1, p. 81 (lines 16—24).

Hölderlin's mind, should have passed the torch to his "favorite Swabian," who then would overcome, surpass Schiller's thought and art.[24]

Particularly striking is the last line above, in which the genius is freed of all mundane cares of everyday living. His work "rewards itself," a turn of speech which he would use in a letter to his mother in 1790,[25] after he had decided that it was his destiny to foreswear any hopes of a rewarding life in the normal sense and had already acted upon his conviction by breaking his engagement to Luise Nast, so that he might devote himself to his true destiny and educate himself for the work of the poet-philosopher, which would "reward itself" — an idea that he probably got from Schiller's *Antrittsrede* at the University of Jena in 1788, which had been published in the *Deutsches Museum* in 1789. The sentiments, the motivations, and the tragic fate that Hölderlin ascribed to Gustav Adolf, Kepler, Thill, and the prototype of virile manhood were to him those of the poet as well. The hero-martyr figure was Hölderlin himself. Not only did he see himself as the hero in the later poems of the period in which he turns his attention away from historical themes and concentrates on himself. Even in the earlier poems this figure is seldom absent.

In "Bücher der Zeiten" near the end of the catalogue of horrors through which he depicts the age of the Antichrist, a number of impressionistic images flit past which suggest preoccupations basic to Hölderlin's self-conception. He writes:

> Da steht geschrieben —
> Der Vater verlassend
> Weib und Kind im Hunger,
> Zustürzend in Taumel
> Dem lokenden süßlichen Lästerarm.—.
> Im Staub das Verdienst
> Zurük von der Ehre
> Ins Elend gestoßen
> Vom Betrüger —
> Im Lumpengewand
> Einher der Wanderer
> Bettelnahrung zu suchen
> Dem zerstümmelten Gliederbau.

---

24 See "An die Klugen Rathegeber" (I, 1, pp. 223f.) and also the letter to Susette in which he expressed his belief that he had been conspired against by those who had refused to contribute to his journal *Iduna* (195.28ff.).

25 34 a.22f.

Da steht geschrieben
  Des heitern, rosigen Mädchens
  Grabenaher Fieberkampf;
  Der Mutter Händeringen,
  Des donnergerührten Jünglings
  Wilde stumme Betäubung.[26]

These are, with a few variations in wording, exactly the themes which Hölderlin employed again and again to represent his own fate. The desertion of the mother and child is slightly varied here, for the father deserts them for the sake of the temptress. The father's infidelity is probably introduced because of the religious tone of the poem. The image of the family suddenly finding itself alone and without a father had already appeared in "An die Seinige" and also appears in "An Thill's Grab" and in "Einst und Jezt." In every instance but this one, the father is taken by death, just as Hölderlin's father was taken, and the bereaved mother bewails her loss. In "Bücher der Zeiten" the father left under less honorable circumstances. The mother could hardly appear wringing her hands, or she would look ludicrous. But, twelve lines later, there she is wringing her hands over the death – of a young girl! It would seem as if the disappearance of his father and the image of his mother wringing her hands and wailing were somehow locked in his mind and that the mention of one automatically compelled him to conjure up the other, even if that required the invention of a completely superfluous death.

Such was the legacy of his childhood. This complex of images had already become a symbol of his fate in his mind. And then, again as if by some inner compulsion, the image of the earthly Hölderlin appears. Uncanny! For what we saw just after the bereaved mother is a fleeting glimpse of the "sunstruck" Hölderlin of later years. Cheated of honor, the victim of men's cruelty, wandering in search of food for his wasting spirit, the youth reels toward his confoundment. An eerie anticipation of his words after he had returned from southern France: "struck down by Apollo."[27]

He had written about heroes before. In Denkendorf he had written a monologue in verse from Alexander the Great to his soldiers. He had written poems about his own fate, modeled after Klopstock and Schubart. But now he had begun to absorb all sorts of images and subordinate historical fact to his view of his own life. More and more it was the poet himself who stepped to the center of the stage and commanded the reader's attention. No longer did he not draw ideas from the figures he chose, but strength, spiritual sustenance and encouragement. The new tone of self-confidence which had appeared in the letters to his mother after his visit to Stäudlin and Schubart appears now in the

[26] I, 1, p. 71 (lines 72–90).
[27] 240.10.

poems. As the months rolled on neither Christianity nor any hero was able to dominate his poems. The poet began to grow and continued to increase in importance until he swallowed up the themes he had taken from history. It was not that the personal inadequacies that plagued him vanished, but rather that he, through ascribing those same inadequacies to every historical figure he used as the subject of his poetry, convinced himself that his very weaknesses and the misery which they caused him were unmistakable signs that he also belonged to the realm of heroes, for which he too was destined.

Now the psycho-biographical weakness was no longer something of which he must be ashamed but was rather the very part of him which was holy and demanded expression. In the poem "An Thill's Grab" we see the poet usurp the role of the historic subject. He becomes a lyricist. He no longer preached as in "Bücher der Zeiten" or passed on the traditional learning that, as he now saw, had nothing to offer but unbearable admonitions to humility. He shakes off the bonds of this world and boldly claims kinship with the hero of the poem.

Johann Gottlieb Thill (1747–1772) was a minor Swabian poet who had also begun as a *Stiftler*. His works, mostly Klopstock imitations, had been published by Stäudlin in 1782. His grave lay not far outside Tübingen. Rudolf Magenau, the third member of the *Dichterbund* has described in his memoirs the three friends' venture to Thill's Valley.[28] Magenau only mentioned the incident in passing.

To Hölderlin, however, the sight of the grave awakened once more the conglomerate of painful impressions surrounding the loss of his father. Thill is already forgotten as the poem begins and is not named until the eleventh line. The inner compulsion surrounding the trauma surges up and displaces his perceptions of real surroundings.

> Der Leichenreihen wandelte still hinan,
>> Und Fakelnschimmer schien! auf des Theuren Sarg,
>>> Und du, geliebte gute Mutter!
>>>> Schautest entseelt aus der Jammerhütte,
>
> Als ich ein schwacher stammelnder Knabe noch,
>> O Vater! lieber Seeliger! dich verlohr,
>>> Da fühlt' ichs nicht, was du mir warst, doch
>>>> Mißte dich bald der verlaßne Waise.
>
> So weint' ich leisen Knabengefühles schon,
>> Der Wehmuth Träne über dein traurig Loos,
>>> Doch jezt, o Thill! jezt fühl' ichs ernster,
>>>> Schmerzender jezt über deinem Hügel,

28   VII, 1, p. 395.

Was hier im Grab den Redlichen Suevias
  Verwest, den himmelnahenden Einsamen.
    Und, o mein Thill! du ließst sie Waisen?
      Eiltest so frühe dahin, du guter? [29]

Thus the poet Thill and Hölderlin's father, who died in the same year, are fused. Hölderlin, the orphaned son in life, becomes a tragic orphan in his world of poetry. He is not writing of the realm of Swabian history but of the "honest ones of Swabia." Spiritually, he is the son of Thill and has his rightful place in the realm of heroes. He too suffers the perennial mockery of the unfeeling world that did not know what it had lost in Thill.

Ihr stille Schatten seines Holunderbaums!
  Verbergt mich, daß kein Spötter die Tränen sieht
    Und lacht, wann ich geschmiegt an seinen
      Hügel die bebenden Wangen trokne.[30]

Already, in the not always very skillfully executed poems of his nineteenth year, we see his later self-appraisal emerging. If we are content with mythology, then we are disposed to accept Hölderlin's explanation of things, which he fully developed later but which was already beginning to emerge now at face value: He was a hero of human history who had a mission to perform that demanded of him the renunciation of normal life. If we are inquisitive and demand a sounder explanation and search diligently for the connections between his life and his works, then it becomes evident very soon that the self-glorification was, to a great extent, rationalization. The facts we have already unearthed — that he was hypersensitive, self-protective, defensive towards others, and yet tormented by his estrangement from his fellows — provide more than sufficient biographical explanation for the autistic preoccupation with himself which increased so sharply during these months. The mythology, which he created himself, resulted from this autism.

The hero might find no fulfillment in this life, but he still could not escape life. Life on earth, among common men, was his cross. His most important asset was, therefore, resolute endurance.

Hölderlin always wanted and sought respect, honor, and recognition. He was never able to turn completely away from real life and slam the door shut. He sought to build bridges across that abyss that separated him from the world of social contacts somewhere beyond. He built them, but, just as resolutely, he tore them down. His letters to his mother are curious mixtures of resentment ("I would be happy if it were not for you") and abject pleas for her understanding ("I ask most humbly your forgiveness").

---

[29] I, 1, p. 83 (lines 1—16).
[30] I, 1, p. 83 (lines 17—20).

His heroic mythology was then not merely an excuse by which he tried to justify escaping from responsibilities towards others, although that was part of it and the most destructive part. More than that, it was the verbal manifestation of a complex psychological process by which he, unable as he was to escape the torment of his isolation, tried to justify it by proclaiming it to be the holiest of holies.

This leads us to another observation about these early poems from Tübingen, which will be valid for almost all his poetry. He never really glorifies the hero's battle with the world. The business of *becoming* heroic, of earning the respect and admiration of others, did not appeal to him. He yearned for fulfillment but doubted that he was strong enough to attain it. In the poem "An die Vollendung," in which the religious tones and the traditional view of one's receiving his reward in heaven, he wrote:

> Vollendung! Vollendung! —
> O du der Geister heiliges Ziel!
> Wann werd ich siegestrunken
> Dich umfahen und ewig ruhn?
>
> Und frei und groß
> Entgegenlächeln der Herrschaar
> Die zahllos aus den Welten
> In den Schoos dir strömt?
>
> Ach ferne, ferne von dir!
> Mein göttlichster schönster Gedanke
> War, wie der Welten
> Fernstes Ende, ferne von dir![31]

To his own frailty he contrasts the sure-footed progress of his forerunners:

> Voll hoher Einfalt
> Einfältig still und groß
> Rangen des Siegs gewiß
> Rangen dir zu die Väter.[32]

In the poem "Die Heilige Bahn" he seems to have been trying free variations of Klopstockian meters. And yet automatically reached for the image of the struggling poet and saw himself stumbling, fighting on, falling, rising again, always struggling though on the verge of defeat, under the watchful eye of Aristotle, the stern judge of all his efforts.

In the last stanzas of the poem "An Thill's Grab," he wrote:

---

[31] I, 1, p. 75 (lines 1—12).
[32] I, 1, p. 75 (lines 21—24).

O wohl dir! wohl dir, guter! du schläfst so sanft
   Im stillen Schatten deines Holunderbaums.
      Dein Monument ist er, und deine
         Lieder bewahren des Dorfes Greisen.

O daß auch mich dein Hügel umschattete,
   Und Hand in Hand wir schliefen, bis Erndte wird,
      Da schielten keine Vorurteile,
         Lachte kein Affe des stillen Pilgers.

O Thill! Ich zage, denn er ist dornenvoll,
   Und noch so fern der Pfad zur Vollkommenheit;
      Die Starken beugen ja ihr Haupt, wie
         Mag ihn erkämpfen der schwache Jüngling? [33]

Here was a new and significant dimension to his internal tension and one that would trouble him for years to come. His need for honor and recognition conflicted with his need for peace and tranquility. Two poems written in the last months of 1789 demonstrate the extent of this conflict. "An die Ruhe" is a celebration of sweet repose and rejuvenation of the spirit following exhaustion. And yet, he seeks not eternal rest but the repose of the champion as he gathers his strength for another battle.

Erquiklich, wie die heimische Ruhebank
   Im fernen Schlachtgetümmel dem Krieger deucht,
      Wenn die zerfleischten Arme sinken.
         Und der geschmetterte Stahl im Blut liegt —

So bist du, Ruhe! freundliche Trösterin!
   Du schenktest Riesenkräfte dem Verachteten;
      Er höhnet Dominiksgesichtern,
         Höhnet der zischenden Natterzunge.

Im Veilchenthal, von dämmernden Hain umbraust,
   Entschlummert er, von süßen Begeist'rungen
      Der Zukunft trunken, von der Unschuld
         Spielen im flatternden Flügelkleide.

Da weiht der Ruhe Zauber den Schlummernden,
   Mit Muth zu schwingen im Labyrinth sein Licht,
      Die Fahne rasch voranzutragen,
         Wo sich der Dünkel entgegenstemmet.

[33] I, 1, p. 83 (lines 21–32).

Auf springt er, wandelt ernster den Bach hinab
Nach seiner Hütte. Siehe! das Götterwerk,
 Es keimet in der großen Seele.
  Wieder ein Lenz, — und es ist vollendet.[34]

"An die Ehre," however, emphasizes the reverse. Here the hero awakes from his slumbers and sets off to do the work of the gods. Hölderlin's portrayal of the struggle makes it clear just how badly the hero needs repose from time to time, for his ordeal is gruesome.

So rief ich — stürzt' im Zauber des Aufrufs hin —
 Doch ha! der Täuschung — wenige Schritte sinds!
  Bemerkbar kaum! und Hohn der Spötter,
   Freude der Feigen umzischt den Armen.

Ach! schlummert' ich am murmelnden Moosquell noch,
 Ach! träumt' ich noch von Stellas Umarmungen.
  Doch nein! bei Mana nein! auch Streben
   Ziert, auch der Schwächeren Schweis ist edel.[35]

The compulsion to ascend into the realm of the heroes, to accept the gloriously tragic fate of the hero in life in hopes of sharing in the hero's rewards and immortality, was growing evermore irresistible. He was now ready to leave his dreams of Stella's embraces. Stella, as we know, was his poetic name for Luise Nast. He meant this turn of speech seriously. Within two or three months he would break their engagement of two years. He was becoming more and more convinced that he was destined for greater things than for the simple life of a preacher. And he needed a better education than that which he was being spoon-fed in the *Stift*.

Ich duld' es nimmer! ewig und ewig so
 Die Knabenschritte, wie ein Gekerkerter
  Die kurzen vorgemeßnen Schritte
   Täglich zu wandeln, ich duld es nimmer!

Ists Menschenlooß — ist meines? ich trag es nicht
 Mich reizt der Lorber, — Ruhe beglükt mich nicht
  Gefahren zeugen Männerkräfte
   Leiden erheben die Brust des Jünglings.

Was bin ich dir, was bin ich mein Vaterland?
 Ein siecher Säugling, welchen mit tränendem
  Mit hofnungslosem Blick die Mutter
   In den gedultigen Armen schaukelt.

[34] I, 1, p. 92 (lines 5—24).
[35] I, 1, p. 94 (lines 13—20).

Mich tröstete das blinkende Kelchglas nie
  Mich nie der Blik der lächelnden Tändlerin,
    Soll ewig trauern mich umwolken?
      Ewig mich tödten die zornge Sehnsucht?

Was soll des Freundes traulicher Handschlag mir,
  Was mir des Frühlings freundlicher Morgengruß
    Was mir der Eiche Schatten? was der
      Blühenden Rebe, der Linde Düfte?

Beim grauen Mana! nimmer genieß ich dein
  Du Kelch der Freuden, blinktest du noch so schön
    Bis mir ein Männerwerk gelinget,
      Bis ich ihn hasche, den ersten Lorbeer.

Der Schwur ist groß. Er zeuget im Auge mir
  Die Trän' und wohl mir wenn ihn Vollendung krönt.
    Dann jauchz auch ich du Krais der Frohen
      Dann o Natur, ist dein Lächeln Wonne.[36]

Now, perhaps just at the time when he was trying to escape from the *Stift,* he found his answer. He, too, like his heroes, must renounce life. For what did life have to offer him? A post in some lonely village with Luise Nast bearing children and growing old by his side, cooking his meals, mending his clothes, and never quite understanding why it was not enough for him. Were the responsibilities of a husband even within his power? Could he ever be a husband and a father? Here one can only speculate. He was psychologically a schizoid type. The absence of a father during his adolescent years had already become an obsession. His dependence on his mother went far beyond the normal adherence of a young boy to a parent's wishes or respect for a parent's opinions. He had imaginary loves at Maulbronn and Tübingen and seems to have been attracted to a young widow at the von Kalb house. But he continually fled from single women whenever he seemed to be getting deeply involved with them.[37] The final test of masculinity he may have instinctively avoided. Only once — in the letter to Nast about Wieland's *Neuer Amadis* — did he ever mention sex. The tone was one of disgust. He took offense and felt that "virtue" had been offended. Love for a woman was for him something soulful, spiritual, a communion of the soul. In a word, it, like so many of his relations with others, was merely verbal. Sex had no place.

It is useless to speculate whether a psychologist, confronted with Hölderlin and his history, would judge him impotent or whether the eternal celebration of

---

[36] I, 1, p. 90f.
[37] Ricarda Huch seems to have been the first to point out that the fact that Susette Gontard was unattainable accounted for much of his intense feeling for her, in her *Die Romantik* (Leipzig, 1924), p. 152.

"friendship" for men might suggest latent homosexuality. The types of "love" and "friendship" about which he wrote were so much the contemporary poet's stock in trade that it would be impossible for us to say how much resulted from the society's influence and how much from the condition of his glands. But the obsessive quality of his enthusiasm for spiritual love and soulful friendship did not belong to the culture — at least not in such an intensive form. All this might suggest a total sublimation of the sex-drive. That too may have perished in its overt form as the rest of the social dimension perished.

Just before 1790 dawned, or perhaps in the first few weeks of the new year, Hölderlin wrote the poem "Einst und Jezt." He had just returned from the disastrous confrontation with his mother, which will be examined more closely in the next chapter. Crushed at his failure to escape, overwhelmed by the knowledge that he was condemned to three and a half years of further torment at the seminary, he compared the golden days before the death of his father with the misery and loneliness of his present existence. The poem is revealing. In Hölderlin's mind there existed "Then" and "Now." The one meant happiness and the carefree joys of childhood. Of the "Now" and of his prospects for the future he wrote:

Jezt wandl' ich einsam an dem Gestade hin,
   Ach keine Seele keine für dieses Herz?
      Ihr frohen Reigen? Aber weh dir
         Sehnender Jüngling! sie gehn vorüber!

Zurük denn in die Zelle, Verachteter!
   Zurük zur Kummerstätte, wo schlaflos du
      So manche Mitternächte weintest
         Weintest im Durste nach Lieb' und Lorbeer.

Lebt wohl, ihr güldnen Stunden vergangner Zeit,
   Ihr lieben Kinderträume von Größ' und Ruhm,
      Lebt wohl, lebt wol ihr Spielgenossen,
         Weint um den Jüngling er ist verachtet.[38]

Now he knew that the time of play was gone forever. Before him he saw only a thorny path which his mother had condemned him to walk. Before him lay not the comradeship of his former playmates but a comradeship of another type. Before him lay the *Dichterbund,* which would give him the strength to renounce life and throw himself into his imagined mission.

Doch nein! ich wag's! es streitet zur Seite ja
   Ein felsentreuer, muthiger Bruder mir.
      O freut euch, seelige Gebeine!
         Über dem Nahmen! Es ist — mein Neuffer.[39]

---

[38] I, 1, p. 96 (lines 25—36).
[39] I, 1, p. 84 (lines 33—36).

8

DICHTERBUND AND DEDICATION

Near the beginning of January 1790, Hölderlin returned to Tübingen. He had hoped that he would never have to come back. His first year in the seminary had been a time of tension and increasing anxiety and had culminated in the rather incongruous spectacle of Hölderlin — the obedient son, the good student who had always received good marks in deportment, the Christian boy who had been so jealous of his purity that his classmates dared not utter a vulgar word in his presence — suddenly confronting a school official on an open street, accusing him of not showing proper respect to a *Stipendiat*, finally knocking the hat from the astonished man's head. This behavior, so completely out of character, could only have resulted from a deep and profound resentment which had been fomenting inside him for months. His indignation, stimulated perhaps by the Herzog's recent demands that school discipline be more rigidly enforced, suddenly boiled over when he was snubbed by the *Mägdleinprovisor*.

Hölderlin recovered from his attack of courage almost immediately. He was courteous when the Ephorus interrogated him about the incident, accepted his punishment rather meekly — and decided that he could not endure another moment in the school. He wrote his mother, begged her to take him out of the *Stift* because the confinement and poor living conditions were dangerous to his health and aggravated his "spiritual condition."[1] He wrote to her of "mistreatment" and "scorn."[2] After he had obtained sick leave and had gone home to Nürtingen, he wrote of "injustice" and "chicanery"[3] to his friend Neuffer. This was, of course, the language that was current among the students that year. The Bastille had been stormed only five months before, heralding the outbreak of the French Revolution. The youth of Germany was just becoming conscious of the revolutionary hero, and Hölderlin, quite naturally, decked himself out, in *his* imagination at least, in a red cap and thought of himself as a champion of human rights. This concern for the rights of man would endure. Several years later, letters from Tübingen to his sister would show him cheering on the armies of France and again playing an imaginary role of the leader in a students' revolt when he proclaimed that he could not stay in Tübingen if the reform of 1792 proved as repressive as he feared.[4]

[1] 27.2ff.
[2] 27.8ff.
[3] 28.4.
[4] In February or March 1792 he wrote Rike: "God knows how dear my family is to me and how very much I desire to live in accordance with their wishes; but it is impossible for me to submit to senseless, pointless laws and to stay in a place where my greatest talents would perish" (49.19ff.).

Nothing came of the revolutionary posing, either in 1789 or in 1792. Many of the other students acted and thought the same way, and, although the Herzog had nightmares about the "republicanism" among his students, it was all more or less harmless. They were, after all, only boys caught up in an historically determined wave of enthusiasm, which was a passing phenomenon. Fifteen years later the German students would be nationalistic, willing to lay down their lives for the very rulers whose arbitrary rule their older brothers had found so oppressive. Their republicanism and revolutionary leanings were confined, for the most part, to extravagant phrases. They were mostly content to discuss freedom and write poems about it. Schelling's really rather tame retort when the Herzog asked him whether he was responsible for circulating a copy of the "Marseillaise": "Sire, we all have many failings" — was probably the most serious incident. They were naive young men who would remember their liberalism in later years with a condescending nostalgia or translate it into an excuse to fight against Napoleon.[5]

All but Hölderlin. He tried to escape, and it was not the first time. Indeed, what happened in the fall and winter of 1789—1790 followed the pattern established in 1787, when he had tried to convince his mother to let him quit school the first time. In both cases months of stress, which affected his nerves, were required to bring him to such a state of despair that he dared pit his will against his anxious mother. He tried to endure hardship manfully, as he had promised that he would, partly because he loved his mother and did not want to disappoint her, but mostly because he dreaded the reproaches that any new attempt to quit school would surely bring on his head.

And yet the knowledge that it might well be impossible to convince her that he was old enough to make his own decisions and that he would encounter unrelenting opposition if he tried to escape again aggravated his well-established penchant for feeling himself martyred — that growing streak of self-pity which made Schiller's heroes, Klopstock's warrior, and the members of the National Assembly so attractive to him. As far as Hölderlin's life is concerned, the particular form his fantasies assumed at different times are not all that important. It is the general type of hero to which he was drawn that is significant. It was, in almost every case, the strong manly type of towering strength. For from these imaginary or real figures he could draw a vicariously attained self-confidence, which he himself did not possess.

Only after months of intense fantasy-identification with such figures was he

---

5 Hegel is perhaps the most famous example of that change from liberalism to extreme support for the Prussian state. It is hard to imagine the same young man who had been such an ardent supporter of the French Revolution delivering the lectures on reason in history in which he proclaimed the individual to be nothing more than a tool of the state, which was, in turn, the tool of the world-will (Georg Wilhelm Friedrich Hegel. *Die Vernunft in der Geschichte,* edited by Johannes Hoffmeister [Hamburg, 1955], pp. 87ff.).

able to confront his mother. This too was the case in both 1787 and 1789. He was finally able to act only because he had learned to rely on his fantasy and block out reality. But this very psychological trick, which he came to play on himself so often in the ensuing years, also condemned him to failure. Facing his mother in reality must have been somewhat like awaking from a dream which had been so real that one has difficulty distinguishing it from real life. But it was, after all, only a dream. He had none of the strength he enjoyed when he portrayed on paper the man he would like to be. Just as he had had the strength to face the *Mägdleinprovisor* and knocked his hat off, but then turned meek and submissive as soon as he realized what he had done — so also did he realize, even as he wrote his mother, that he could not actually stand up to her because he was still psychologically dependent on her approval. Near the end of the letter to his mother, he wrote: "If my request is weakness, then have pity with me; if my request is reasonable and well-considered, then let us not be deterred by over-anxious doubts about the future from taking a step that may still bring you so much happiness in your old age."[6]

Already wavering in his resolve when he left for Nürtingen, he had to fail. He spent a month with his mother. Those four weeks must have been terribly shameful for him. His dream of himself as a man of strength and endurance, the equal of Karl Moor, had no substance. There were no great monologues and no poetry. There was only the disgrace of being dragged all over the little town while mother sought advice from men whose opinions she respected. Should she let her son desert his theological studies and change to the study of law? Or should she insist that he continue at the seminary? The issue was never really in doubt. *She* opposed the change, and that was enough.

Near the beginning of January 1790, after he had returned to Tübingen, he wrote her: "You will soon guess why I am writing you at this time. I believe this letter will not be unpleasant to you.

"I have decided to stay in my present situation from now on. The thought of causing you anxious hours, the uncertain future, the reproaches that I would deserve from my loved ones, and which I would make of myself in proper measure if my hopes had deceived me, the advice of friends, the disgusting study of law, the foolishness which I would be letting myself in for as a lawyer, and, on the other side, the joys of a quiet parsonage, the hope of certain, not too distant advantages, the idea of remaining indifferent to adversity through four short years for the sake of His flock and of laughing at foolishness — all this finally compelled me, dear Mamma, to follow you. Parental advice is soothing in any case. However it turns out, I still have that consolation."[7]

---

[6]   27.12ff.
[7]   29.2ff.

Wilhelm Böhm has observed that this incident marked a turning-point in Hölderlin's relationship with his mother. This was, according to Böhm, the last time that he would ever be able to communicate openly with her.[8] This is true. From that point on he constantly protested that he was being honest with her and grew quite agitated whenever she let him know that she knew better.

But the consequences of this misunderstanding went much deeper than that. For he had not wanted merely to escape from school but also to prove that he was mature enough to choose his own profession. By then he had realized that he would never be able to comply with his mother's wishes for his life.

Something quite uncanny was going on in Hölderlin during those winter and spring months of 1790. Back at the *Stift,* he had given up any hope of ever being able to accept the life his mother had planned or the career for which he was being educated. He needed something more, a life that would be more rewarding and bring him more respect and admiration. He needed a profession in which he would be able to play out the fantasies all his life and in which he would occupy such an exalted position among men that he would no longer be subject to their demands.

All this had compelled him to try to change to the study of law. He had promised his mother in 1787 that the thought of giving up his studies would never occur to him again *unless* he could suggest an acceptable alternative profession. Hence his suggestion that he study law. Through suggesting that he study law instead, he had kept his word. And yet, within four weeks, he was writing that the reality of a legal career disgusted him. He wrote, "I have decided," which would indicate that he made the final decision himself.

Why the change? Partially he was yielding to his mother. That would have been enough in itself. But, beyond that, it seems doubtful that he had ever really considered what being a lawyer would mean. Once more he was following an example blindly. This time, however, his example was real. He wrote Neuffer while he was in Nürtingen: "Stäudlin is truly a splendid man. When my mother has heard the evidence of a few more knowledgeable men, and if they advise her as I hope they will, then I will be able to take him as my model even for my professional studies [*Brotstudium*]."[9] Neuffer had introduced Hölderlin to Stäudlin during the Easter vacation of 1789. Stäudlin, a lawyer in Stuttgart, had succeeded in combining a legal career with considerable literary activity. His publications, such as the *Schwäbischer Almanach,* had brought him a good deal of local fame. He would, within two years, become the first editor to publish poems by Hölderlin. Now Hölderlin followed, or hoped to follow, him as an example "even" for his professional ambitions. The word "even" would suggest that Hölderlin saw the editor as his model primarily in another sense. His dreams

8   Böhm, I, p. 24.
9   28.32ff.

of becoming a poet, of commanding the respect of others, and of finding an alternative profession, thus providing himself with the excuse he needed to effect his escape from the Stift, would all be realized (or so it seemed to him) if he but modelled his life after Stäudlin's. It was not really the lawyer Stäudlin but Stäudlin the poet who attracted him and helped mold his idea of studying law. When he failed to convince his mother that a legal career was an acceptable alternative, he realized that he would actually never be able to convince her that he should be allowed to make up his own mind and that she was determined that he must bend to her will.

In 1790 something began to change. The third stage of the two-year old behavior pattern set in. In 1787 he had withdrawn into his books when he realized that he would have to stay in school. Something similar happened now, except that this time his withdrawal was so thorough, his fantasies so pronounced, that it had a profound effect reaching beyond his student years and molding his attitudes for the rest of his life. Soon he came to include family, marriage, children, and the ministry in the category of a mother-dominated existence. None of these could he accept. Almost systematically, he began to disrupt the lines of communication with his mother and break all ties which might entangle him and force him to follow the path that led to an eventual acceptance of all the things he wanted to avoid.

He broke his engagement to Luise Nast. In January 1790 he played the role of the moody lover once again. We learn that again his preceeding letter, which has been lost, had disturbed her. He wrote now: "Oh, if I could plead at your feet, blot out the dismal moments which my dark moods may well have caused you; if you could see how very unworthy of your indescribably noble love I feel when I think that my moods have caused me to disregard the respect which I should have for you and do have."[10]

The bonds which had held them together had been very tenuous at best. His pose of the moody lover corresponded to his needs so well that he never seems to have considered what effect it might have on his fiancée until it gave him the opportunity to justify himself indirectly through his apology. This was all well and good in letters. Marriage, however, would have made necessary a change in their relationship that he was unable to make. He must have known that months before he broke with her. He wrote: "I promise you, dear sweet girl, that, from now on, I will never write you so offensively if I still want to be your Hölderlin."[11]

Then, in the spring of that year, he returned her ring and letters. He repeated his belief that he was really unworthy of her and wrote: "It is and will remain my unshakeable resolve never to ask for your hand until I have attained a

10   30.4ff.
11   30.21ff.

position worthy of you."[12] He realized, of course, that she could never have been happy with him, for he wrote: "You will then [when you have found another] see clearly for the first time that you could never have been happy with your sullen, discontented, sickly friend."[13]

The logic of this farewell letter reveals quite clearly that Hölderlin was still clinging to the idea of his own holiness. That this quality was obvious to no one but himself was because he had been so mistreated, spiritually mangled by life in the schools. This is implicit in the idea that he was not worthy of Luise, who had always been in his mind the ideal sweetheart of the great man which he had, unfortunately, not yet become; this is the "position worthy of you" of which he wrote. And he went on later: "The unrelenting melancholy in me — please do not laugh at me — is, probably not completely, but mostly — unsatisfied ambition. If this is ever satisfied, then, and only then, will I be completely happy, completely cheerful, and healthy."[14]

What do these examples of twisted logic reveal? First he said that he was unworthy of her because she was so perfect and then implied that his ambition was compelling him toward greater things than he could ever expect if he married her. She was both good for the real Hölderlin and, at the same moment, not good enough for the Hölderlin which was to be. For he wrote: "I would think my love is not of this world."[15] There was no opportunism behind all the sophisms. He believed it all and seems to have thought that she should find it perfectly normal for him to desert her merely because he had some vague notion that he was destined to be great someday.

He had already reached the point at which he found it necessary to hold contradictory images of himself and opposing interpretations of reality at the same time. That he *did*, according to our appreciation, become a great poet, does not make it any less bizarre that he should have been convinced that, although he was "sickly," although he was incapable of discharging social obligations, he was, nevertheless, destined to become the greatest of men and satisfy an ambition which was, like his love, out of this world. That he was able to manipulate so naively his opinions and believe all the while that he was being honest with himself and others, reveals how much he needed to maintain at all costs that exaggerated self-appraisal in order to protect his evermore precarious psychic balance.

Luise, shocked by the letter, wrote Hölderlin's mother, who had known of the engagement and had approved. That Hölderlin had not expected. When called to give an accounting, he wrote: "And that I must now hear reproaches from a person who was so dear to me about changes which she saw as necessary

12 31.8ff.
13 31.17ff.
14 31.20ff.
15 31.45.

herself; and that I now have to think to myself, 'You are making the girl unhappy' — oh, dear Mamma, that I do not deserve!!" "I know you agree with me in this matter; for whenever I want to endure silently I have only to follow your example. Of course, it is also part of my nature that I take everything to heart so; but I thank God for that, for it protects against frivolity."[16]

What was that? Luise had seen the "change" as necessary? Probably so. But she must have been surprised that her fiancé had taken that as authorization to break the engagement altogether.

Yet the following months showed that there was a warped, yet perceptible, logic to Hölderlin's actions. He did indeed undergo a profound change and passed into a period in which he succeeded in avoiding the terrible conflicts that he had had to endure up until then. He changed in the only way possible for him: He limited his contacts with others and avoided all situations in which he would have to debase himself and play the obedient son again. His letters to his mother were fewer after that. Many of the letters home were written to Rike. In them he could play the big brother and communicate with his mother indirectly. But whenever he was questioned directly, his reactions were extreme. When she questioned his financial behavior, he wrote: "I beseech you, dear Mamma, to show my letter to a man who has gone to school himself or is at least aware of the situation. Maybe he can convince you that I cannot possibly get by on less. Of course, it is annoying in that the whole business is so useless. As far as I am concerned, all *Magister* and Doctoral degrees, together with 'learned' and 'wellborn' can go to Morea."[17]

Even in the letters directed toward his sister he frequently made excuses for his failure to write or for the brevity of his letters.

"This time I am ashamed. My head is so heavy from staying awake so much at night that I am having difficulty in getting anything down on paper, not to mention that this something should be as jolly as your clever letter was" (November 1790).[18] "Forgive me! I overslept. Have barely time for a few lines" (December 1790).[19] "Today I must write you rather hurriedly for the simple reason that I stayed in bed later than usual because it is so terribly cold; and now the post is about to leave" (March 1791).[20]

It could hardly have escaped his mother that he had little time for her any more. But, when she accused him of ignoring her, he retorted: "Your suspicion that I am not reading your letters I hardly deserve. And as far as short letter-writing is concerned, I have seen many [students] write letters to parents

16   32.28ff.
17   34.16ff.
18   36.2ff.
19   38.2f.
20   42.3ff.

who live very far away and who were certainly dear to their sons, but they usually expressed themselves briefly.

"I will certainly never measure your love according to the length of your letters. Karl has not written me for a long time, nor asks why I do not write; should I therefore believe that he does not love me any more? Forgive me, dear Mamma, if I write something improper!"[21]

Such straightforward expressions of resentment at her probings are few. More often than not, he was successful in avoiding communication. The shorter his letters were, the more confident was his tone; the less substance they contained, the more glibly he expressed himself. He had learned that his peace of mind depended on remaining aloof and avoiding conflicts. For if he let his resentment show, he came into conflict with her once again; and the results were always as destructive as his last visit to Nürtingen. The above passage was the occasion for such an incident. One week later he was writing her: "You have quite shamed me with your goodness. I am still so far behind you in goodness, and you give me so many opportunities to profit from your example. Forgive me, dear Mamma! if a word slipped out in my last letter which is not in keeping with a child's respect."[22]

The distance between them increased with each day that passed. The same cold aloofness had crept into his letters home in 1787. Then he had lost himself in his day-dreams about Luise Nast and had consoled himself with his poetry and his fantasies of "love" and "friendship." But in the intervening two years life had profaned love. Love had tumbled from its pedestal and had been absorbed by the vulgar reality of marriage plans and nightmares about parsonages, children, and the like. His mother had approved of his engagement.[23] For her it was quite compatible with the proper career she envisioned for him.

Only his books and the "friendship" of which he dreamed remained now. It is true that he entered into a neither-here-nor-there liason with Elise Lebret, the daughter of a school official. But she played no role in his dreams and poetry comparable to Luise Nast in former years.[24] There are indications that he came dangerously close to becoming a woman-hater. For he accepted friend Neuffer's advice against marrying too early and referred to a passage in the lost *Hyperion* fragments of those next years, which he called the "hard passage" about

21   40.10ff.
22   41.2ff.
23   Shortly before Hölderlin broke his engagement with Luise, she wrote him: "How happy I am that your mother — oh, may I say my mother, spoke so kindly about our situation" (VII, 1, pp. 20f.).
24   The three poems to Elise: "Meine Genesung" (I, 1, pp. 120f.), "Melodie / An Lyda" (p. 122ff.), and "An Lyda" (p. 128f.) show much the same adolescent notion of love that appears in the letters to and concerning Luise Nast and also anticipate the poems to Susette Gontard.

women.[25] This was a passing stage. But now he flung himself once more into exclusively male company.

When he had catalogued his reasons for staying in Tübingen in the letter to his mother he had included a passage which read: "Aside from that, I have friends in my Cloister which I would hardly find anywhere else. My Neuffer does his duty manfully whenever my moods come upon me. And they hardly ever come upon me any more when I am busy."[26] When he had given all his reasons for not feeling guilt at having to break the engagement, he had continued: "But I still have a clean conscience and know how to console myself in my books, and that is wonderful. I would have already strayed often from the right path, perhaps, if it were not my fate to suffer more than others."[27]

In June he had written that a student had been expelled for "disorderly conduct," which he called "more than strict." He went on: "In general, the pressure on the *Stipendium* is indescribable . . . . . Incidentally, I can assure you that I and my friends, particularly Neuffer and Magenau, pass our days as content as possible. We sit industriously at our desks, not because we have to, but because the joy of studying increases with each day in which I learn more."[28] And in August he wrote his mother: "I have many plans. As your son, I can tell you without appearing immodest that a continued study of philosophy has recently become a necessity for me. If I encounter small annoyances here and there, then I return all the more resolutely to my books. If I received no reward for it, if I am misunderstood and slighted sometimes in life, that's all right! I wanted no reward. My work rewards itself through itself."[29]

His new love of study had little to do with writing his *specimina* or preparing for his examinations. Study meant something else to him and was intimately connected with his determination to find a better life, whatever the cost. In the spring of 1790, he, along with Neuffer and Magenau, the only really close friends he had, founded the "Allemannsfreunde," a poetic circle which can only be designated by that untranslatable word *Bund*. Hölderlin later wrote of "the golden days of our *Bund*,"[30] after Neuffer and Magenau had left Tübingen. A *Bund* was a literary club, a debating society, and a fraternity, all in one. It had become popular after Klopstock published his "Gelehrtenrepublik" and was based on the soulful type of friendship between young men about which not only Hölderlin, but the entire generation never tired of talking and writing.

---

25 60.41.
26 29.17ff.
27 32.32ff.
28 33.7ff.
29 34 a.15ff.
30 To Neuffer he wrote on 28 November 1791: "If you wish, Dear! we will criticize our verses in writing, like in the Golden Days of our *Bund!*" (47.51ff.); in May (?) 1793: "How often we said to each other that our *Bund* is a *Bund* for eternity" (57.6f.); in April (?) 1794: "What more do we want to believe that our *Bund* is eternal? " (75.21f.)

Membership in a *Bund* was an acceptable form of association in the eighteenth century. This peculiar German institution, which has since then influenced so much of the intellectual and political life, was celebrated, after Klopstock, by Bouterwek in his *Graf Donamar* and von Meyern in his *Dya-Na-Sore*. It also existed in fact, beginning with the *Göttinger Hainbund* of Voss and Bürger and continuing in its literary form in the Berlin and Jena Romantic circles, and probably made possible the quick growth of Jahn's *Turnerschaften*. This type of friendship between boys and young men continued well into the twentieth century in the Youth Movement. Gradually the *Bünde* became largely political. In the last years of the Weimar Republic they became a potent political force both for the Communists and the National Socialists, as well as for other splinter groups. In Hölderlin's day they were largely poetic, although the element of comradeship and the attachment to and idolization of spiritual leaders unite both the political and poetic types of *Bünde*.

The *Bund* always appealed most strongly to adolescents. Young men in search of truth, freedom, beauty, and service to their country found those ideals realized spiritually, if not actually, in each other's arms, in kisses exchanged, in tears shed jointly over favorite poems, or in political rallies and demonstrations. The *Bundesbruder* was something more than a mere friend. He became the object of intense love and devotion. This relationship is almost mystic and defies very close analysis. Interdependence was strong. In a sense one's *Bundesbruder* actually owned one. Partially because of the youth of most of the *Bundesbrüder*, there was generally a spiritual leader, who may not even have known of the particular *Bund's* existence. Klopstock presided over the *Göttinger Hainbund* in spirit. The words of the spiritual leader became a holy scripture. When Baldur von Schirach composed the prayer of the Hitler Youth, which began "Adolf Hitler, we believe in Thee; without Thee we would be alone," he was simply perverting to political ends a traditional attachment of German youths to a spiritual "Führer" which had been going on for 150 years. If Schiller were substituted for Hitler, Hölderlin could have repeated the prayer with enthusiasm.[31]

---

31   The following is a partial list of those passages from Hölderlin's letters to Schiller which show his total subservience to the older man: "great man" (76.1); "the deep respect for you with which I grew up, with which I have so often been either strengthened or humbled" (76.35f.); "great, noble man!" (76.50); "a great man" (102.20); "this dependency is sacred to me" (102.34); "I belong to you — at least as *res nullius* — and thus so also do the bitter fruits that I bring" (104.7f.); "It is almost my only source of pride, my only consolation that I may say anything to you, and something about me" (104.36f.); "I wanted to appear before you once again in all my poverty . . . and wanted to steal for myself a few friendly words from you through all sorts of round-about ways" (124.13ff.); "a dependency on you, which I have often attacked in vain, a dependency which still has not left me . . . ." (129.23ff.); "I would reproach myself for it if you were not the only man to whom I have thus lost my freedom" (129.27f.); "Say one friendly word to me and you will see how I am transformed" (129.39f.); "on you I am incurably dependent" (139.6f.); "I am

The activities of the three friends in Tübingen were rather restrained. They met periodically, read poems, and criticized each other's verses. One of them was always the leader of the day and proposed the topics for the next meeting. The best poems were copied neatly in the *Bundesbuch*, which has been preserved. And yet, this summary of their activities gives no indication of the intense devotion which the three friends felt for each other and for the *Bund*. Rudolf Magenau's memoirs, which he wrote in old age, give some idea of how a student gravitated to other like-minded friends, the function of the *Bund,* and the intense devotion to the *Bund* which continued into later life.

"At the beginning of my period in Tübingen I had made very few friends. Among these, I name you, noble Neuffer! Death will not destroy our *Bund.* Neuffer sacrificed to the Muse on the same altar as I; our studies were the same, our attitudes even more so. We loved each other as brothers, and I never had any idea that we would separate. Later on I got to know Hölderlin, and the bond of friendship wound about us as tightly as it did around Pylades and Orestes. We three lived together peacefully and quietly. Not a day went by that we did not talk, not an evening that we did not see each other. On the same path we struggled toward the same goal — the blessing of the Muse. My best songs are from this time. We criticized each other, and no one refused to strike out whole pages even on the advice and at the command of the others. Oh, that I might conjure up those blessed days once more! But even their memory elevates my soul to joy. Tübingen was not receptive to poetry's song. Our art was not infrequently the object of mockery, and only a noble dedication endured through the wasp-swarms of foolishness."[32]

Here we catch a glimpse of the boys in their *Bund* and get some idea as to *why* they are there. Few other friends; the yearning for brotherhood; the intense desire to become poets; the playing at being martyrs — these elements convinced each of them individually that in ostracism was nobility.

Hölderlin was the most passionate of the three.

"How Neuffer and I battled against Hölderlin's moods! He studied the material for a poem thoroughly before putting pen to paper. His imagination is

not ashamed to need the encouragement of a noble spirit" (139.50f.); "noble man! It [your letter] has given me new life" (144.1f.); "As long as I was before you, my heart was almost too small; and when I was away, I could not keep it from breaking [*es zusammenhalten*]. Before you I am like a plant that has just been put into the earth. It must be covered at noon" (144.6ff.); ". . . I cannot bring myself to stay away out of fear of reproach from a man whose singular spirit I feel so deeply and whose strength would have perhaps long ago robbed me of my courage if knowing you were not just as much pleasure as pain" (159.7ff.); ". . . I am at times at war with your genius in order to preserve my freedom . . . ." (159.17f.); "I withdrew from your presence and reserved approaching you again until I could justifiably claim the attention of which you deem me worthy and have, therefore, cheated myself out of the beneficial influence of your teaching which I could do without less than others, because my courage and convictions are only too easily confused and weakened by unfavorable influences of normal life" (194.9ff.).

32   VII, 1, pp. 394f.

not lacking in fire, but is merely somewhat wild. He trembles whenever a thought excites him. He already had a good knowledge of Greek and philosophy. Whoever saw him loved him, and whoever got to know him remained his friend. Unhappy love, *amor capriccio*, sometimes embittered him at Tübingen. Yet he was not deaf to the warnings and reproaches of his friends. A small party with Rhinewine was immediately soothing to his spirit, and he loved these gatherings more than anything else."[33]

These passages reveal a quite different Hölderlin from the traditional image of the stormy poet who wrote on sheer inspirations from on high. He studied and worked out his ideas before he began to compose. This is one of the basic aspects of his creative process in which he was akin to Schiller and so different from Goethe. His poetry was a conscious art, an intellectual endeavor, and had little to do with sudden inspiration. His composition was an act of the will and cost him intense effort and concentration. Hence the many versions of individual poems which he tried and discarded. Hence the laborious process by which he first tried to write *Hyperion* in prose and then recast it in verse, while he was in Jena. Hence the complicated sentence structure of his essays for the journal *Iduna,* which he wrote while in Homburg, as well as the elaborate syntax of the late poems. The psychological paradox of his poetry is simply this: How is it that works so painstakingly written, so carefully planned, so cerebral in conception, glow with that intense fire that we associate with the impassioned poet driven by a creative fire and visited periodically by divine inspiration? The answer lies, most of all, in the intense stress under which he lived all the time and in the resulting psychic aberrations which affected even his conceptual thought patterns very early.

"We sang "Lied an die Freude" all the way through. We had saved Schiller's "Lied an die Freude" until we had a bowl of punch. I went to fetch it. Neuffer had gone to sleep. Hölderlin stood in a corner smoking. The bowl sat steaming on the table and the song was about to begin. But Hölderlin wanted us to cleanse ourselves of our sins at a Castalian Spring. Near the garden ran the so-called 'Philosopher's Spring,' and that was Hölderlin's Castalian Spring. We went through the garden and washed our faces and hands. Neuffer walked solemnly. 'No impure person must sing Schiller's song,' said Hölderlin. And then we sang. At the verse, 'A glass to the good spirit,' clear, glowing tears appeared in Hölderlin's eyes; all aglow, he held the glass toward the open window and bellowed, 'This glass to the good spirit,' into the open air, so that the whole Neckar valley resounded. How happy we were! Oh, academic friendship, where is the old man who does not grow stronger each time he thinks back on your joys!"[34]

[33] VII, 1, p. 396.
[34] VII, 1, p. 396f.

This is the world in which Hölderlin lived as he wrote less and less to his mother. He moved among his "brothers" in the *Bund*. The world beyond the walls of the school had little claim on him now.

The studies which he loved were those which belonged to the interests and activities of the *Bund*. He had found his element. When he wrote his mother that he did not even care whether she let him spend the money necessary to earn his degree, he was referring again to the idea that his studies "reward themselves through themselves." He had now discovered Schiller.

Not only in the sense that he now began to imitate Schiller's verse, but also in the sense that Schiller was the "Führer" of the *Bund*. Schiller, who would later prove such a disappointment when he tried to help Hölderlin, now became his model for everything. He provided the formula through which Hölderlin expressed his changed attitude toward his studies. It was natural that he should be attracted to Schiller, for the man was everything Hölderlin one day hoped to be. Schiller too had felt the oppression of school life under Karl Eugen. But he had been strong enough to break all ties and flee the Duchy. He had not been deterred from pursuing his ideals. He had asserted himself and made his name despite great hardship. He had written the play portraying Karl Moor's revolt against the society that had cheated him and then had fled himself. Determination, dedication to his dreams – all these made a profound impression on the young man who had recently been laid low in his own attempt to escape by his own mother!

Hölderlin saw himself now as the exceptional student. He studied, not because he wanted degrees or titles, but because, through studies, he served his ideals and prepared himself for another life.

His studies "reward themselves through themselves." These very words were Schiller's. He had found them in Schiller's inaugural lecture at Jena in 1788, which had been published in Wieland's *Deutsches Museum* in 1789. The themes Schiller struck in an attempt to convince his students that the truly exceptional students developed a love of study independent of any hope of worldly reward so closely parallelled Hölderlin's own thinking that it is worth quoting at some length. Schiller spoke of two types of students: the one who studied in order to meet a professional requirement – the *Brodgelehrter* – and the "philosophical mind," who found his studies rewarding in their own right.

"The plan of study which the *Brodgelehrter* sets for himself and that which the philosophical mind draws up are quite different. The former, who, with all his industry, is concerned only with fulfilling certain requirements in order to qualify himself to hold a certain post and enjoy its material advantages, and who only sets his mental powers in motion in order to improve his material situation and satisfy a narrow-minded mania for recognition, will, when he begins his studies, have no more important task than the careful isolation of the disciplines which he calls 'practical studies' *(Brodstudien)* from all the others which give spiritual satisfaction. Any time that he devotes to the latter he will look upon as wasted in terms of his future profession, and he will never forgive himself such larceny. He regulates all his industry according to the demands that the future masters of his destiny will make upon him and will believe that he has done the job when he has qualified himself to the point that he does not have to fear those requirements."[35] The *Brodgelehrter* is thus, by nature and self-discipline, narrow-minded. ". . . no more implacable enemy, no more subversive colleague, no more zealous intolerant than the *Brodgelehrter*. The less his knowledge *rewards itself through itself,* the more payment he demands from others; he has only one criterion for both manual and intellectual labor: sweat [*Mühe*]."[36]

Schiller saw only disappointment ahead for the young man who followed such a course of study, particularly if he happened to be talented and had a potential for great accomplishments. Hölderlin must have thought that Schiller was speaking directly to him when he said: "Even more lamentable is the young man of genius whose development, naturally beautiful, is side-tracked onto this sad course by harmful teachers and bad examples, who allows himself to be convinced that he should prepare himself for his profession with such painstaking pedantry. Soon his professional knowledge will disgust him as patchwork; desires will awaken within him that his knowledge is unable to quench, and his genius will rebel against its task."[37] "He feels ripped out of the cohesiveness of things because he has failed to relate his activities to the great whole of the world."[38] ". . . the theologian [for example] loses all respect for his own kind as soon as his faith in the infallibility of his house of knowledge is shaken."[39]

All this awaited him if he continued to allow his mother to dictate his decisions, if he worried about degrees and titles, and if he allowed himself to be limited to studies and interests which were of service only to the preacher but not to the intellectual in general or the poet. Against the *Brodgelehrter* Schiller held up the "philosophical mind," and his description must have struck the poetic chords of Hölderlin's heart. "His efforts," wrote Schiller, "are directed toward the completion of his knowledge, his noble impatience cannot rest until all his concepts have been ordered into an harmonious whole, until he stands at the midpoint, surveys its expanse with a satisfied eye."[40] At the same time, the "philosophic mind" was a character of great strength and determination. He stood apart from the common herd. Most important of all, the single-minded dedication of the philosopher to his studies justified a lonely, isolated existence.

---

35 Schillers Werke, edited by Alfred Richter (6 vols.; Berlin: Verlag von R. Trenke, n.d.), V, p. 4.
36 *Ibid.,* pp. 4f.
37 *Ibid.,* p. 5.
38 *Ibid.*
39 *Ibid.*
40 *Ibid.,* p. 6.

". . . and however far the objects of his endeavor separate his from his brothers, he is akin to them and *close* to them by virtue of the harmonizing intellect; he encounters them where all bright minds meet."[41]

This is the self-appraisal that Hölderlin projected in his letters at that time. The idea of self-rewarding study, the need to pursue his studies throughout his life, the notion that, through a life devoted to intellectual pursuits, he would be able to win the companionship he needed so badly and extend the fellowship of the *Bund* indefinitely — these were the attitudes and longings which would exert a profound influence for years to come.

It is difficult to say exactly when his reading and preference for books over social life began to assume such extensive and sinister proportions. When he tried to justify his recent rupture of his engagement in April, he had written his mother "I am to console myself with my books."[42] In June he had written of the "joys of study" and had emphasized that the three friends were not studying because they had to.[43] Escape still played a role, but the idea that they enjoyed studying might indicate that he had already found Schiller's lecture. By August he was undoubtedly appropriating Schiller's thought, for it was then that the "rewards itself through itself" formula appeared.[44] From that point on the theme was emphasized more and more — at exactly the time when his letters were directed exclusively to his sister! For it was easier to play the learned man in letters to her than it would have been, had he been writing his mother directly.

During the last week of November 1790 he responded to the news from home that his half-brother Karl was having difficulty in his studies. "I am sorry for Karl," he wrote, "that he has found the scribe's post to be such a bitter weed. Tell him I have found a plant which makes one forget the bitter one. And that is — the occupation of the thinking mind."[45] He went on to suggest that they should exchange essays, so that Karl would get a chance to practice. The topic he suggested was: "How does one attain true satisfaction? " In the next letter home, written sometime near the beginning of December, he mentioned an essay which he had sent or was perhaps enclosing with the letter. But instead of writing simply so that his brother might actually profit from the exchange, he seems to have used the opportunity to parade his erudition before the family. "You will not find much that is elevating in the beginning of my essay. I was careful, now and again, to choose expressions which are encountered only in the so-called scholarly language, or at least very seldom anywhere else, in order to acquaint Karl with them."[46]

41   *Ibid.,* p. 7.
42   32.32ff.
43   33.13.
44   34 a.22f.
45   37.21ff.
46   38.12ff.

Near the end of 1790 he wrote home more frequently, although almost always to his sister. This increased incidence of letters home stood in marked contrast to the earlier months of 1790, when he had written very seldom. Now he used his letters to impress his family with his love of knowledge and with his scholarly accomplishments. The sudden expansiveness, which actually takes the form of letters that are shorter but contain more information than before, appeared, significantly, when he had hit upon the self-conception that would eventually allow him to escape from the mother-dominated world of family and theology.

He wrote in the middle of December 1790: "Everything is quite peaceful and quiet here. Or rather it is so only for me. One can change very quickly. If I had made it my nature earlier to live only for myself, I would have been able to avoid many annoyances."[47]

By February 1791, after he had defended himself for ignoring his mother's letters, he showed off his learning even to her. He devoted a good deal of space to a demonstration of how he had proven in a sermon that Spinoza's pantheism must of necessity lead to a belief in Christ and His divinity.[48]

These characteristics are completely new. Before he had discovered the joys of the *Bund* and the rewards of knowledge his letters home had never exuded such confidence. Never before had he waxed eloquent about the virtues of his classmates as he now did about Neuffer, who did his duty "manfully." Nor had he ever before given any sign that he was really very enthusiastic about his studies even though he had always received good to superior marks.

When he was twenty-two he abandoned the sorrowful, tortured, misunderstood tone of earlier years. He may have believed that it was for good, that he was now on the path to health. He would no longer be "sullen, morose, sick." Now he would be the "philosophic spirit" of whom Schiller had written.

But, at bottom, it was all the same. The *Bund* was not really a satisfactory substitute for normal relationships with boys his own age. It was a defense against loneliness. His assertions that he had now learned to live for himself alone occur for the first time during the period in which the *Bund* was flourishing. Magenau said later that the *Bund* attracted three boys who were enthusiastic about poetry, who had few other friends, and who thought they were being laughed at because of their dedication to poetry. This is the main point, as we shall see, in the letters to Neuffer: the search for a Klopstockian friend who would confirm him as a great poet — and to whom he would have to discharge no greater responsibility than correcting the friend's poems.

Normal men outgrew the adolescent attachments of their *Bund*. Neuffer and Magenau outgrew it, even if they later looked back upon it nostalgically. Only

<hr>

47   39.5ff.
48   41.14ff.

Hölderlin was unable to make the transition to adulthood. Only Hölderlin wrote his old schoolmates again and again that he still remained true to the spirit of their *Bund* and urged them to do likewise.

It was not Hölderlin's exaggerated enthusiasm for the *Bund* or the depth of his affection for his friends that set him apart, but rather the way in which he continually associated the *Bund* with isolation. By the same token, there was something about his love of his studies that was not quite right. For those studies led nowhere; they led only away from theology and the ministry. His dreams had now become hopelessly confused with reality. The apparent realization of his dreams, which were, at bottom, dictated by his need for more respect and a more elevated stature than most and by his need to attain those things without giving anything in return, convinced him that he was right, that the world of Klopstock and Schiller was not merely an appealing dream which he would eventually have to discard, but could really be attained and might provide a workable alternative to normal life – if he but had the will. Until then, for all his enthusiasm, he seems to have realized more or less clearly that these were only dreams and that he would have to face adult life and compromise with real life when the time came. Frequently, when he wrote of his dreams to his friends, he made note of his own childishness for still believing in such things.

By the beginning of 1791 all this had changed. He wrote his sister in March: "I am less and less concerned about myself when I think about my future; for each day I become more and more convinced that no one else can become so arrogant when things go well and, on the other hand, can become such a good person with such a limited amount of good fortune as do I. And so my greatest wish is to be able to live in peace and write books, without going hungry while doing it.

"Do not laugh at me, little sister! Joseph's brothers – and I say this without comparing you to them in the slightest – Joseph's brothers called him a dreamer – and yet the lad became a real man! And so I am little concerned about myself as regards eventual employment – and eventual marriage and family, as long as you are happy."[49]

It must have been clear to his family by February where this sudden interest in studies was leading. He had gained confidence in the *Bund* – so much so that, when his mother wrote him in June that Luise Nast was now engaged to someone else, he no longer concealed his true attitudes toward his future. He wrote: "The news which you write me *relieves* me very much – for reasons you can probably guess. Old love does not die! The good child was always thinking of me, as I had several occasions to learn – and if my twenty-one year old wisdom had not guided me, I might have suffered relapses. Of course, I admit that the news made my poor heart pound for a few minutes. But that's beside

---

49   43.18ff.

the point! I must take this opportunity to tell you that I have been determined for more than a year never to marry. You may believe me in any case when I say that I am serious. My unique character, my moods, my penchant for projects, and (to be quite honest) my ambition — all traits which cannot safely be rooted out — do not allow me to hope that I will ever be happy in a quiet marriage, in a peaceful parsonage."[50]

He had at last found the arguments which he would use against his mother for years to come. "I cannot do what you ask of me; I am what I am and cannot change." This was, however, not merely an excuse for not serving a church. It was the whole spectrum of normal life that he wanted to avoid and that, as he now believed, he could avoid. The church was only one aspect of that withdrawal reaction which permeated his behavior from this point on. A battle raged within him between the forces pulling toward maturation and the lures which a continuation of adolescence and the sheltered student's life held out for him. In Schiller he thought that he had found a way to have the best of both worlds: the respect and companionship he needed so desperately and the protection of a lonely and secluded life. What he found in words in Schiller's first lecture in Jena, he found in pseudo-fact in the *Bund*.

But, in reality, all this was self-deception. The solution that he had discovered was frail and delicate; it presupposed that nothing would change, that the *Bund* would always exist, and that the other two young men would be as willing as Hölderlin to stunt their own growth in order to preserve the *Bund*. It was a beautiful dream. The poems of that period will show just how enticing it all was.

But it could not last.

Neuffer and Magenau were two years older than Hölderlin. In September 1791 they left the *Stift* forever. Hölderlin could look forward to two more years of loneliness and dejection, during which he would flee ever more resolutely into the verbal solutions of Schiller.

That too would have to end. In the autumn of 1793 he would emerge from the *Stift* himself and have to face real people and real-life situations. By then the process of self-aggrandizement and self-deprecation, of yearning for other's support and shunning close contact with them, would have become irreversible.

50   45.7ff.

9

THE TÜBINGEN HYMNS

The hymns which Hölderlin wrote from 1790 to 1793 are the earliest of his poems which have been of continued interest to the literary historian. In the nineteenth century they were the best known of all his works. It was because of the disproportionate attention paid to the poems from Hölderlin's "Schiller Period," roughly from 1790 to 1797, that he was, for a long time, thought to be nothing more than Schiller's most talented imitator. Throughout those seven years he composed almost exclusively in the metrical patterns that he had learned from Schiller's idealistic poems such as "An die Freude," "Die Künstler," and "Die Götter Griechenlands." Moreover, he demonstrated in his choice of themes, and particularly in his predilection for abstract substantives common to the philosophical publications of that period, tendencies that the nineteenth century took for unmistakable evidence of his spiritual subservience to Schiller.

We now recognize that his poems from 1790 to 1797, and certainly those written while he was still in Tübingen, were not his best; for he had not yet succeeded in breaking Schiller's spell and liberating his own poetry from the category of philosophically oriented verse based on abstract concepts and flamboyant rhetoric. Nevertheless, we have not yet been able to break the historically ingrained habit of paying more attention to the Tübingen Hymns than to the earlier poems, even though they show not much more originality than the poems written from 1787 to 1789. It seems that we have concluded that the Tübingen Hymns are somehow more important than anything that he had written before 1790 simply because his Schillerian poetry more readily lends itself to discussion within the framework of "literary history." All of Hölderlin's biographers have treated his life and poetry before 1790 as something of a prelude — as a necessary, but largely irrelevant, introduction to the real life of the poet. Because we have been conditioned to transpose the categories and values in which the authors of intellectual history have taught us to think onto all subjects dealing with things past (even onto the private life of individuals), we have underestimated the biographical importance of everything prior to 1790, as if we believed that Hölderlin's life really began only when he began imitating Schiller, thus making it possible for us to assign him and his works to a prearranged slot in an historical scheme.

So it seems to us from our historical vantage point. We have already seen, however, that it is a mistake to pass over the poems of the Denkendorf and Maulbronn years with a few casual remarks about how derivative they are. Closer analysis of the way in which he developed the unoriginal themes that he had appropriated from Klopstock and Schubart has revealed characteristic thought-forms which reappear in poems of a much later date, when he was, from the literary historian's point-of-view, far ahead of his time. Similarly, the fact that the Tübingen Hymns meet our expectations of what we should find in works written in 1790 is no guarantee that they are more important than any others to an understanding of the poet's growth. Even more important, the similarity or dissimilarity of any work to the intellectual historian's model is irrelevant to biography.

When we reach 1790 and realize that Hölderlin has abruptly abandoned Klopstock's antique meters in favor of the six to eight line stanzas of rhymed trochee and that he owed his choice of metrics, along with his themes and diction, to Schiller — then we are tempted to fill many pages with an erudite narrative about how those changes in Hölderlin's poetry are microcosmic reflections of transitions taking place in the macrocosm of German intellectual history. Nothing would be easier to write than such a narrative. We could say, for instance, that Klopstock's sentamentalism and the rantings of the *Sturm und Drang* hero, which he had helped inspire, gave away to the quiet, reflective search for absolute values, to which such former *Stürmer und Dränger* as Schiller and Goethe devoted themselves when they realized that the havoc they had wreaked in their youthful zeal to assert their freedom from Enlightenment orthodoxy made it necessary for them to find new articles of faith in keeping with their newly won freedoms. Having once said that, we could go on to suggest vague spiritual connections between Kant's Critical Philosophy, Schiller's carefully Kantian essays and historical writings, and Goethe's studies in the natural sciences. Within such a framework we could confidently assert that the Tübingen Hymns were Hölderlin's attempt to lend a hand in the historical process. We could then assure — (read: "decive") — ourselves that we have understood the poems because we had succeeded in placing them — however arbitrarily — within the context of "history" and could view them as part of a great historical tidal wave carrying "the German spirit" to new cultural heights.

Such constructions are very satisfying to many people because everything seems to be accounted for. There are no loose ends. They are gratifying because they appeal to the basic human intellectual impulse to organize the confusing, often contradictory, manifold of experience into some sort of whole, some unity.

There are two objections that we shall raise against such constructions here. First, as a general criticism, they are absolutely wrong; secondly, as a specific criticism, they are not biography and have no place in a biographical study.

The whole historical scheme is absurd. It is the troublesome and (as we have had ample opportunity to learn by experience in the twentieth century) often tragic legacy of the Hegel-inspired historicism that we insist upon seeing history as a single line of development from one stage through a second (higher) and on to a third (still higher). Such oversimplified "history" is a convenience to the apostle of mass education and a God-send to the charlatan. But the more one reads of the writings dating from the historical period in question, the more one realizes that all the much-debated "mainstreams" and "movements" are largely the arbitrary constructions of historians living afterwards. They are confirmed as truth when enough schoolboys have been forced to read a carefully selected list of works from the "period." Only because the "Classics" have been so carefully chosen does it appear that there has always been only one strand of development, which has made the present the inevitable, and therefore legitimate, child of the past, and which makes the past so simple to master. "Die Bewältigung der Vergangenheit" should read "die Verfälschung der Vergangenheit," because such constructions so often violate objectively verifiable fact. There is never a single-strand historical development making the course of thought and events ineluctable; at any given time there is no clearly defined profile of intellectual life within a culture. Only selection from the wealth of publications from the late eighteenth century makes it appear that the thought of Kant, Goethe, and Schiller (which is not really one coherent line of thought anyway) was dominant. To assert that, through adopting Schiller's themes, vocabulary, and meters, Hölderlin somehow stepped out of some intellectual backwater province and into the thriving and bustling marketplace of German intellectual and literary history comes very close to saying just the opposite of the truth. Neither Goethe nor Schiller were widely read in 1790. Goethe's popularity was almost non-existent, while Schiller's journals were not great financial successes throughout the 1790s. While Goethe's critical writings direct our attention to a number of works undeservedly forgotten, his taste in literature varied markedly from that of future literary historians, which would indicate that the Zeitgeist was to Goethe indeed "a book with seven seals." The popular poets at that time were such men as Klopstock, Schubart, Matthias Claudius, and Voß — men who, in the main, wrote the type of poetry that Hölderlin had been imitating, but was now giving up. While it is true that Schiller was more popular in his Swabian homeland than in other parts of Germany and was being read more enthusiastically by the Stiftler than by the general reading public, Hölderlin could not have known that he, in taking Schiller as a model, was getting into the "mainstream" that future historians would invent.

This brings us to our second, and more pertinent, objection. Over and above the fact that many historical explanations rest on gross distortions of verifiable fact, they have nothing to do with biography. Even if Hölderlin had known that Schiller would someday be considered one of the giants of German writers and that Kantian philosophy would prove basic to much subsequent western thought, that knowledge would not have been enough to make him accept that vision of Schiller and Kant. If one suggests seriously that Hölderlin adopted Schiller as a model and began studying Kant because he realized that the Zeitgeist demanded it as the price of immortality, then one must be ready to show that Hölderlin was so shrewd, so calculating, so indifferent to the truth of his poetry, and so lacking in personal integrity, that he was willing to prostitute his talents by latching onto Schiller's coattails in order to win for himself a place in the history books. Such opportunism would suggest a hard-headed realism that manifested itself in Hölderlin's behavior only once in his entire life. Of course, one can assert that he followed the dictates of the *Zeitgeist* unconsciously. But that assertion rests on the already mentioned fallacy of assuming that the "mainstream" of a given time is discernible at that time. Naturally Hölderlin was affected by his culture; it is obvious that he would neither have written nor lived as he did, had he been born in China during Confucius' lifetime, because the thought-forms that he found in Kant, Schiller, Herder, and others would not have been available to him. But, as we pointed out before, one's intellectual environment is never a single, coherent bundle of ideas which force themselves on the individual, but rather a heterogeneous mass of often very contradictory ways of thinking. One's intellectual environment only makes certain ideas, certain modes of expression, certain ways of organizing and synthesizing one's experience of reality, available. The individual, and above all the artist, who possesses the ability to create completely new alternatives, chooses from what is available. Why he chooses one set of ideas or one system and rejects others; why, for example, Hölderlin chose Klopstock and Schiller and rejected Wieland, cannot be explained by appealing to intellectual history. He chose this over that partly because of his training — but only in part, because men can reject cultural influences, just as Schiller and Goethe rejected the medical and legal professions. Basic to the eclectic process of assimilating suggestions coming from without is the personality of the individual with its special set of spiritual needs. He accepts or rejects because one set of ideas seems true and is comforting; others either do not fulfil his needs or aggravate his wounds. And if he changes his mind, as Hölderlin did in 1790, it is because his needs changed — not because history moved on.

We shall, therefore, examine the Tübingen Hymns from three points of view: First, we shall compare the changes in his poetry which took place in 1790 to changes in his attitudes and behavior, as we have determined them in the last chapter; secondly, we shall show the development of the poetic vision, which will involve a general comparison of the poetry before and after 1790; finally, we shall attempt to demonstrate why and how he assimilated the forms he appropriated from others and synthesized them into a mythology that corresponded to his personal needs and experiences.

We have already seen how his attitudes toward his family, his fiancée and his friends changed following his visit to Nürtingen in late 1789 and how these changes in attitude brought about alterations in his behavior. His withdrawal into his studies, his reaffirmation of "Friendship" through his enthusiastic participation in the *Bund* with Neuffer and Magenau, and his conviction that he could never hope for a normal life were all part of a new phase of self-isolation. On the surface, he reacted to disappointment in 1790 similar to the way in which he had reacted in 1787. But there were also significant differences. In 1787 he had developed the compensatory image of himself as a stormy, passionate lover and, while playing that role, had won the hand of Luise Nast; now he rejected love for a specific "sweetheart," broke his engagement, and declared that he would never marry. Thus, while he had developed two compensatory self-images in 1787 and had alternately thought of himself as a lover and then as a friend, in 1790 he dropped the role of the lover and devoted himself almost exclusively to the man-to-man companionship of the *Bund*. Friendship, as we shall see, became the dominant human relation in his thinking. This shift of emphasis to male relationships is also mirrored in the fact that, while in 1787 he had communicated with his best friend through letters and saw his imagined love quite often, in 1790 just the reverse was true. Elise Lebret, his sweetheart of the Tübingen years, seems to have played a very minor role in his thinking; Neuffer and Magenau, and, to a lesser extent, Hegel and Schelling, occupied his mind entirely.

The character of this new period of isolation can then be summed up in a few words. It was similar to what had gone on in 1787 in so far as it was a time of searching for a new self-image and a new definition of his relationship to the world following a severe blow to his self-respect. Moreover, he again carefully limited his social contacts to those people who posed no threat to him and who made only those demands on him that could be met through the production of poems. The fact that a new period of isolation and a new search for personal identity was necessary implies that the heroic self-image that we encountered in his poems, which, through a process of self-delusion, was made possible by an artificial and extreme limitation of his social contacts, had proved untenable as a result of his trying to live out the role in life. When he discovered that he did not have the self-confidence necessary to oppose the world and defy Mother and Church, he was utterly destroyed. He began talking about his new capacity of resignation and about his love of studies; and he emphasized that he wished to be left alone and spend his life in solitude writing books.

In the foregoing chapter we have shown how Schiller's "philosophic mind" was the self-image that he projected in his letters in order to justify his aloofness from others. That pose was not, however, merely propaganda. He seized the set of attitudes suggested by Schiller because it perfectly corresponded to his needs. As a philosopher he would not have to compromise with the corrupt world — but neither would he have to openly defy it. He had only to contemplate, devote himself to a search for meaning in life (while assiduously avoiding real life), and express the truths he discovered in books and poems.

Such was the advantage of presenting himself as the devoted student, the budding philosopher, rather than as the would-be social reformer. We should not forget, however, that his negative aspect to his behavior was only part of the subconscious motivation leading him to act as he did. For, while he, of course, exploited the image of the "philosophic mind" to excuse himself for his coldness toward others, he also demanded of himself that he live up to the image. He was compelled to reach a new synthesis of his experience, and that entailed becoming what he claimed to be.

This rigid sense of honor by which the excuses he used to escape invariably became traps themselves, is the characteristic that distinguishes Hölderlin from the ordinary misfit. Through his propaganda he succeeded in convincing himself more firmly than he managed to convince anyone else. That morbid bent toward endless self-analysis, which we have encountered earlier, made it impossible for him to try consciously to hoodwink others for his own comfort, as a more superficial spirit would have done. When his sense of personal impotence made his heroic image of self no longer tenable and he reached for the new costume of the academician, who would not have to rebel openly to maintain his self-respect, his need to harmonize his feelings with reality forced him to delude himself and live himself completely into the new role. Thus he set for himself the task of working out anew his relationship to reality. It is significant that he now conceived such a task as a specifically intellectual problem, whereas earlier he had seen it as the problem of his ambivalent social attitudes. Before then he had wanted to change his real self; now he was compelled to change his appreciation of both himself and the whole of reality in order to establish the illusion of harmony that he needed so badly. His dilemma was, of course, at bottom, the type of unacademic problem that most people resolve unconsciously by changing their behavior to fit their situation. It is the type of problem that does not lend itself to theoretical solutions. Only during times of stress do most men consciously face questions concerning their own worth and their place in the world. With Hölderlin, however, stress and tension were such constant states of mind that the problem of alienation attained an urgency unknown to most of us. Thus he was susceptible to philosophic solutions and identified personally — almost frenziedly — with the general theories that he found in the philosophy of his time. Philosophy was then, for him, a matter of spiritual life and death. When he turned to philosophical speculation in search of a new definition of life, he did so with a sense of desperation. In the clichés that Kantian thought had already become under the hands of Reinhold, Maimon, and — not least of all — Schiller, he would search for years for clues which might help him learn to cope with a purely personal dilemma.[1] Hence the intense

---

1 On New Year's Day, 1799, Hölderlin wrote Karl about the influence of the new philosophy on the Germans. He identified the limitation of the German national character as "obtuse domesticity" [bornirte Häuslichkeit] (172.52) and went on to describe German provinciality in a way which reminds us of his antipathy to normal life in the way others conceived it. Kant, however, was seen as "the Moses of our nation who is leading them out

emotion with which Hölderlin speaks of sheer abstractions in the Hymns. Hence, also, his inability to isolate a theoretical problem and treat it disinterestedly and thus become anything more than a gifted *student* of philosophy. He did not, after all, ever succeed in presenting his philosophy in discursive prose; when he tried to do so, he could only produce fragments. Conceptual reasoning was difficult for him because the concept, which to the philosopher is but a means of representing elements in a problem to be solved, attained for Hölderlin a reality in its own right. They became poetic symbols, and the meaning could not be reproduced in other words because the words themselves had become bearers of the poet's intense emotion. It was emotion — not thought — that determined his treatment of abstractions and the conclusions he drew.

In 1790 he redefined for himself his isolation with the only tools at his command — through the medium of poetry. The changes in his attitudes toward himself and others were so profound that he had to reevaluate and restructure his entire perception of the world. The result was the Tübingen Hymns.

He settled on the Hymn form by late 1790. But elements of his changing attitudes were already visible in the poems written in the early months of that year, roughly at the time at which he was breaking his engagement, establishing the *Bund* with Magenau and Neuffer, and writing of his love of studies to his family. It was in about April that he wrote his first poems in Schillerian metrics: "Lied der Freundschaft" and "Lied der Liebe." They, together with "An die Stille," which he wrote in the summer, show what changes were entailed in his metamorphosis from the heroic rebel to the more restrained philosopher in search of beauty behind everyday life with its suffering. The contrast between the old and the new is particularly striking in these transitional poems because he was treating themes that he had dealt with before.

On first reading, "Lied der Freundschaft" seems no more than a recapitulation in Schillerian poetics of the Friendship theme under the influence of "An die Freude." Just as in 1788, in the poem "Am Tage der Freundschaftsfeier," the poet sings his song in a banquet of friends who, through their relationship to each other, are drawn into a mystic union with heroes of the past.

> Wie der Held am Siegesmahle
> Ruhen wir um die Pokale
> Wo der edle Wein erglüht,
> Feurig Arm in Arm geschlungen
> Trunken von Begeisterungen
> Singen wir der Freundschaft Lied.

---

of their Egyptian stupor into the free, lonely desert of his speculation . . . (172.93f.). Here we encounter that idea that appears in so much of the poetry of those years: that the German people would soon, he hoped, become receptive to his poetry and prophecy.

Schwebt herab aus külen Lüften
Schwebet aus den Schlummergrüften
Helden der Vergangenheit!
Kommt in unsern Krais hernieder
Staunt und sprecht: da ist sie wieder
Unsre deutsche Herzlichkeit![2]

The poet's hostility to the external world was still basic to his conceptions of Friendship. He restates his conviction that Friendship, through giving strength to the warrior, makes it possible for him to endure life within the real world.

Stärke, wenn Verläumder schreien
Warheit, wenn Despoten dräuen,
Männermuth im Misgeschik
Duldung, wenn die Schwachen sinken
Liebe, Duldung, Wärme trinken
Freunde von des Freundes Blik.[3]

But, on closer examination, significant, if slight, variations appear. In "Am Tage der Freundschaftsfeier" the mood had been one of extreme melancholy. The strength that the poet gathered during the hours spent with his friends in the banquet hall had been strangely impotent. At best, companionship with his chosen friends was a refuge from reality. Those stolen moments were a poor substitute for a more fulfilling life, for the celebration was permeated with the knowledge that real life with all its cruelties and strife was always threatening to break in. Indeed, the corrupt smell of real life was brought into the banquet hall by the poet—warrior himself, who dwelt on the horrors he had seen, and who could not, even for a little while, rid himself of the awful dread,

Daß er vieleicht noch lange
Verweilen müsse unter diesem Geschlechte.

"Am Tage der Freundschaftsfeier" is illustrative of the deeply negative attitude toward life in general that characterized his feelings prior to 1790. It ran as an undercurrent throughout his heroic poetry in 1789; and it was just this negativism that had made it necessary for him to intensify that self-image and to try to live out his role in life.

In "Lied der Freundschaft" the same underlying hostility is still very much in evidence. But something is different. Most obviously, there is a new tone of confidence, which the Schillerian meters so perfectly express, but which also appears in the conceptual treatment of the Friendship theme. The last few stanzas are remarkable in contrast to "Am Tage der Freundschaftsfeier."

[2] I, 1, p. 107 (lines 1—12).
[3] I, 1, p. 108 (lines 37—42).

Rufet aus der trauten Halle
Auch die Auserwälten alle
In die Ferne das Geschik,
Bleibt, auf freundenlosen Pfaden
Hinzugeh'n mit Schmerz beladen
Tränend Einer nur zurük.

Wankt er nun in Winterstürmen
Wankt er, wo sich Wolken türmen
Ohne Leiter, ohne Stab;
Lauscht er abgeblaicht und düster
Bangem Mitternachtsgeflüster
Ahndungsvoll am frischen Grab;

O da kehren all die Stunden
Lächelnd, wie sie hingeschwunden
Unter Schwüren, wahr und warm,
Still und sanft, wie Blumen sinken
Ruht er, bis die Väter winken
Dir, Erinnerung! im Arm.

Rauscht ihm dann des Todes Flügel,
Schläft er ruhig unter'm Hügel
Wo sein Bund den Kranz ihm flicht
In den Lokken seiner Brüder
Säuselt noch sein Geist hernieder,
Lispelt leis: vergeßt mich nicht![4]

His view of his own life was now beginning to change. The image of the warrior completely disappeared because *he* would no longer try to act in the world. In earlier poems the warrior had always ventured forth to do battle after he had regained his strength through communion with his friends. Now, however, all the others go out into life; *one* stays behind and remains forever faithful to the spirit of the *Bund*. He shares vicariously in the glories that his more active comrades win for themselves, but he does not seek to win the laurel wreath in direct competition. He had by now recognized that he could not endure the life of which he had dreamed before with its alternating times of conflict and recuperation and still live in a rarified atmosphere of complete joy and harmony. This was far removed from "Am Tage der Freundschaftsfeier," in which he had been the active member of the *Bund* while his companions shared in his glory only through associating with him and listening to his song. This was the first expression in his poetry of what we noticed in the last chapter: that, after his return to the *Stift* in January 1790, he had come to realize that he could maintain his stability only in an atmosphere of harmony; and that, in order to survive, he would have to severely limit his contacts with other people — and thus live, spiritually at least, in the *Bund* for the rest of his life.

How was he to accomplish such an unrealistic objective? How could he fulfill his need for continuous insulation from normal life when it was inevitable that his Church would, upon his graduation, assign him to a congregation and thus force him into the life of conflict and compromise that he could not endure? How could he console himself with the hope of spending his entire life in the *Bund?*

First of all, it might be objected that Hölderlin did not mean that at all and that the idea of staying behind referred to the fact that Neuffer and Magenau were two classes ahead of him and would be graduated in 1791. That fact was,

---

[4] I, 1, p. 109 (lines 55—78).

of course, in his mind. But that cannot have been all. He spoke unequivocally of staying in the *Bund* until he died. And there are too many references in his letters pointing to his intention of continuing his solitary existence throughout his life, too many passages in which he traced his new sense of well-being to the fact that he had learned to live "for myself" to allow us to conclude that the poem merely exaggerated the feeling of loneliness that he would experience when his friends deserted him. The other two poems from the early months of 1790 make it quite clear that the same attitude that we have seen in the letters was basic to his newly developing interpretation of life in general.

This is most striking in "An die Stille." Here also he treated a theme that had concerned him for some time. It might be said without exaggeration that the search for "Stille" (peace and solitude) was the basic theme of all his poetry. Once more he was treating a theme that he had already defined before he had arrived at Tübingen; so we can again distinguish the new tone of confidence in contrast to his earlier works. And it is his new definition of "Stille" that we discover the thought processes that led him to conclude that he might be able to perpetuate his isolation from life indefinitely. In an earlier poem he had written:

> O wie pflegtest du den armen Jungen,
> Teure, so mit Mutterzärtlichkeit,
> Wann er sich im Weltgewirre müdgerungen,
> In der lieben, wehmutsvollen Einsamkeit.[5]

And later in that same poem he had written:

> Drum, wenn Stürme einst den Mann umgeben,
> Nimmer ihn der Jugendsinn belebt,
> Schwarze Unglükswolken drohen ihn umschweben,
> Ihm die Sorge Furchen in die Stirne gräbt;
>
> O so reiße ihn aus dem Getümmel,
> Hülle ihn in deine Schatten ein,
> O! in deinen Schatten, Teure! wohnt der Himmel
> Ruhig wirds bei ihnen unter Stürmen sein.[6]

Before 1790 he had thought of "Stille" as simple physical aloneness, as the absence of other people. It was the opposite of life in the world and was, therefore, closely related to Friendship in that it meant refuge from conflict and strife. And, like Friendship, "Stille" depended on physical surroundings. Its prerequisite was actual physical removal from society. Hence his treatment of both themes in relation to the warrior in need of rest. He was again polarizing experience into mutually exclusive categories. He polarized his physical

---

5 I, 1, p. 43 (lines 45—48).
6 I, 1, pp. 44ff. (lines 77—84).

circumstances just as he polarized his acquaintances. The distinction of "Stille" rested in the absence of all strife. He was only happy when he enjoyed the complete isolation of "Stille" or the semi-isolation of Friendship.

But now, in the summer of 1790, he wrote:

> Dort im waldumkränzten Schattentale
> Schlürft' ich, schlummernd unter'm Rosenstrauch
> Trunkenheit aus deiner Götterschaale,
> Angeweht von deinem Liebeshauch.
> Sieh' es brent an deines Jünglings Wange
> Heiß und glühend noch Begeisterung,
> Voll ist mir das Herz vom Lobgesange,
> Und der Fittig heischet Adlerschwung.
>
> Stieg ich künen Sinns zum Hades nieder
> Wo kein Sterblicher dich noch ersah,
> Schwänge sich das mutige Gefieder
> Zum Orion auf, so wär'st du da;
> Wie ins weite Meer die Ströme gleiten
> Stürzen dir die Zeiten alle zu
> In dem Schoos der alten Ewigkeiten,
> In des Chaos Tiefen wohntest du.
>
> In der Wüste dürrem Schrekgefilde,
> Wo der Hungertod des Wallers harrt,
> In der Stürme Land, wo schwarz und wilde
> Das Gebirg' im kahlen Panzer starrt,
> In der Sommernacht, in Morgenlüften,
> In den Hainen weht dein Schwestergruß,
> Über schauerlichen Schlummergrüften
> Stärkt die Lieblinge dein Götterkuß.[7]

Clearly this is quite at odds with his earlier definition of "Stille." For now he no longer insists on physical aloneness or removal from the arena of life. No longer does life consist of alternating periods of strife and withdrawal, because now "Stille" is an attitude and can thus exist in the mind of the poet independent of external conditions. The mutually exclusive spheres of society and solitude, between which the warrior had passed back and forth in his earlier works, were now merged. Or so it would seem. It would appear that the forced polarization of life, which we have encountered so often, was no more and that, in a sense at least, the poet and the world had been reconciled.

---

[7] I, 1, p. 114 (lines 1—24).

This curious, sleight-of-hand reconciliation, which allowed the poet to speak in tones of supreme self-confidence while still conceiving normal life as a confusing and chaotic stage on which the human being goes about the business of suffering, is characteristic of the Tübingen Hymns. He would never be able to leap into life with both feet and participate whole-heartedly in the boisterous business of living; and because he was a genuine poet and thus expressed in his poems solutions to problems that he actually faced in life, he could not, even in his poems, embrace real life or depict it with as much enthusiasm as Wieland any more than he could accept the life that his mother had planned for him. Thus he could not now — and would never be able to — do away with the old polarization of life into distinct realms of frozen ideals over against the world of men in action. And so, when he found that he could not pass over periodically into the world of action, strike a few blows for idealism, and retreat unscathed into solitude, he conceived a strange sort of realization for his ideals: He proclaimed that he was bringing his ideals with him into the realm of action as an attitude and thus relieved himself of all obligation to act. How he was able to maintain such an attitude is revealed in the Hymns. "An die Stille" indicates what direction his thoughts were taking. He would carry his ideals with him into life; he would not strike out at what was evil in the world, but would bring goodness in the form of his Ideals — those articles of faith which had sustained him for so long — into life, and reveal to men no longer merely the meaninglessness of their way of life but the principles which make sense of the confusion of events.

In other words, the changes that Hölderlin underwent during 1790 were primarily changes of attitude. When seen on the plane of everyday life, from his letters of 1790 and 1791, those changes consisted primarily of increased devotion to his studies and the establishment of relationships with his family that were purposefully strained because he wanted to distance himself from his mother, hold himself aloof from her influence, and thus prepare her for the time at which he would set out on his own and pursue his "education" in his own way. To Frau Gok, who could follow the changes in her son only through his letters, the new tone of heightened aloofness must have been confusing. There were, of course, hopeful signs. He seemed, in a way, to have mellowed; he no longer confronted her with frantic ultimata to take him out of school or accept responsibilities for the consequences. He was studying and he had found friends in the *Stift*. And yet, there were also disturbing signs, which she could not understand. The way in which he wrote of his plans to pursue his education and write books as pursuits that were somehow irreconcilable with a settled life with a wife and children must have been incomprehensible to her. It would have been confusing to anyone who could not see that the letters represented only the outer shell of his thoughts and that in his letters he was trying to express realistically adjustments in his views that he was making on an unrealistic intellectual or poetic plane. When he spoke of "education" he did not mean practical training for professional life, such as his mother would have understood. That was only his *Brodstudium.* He meant rather a continuous period of isolation in which he might prepare himself for a great prophetic mission; and his long range hope was that, through performing that mission, he might write his way into a position of preeminence among men so that he would never be called upon to live a normal life and meet normal responsibilities of the everyday world. For only in a state of isolation could he take comfort in his Ideals. He had taken Schiller's assertion that the "philosophic mind" did not prepare himself only for his profession to mean that the true philosopher did not prepare himself for professional life at all.

His work "rewards itself." His self-rewarding work was the writing of the Hymns. It was in those poems that Hölderlin transformed his earlier poetic themes into "Ideals" and thus brought them out of the realm of escapist withdrawal, where they had first been experienced, into the world of men. The process of reevaluation, which went on throughout 1790, can be summed up in a few words: Hölderlin declared that the dreams of his youth, which he had hitherto sought to defend as private possessions against the mockery of the world, were actually principles of order that underlay all human life in so far as it is meaningful. This purely semantic postulate enabled him, in his imagination, to escape the obligation of the heroic rebel to attack the evil in life. He could now don the mantle of the philosophic spirit, who approached the problem positively by fostering within his fellow men an awareness of those principles that others *(Brodgelehrte)* did not perceive because of some tragic historical event. Now this new self-image in the poems, which corresponds so perfectly to the image he was now projecting in his letters, did not really approximate Schiller's "philosophic mind" at all. Schiller's construction was used by Hölderlin as a verbal designation. He now thought of himself as a teacher, it is true, but never in the sense of one who opens up new lines of thought to his pupils. He was, therefore, not a teacher, as Schiller would have understood the word, but a prophet, thrilled by the beauty of the better life that he alone had seen and that could not be revealed by conceptual argument, but only *felt* by him who opens his heart to the poet's song. As we shall see presently, he was adopting the image of "the artist," which Schiller considered to be of historical significance, but which Schiller now thought to be a philosophic anachronism.

"Lied der Liebe," written as early as April 1790, had many of the elements of the Hymns. Characteristic for his newly evolving self-image were the first few lines in which the new tone of confidence, which we noted in "Lied der Freundschaft," allowed him to play his new role of the prophet, opening up new perceptual dimensions to his companions.

Engelfreuden ahndend, wallen
Wir hinaus auf Gottes Flur,
Daß von Jubel wiederhallen
Höh'n und Tiefen der Natur.
Heute soll kein Auge trübe,
Sorge nicht hienieden seyn,
Jedes Wesen soll der Liebe
Frei und froh, wie wir, sich weih'n!

Singt den Jubel, Schwestern, Brüder,
Fest geschlungen, Hand in Hand!
Hand in Hand das Lied der Lieder,
Seelig an der Liebe Band!
Steigt hinauf am Rebenhügel,
Blikt hinab ins Schattenthal!
Überall der Liebe Flügel,
Hold und herrlich überall![8]

Here he had already moved to the "Lied"-form, which Schiller had used. He calls upon his brothers and sisters to come with him out into nature and perceive the spirit of love in all things. Once more it should be noted that his invitation is not to a philosophical discourse but to a religious nature-festival, complete with embracing, the touching of bodies, and the sharing of song. It is through the awakened senses that man is to perceive the power of love permeating the order of nature.

The *order* of nature. Instinctively Hölderlin sought harmony for the sake of self-preservation. Love is, most of all, an ordering principle.

Liebe lehrt das Lüftchen kosen
Mit den Blumen auf der Au,
Lokt zu jungen Frühlingsrosen
Aus der Wolke Morgenthau,
Liebe ziehet Well' um Welle
Freundlich murmelnd näher hin,
Leitet aus der Kluft die Quelle
Sanft hinab ins Wiesengrün.

Berge knüpft mit ehrner Kette
Liebe an das Firmament,
Donner ruft sie an die Stätte,
Wo der Sand die Pflanze brennt.

---

[8] I, 1, p. 112 (lines 1—16).

Um die hehre Sonne leitet
Sie die treuen Sterne her,
Folgsam ihrem Winke gleitet
Jeder Strom ins weite Meer.

Liebe wallt durch Ozeane,
Durch der dürren Wüste Sand
Blutet an der Schlachtenfahne,
Steigt hinab ins Todtenland!
Liebe trümmert Felsen nieder,
Zaubert Paradiese hin,
Schaffet Erd und Himmel wieder –
Göttlich, wie im Anbeginn.[9]

Now the place of the Ideal was fixed. It was to be, from then on, an ordering force, a principle of meaning which ran throughout the confusing manifold of life. Hölderlin started from harmony that he perceived in the natural world and sought to demonstrate that harmony was not only possible in human life but was, in fact, the natural state of *all* things. Throughout the Tübingen Hymns, the order of nature provides a constant source of faith and confidence. In 1791, for example, when he wrote "Hymne an die Göttin der Harmonie," he again had the Ideal, which had since become a goddess, initiating the natural order.

Thronend auf des alten Chaos Woogen,
Majestätisch lächelnd winktest du,
Und die wilden Elemente flogen
Liebend sich auf deine Winke zu.
Froh der seeligen Vermälungsstunde
Schlangen Wesen nun um Wesen sich,
In den Himmeln, auf dem Erdenrunde
Sahst du, Meisterin! im Bilde dich. –[10]

And the theme is developed for three more stanzas.

Hölderlin was, of course, no mere nature poet. He did not make his observations concerning natural harmony for their own sake. He used them as the starting point from which he sprang into human life and pointed to the striking contrast between the harmony of nature and the chaos of human existence. He extracted a principle from nature and measured man against it. But the words he used to designate his Ideals denoted specifically human qualities. "Love," "Freedom," "Immortality," "Beauty," "Friendship," "Boldness," are all human attributes and do not relate to inhuman nature. His goal was an

<hr>

[9] I, 1, pp. 112f. (lines 17—40).
[10] I, 1, p. 131 (lines 25—32).

introduction of the Ideals into human life and thus the creation of a better world. In "Lied der Liebe" there was only a faint suggestion of that vision; within a few months he saw it as a natural outgrowth of his devotion to the Ideal. He had said in "Liebe der Liebe" that love was "recreating Heaven and earth anew — divine — as in the beginning of time."[11] In the last two stanzas, however, he reverted to traditionally Christian thought, abandoned the thought of the rebirth of the world, and began speaking of life after death and praising love for assuring eventual triumph over time and the grave. The idea of remolding human life on earth through the prophetic revelation of the Ideals to mankind became a dominant theme only when Hölderlin turned to the Hymn-form in October 1790.

What differentiates the Hymns from everything he had written before, including the *Lieder* just discussed, was the appearance of a characteristic structure, which reflects and accentuates the poet's role as a prophet *vis-à-vis* those who listen to his song. Although Hölderlin would pursue the study of philosophy intermittently for some years still, and, even more irregularly, try to formulate his perceptions in philosophical essays, he had, by late 1790, already solidified his view of himself in the world. His perceptions of human life had assumed such a non-philosophical form that it would be a mistake to take the poems apart and rearrange his thoughts in order to pass them off as a philosophical system. From that point on his major efforts were directed to the expression of his view of world and self through that extremely varied imagery, ranging from the most abstract to the most sensual, that is the stock-in-trade of the mythological poet. That he experienced his world-view as mythology and not as philosophy was inevitable, because he was primarily concerned with issues arising from his own experience. The way he treated them was determined by his emotional reaction to them. It is true, of course, that his expression was, at that time, profoundly influenced by his philosophical readings. But the evolution and expansion of his views did not progress as they did because logic demanded it but because his personality demanded commitment to a certain line of thought and expression.

The Ideals became "the Gods," as we are wont to say, or, more correctly, the goddesses. They are, of course, still Ideals in the Kantian sense, for they still represent the outposts of knowledge, the goals of human inquiry and hope, the regulative ideas that control human thinking and longing. But Hölderlin made one important change when he defined the Ideals. To Hölderlin the Ideals were *accessible to the enthusiast* — an innovation that would have seemed as untenable to Kant as Goethe's *Urpflanze* seemed to Schiller. To Hölderlin, who so desperately needed the fulfillment of his dreams in this life, the Ideals ceased to be "bloße Ideen" comprehensible only as the precepts of Practical knowledge.

11   I, 1, p. 111 (lines 39f.).

By 1791 they had become for him the stuff of real life; without them human life was meaningless and, therefore, inconceivable.

Most human life he still regarded as meaningless because he was convinced that most people had never experienced the Ideals. They were accessible only to the enthusiast who, through the power of his love, transcended the sensible manifold and entered into the realm of pure meaning. This accounts for the fact that he began almost all the Hymns with the enthusiast's experiencing the beauty of nature and then, thus inspired, moving on to a perception of the Ideal. In "Hymne an die Unsterblichkeit" he expressed the enthusiast's flight to the realm of the goddess as an ascent into the skies.

> Froh, als könnt' ich Schöpfungen beglüken,
> Stolz, als huldigten die Sterne mir,
> Fleugt, ins Stralenauge dir zu bliken,
> Mit der Liebe Kraft mein Geist zu dir.
> Schon erglüht dem wonnetrunknen Seher
> Deiner Halle gold'nes Morgenroth,
> Ha, und deinem Götterschoose näher
> Höhnt die Siegesfahne Grab und Tod.[12]

Later he used the same set of images in "Hymne an die Göttin der Harmonie," varying the words to read:

> Froh, als könnt' ich Schöpfungen beglüken,
> Kün, als huldigten die Geister mir,
> Nahet, in dein Heiligtum zu bliken,
> Hocherhab'ne! meine Liebe dir;
> Schon erglüht der wonnetrunke Seher
> Von den Ahndungen der Herrlichkeit,
> Ha, und deinem Götterschoose näher
> Höhnt des Siegers Fahne Grab und Zeit.[13]

That variation was significant, for it indicated that he was less concerned with overcoming death than with overcoming the time separating modern man from the golden age of communion between gods and men.

Similarly, "Hymne an die Muse" begins:

> Schwach zu königlichem Feierliede,
> Schloß ich lang genug geheim und stumm
> Deine Freuden, hohe Pieride!
> In des Herzens stilles Heiligtum;

[12] I, 1, p. 116 (lines 1—8).
[13] I, 1, p. 130 (lines 1—8)

Endlich, endlich soll die Saite künden,
Wie von Liebe mir die Seele glüht,
Unzertrennbarer den Bund zu binden,
Soll dir huldigen diß Feierlied.[14]

"Hymne an die Menschheit" opens:

Die ernste Stunde hat geschlagen;
Mein Herz gebeut; erkoren ist die Bahn![15]

These opening lines, chosen from some of the earliest hymns, are striking for their thematic unity. In each the poet begins singing when he sees the realization of the Ideal in nature and is then spurred on by his love to approach the pure Ideal, the deity herself. "Drunken," filled with enthusiasm *(Begeisterung)*, he ascends into the realm of the deities, enters into the consecrated temple of the goddess, and discovers the pure Ideal *beyond the sensible manifold*. He had now reached the heights from which he can see all creation, distinguish its order, and perceive the principles of life that make existence not only meaningful, but possible. Admission to the realm of meaning and truth is gained by the poet because he loves the "life never enjoyed."[16] The Ideals then become accessible to the theoretical faculty (in Kant's terminology), not through reason, but through reverence and spiritual yearning.

On this level of prophetic perception the poet is able to see that the Ideals are not merely abstract goals posited by man but vital forces running throughout all being. In "Hymne an die Unsterblichkeit," probably the earliest of the Hymns, immortality is still treated as only an idea, but an idea that would survive when the natural order perished. It was the Ideal as a belief that made life good. Without it man would exist in confusion and uncontrolled license.

Müßte nicht der Mensch des Lebens fluchen,
Nicht die Tugend auf der Dornenbahn
Trost im Arme der Vernichtung suchen,
Täuschte sie ein lügenhafter Wahn?
Trümmern möchte der Natur Geseze
Menschenfreiheit, möcht' in blinder Wuth,
Wie die Reue die gestohlnen Schäze,
Niederschmettern ihr ererbtes Gut.[17]

With the assurance of immortality, however, friendship, love, poetry, and justice are possible.

14 I, 1, p. 135 (lines 1–8).
15 I, 1, p. 146 (lines 1f.).
16 I, 1, p. 139 (line 5).
17 I, 1, p. 117 (lines 41–48).

Wenn im Heiligtume alter Eichen
Männer um der Königin Altar
Sich die Bruderhand zum Bunde reichen,
Zu dem Bunde freudiger Gefar;
Wenn entzükt von ihren Götterküssen
Jeglicher, des schönsten Lorbeers werth,
Lieb' und Lorbeer ohne Gram zu missen
Zu dem Heil des Vaterlandes schwört!

Wenn die Starken den Despoten weken,
Ihn zu mahnen an das Menschenrecht,
Aus der Lüste Taumel ihn zu schreken,
Muth zu predigen dem feilen Knecht!
Wenn in todesvollen Schlachtgewittern,
Wo der Freiheit Heldenfahne weht,
Muthig, bis die müden Arme splittern,
Ruhmumstralter Sparter Phalanx steht.[18]

In the last stanza of "Hymne an die Unsterblichkeit" Hölderlin defied his own admonition, several times earlier, to "turn ... to the hall where life dwells,"[19] and reverted to the theme of life after death. "Hymne an die Unsterblichkeit" was the last poem in which the specifically Christian view, which placed its better life safely beyond the grave, played a major role. From then on he did not treat the Ideals as promises that could never be fulfilled in this life (as they appear in both Christian faith and Kantian ethics) but as active forces which must someday come to guide life on earth. With this change we can properly begin speaking of Hölderlin's mythology. The poet who, through the power of his love, ascends to a realm of perception from which he can discern the guiding principles of human life attains his goal because he *needs* the knowledge he acquires. But, having acquired that precious knowledge, he is able to understand what is missing in ordinary human life and is thus obligated to reveal his knowledge to others. The poet becomes the link between the realm of the Ideals, turned deities, and the world of men who suffer because they lack his knowledge. And the poet hears the very words of the goddess.

Sanftbegrüßt von Paradiesesdüften
Steht er wonniglichen Staunens da,
Und der Liebe großen Bund zu stiften,
Singt entgegen ihm Urania:

---

18 I, 1, p. 118 (lines 65—80).
19 I, 1, p. 116 (lines 25f.).

"Komm, o Sohn! der süßen Schöpfungsstunde
Auserwählter, komm und liebe mich!
Meine Küsse weihten dich zum Bunde,
Hauchten Geist von meinem Geist in dich. —
Meine Welt ist deiner Seele Spiegel,
Meine Welt, o Sohn! ist Harmonie,
Freue dich! Zum offenbaren Siegel
Meiner Liebe schuf ich dich und sie.

Trümmer ist der Wesen schöne Hülle,
Knüpft sie meiner Rechte Kraft nicht an.
Mir entströmt der Schönheit ew'ge Fülle,
Mir der Hoheit weiter Ozean.
Danke mir der zauberischen Liebe,
Mir der Freude stärkenden Genuß,
Deine Thränen, deine schönsten Triebe
Schuff, o Sohn! der schöpferische Kuß.

Herrlicher mein Bild in dir zu finden,
Haucht' ich Kräfte dir und Künheit ein,
Meines Reichs Geseze zu ergründen,
Schöpfer meiner Schöpfungen zu sein.
Nur im Schatten wirst du mich erspähen,
Aber liebe, liebe mich, o Sohn!
Drüben wirst du meine Klarheit sehen,
Drüben kosten deiner Liebe Lohn."[20]

The self-revelation of the goddess to the poet indicates Hölderlin's new self-image most clearly. He, of all men, was "the chosen one," the darling of the goddess, because he alone had been imbued with her breath. Moreover, he belonged to the Ideal life more than to the realm of everyday, transitory existence. His soul was united with her in a deep and enduring harmony. What the goddess revealed to him, the knowledge that she gave him, was that all beings, however attractive their external appearance might be, are "ruins" unless they partake of the Ideals. The poet was summoned to recreate the world in the image of the goddess. She admonished "to found love's great *Bund*."[21] He was to work constantly to bring about a new age of harmony in which man might once more perceive, serve, and, therefore, be united with the gods; his work was to be a resurrection of the past, a restoration of the "ruins."

In one sense, Hölderlin's new image of self was just the reverse of his self-image before 1790. Because he no longer felt called upon to oppose social

20 I, 1, p. 132 (lines 57—80).
21 I, 1, p. 131 (line 55).

life or lash out in defense of himself and his dreams, the destructive tone that appeared so often in the earlier poems has now vanished. There was no need for the heroic destroyer now. Man had destroyed his own life; and human life consisted of "ruins" because it was meaningless. Opposition was not called for; there was nothing in human life worth opposing any more. The sense was gone. Mankind needed a reawakening, a rediscovery of meaning. Thus Hölderlin could forego his opposition to life as he saw it being lived all around him and become the prophet, whose mission was not to destroy, but to rebuild, to restore, and to work toward a realization of the Ideals.

The mythology was then, at bottom, the frame of reference for his new self-image. It deserves to be called a mythology because through it Hölderlin provided an explanation of man's place in the manifold of being and indicated in what sense man's life has meaning above and beyond the mere satisfaction of animal needs. It is mythological rather than philosophical because one either accepts or rejects it depending on whether it fulfills subconscious needs, not because the argument convinces or fails to convince. There is, in fact, no real argument at all; there is only the testimony of the religious ecstatic. Finally, it is essentially an historically oriented mythology. The deities, one after the other, reveal themselves to Hölderlin in an age in which only a very few could hear them, simply because men were isolated from the natural order. This historical dimension was suggested as early as "Hymne an die Unsterblichkeit," when the image of reshaping the world at some time in the future first appeared. As we have seen, it was more fully developed in "Hymne an die Göttin der Harmonie." In "Hymne an die Freiheit" the mythology assumes definite historical form.

"Als die Liebe noch im Schäferkleide
Mit der Unschuld unter Blumen gieng,
Und der Erdensohn in Ruh' und Freude
Der Natur am Mutterbusen hieng,
Nicht der Übermuth auf Richterstühlen
Blind und fürchterlich das Band zerriß;
Tauscht' ich gerne mit der Götter Spielen
Meiner Kinder stilles Paradieß.

Liebe rief die jugendlichen Triebe
Schöpferisch zu hoher stiller That,
Jeden Keim entfaltete der Liebe
Wärm' und Licht zu schwelgerischer Saat;
Deine Flügel, hohe Liebe! trugen
Lächelnd nieder die Olympier;
Jubeltöne klangen — Herzen schlugen
An der Götter Busen göttlicher.

Freundlich bot der Freuden süße Fülle
Meinen Lieblingen die Unschuld dar;
Unverkennbar in der schönen Hülle
Wußte Tugend nicht, wie schön sie war;
Friedlich hausten in der Blumenhügel
Kühlem Schatten die Genügsamen —
Ach! des Haders und der Sorge Flügel
Rauschte ferne von den Glüklichen.

Wehe nun! — mein Paradieß erbebte!
Fluch verhieß der Elemente Wut!
Und der Nächte schwarzem Schoos' entschwebte
Mit des Geiers Blik der Übermuth;
Wehe! weinend floh' ich mit der Liebe
Mit der Unschuld in die Himmel hin —
Welke, Blume! rief ich ernst und trübe,
Welke, nimmer, nimmer aufzublüh'n!

Kek erhub sich des Gesezes Ruthe,
Nachzubilden, was die Liebe schuf;
Ach! gegeißelt von dem Übermuthe
Fühlte keiner göttlichen Beruf;
Vor dem Geist in schwarzen Ungewittern,
Vor dem Racheschwerdte des Gerichts
Lernte so der blinde Sklave zittern,
Fröhnt' und starb im Schreken seines Nichts.

Kehret nun zu Lieb' und Treue wieder —
Ach! es zieht zu langentbehrter Lust
Unbezwinglich mich die Liebe nieder —
Kinder! kehret an die Mutterbrust!
Ewig sei vergessen und vernichtet,
Was ich zürnend vor den Göttern schwur;
Liebe hat den langen Zwist geschlichtet,
Herrschet wieder! Herrscher der Natur!"[22]

Such a mythological history was, of course, nothing new; it was almost as old as religion. The myth of the three-stage history of mankind in which everything turned on man's relationship to the gods echoes countless other mythologists. Thinking of man's life on earth as a three-step development from an original state of paradisaical innocence through a time of confusion and discord to a final stage of joyful reunion with God would have been natural for a theology

22 I, 1, pp. 139ff. (lines 17—64).

student; his Christian upbringing would have made him susceptible to such constructions. In "Hymne an die Freiheit" the goddess says specifically that man's case is unique in that he alone has isolated himself from the rest of creation.

> Einer, Einer nur ist abgefallen,
> Ist gezeichnet mit der Hölle Schmach;
> Stark genug, die schönste Bahn zu wallen,
> Kriecht der Mensch am trägen Joche nach."[23]

It is unnecessary to trace each mythological image in the Hymns back to specific publications of his time. The whole Rousseau-inspired worship of man in the natural state was echoed in his poems, particularly in those lines reproduced above in which the original state of innocence is represented as a pastoral scene. Indeed, it would not be invalid to say that Hölderlin's mythology in Tübingen was perfectly consistent with traditional Christian thought, which he then recounted in Hellenic trappings supplied by his reading — were it not for the fact that, in Hölderlin's view, man's aesthetic sense, not his moral sense or his behavior in terms of orthodox ethical prescriptions, determined whether he can gain access to the gods. It is true that certain words imply moral judgments. But the emphasis is clearly on man's insensitivity rather than on his sinfulness. Sin is not absent, it merely results from the dullness of man's aesthetic sense.

This brings us back to the problem that we declined to discuss at the beginning of this chapter: Hölderlin's position within the intellectual climate of his day. For it was precisely in the subtle shift of emphasis from the moral to the aesthetic that Hölderlin defined his place in the Kantian, Schillerian intellectual "tradition" of his time. More specifically, it was in his synthesis of the Semitic-Germanic thought, in which moral judgments predominate, with the Hellenic world-view, in which aesthetic values are basic, that Hölderlin defined his place within the so-called intellectual traditions of his time. We have delayed this discussion up until now because we wanted to demonstrate why Hölderlin felt compelled to change so many of his opinions and restructure his view of himself and the world. We have already shown that the mythology that he produced was not an end in itself but another means of rationalization by which he succeeded in defining himself in such a way that he could go on avoiding normal life and yet not be obligated to actively oppose it. His mythology made it possible for him to continue in his self-imposed isolation and yet avoid the stigma of sin which, according to his mother's point of view, he would have deserved because of his aloofness. We feel called upon to repeat that the Tübingen Hymns arose as symbolic struggles with problems with which he could not cope in real life. We have, up until now, indicated why Hölderlin began

---

[23] I, 1, p. 159 (lines 61–64).

writing a new kind of poetry in 1790 and why he was drawn to Kant, Schiller, and the Greeks. Now it is necessary to define Hölderlin within the framework of his time. We undertake this now, not as a study in *Geistesgeschichte* but as part of our study of Hölderlin's personality. For that reason we still decline to evaluate Hölderlin's place in the intellectual history of his time; we measure him against his models only because the way in which he changed the themes and thought forms that he borrowed from them will allow us to further refine the answers we have already posited in rough form.

In the second version of "Hymne an die Schönheit" Hölderlin prefaced his poem with Kant's words: "Nature in its beautiful forms speaks to us in signs [figürlich], and the talent of interpreting her hieroglyphics is given to our moral sense."[24] Kant's words indicate that he recognized the difficulty of bringing two such diverse aspects of human knowledge into harmony within his system. Indeed, it is *The Critique of Judgment* that is the least satisfying. Why his account of aesthetic judgments was so unsatisfactory – and was felt to be so by his immediate followers – is imbedded in the system itself. However seriously Kant warned against taking the primacy of Practical Reason too seriously and making of duty a tyrant, destructive of human freedom, the system has the Christian, orthodox, moralistic bent built into it. His definition of duty, by which one acts out of duty only when one acts in a manner that contradicts one's natural inclinations, made reconciliation of moral and aesthetic judgments extremely difficult. The solution in *The Critique of Judgment*, which appeared in 1790, is, at best, forced. As time went on, the carefully constructed synthesis proved less and less acceptable to Kant's followers. Its rapid collapse came about when diametrically opposed points of view were espoused by Fichte, on the one hand, and the Romantics on the other, each of whom looked upon himself as the legitimate heir of Kant. Fichte's insistence on the Primacy of Practical Reason to the point that duty became the tyrant of human reason was justly opposed by the Romantics, who, on the other hand, committed a similar error of extremism in abolishing, in effect, morality for the sake of beauty. It is hard to say which point of view was less wrong. Certainly Fichte was correct in insisting on the Primacy of Practical Reason and in claiming that he was the legitimate heir of Kant, because Kant had created the *Urtheilskraft*, and with it aesthetic judgments to serve merely as a link between Theoretical and Practical Reason; the Romantics could, on the other hand, point to Kant's sensitive treatment of the Ideal of beauty and assert rightly that Kant's sensitivity was not shared by Fichte, who left no room for the original genius whatsoever. At bottom they were, of course, both wrong, partly because the moralistic passion of Fichte and the Romantictists' aesthetic mania were extreme, and partly

---

[24] As Beck points out, Hölderlin's preface to the poem is a free adaptation, probably from memory, of § 42 of *The Critique of Judgment* (I, 2, p. 457).

because Kant's reconciliation is based on such a carefully (precariously, one is tempted to say) balanced argument that any tampering with it, any change in the prescribed weights of the various parts, inevitably results in the collapse of the whole system. Consequently Kant's system was transformed into a junkyard of clichés from which anyone could gather in the broken parts that suited his fancy, construct his own makeshift system, and, because he had used a few of the original parts, claim that he had "completed" Kant's work.

These questions would concern Hölderlin later, particularly when he studied Kantian aesthetics in detail and listened to Fichte's lectures in Jena in 1795. They did not really concern him at all during his Tübingen years because he was unaware of the complexities involved. He turned to the watered-down version of Critical Philosophy that he found in Schiller and which he heard from his professors at the *Stift,* not because the logic or profundity of thought that he encountered was particularly compelling, but because he found in Idealism a way of reconciling himself with the world by denying the world, in the form in which he encountered it, any validity at all. If he really knew much about Kant's treatment of aesthetic judgments in *Critique of Judgment,* he was probably attracted by certain elements of Kant's theory. First, he would have been struck by the proposition that beauty is found in the disinterested contemplation of the harmonious object.[25] This he would have taken to mean that he was right in not seeking fulfillment in professional life; it would have reenforced his warm acceptance of Schiller's "philosophic mind" and the work which "rewards itself." Although we see now, from a psychological point of view, that Hölderlin was not really involved in the disinterested contemplation of beauty, and could not have been, since his self-preservation depended upon his success in separating the good and the beautiful from the world of action, he would, nevertheless, have considered his refusal to consider his future in realistic terms a fulfillment of Kant's prerequisite of "disinterestedness" as the prerequisite for the perception of beauty. Moreover, Kant's assertion that the beautiful was a symbol of the good and that the faculty of the mind that makes aesthetic judgments is the binding link between Theoretical and Practical Reason (speculative knowledge and morality) would have been grist for Hölderlin's mill. For fundamental to his mythology was the proposition that the perception of beauty was a prerequisite to knowledge of the gods. The great difference was Hölderlin's assertion that one really knew the gods, that the gods became the object of Theoretical Knowledge, and that such knowledge was necessary for life to be meaningful and good.

Only later, when at Waltershausen he read Schiller's *Anmut und Würde,* did Hölderlin recognize that Kantian ethics was a much more rigorous system and that Kant had left far less room for the creative spirit, the prophet, than he had

25 *Kritik der Urtheilskraft* (1790 Edition), p. 16.

supposed. In this sense, Hölderlin exaggerated the importance of the creative spirit, much as the Romantics would do a few years later. He was able to do that naively, without the cerebral contortions of the Romantics, because he had, in no sense, mastered, or even thoroughly studied, Kantian philosophy. He simply appropriated the clichés and proceeded to breathe life into them and construct from them a mythological interpretation of life which Kant would have rejected as surely as he rejected Herder's *Ideas on the Philosophy of the History of Mankind* in the 1780's.

Hölderlin's philosophical weakness, which made it unnecessary for him to come to grips with all the reasons why Ideals could not be realized in life and were inaccessible to the faculty of Theoretical Knowledge, was of little consequence as far as his poetry was concerned. The dimensions of faith, which had been missing in Kant — simply because Kant was a philosopher — gave Hölderlin the assurance that the Ideals not only existed but were basic to a meaningful life; Hölderlin was not hampered by Reason's objections which would have stopped the philosopher cold. Faith dictated that one believe in the Ideals. The enthusiast's *experiencing* the Ideals silenced all of Reason's objections. The Ideals became the only worthy object of knowledge, a truth that the creative genius, the enthusiast, the prophet, was obligated to proclaim to all men. He was not then betraying his God when he refused to become the shepherd of His flock. He was rather serving God in a way in which no one else could by maintaining his "disinterested" posture toward the world of men so that he might continually go up to the mountain and spread the Word. In that way he was the forerunner of the Kingdom of God on earth. Only if he remained aloof from men could he see the meaning of all life, broaden his vision, and catch glimpses of God in nature — a God operating through principles that were at once natural and divine. It was through his pronouncedly unphilosophic attitude that he was able to perceive the Ideals as both natural and divine, both moral and aesthetic, both part of the realm of nature and yet making possible the exertion of freedom.

Finally, it was his unphilosophic, highly uncritical stance that made it possible for him to accept the historical scheme, which was Rousseau's legacy, as an article of faith. Here, once again, he used the clichés at hand to express his own highly original thought. The Rousseau-inspired belief — that the attainment of perfection in human life would be something quite at odds with the Enlightenment idea of man's having at least established his mastery over the natural world and having subjugated it to his pleasure — had culminated in the notion that the Golden Age of mankind was to be found in the past and that man must *return*, not progress, to perfection. Through the years the Golden Age had been associated more and more with Greece rather than with the primitive state of man's origins.

Hölderlin's mythology was most original in his handling of this very theme.

He accepted the view that the goal of human history was in the past. But more than the *Stürmer und Dränger,* who had so ardently accepted Rousseau's indictment of modern culture, Hölderlin recognized that the return to the lost time of innocence must be primarily religious. The message of the Hymns is that the world must experience a "Verjüngung." In "Hymne an die Muse" the theme was first developed in detail. The knowledge of the present is contrasted with the knowledge that man can attain through following the prophet in search of the revitalization of the world.

> Öde stehn und dürre die Gefilde,
> Wo die Blüthen das Gesez erzwingt;
> Aber wo in königlicher Milde
> Ihren Zauberstab die Muse schwingt,
> Blühen schwelgerisch und kün die Saaten,
> Reifen, wie der Wandelsterne Lauf,
> Schnell und herrlich Hofnungen und Thaten
> Der Geschlechter zur Vollendung auf.[26]

The poet is dedicated to the knowledge that poetry can give. To the Muse he called: "Dieses Herz ist dein!"[27] For he can see a life to which that of those who have not yet perceived beauty stands in frightening contrast.

> Wehe! wem des Lebens schöner Morgen
> Freude nicht und trunkne Liebe schafft,
> Wem am Sklavenbande blaicher Sorgen
> Zum Genusse Kraft und Muth erschlafft.[28]

The poet cannot bring about the rebirth of the world alone. Once again friendship makes its appearance. Now, after he has worked out his mythology in detail, we are able to see how the magic word *Bund* made friendship an essential part of his thinking. His friends, those who have heard and hearkened to his song, now become the priests of the goddess.

> Deine Priester, hohe Pieride!
> Schwingen frei und froh den Pilgerstab,
> Mit der allgewaltigen Aegide
> Lenkst du mütterlich die Sorgen ab;
> Schäumend beut die zauberische Schaale
> Die Natur den Auserkornen dar,
> Trunken von der Schönheit Göttermahle
> Höhnet Glük und Zeit die frohe Schaar.

---

[26] I, 1, pp. 136f. (lines 57—64).
[27] I, 1, p. 137 (line 80).
[28] I, 1, p. 137 (lines 85—88).

Frei und muthig, wie im Siegesliede,
Wallen sie der edeln Geister Bahn,
Dein Umarmen, hohe Pieride!
Flammt zu königlichen Thaten an; —[29]

The message of the new Hölderlin is then the call to his friends to dedicate themselves to the *Bund* — the priesthood of the Ideals.

Kommt zu süßem brüderlichem Bunde,
Denen sie den Adel anerschuf,
Millionen auf dem Erdenrunde!
Kommt zu neuem seeligem Beruf![30]

Similarly, when he wrote "Hymne an die Freiheit," the goddess proclaims that the time of reunion is dawning, to which the poet replies:

Froh und göttlichgroß ist deine Kunde,
Königin! dich preise Kraft und That!
Schon beginnt die neue Schöpfungsstunde,
Schon erkeimt die seegenschwang're Saat.[31]

Once more the result is the rebirth of the world:

Staunend kennt der große Stamm sich wieder,
Millionen knüpft der Liebe Band;
Glühend steh'n, und stolz, die neuen Brüder,
Stehn und dulden für das Vaterland.[32]

Now the old vices fall away:

Ha! getilget ist die alte Schande!
Neuerkauft das angestammte Gut!
In dem Staube modern alle Bande,
Und zur Hölle flieht der Übermuth![33]

The same close union between the poet and his converts is indicated in "Hymne an die Menschheit." The friends dedicate themselve to the goddess and to each other.

---

[29] I, 1, p. 138 (lines 89—100).
[30] I, 1, p. 138 (lines 109—112).
[31] I, 1, p. 141 (lines 65—68).
[32] I, 1, p. 141 (lines 73—76).
[33] I, 1, p. 142 (lines 93—96).

Schon lernen wir das Band der Sterne,
Der Liebe Stimme männlicher versteh'n,
Wir reichen uns die Brüderrechte gerne,
Mit Heereskraft der Geister Bahn zu geh'n;
Schon höhnen wir des Stolzes Ungebärde,
Die Scheidewand, von Flittern aufgebaut,
Und an des Pilgers unentweihtem Heerde
Wird sich die Menschheit wieder angetraut.[34]

Here, as we noticed in the last chapter, the *Bund* is isolated from others. But, once more, because the friends have now disassociated themselves from the world and its vices, friendship is responsible for bringing about the rebirth of the world.

So jubelt, Siegsbegeisterungen!
Die keine Lipp' in keiner Wonne sang;
Wir ahndeten — und endlich ist gelungen,
Was in Aeonen keiner Kraft gelang —
Vom Grab' ersteh'n der alten Väter Heere,
Der königlichen Enkel sich zu freu'n;
Die Himmel kündigen des Staubes Ehre,
Und zur Vollendung geht die Menschheit ein.[35]

The promise of the rebirth of the world, of the rebuilding of human life in accordance with the Ideals, of the realization of the Ideals in life on earth — is the culmination of the Tübingen Hymns. These proclamations that the world can indeed be transformed and that human life, which is now cruel and meaningless, will someday approximate the original state of harmony and innocence give purpose to the poet's call to his friends to remain true to him and the *Bund*. It is this promise of salvation that imparts to Hölderlin's Hymns the tone of religious ecstasy that differentiates his treatment of the imagery he got from Schiller's poetry from Schiller's own.

Schiller's poem "Die Künstler" was perhaps the most important single work influencing the structure and imagery of the Tübingen Hymns. In that poem Schiller had described man's progress from his original animal state to his position as "the ripest son of time," a position he had attained, in Schiller's eyes, because of a long process of aesthetic maturation. Appreciation of beauty was seen as the anticipation of knowledge, and growth of the aesthetic faculty always preceded intellectual growth.

---

[34] I, 1, p. 146 (lines 17—24).
[35] I, 1, p. 148 (lines 81—88).

was wir als Schönheit hier empfunden,
wird einst als *Wahrheit* uns entgegen gehen.[36]

The artist was, therefore, the spiritual pioneer of mankind whose historic mission was to create visions of ever more elaborate harmony and thus to point the way for science. Not only this glorification of the artist and the enthroning of the aesthetic sense would have appealed to Hölderlin, but also Schiller's hint that there had indeed been an original state of grace from which man had fallen. For that assertion implied that it was the task of the artist to lead man *back* to perfection.

Als der Erschaffende von seinem Angesichte
den Menschen in die Sterblichkeit verwieß,
und eine späte Wiederkehr zum Lichte
auf schwerem Sinnenpfad ihn finden hieß,
als alle Himmlischen ihr Antlitz von ihm wandten,
schloß sie, die Menschliche, allein
mit dem verlassenen Verbannten
großmüthig in die Sterblichkeit sich ein.
Hier schwebt sie, mit gesenktem Fluge,
um ihren Liebling, nah dem Sinnenland,
und mahlt mit lieblichem Betruge
Elysium auf seine Kerkerwand.[37]

Hölderlin would have been thrilled at the promise of a return to the original perfection through the work of the artist. It is unnecessary to point out all the elements in Schiller's long, and often obscure, poem that Hölderlin adopted. More important to our understanding of the Tübingen Hymns is the immense gulf that we see opening up between the two poets on closer analysis, even though Hölderlin's themes and form were so similar to Schiller's at that time. For the themes and images that proved to be most important in Hölderlin's mythology seem, on first glance, to be little more than embellishments of Schiller's verse essay in the philosophy of history. And yet, on closer examination, one discovers a number of significant differences.

First, there is a great difference between Schiller's and Hölderlin's attitudes toward their listeners. As we have already seen, Hölderlin issues an evangelical admonition to his audience to hearken unto the words of the goddess and dedicate themselves to her service. Schiller's poem, on the other hand, is anything but religious. At bottom it is a rather dry lecture masquerading as a poem. The gods play a largely decorative role. The poet, absorbed by the theme

---

[36] *Schillers Werke. Nationalausgabe,* edited by J. Petersen and H. Schneider (33 vols.; Weimar: Hermann Böhlaus Nachfolger, 1943ff.), I, p. 202 (lines 64f.).
[37] *Ibid.,* pp. 202f. (lines 66—77).

of the historical importance of the artist in the story of human progress, uses the gods, in good Kantian form, as the postulates of Practical Reason, *bloße Ideen,* images of the perfect man, which the artist, once he has constructed them, must call gods because they cannot be found in the world of experience. Under Schiller's hands the gods become, at best, allegories of an intellectual theme and, at worst, pedagogical hypotheses. The image of the gods turning away from man at the beginning should not be taken too seriously; that image, which would be of crucial importance in Hölderlin's mythology, was treated by Schiller as nothing more than a fairy-tale. It could hardly have been otherwise, for Schiller's aim was not to provide the reader with a religious experience, but rather to impart to him a specific philosophy of history.

This implies a second and perhaps even more crucial difference between the two men. Schiller, the philosophically inclined spirit to whom the divinities — those principles of meaning in life — had validity only in the Kantian sense, only as hypothetical postulations which served man as a visual representation of the goals of all his striving, and who was thus unable to believe in the gods or in the myth of the Golden Age to come, which would be a return to an earlier condition, was imbued with a fundamental optimism about the direction of human history which Hölderlin could not share. "Die Künstler" is an apology for modern man. To Schiller life in the eighteenth century was the highest form that human life had ever assumed up until then; anything surpassing the accomplishments of his age was a fairy-tale. The artist, as Schiller saw him, could, therefore, not be a prophet in Hölderlin's sense; the visions he presented to man were not real and could never become real. The artist accomplished an historical purpose through inventing a dream world that could never be attained, but toward which man could be impelled to strive. Schiller says specifically that the work of the artist "loses the crown it wore as soon as it achieves reality."[38] Thus, although the artist is a spiritual pioneer, his vision is always changed by science. He has helped bring man to his present elevated state by painting beautiful, utopian pictures on the walls of his dungeon. But reality remains for Schiller the world of science and philosophy — the dungeon walls. Schiller goes on to say that "thought," which he calls "the illustrious stranger," arose from the free spirit when it had been liberated from the prison of the senses by the artist. Thought is, therefore, progress beyond art. There lies inherent in Schiller's view the elevation of abstract reasoning above artistic creation. He shares Kant's disdain for all pretentious metaphysics based on aesthetics; to him art paves the way for philosophy but remains the handmaiden of Practical Reason. In another sense, Schiller shares the notorious optimism that infected the philosophers of his age, which we are all too often willing to pass off as an affliction limited to dogmatic rationalists, but which we also find in Kant's foreword to *The Critique of Pure*

[38] *Ibid.,* p. 205 (lines 159f.).

Reason: "Now metaphysics, understood as we shall define it here, is, of all the sciences, the only one that can promise itself such a completion, and indeed in a short time and with but little, albeit concentrated effort, so that nothing will remain for posterity but to dispose of everything didactically in accordance with their intentions, without, however, being able to increase the content in the slightest."[39]

Hölderlin's views were quite at odds with Schiller's in almost every aspect mentioned above. The direction of his thought was not toward a conceptualization of the process by which man had progressed to the elevated heights of the Kantian philosopher; rather he used Schiller's themes and poetic forms to condemn his time utterly. Where Schiller saw man's future greatness as the inevitable result of his traveling further down the road along which he had been traveling since he had become man, Hölderlin called for a break with the present — and with the entire direction of history up until his time. It was, in his view, the artist — not the philosopher — who must save mankind. In this sense, the roles of the artist and the philosopher are reversed when we go from Schiller to Hölderlin. To Schiller, the artist will continue to paint his utopian pictures and thus set impossible goals for thought and science; the philosopher's attempt to achieve the vision, even though he fails, will result in progress to a higher level. Hölderlin, on the other hand, saw the artist moving through the works of the philosophers eclectically and selecting those forms of thought, those conceptual arguments, that might make it possible for him to persuade his fellow men that a new world, a world more like the Golden Age that had been lost, was possible. Hölderlin, in the end, came to believe that the Ideals would indeed be realized on earth when men heeded the poet and devoted their lives to his dreams.

From these very fundamental differences between Hölderlin and Schiller, which the formal similarities of their works tend to conceal, it is easy to understand why they were committed to such divergent views concerning the significance of Plato's Greece. There were many reasons why Hölderlin would have been more enthusiastic about Greek art and thought than Schiller. Hölderlin knew Greek and was, therefore, more susceptible to the graecomania that was infecting German youth at that time. Schiller, on the other hand, had forgotten most of the little Greek he had learned in the *Karlsschule*. When he studied the Greek tragedians in the late 1780's, he was primarily interested in learning how he might attain, in his own dramas, the simplicity of the Greek model. He was looking for a technique. He never succumbed to the idolizing of antiquity, which was rampant at the time. He did not deny its beauty; he merely doubted that the unity of man and nature, which German youth saw in Greek art, could be attained in the modern age. At bottom, of course, he did not believe that such a renaissance was needed.

39 *Kritik der reinen Vernunft* (1781 Edition), p. XX.

Schiller expressed his feelings toward Greece of Classical Antiquity in the poem "Die Götter Griechenlands" in 1788. The poet within him sincerely mourned the passing away of the pantheistic view of life.

> Schöne Welt, wo bist du? — Kehre wieder,
> holdes Blüthenalter der Natur!
> Ach! nur in dem Feenland der Lieder
> lebt noch deine goldne Spur.
> Ausgestorben trauert das Gefilde,
> keine Gottheit zeigt sich meinem Blik,
> Ach! von jenem lebenswarmen Bilde
> blieb nur das Gerippe mir zurück.[40]

And yet, however much the poet within him mourned the loss, the philosopher Schiller — that part of him which always had the last word — pronounced the hard and bitter verdict that the death of ancient pantheism was an irreversible fact.

> Unbewußt der Freuden, die sie schenket,
> nie entzückt von ihrer Treflichkeit,
> nie gewahr des Armes, der sie lenket,
> reicher nie durch meine Dankbarkeit,
> fühllos selbst für ihres Künstlers Ehre,
> gleich dem todten Schlag der Pendeluhr,
> dient sie knechtisch dem Gesetz der Schwere
> Die entgötterte Natur!
>
> Morgen wieder neu sich zu entbinden,
> wühlt sie heute sich ihr eignes Grab,
> und an ewig gleicher Spindel winden
> sich von selbst die Monde auf und ab.
> Müssig kehrten zu dem Dichterlande
> heim die Götter, unnütz einer Welt
> die, entwachsen ihrem Gängelbande,
> sich durch eignes Schweben hält.[41]

Hölderlin recounted the same loss of the gods of Greece in the poem "Griechenland," which he seems to have written shortly after he left the *Stift*. That poem stands at the very end of the Tübingen Hymns and was a fitting response to Schiller's "Die Götter Griechenlands." For, after he too had bewailed the loss of the gods, Hölderlin concluded with the words:

---

[40] Schiller, *Nationalausgabe,* I, p. 194 (lines 145—152).
[41] *Ibid.,* pp. 194f. (lines 161—176).

Mich verlangt ins ferne Land hinüber
Nach Alcäus und Anakreon,
Und ich schlief' im engen Hause lieber,
Bei den Heiligen in Marathon;
Ach! es sei die lezte meiner Thränen,
Die dem lieben Griechenlande rann,
Laßt, o Parzen, laßt die Scheere tönen,
Denn mein Herz gehört den Todten an![42]

The tone of despair, which had once again returned to his poems in "Griechenland," stands in bold contrast to the poems that he had written at Tübingen. But, however different it may have been from the vigorous and resounding call to victory than ran through the Tübingen Hymns as far as the tone is concerned, it points out once again the one quality which made Hölderlin unique. The mythology which he constructed was not, as it was for Schiller, merely a fairy-tale, a way to impart reason's knowledge. With Hölderlin the forms and expressions are not merely embellishments of an intellectual theme, but are symbolic utterances that are to be interpreted intellectually and, at the same time, are to be understood literally. In the intellectual life of his time, Hölderlin stands apart. He was one of the few artists — the only other who comes to mind at once is Kleist — who clung to the symbol or the form as an article of faith, who believed in the mythological fairyland they created. And, again like Kleist, the reason for the creation of a mythology that was to be taken as it appeared and that meant exactly what it said, was that the creation of a mythological world was not for Hölderlin mere participation in the intellectual parlance of the age but the creation of a dream-world in which he needed to live. In his dream-world he could play an historic role — a role that he could not play in life. And so Hölderlin stands alone as the only German poet who seriously believed in the mythology of Greece and who believed that he, as a modern poet, could actually lead mankind out of the wilderness and into a new age in which the original harmony of man and nature would be restored.

We have compared Hölderlin directly to Schiller, and we have given some indication as to how his thinking conflicted with that of Kant. A full exposition of how Hölderlin fits into the intellectual life of his time has been reserved for a later chapter. We could have gone further in this discussion and demonstrated how he seized upon the vision of the "Verjüngung" of the world offered by Herder in *Tithon und Aurora* or related Hölderlin's vision of the Golden Age to Herder's translation and discussion of Hemsterhuys' essay.[43] All of these

---

42 *Ibid.*, p. 180 (lines 49–56).

43 Herder wrote in the appendix to his translation of Hermsterhuys' letters "Über das Verlangen": "It is a beautiful legend of the most ancient poetry that Love drew the world out of chaos and joined the creatures to each other with reciprocal bonds of yearning and longing; that she — Love — keeps everything in order with those tender bonds and leads

comparisons would have been relevant. But it would be a mistake to make too much of them. For Hölderlin was not the follower of Kant, Schiller, Herder, or anyone else. He took from each of them those elements which he could use to create the vision of an harmonious world of motionless, frozen life. Only if one has recognized that Hölderlin was not just another follower of Kant or part of any "intellectual tradition" of his time, save in the very limited sense that he chose from those forms of thought and expression which were available to him, can one grasp the importance and the meaning of the Tübingen Hymns. In wrestling with the problems of life, which he could not overcome, he was compelled to construct a vision of harmony with everything around him and to conjure up the promise that such an ideal state of being would eventually come into being. He had to make sense of his suffering, and so he saw himself suffering in the service of the Ideals in the company of a few other young men. They, along with him, were the forerunners of a Golden Age. His enunciation of his dream is so overwhelming, I think, because he sang with the unmistakable earnestness of an archetypal myth that runs throughout all thought and poetry. The mythology of Yin and Yan, the alternating times of strife and love, occurs in Oriental mythology. Eastern thinkers called the time of Yin the age of softness and warmth, while the age of Yan was a time of hardness and coldness. Hölderlin's poetry creates the vision of the Golden Age in such a way that those poems literally breath softness and warmth. In 1795 he wrote of his time, the time of Yan: "How iron is my heaven, how I am made of stone!"[44] Later, when he was succumbing to Yan, he began to speak of "a certain coldness."[45] As he

---

everything to the One, to the great source of all light and love" (*Sämtliche Werke* edited by Bernhard Suphan, V, p. 58).

He also wrote of the friendship of the soldiers in the Greek phalanx much as Hölderlin would write of his "priests": "A common purpose joined them together; danger bound the knot; proven fidelity, continuous, growing zeal, glorious toil, common partaking in toil, hardship and death finally bound the knot forever (p. 311). Similarly, Hölderlin's image of the poet's awareness of a lost paradise being awakened through his encounter with a beautiful object was anticipated by Herder when he wrote: "I do not recall in which Asiatic mythology the most ancient time is treated in such a way that men (still spirits in paradise at that time) are supposed to have loved each other first with glances, then with kisses, with mere touching, until in the slow passage of time they finally descended to the lower types of pleasure. The moment of intellectual cognition, that betrayal of the soul through *one* glance transports us, as it were, back into that time ans so into the joys of its paradise. There we enjoy *reflectively (zurückempfindend)* what we have searched for for so long and dare not say to ourselves that in this moment we experience through precognition *(vorempfindend)* all the joys of the future. ..." (p. 314). Herder also presented love as the auther of all creation (p. 317). Also, the new, revolutionary image of the renewal of the world through organic development, which was already apparent in Hölderlin's hymns of this time, and which would find expression in *Hyperion*, was anticipated in *Tithon und Aurora* (XVI, pp. 177ff.).

[44] 104.29f.

[45] "I fear the warm life in me will freeze in the ice-cold history of this day" (167.58f.).

knew himself, his kinship to Empedocles was very close; for Empedocles also had spoken of a time of love and time of strife.[46]

All mythologies require some support in experience. Hölderlin would seek, from that point on, to live his life in such a way that he might fulfil his own prophecy. When he really began to penetrate Kantian thought, heard Fichte's lectures, and came to realize that Schiller was not the perfect traveling companion on the way to the Golden Age, he rejected them all. He needed confirmation for his mythology *in life,* in some symbol of living beauty in which he might find embodied the promise of eternal harmony and peace. He would find that symbol in Susette Gontard and celebrate his reawakening to life in the poem "Diotima," to which we have referred before. As we have already seen, the perfect woman would always remain the final confirmation of his dream. Even now he selected a girl to represent, in his poetry at least, the image of the beloved. Elise Lebret, who seems to have been anything but the incorporation of harmonious love of which he dreamed, was now the object of a poem strangely like "Diotima."

> Jede Blüthe war gefallen
> Von dem Stamme; Muth und Kraft,
> Fürder meine Bahn zu wallen,
> War im Kampfe mir erschlafft;
> Weggeschwunden Lust und Leben,
> Früher Jahre stolze Ruh;
> Meinem Grame hingegeben,
> Wankt' ich still dem Grabe zu.[47]

And then, when he finds her:

> Daß ich wieder Kraft gewinne,
> Frei wie einst und seelig bin,
> Dank ich deinem Himmelssinne,
> Lyda, süße Retterin![48]

In those years he wrote the first fragments of *Hyperion*. He had now reached the view of self and his relationship to life which, in life, he would defend to the end.

[46] Eduard Zeller, *Die Philosophie der Griechen in ihrer geschichtlichen Entwicklung* (Reprinted: Hildesheim, 1963), I, pp. 969ff.
[47] I, 1, p. 120 (lines 1–8).
[48] I, 1, pp. 120f. (lines 25–28).

10

THE PROPHET ALONE

Between 12 February and 14 March 1798, Hölderlin composed a letter to Karl Gok in which he cautioned against venturing out too early into life, thereby exposing oneself to hurt through daring to commit oneself to any person or any goal with one's whole body and soul. "Dear Karl! It is to be hoped that we might be occupied superficially rather than always exposing our whole soul, be it in love or work, to destructive reality."[1] His admonition to avoid reality, to avoid all involvement in real life, came from experience. "Dear Karl! I speak as one who has been shipwrecked. Such a person is only too happy to advise staying in port until the best season for a voyage is at hand. I had obviously ventured out too early, striven too soon for something great, and will probably have to pay for it for as long as I live; I will hardly succeed in anything, because I did not allow my nature to mature in peace and in an undemanding absence of care."[2] "I seek peace, my Brother! I will find it in your heart and in association with our dear family. Best Karl! I seek only peace."[3]

When Hölderlin wrote that letter, his position within the Gontard household was rapidly becoming unbearable. But he did not blame his embarrassing position on his employer — nor on anyone else. "I know my heart and know that things had to happen as they did. I passed so many precious days in mourning in the most beautiful time of my life because I had to endure thoughtlessness and disdain as long as I was not the only competitor. Afterwards I found and returned kindness, but it was not hard to see that my first, rather deep commitment had perished in the undeserved sorrow that I suffered. By my third year in Tübingen, it was finished. The rest was superficial, and I have paid enough for living the two remaining years in such an uninterested interest [*interesseloses Interesse*]. I have paid for it in full through the frivolity which, in that way, crept into my character, and from which I escaped only through unspeakably painful experiences."[4] That was the conclusion of his ruminations. Earlier in that letter he had given a clue as to what he meant when he spoke of the state of "uninterested interest." "Do you know the root of all my woe? I would live for art, to which I am completely devoted, and must work myself around among men [*mich herumarbeiten unter den Menschen*] so that I am often dreadfully tired of life. And why? Because art nourishes her masters, but

---

[1] 152.19ff.
[2] 152.32ff.
[3] 152.59ff.
[4] 152.87ff.

not her pupils."[5] "So be it! After all, many a one who had the stuff of an artist has already perished. We do not live in a poetic climate. For that reason, out of ten such plants hardly one survives."[6]

The letter is at once an obscure mixture of perceptive, ruthlessly honest self-analysis and self-excusing rationalization. He could never blame others for his trouble directly. Even after he had left the Gontard house under mysterious, but evidently unpleasant circumstances, he never breathed a word of reproach about his former employer.[7] Only now and then did he bring himself to blame a rather nebulous "them" for his predicament in Frankfurt.[8] His sorrow and the tragedy of his life were seen as the result of the cruelty of the impersonal age in which he lived. It was not an age for poets, and so he was perishing. Or he blamed himself, but always in a way that allowed him to appear to be the victim of his own greatness. "I ventured forth too early and did not give myself time to mature," he explained. Surely he was thinking of his hopes of collaborating on equal footing with Schiller in 1795, which had been dashed. Behind these rationalizations lay his hypersensitivity, which led him to the not inaccurate conclusion that he had failed because he had exposed himself to the hardships of real life before he was able to cope with them. In fact, in 1793, when he finally had to face real life, he had already been able to isolate himself for so long that he was quite incapable of coping with everyday problems. By then reality was, in his view, simply "destructive."

"By my third year in Tübingen, it was finished. The rest was superficial. . . ." That much was true. Those last two years in Tübingen had been a time of loneliness so intense and a spiritual isolation so profound that he never recovered completely from that period of solitude.

Neuffer and Magenau left the *Stift* in 1791. Magenau describes his own departure in the late summer in his *Lebensabriß*.

"My farewell from Tübingen and from most of my friends was near. I left eight weeks before my graduation.

"It was a beautiful, moonlit night when I left Tübingen. I had torn myself from my friends' arms at a brotherly feast. Our tears sank into the trembling goblet as we began to sing

'Traurig sehen wir uns an'

the heartfelt song by Miller. We parted; at the Cloister gate we embraced each

---

5   152.66ff.
6   152.73ff.
7   Of his last interview with Gontard, Hölderlin wrote: "We parted politely" (165.109).
8   In his letter to his mother in which he explained why he had left Frankfurt, he spoke nebulously of "the rich businessmen in Frankfurt" who, "embittered by the present state of affairs," were guilty of "a deprecation of all science and all learning" and who had insulted him by saying that a *Hofmeister* should not expect special treatment because he was, after all, nothing more than hired help (165.74ff.). To what degree Gontard shared those opinions, or whether he expressed himself concerning the matter, is not known.

other once more, and I moved off with Klopstock's great 'silver tone of freedom' ringing in my ears. It seemed as if the little stars in heaven had waited to witness the triumph of our friendship; for they were all there in the dome of the bright heavens. I was so happy and sad; separation and freedom — never did I feel those mixed feelings so deeply. I went most of the way through the woods and fields to Waldenbuch singing. Round about me nature was sleeping. Only here and there a timid roe rustled through the foliage, or a village bell rang from far away. Everything, everything provided nourishment for my melancholy fantasy. Once more I looked back at Tübingen from the hill at Lustnau; a gray mist hung over it. 'Farewell, Brothers,' I shouted over to them once more, and went on my way."[9]

Shortly after that, Neuffer moved to Stuttgart. Now Hölderlin was quite alone. The letters from his last two years at the seminary bear witness to the ever widening gulf between the fantasy world of the poet-prophet, which we examined in the last chapter, and the world of friendless loneliness in which he really lived. The assertion that Hölderlin was now, after Neuffer and Magenau had left Tübingen, more alone than ever before, requires some qualification. We know that Hegel and Schelling became his partners in study and that much of Hölderlin's somewhat desultory study of philosophy during those years was the result of the influence that the two boys, who were now just about his only friends among those left in Tübingen, exerted upon him. But it seems that they were never able to compensate him for the loss of Neuffer and Magenau. He mentioned Hegel and Schelling only very seldom in his letters.[10] More and more he was giving himself over to the world of fantasy and memory. Only after he had left Tübingen did he begin to give any indication that he considered Hegel the kind of friend that Neuffer had been. In fact, the period of his really close association with Hegel did not come until Hegel moved to Frankfurt and became Hölderlin's confidant and, perhaps, consoler during the latter part of his stay in the Gontard house which had become more and more unendurable. In Tübingen, Hegel and Schelling, the young philosophers, could inspire Hölderlin in his philosophic studies; they could not, however, replace Neuffer and Magenau in his heart, because they were not poets. They inspired him in, and directed his readings in, the philosophers. Hölderlin swore to work with them in order to bring about the Kingdom of God on earth. Their communal study of Kant and Plato influenced many of the Tübingen Hymns. But Hölderlin yearned for the companionship of other poets and for the lost days of the Bund.

9   VII, 1, p. 421.
10   Hölderlin's first reference to Hegel was negative; he wrote in January 1790 that he was upset because Hegel and Märklin had made better grades than he (32.24ff.). The fact that he said little about Hegel or Schelling after Neuffer's and Magenau's departure was perhaps in part due to the fact that he wanted to play on Neuffer's sympathy in an attempt to hold his friendship. But that in itself indicates that he did not a first find Hegel's friendship as rewarding as Neuffer's.

"... you must have known that I need your sympathy and that there could only be a wilderness about me and in me," Hölderlin wrote Neuffer on 28 November 1791, "and it must have annoyed you that I was too lazy to make one happy hour for myself and pour out all my thoughts to you [*mich erleichtern*]. Brother! It has seemed to me, since I have been back here, as if my dear ones have taken their strength away with them; I am indescribably stupid and indolent. Seldom are there *lucida intervalla.* And when I think of how you [two] now awaken, you and our Magenau, gaining in strength through love and happiness, and how I was so full of pride and courage in the divine hours that I celebrated down there with you, and that I could be another person if it were not for my situation [*Lage*], which suits me least of all — then, of course, I would like to get far away from this place."[11] "That I am still in the seminary is due to my mother's request. For her sake one can surely pass a few years in bitterness."[12]

Now that his friends had finally escaped from the school, his own fate, which he knew at bottom to be the result of his own impotence and inability to assert himself against his mother, was all the more depressing. How different in tone was his letter to Neuffer in April 1792 from the buoyant self-confidence of the Hymns that he was writing at that time! "You and the dear image appear before me, of course, in my brighter hours. But the dear guests do not find a particularly gracious host. I have relinquished all my hopes, as I wanted to. Believe me, the beautiful flower that blooms even for you, the most beautiful in the wreath of life's joys, will never bloom for me on earth. Of course, it is bitter to know that such beauty and magnificence is on earth and to have to say to oneself — it is not for you! But is it not foolish and ungrateful to want eternal joys if one has been fortunate enough to have a little happiness! Dear Brother! I have lost my courage, and so it is not good to want much. I cling to everything that I believe might give me forgetfulness and feel, each time, that I am out of sorts and unable to be happy like the other children of men. I think a thousand times that it should be different, if only I had you with me. You cannot imagine how often I miss the glorious days that we lived here together."[13]

This letter set the tone for all of his letters to Neuffer from Tübingen. When he thought of how his friends were enjoying life, he found that it was really not so romantic to be the "one alone" who "stays behind," as he had characterized himself in the poem "Lied der Freundschaft." It was, of course, inevitable that he would begin to resent his friends' happiness. In the same letter to Neuffer, he wrote: "When you are among your friends, think how nice it would be for the poor boy in Tübingen if he were also there."[14]

11   47.9ff.
12   47.55f.
13   50.3ff.
14   50.38ff.

It was just as inevitable that his resentment would increase when his friends found sweethearts and fell in love. Magenau fell for Caroline von Olnhausen from Weinsberg in the spring of 1792. In March he wrote Hölderlin of his love: "She loves me; that is all I can say to you. I hardly know any more myself and want to know nothing more."[15] That letter, which Hölderlin received in March, must surely have had something to do with his assurances to Neuffer, one month later, that he himself had given up all hope of enjoying the rewards of love in this life.[16] But, in reality, that was only a repetition of the same theme upon which he had been playing in letters to his mother for more than a year. It was not that he did not have any interest in girls but rather that the vow he had made to himself never to marry made it difficult for him to relate to young girls. He may have been afraid that one of them would trap him just as Luise Nast — as he now saw it — had trapped him earlier. This made it difficult for him to adapt to people his own age or take advantage of the social life available to a student in Tübingen. His "loneliness," which he had cherished when Neuffer and Magenau had been there to share in his lonely pursuits, now weighed heavily upon him. He wrote to Rike soon after she had become engaged: "You have reached your goal. Who knows where the wind will yet blow my little ship? I am assured that I will always find a port with our dear Mother and with you, Sister of my heart! Oh, I have often thought of you! It was not right that I did not stay [at home] until you had announced your engagement. But I would have remained an unimportant person at the affair. Is our dear Mother, in the midst of the sorrows that may, of course, afflict her tender heart, still happy about the step you are taking? Heaven knows that it is my sincere, firm intention to make up to her through joys all the pains she has taken with me for so long."[17] His regret at having failed to stay at home for the announcement of Rike's engagement because he would have been "an unimportant person" corresponds perfectly to the confession he made to his mother two months later: "I can hardly demand of myself that I adjust to some circles — acceptance into which I am supposed to consider an honor, as people say — with their foolishness and dishonesty. That does not mean, however, dear Mamma, that I do not make my social calls dutifully. The circles of which I am speaking consist mostly of younger people."[18] In September he had written Neuffer ". . . I simply have no joys here. There I sit almost every night in our old cell and think of the many vexations of the day and am happy that it is over. Because I do not adapt to the fools, they do not adapt to me."[19]

15   VII, 1, p. 24.
16   50.5ff.
17   52.7ff.
18   55.8ff.
19   54.11ff.

He was remaining true to the *Bund*. The love affairs of his friends and the ease with which they were adjusting to life in regular society seemed treasonous to him. He even grew jealous of Neuffer's flirtations and was, at least to some extent, relieved when he learned that his friend had fallen in love with Rosine Stäudlin. "Our hearts cannot endure love for mankind if it does not have near it those it loves. How often we said to each other that our *Bund* was a *Bund* for eternity. I — fool that I am — had forgotten that. Truly I am a petty person to let childish things turn me against you. At bottom, however, it was no unimportant misunderstanding. You were changed; your affairs of the heart had made you so uncertain. You did not know yourself; how was I to know you as the one who was my first friend and whose friendship was dearer to me than my first love? You had to once again become the person you were in the happy time of our common joys and hopes and undertakings; otherwise our friendship was done for. But, praise God! now I know you once again! And I believe that we owe it mostly to beneficial love."[20] He assured Neuffer that an earlier affair with a girl of whom Hölderlin had not approved was nothing. "Now," he concluded, "you are, of course, on a better path. Just send me news from your paradise once in a while."[21]

In those same waning months of 1792, Magenau wrote Neuffer that Hölderlin had visited him and had told him of his plans to write a novel about a modern Greek youth.[22] Then he continued: "Holz spoke warmly of you, but his phlegmatic nature inhibits the warm utterances that, nevertheless, lie like embryos in his soul."[23]

The three friends were growing apart. Neuffer and Magenau were not the same. They had now gone out into life and were meeting adult responsibilities. For all Neuffer's talk about the danger of marrying too early, which Hölderlin had taken seriously, he had involved himself quite readily in the social life of Stuttgart and was engaged within less than two years after he left Tübingen. Hölderlin approved of Rosine Stäudlin as a match for Neuffer. He may have thought that Neuffer's marriage to the daughter of their publisher would keep the friends close together. But that his *Bundesbruder* would share in the frivolous flirtations of just those "circles" of young people to which Hölderlin refused to conform was a blow for him. Neuffer seems to have recognized his mistake and reverted to the role of "friend" for Hölderlin's sake.[24] Hölderlin asked for pity and got it. But the *Bund* was finished. The priesthood into which the *Bund* was supposed to develop was not to be realized in the company of Neuffer and Magenau.

20   57.5ff.
21   57.27f.
22   III, p. 296.
23   VII, 1, p. 435.
24   See Neuffer's letter of 20 July 1793 (VII, 1, pp. 33f.).

"I do not know what will become of our correspondence," he wrote his sister in June 1792. "There are always a thousand things running through my head, with which I cannot entertain you. I believe that it is the fortune and misfortune of loneliness that everything that one reads or writes is worked over more in one's soul; but it is, of course, bad when there is something else to be done that the inopportune guests, the thoughts about that which one has read or composed, block out those for which it is time."[25] There is no more illuminating passage in his letters from that time. He had once again given himself over entirely to his reading, his poetry, his dreams. He had sworn off life, and he had decided, as he would soon write his brother, to devote himself entirely to the betterment of "mankind" in the hope of "exerting a general influence."[26] As our study of the Hymns suggested, he had, by the end of his student years, become totally absorbed in his "mission" of revitalizing the world. His first task was to finish *Hyperion,* into which he hoped to breathe the spirit of Socratic Friendship, so that he, like Socrates, might "teach them all what love is."[27]

The more he lived himself into the role of prophet, the more he was forced to admit that he had no companions in his quest, that there were no fellow priests, and that he was a prophet alone. Almost as if in a dream, he prepared and submitted his *specimina.* The first: "Parallele zwischen Salomons Sprüchwörtern und Hesiods Werken und Tagen" — was almost completely mechanical. The other: "Geschichte der schönen Künste unter den Griechen" — showed only a modicum of reading on his part. It is interesting only in one aspect: Among all his judgments about Greek art, which were not his at all but were taken straight from Winkelmann, he continually emphasized the position of respect that the poet supposedly held in Greek society.[28] His mind and heart were concentrating on the mythology of another time. He had better things to do than waste his time on his schoolwork.

"My heart belongs to the dead," he wrote. But, very soon now, he would be propelled into the realm of the living.

---

25 51.2ff.
26 65.29f.
27 60.26.
28 IV, 1, p. 189 (lines 10ff.), p. 190 (lines 22f.), p. 191 (line 31), p. 194 (lines 10ff.), p. 198 (lines 15ff.), p. 201 (lines 1ff.), p. 202 (lines 21ff.), p. 204 (lines 1ff.).

11

HOFMEISTER HÖLDERLIN

In August 1793, little over a month before he was to leave the seminary for good, Hölderlin touched on his progressive withdrawal from the social realm in a letter to Karl. Since Litzmann first based a presentation of Hölderlin's life on his correspondence in 1890,[1] this passage has been one of the most famous. Here, for the first time, Hölderlin revealed to a member of his family how firm was his intention of living apart from others as much as possible and how firmly he was convinced that he could best serve humanity by avoiding individual human beings.

"I know it well," he wrote, "this awakening of the youthful heart; I too have experienced them, the golden days when one attaches oneself to everything with such sincerity and brotherly love, and when interest in everything still does not satisfy, when one wants *one* thing, *one* friend in whom our soul might find a reflection of itself and rejoice. Were I to tell you the truth, [I would say] that I will soon have outgrown that period. I am no longer so devoted to individuals. My love is mankind — not, of course, the depraved, enslaved, slothful mankind, as we only too often find it even in our most limited experience. But I love the great, beautiful trait even in depraved men. I love the race of the coming centuries. For this is my most cherished hope, the belief that keeps me strong and active: Our grandchildren will be better than we; freedom must come sometime, and virtue will thrive more readily in freedom's warming, holy light than in the ice-cold zone of despotism. We are living in an age in which everything is working toward better days. The seeds of enlightenment, these quiet desires and exertions of individuals toward the education of the human race, will spread and grow in strength and bear magnificent fruit. Behold, dear Karl! It is that to which my heart is devoted. That is the holy goal of my desires and activities — this: that I might awaken seeds in our age that will bring forth fruit in a future one. And so it happens, I think, that I attach myself to individuals with somewhat less warmth. I would like to exert a general influence [*Ich möchte ins Allgemeine wirken*]; the universal does not let us simply ignore the individual, but, at any rate, we do not live for the individual with our whole soul once the general has become the object of our desires and endeavors. But I can, nevertheless, still be the friend of a friend, perhaps not so tender a friend as before, but a faithful and active friend. Oh! When I find a soul that strives, as I do, for that goal, that soul is holy and precious to me, precious above all. And

[1] Carl C.T. Litzmann, *Friedrich Hölderlins Leben. In Briefen von und an Hölderlin* (Berlin, 1890).

now, Brother of my heart! that goal, the education, the improvement of the human race, that goal that we will perhaps only imperfectly attain during our life on earth, which will, however, be attained the more easily in later times the more we have laid the foundation in our sphere of influence, that goal, my Karl, lives, I know, (perhaps just not as clearly defined) in your soul. If you want me for a friend, then that goal shall be the bond that unites our hearts more firmly, more deeply, more inseperably from this point on. Oh, there are many brothers; but there are few brothers who are such friends."[2]

What are we to make of this mixture of incompatibles? On the one hand, a pronounced, apparently not completely unconscious, arrogance ("I am no longer so devoted to individuals"); on the other hand, an enthusiastic dedication of self to the cause of improving mankind. We might, of course, proceed in the traditional way, arming ourselves with all the time-honored clichés about Hölderlin's future significance to philosophy and art and then bend all our energies to the task of manufacturing lofty phrases with which to portray (tearfully, of course) that splendid moment at which the youth was first awakened to a consciousness of his own potential greatness and of the as yet unrealized possibilities for mankind. We could then proceed to portray the young hero girding himself for the hard struggle that lay ahead of him and humbly accepting the mission imposed upon him by fate — in pursuit of which he wandered from town to town, menial task to menial task, from disappointment to despair, as men failed over and over again to recognize and appreciate his genius, from misunderstanding to persecution, from deepening despondency into madness.

But we know that the truth was more prosaic. We have traced the growth of his autistic self-estimate and know quite well that there was no such moment of awakening to a sublime truth, but rather a torturous process of growing insecurity, which made it necessary for him to write letters like the above in order to bolster his flagging self-confidence. It would be much easier for us to accept the traditional view of his life; for, if we did, we would be able to fit all the pieces together neatly, like in a jig-saw puzzle. We could speak of the coldness, feelinglessness, and unspeakable cruelty of the world, which cared so little for its savior that it proceeded to crucify, little by little, the man who cared so much for mankind. But we know that it was not so. For we have seen that the notion of a mission, which first appeared in his letters and poetry as early as 1790, was part of a defense mechanism, a rationalization for his progressive, self-imposed isolation from others.

However famous his letter to Karl in August 1793 may be, there is good reason to believe that it has never been read closely by those who seek to praise

2 65.6ff.

the sentiments expressed therein.[3] An analysis of the letter reveals quite unequivocally that self-protectiveness prompted the sentiments expressed in the passage quoted above and moved him to reveal his feelings to Karl. The way in which he structured his remarks indicate that he intended primarily to justify his antisocial attitudes to Karl — and then influence his brother to interest himself in the very things that Hölderlin found so edifying, dedicate himself to the same cause, withdraw from companionship with other men (as he would later suggest to Neuffer when Rosine Stäudlin died), and thus become the "one friend" he was always seeking.

He began with the sentence: "I am no longer so devoted to individuals"; then followed the famous passage about his concern for future generations. But the latter remark is clearly intended to justify his former expression of a lack of interest in others. He did not say: "I think one should devote oneself to the betterment of mankind in general, *therefore* I am trying not to let myself be swayed so much by my concern for individuals." Rather his reasoning ran: "I have outgrown the stage of life in which you find yourself, where one is enthusiastic for everything and everybody. I really care less for individuals now than before. I *think* this is because I have devoted myself to mankind." This reading is correct, I think, because it is his lack of interest in individuals of which Hölderlin is sure, while the "I think" refers specifically to the role of his devotion to the general welfare of the human race. In this sense, the passage represents a culmination of nine years of dwelling on his moral superiority to his classmates. In 1784, when he had written his former teacher, Köstlin, that he could not get along with the other boys at school because he considered them sinful and found fellowship with them degrading, he had felt ashamed of those feelings.[4] But much had happened to him during those intervening nine years. He had learned that one could justify rejecting society through the thought of Rousseau and the young Schiller. He had gradually come to believe that it was possible for him to be a misfit simply because he was more perceptive than others. He also had learned to justify rejecting the society of his day by swearing allegiance to a better world in the future.

This is really central to his love for mankind, which he carefully defined so as to exclude all living people, unless, of course, Brother Karl agreed to foreswear life also and become the "one friend" of the poet. He loved "the race of the coming centuries" and rejected the "depraved, enslaved, slothful" men of the present. This, of course, made it impossible for him even to consider seriously the prospect of becoming a preacher and thus exerting an influence on real people. But, characteristically, he seems never to have considered a position as a

---

3   Michel, for example, already sees the letter as an expression of the "hopes, goals, expectations assured of victory with which the whole German intellectual class had been seized," but says nothing about what the letter tells us about Hölderlin himself (p. 93.).

4   1.8ff.

teacher in the Duchy, in which he might, over the years, have influenced the educational practices and thus have made school life more tolerable for other sensitive young men than it had been for him.[5] Such a liberalization of the educational system might have been a real, tangible contribution to the growth of freedom, which he considered all-important in the improvement of mankind. He considered none of those possibilities because, unlike Schiller and Rousseau, Hölderlin did not think as much about improving man through bettering the human situation as about simply changing the very nature of man altogether. In order to accomplish his aim, he sought to "exert a general influence." That meant, as he had already indicated in his letters to Rike, living as far away from other people as possible and writing books, which others would then read and at which they would marvel. When all the poeticizing is stripped away, he was really devoting his life to — not much at all. He loved no one at all, unless one really believes that one can love people who are going to inhabit the earth at some future time.

So much for his commission to the service of mankind. It too was a poetic embellishment of self-centered thoughts. And yet — Hölderlin believed every word of it. His need to insulate himself against social pressures and, at the same time, to prove to himself (as well as Karl) that he had no real reason to feel guilty for needing such security resulted in the curious inversion of values that made possible such passages as the above, in which washing one's hands of mankind was, quite sincerely, proclaimed to be the highest service that one human being could render his species.

Such complex psychic needs did not let him consider fulfilling his legal obligation to the State Church that had housed and fed him for nine years.[6] And so, when he wrote his mother about his plans for the future in August 1793 — in a letter that, unfortunately, has been lost — he seems to have put forward two possible courses of action. Most of all he wanted to move to Jena immediately and try to establish his financial independence from Mother and escape the Church once and for all by earning his living as an independent journalist. This plan was quite unrealistic, but may not have seemed so to Hölderlin, who, for the rest of his life, would repeatedly underestimate the difficulties involved in pursuing his impulses. Seventeen months after this, in January 1795, he would assure his mother that he would have no trouble in subsisting until Easter on the money that Frau von Kalb had provided for him and that by then he would have completed enough contributions to Schiller's journals to have established himself

---

[5] When he might have been employed as a teacher in Tübingen in late 1795, he wrote Hegel: "I . . . am simply not suited for it" (107.11f.).

[6] When Hölderlin had enrolled in the Upper Cloister School at Maulbronn, both he and his mother had to sign a document in which it was promised that he would not consider taking up any profession other than the ministry and that he would serve wherever the Duke commanded (VII, 1, pp. 355f.).

on firm financial footing.[7] Both assurances turned out to be much too optimistic. Similarly, in 1798, he would assure her that he would be able to live off the money that he had managed to save at Frankfurt until his journal was flourishing.[8] But his funds ran out more quickly than he had imagined, and the journal was never published.

When he suggested that he be allowed to move directly to Jena in 1793, he may have also been overestimating the reputation he had gained locally through his poems, which had appeared in Stäudlin's journals; he may also have thought that his publisher's recommendation would bring him to Schiller's attention and that a man of Schiller's insight would surely recognize his talents. When he did meet Schiller in the fall, however, Schiller's estimate of his character and intelligence was that they were, at best, mediocre.

He knew that Mother would not be as optimistic as he about the probable outcome of such a daring venture, and so he proposed an alternative. He suggested that he might take a job as a *Hofmeister,* that is, a private tutor for the son of a well-to-do family who received room, board, and a modest salary for his services. This plan was much more realistic. It was an accepted way of earning a living for young men who had literary or academic ambitions because, as a *Hofmeister* one had time to study and write. Kant had served as a *Hofmeister* for several years until he earned his doctorate. Fichte had held a similar post until Kant helped him. Hegel, who would graduate from the *Stift* with Hölderlin, had already accepted such a post in Bern.

Frau Gok, probably to her son's delighted astonishment agreed to the latter plan. Elated, Hölderlin wrote: "I wanted to ride over to Nürtingen for an hour today in order to thank you personally for your goodness and motherly care, your letter made me so jubilant. But chores prevented me. Believe me, dear Mamma, I learn with each day to know and honor more the spirit and heart to which I really owe what I am. It is often compellingly clear to me, whenever I have read such a sincere, wise letter, once more, that few have such a mother as I; and, you see, that is my familial pride — that is worth infinitely more to me than if my mother signed herself Baroness of someplace or other."[9]

But he had not forgotten that Jena was his real goal, and he did not let her forget it either. Soon he let her know that he was planning to move on to Jena as quickly as possible. Around the beginning of September he wrote: "If I can find a good position as *Hofmeister,* then I will put off my Jena project until I have perhaps earned (at least) one half of the necessary amount through tutoring and writing."[10]

---

7 92.81ff.
8 He had saved 500 florins in Frankfurt, which he hoped would last "at least a year" (165.15). Ten months later, in August 1799, Frau Gok, according to her accounts, sent 133 florins to him in Homburg and then another 100 florins on 10 October (VII, 1, p. 290).
9 63.2ff.
10 64.13ff.

He hoped to accomplish his goal even more quickly by finding a position in Jena. Failing in that, he hoped to locate in Switzerland, perhaps to be near Hegel.[11] Neither in the letter to Karl nor in the exchange of letters with Mother was there anything that would indicate that Hölderlin considered a job as *Hofmeister* anything other than a way-station on the road to Jena and Schiller's side. Several factors played a role in his search for a suitable position. It was, first of all, important that he find a position as quickly as possible so that he could obtain leave from the Church Council; otherwise, as soon as he successfully completed his State Examination, he would be subject to a Church appointment, which in Württemberg was legally binding.[12] Second, he wanted to locate near or in an intellectual center (Jena, of course, being his first choice), where he might make the right contacts and be stimulated to work hard on his novel. Third, through leaving the Duchy and rupturing his family ties he hoped to alter radically his relationships with others and thus regain his self-respect.

This last consideration, though unexpressed, was implicit in all his planning and was perhaps the single most important motivation during the next few years. His determination to escape from Mother, Church, and friends was basically a need to escape from himself — from the shy, reticent Hölderlin who suffered so much from his largely self-imposed ostracism. During his school years it had not been merely his loneliness or his peculiar position among his fellow students that depressed him. During the period of the *Dichterbund* he had revelled in being different from others. What tormented him was the knowledge that his classmates did not long for his friendship and did not recognize his voluntary withdrawal from them as a sign of his superiority — or as voluntary at all. All this he hoped to change by starting over somewhere else. This too was to become a behavior pattern that would stay with him: Whenever he felt that he was failing and was not respected as he needed to be, he began to feel restless. At last he would move on. His departures from the employ of the von Kalbs in January 1795, from Jena six months later, from Frankfurt in 1798, from Hauptwyl in 1801, and from Bordeaux in 1803 were all somehow flights from reality. The only case in which this may not have been technically correct was when he left the Gontard house. Legend has it that he was run out of the house by a jealous husband. But Susette's letters indicate that, while the situation had surely become rather unpleasant, Hölderlin left on his own volition. That he also left with her blessing may indicate that she had recognized how agitated he became under the constant strain.[13]

---

11   He mentioned both Jena and Switzerland in the missing letter: for in the letter in which he thanked her for her acquiescence, he wrote: "Neither Jena nor Switzerland have to fear the war" (63.24ff.).

12   VII, 1, pp. 355ff.

13   In her first letter to him, which she seems to have written between 28 September and 5 October 1798, she wrote: "I have already often regretted that, when we parted, I advised you to leave at once. I still have not grasped what feeling moved me to entreat you

What did he demand from life that he was unable to find anywhere? Not success in the normal sense. Fame, which he certainly desired, would not have meant to him an escape from his isolation but rather an escape *into* isolation and justification for it in his own eyes and in the opinions of others. This was probably why Schiller's example so fired his imagination. Schiller had fled the Duchy and had established himself as a respected professor in Jena. His fame was spreading across Europe. He saw in Schiller's situation in Jena the utopian union of respect and aloofness. Respected by all, the "philosophic spirit" could cut himself off from all those with whom he did not want to associate, and they would suffer from the separation — not he. Presumably the common herd would then benefit from the "general influence" that his books would exert upon historical development. They were to be eternally grateful, but they would not be in a position to make personal claims on him. He could limit his social contacts to those precious few individuals who, like him, belonged to the poetic aristocracy.

In September 1793 Hölderlin received the most unbelievable bit of news: Schiller, who was recuperating from one of his periodic bouts of illness, was in Stuttgart and had offered Hegel a position as *Hofmeister* near Jena. Hegel had already accepted a position in Bern and thus declined. We can imagine Hölderlin's reaction to the news! Now, at last, fate seemed to be opening up doors for him. Now he had the opportunity of locating near Jena and bringing himself to Schiller's attention at one blow. We may be sure that his mind was filled with things quite different from tutoring a little boy when he prevailed upon Stäudlin to write Schiller on his behalf. Stäudlin knew what was in his young friend's mind also, for, when he wrote Schiller, he emphasized Hölderlin's artistic ambition and talents. He referred to Hölderlin as "the hymn-writer, who shows no little promise" and said that it was his ambition "to transcend the narrow sphere of his homeland and a vicarage therein." "I do not have to speak of his poetic talents," Stäudlin added, "for his works give adequate testimony of that."[14]

In that same month Hölderlin was interviewed by Schiller. In that interview he learned that, if he was hired, he would be *Hofmeister* to Fritz von Kalb, the nine-year-old son of Schiller's close friend Charlotte von Kalb. From Schiller's conversation the awe-struck Hölderlin would have gathered that the von Kalb family had connections with Schiller.

---

so earnestly. I believe, however, it was fear for the entire feeling of our love, which grew too loud within me at this violent rupture, and the power which I felt made me at once too yielding. I later thought how much we might have planned for the future, had only our separation not assumed this hostile tone; no one could have denied you entrance into our house" (Carl Viëtor ed., *Die Briefe der Diotima* Leipzig, 1922, p. 15).

14 VII, 1, p. 467.

The interview lasted less than a half hour.[15] No record exists of Hölderlin's initial reaction to his first meeting with his hero. Schiller, however, was not exceedingly impressed. He wrote Charlotte that Hölderlin seemed qualified for the job and had good recommendations from everyone who knew him. But then he added: "They speak highly of his character; and yet he does not seem quite mature [*gesetzt*], and I do not expect much profundity from him in his knowledge or conduct. It could be that I am misjudging him, because I am relying merely on . . . his speech and appearance."[16] Nor does Schiller seem to have been more than moderately impressed with Hölderlin's poetry. He wrote as if he had read the poems in Stäudlin's almanac, but limited his remarks to the rather non-committal "not lacking in poetic talent."[17]

Hölderlin, probably filled with excitement and enthusiasm for what he hoped lay ahead for him, gave up the trips he had planned to friends and relatives and returned home to await word from Charlotte von Kalb.[18] His letters during the following weeks show just how desperately he wanted the job. In early October he wrote Neuffer: "I am counting the minutes until I learn that and if I am allowed to go out into the world. Here I am as active as possible. But nothing will bear fruit."[19] Still afraid that the opportunity might slip away and that he might, after all, be appointed to a vicarage, he was preparing for the worst. "I preach as much as possible in the surrounding villages in order to stay in practice as long as I still have time."[20]

By 20 October he was desperate. "I am still up in the air about my *Hofmeister* position [*Ich bin mit meiner Hofmeisterstelle schlimm daran*]. I still have no definite answer and, therefore, cannot make my preparations and buy my supplies. My mother would have to get a lot of things for me ahead of time, and I am as curious as she, for the uncertainty of my future situation does not put me in a good mood."[21]

Neuffer knew his old friend and probably recognized the signs of dangerous irritability. He turned to Stäudlin, who wrote Schiller, asking why there should be such a delay.[22] In the meantime, however, Schiller had received a definite answer from Charlotte von Kalb on 29 October. He informed Hölderlin immediately.[23]

---

15 According to Schiller's letter to Charlotte von Kalb of 1 October 1793 (VII, 1, p. 469).

16 *Ibid.*

17 *Ibid.*

18 VI, 2, pp. 641f.

19 67.11ff.

20 67.20ff.

21 68.12ff.

22 Stäudlin wrote: "Since he is curious in any case about the determination of his fate, but particularly would like to be informed about it because of the preparations necessary for such a trip, he has urgently requested that I inquire of you whether you have received as yet any answer from Saxony? " (VII, 1, p. 472.)

23 VI, 2, p. 641.

Several aspects of Hölderlin's behavior during those weeks of indecision between the interview with Schiller and the final verification of the offer are striking. Although he obviously wanted the job rather badly, there is nothing in any of his letters to indicate that he ever once considered what tutoring a nine-year-old boy would mean. He wrote Neuffer about the prospect of "going out into the world." The next passage of that same letter, in which he spoke of how "active" he was, must refer to his writing, for thoughts about literature would explain the transition to the next sentence in which he asked for copies of Bürger's and Voß' journals.[24] On 20 October, when he wrote Neuffer the letter that caused his friend to intercede with Stäudlin on his behalf, he began with the symbolic passage: "Winter has arrived in my head sooner than out of doors. Daytime is very short. The cold nights so much longer. Yet I have written a poem to

— the playmate of heroes,
Iron necessity."[25]

Poetry and the hope that he would get the job and thus escape — these things alone were in his mind. There was no mention of Fritz von Kalb or indication that he wondered how he would fare as an educator. All that seems to have been beside the point. What mattered was whether he would escape, what kind of an impression he had made on Schiller, and his own future.

Soon he was disappointed. Through the long weeks of negotiations with Charlotte von Kalb through Schiller, the lady herself had been in Jena. Hölderlin knew this, for he wrote his acceptance of her offer to Jena. Through the conversation with Schiller and the second-hand correspondence with Charlotte he had gotten the mistaken impression that Waltershausen was on the outskirts of Jena. He still assumed that to be the case early in December, when he wrote his State Examination and applied for official leave to take the job. Church archives show that he applied for, and was granted, leave for a period of three years in order to accept a *Hofmeister* position "at the home of von Kalb in near Jena."[26] Thus, as late as two weeks before he was to leave for Waltershausen, he did not even remember the name of the town for which he was destined and still confidently believed that he would be quite near Jena and Schiller. He may well have envisioned the town as being so close that Schiller would be a frequent visitor in the von Kalb home.

Waltershausen was actually the antithesis of everything that Hölderlin had been hoping for. It lay more than 100 kilometers from Jena in an out-of-the-way corner of Thüringen. This might be relatively insignificant, were it not for the

24 67.13ff.
25 68.4ff.
26 VII, 1, p. 478.

fact that it has always been assumed that Hölderlin was perfectly satisfied with his life in Waltershausen until the summer of 1794. His ignorance of the true location of the town, coupled with the mystery surrounding his journey there during the Christmas holidays of 1793, throws a dim but suggestive light on his attitude toward his job and destined surroundings *before* he ever arrived at Waltershausen and suggests that dissatisfaction may have arisen while he was underway.

Adolf Beck, while editing and annotating Hölderlin's letters for Volume VI of the *Stuttgarter Ausgabe,* discovered that Hölderlin's account of his trip to his mother, which has been preserved in his letter to her from Coburg on 28 December and which he repeated in substantially the same form when he wrote Neuffer and Stäudlin two days later, can hardly be accurate. According to that account, he left Nürtingen on the morning of 20 December (Friday), departed from Stuttgart that afternoon, arrived in Nürnberg on the 22nd (Sunday), left for Erlangen on Christmas Eve, where he then attended services on Christmas morning before leaving for Bamberg that same afternoon. He said that he had arrived in Bamberg "long after midnight" (therefore on the 26th) because of "the cold and the unsafe road."[27] He said that he traveled to Coburg on the 26th, whence he wrote his mother that he had been somewhat delayed "due to the bad road."[28] This timetable would have put him in Waltershausen on Friday the 27th, one week after he had left Nürtingen.

Judging from the letters alone, something is obviously wrong. The run from Erlangen to Bamberg was made easily in one day, and the trip would hardly have lasted until "long after midnight." Moreover, he wrote his mother on 3 January that he would have been in Waltershausen a week "tomorrow," which, in order to agree with his account of the trip, should read "today."[29]

In an effort to solve the worrisome discrepancies, Beck unearthed two new bits of evidence which indicate that Hölderlin's account of the trip was not merely mistaken but probably untruthful. First of all, the newspaper: *Nürnbergische Frage- und Anzeige Nachrichten* reported that "Herr Professor Hölderlin from Stuttgart" arrived and took rooms in an inn *on Christmas day* — at the very time he was supposed to be traveling by public coach between Erlangen and Bamberg.[30] Even more puzzling is an entry in the "Visitors' Book" of the *Nürnberger Lesekabinett* (Nürnberg Reading Room): "M. Hölderlin from Württemberg. / Introduced by Herr Legationssekretär Schubart. / the 26th of December 1793."[31]

27　70.30.
28　69.5.
29　71.6.
30　VI, 2, p. 647.
31　*Ibid.*

Ludwig Schubart, the son of the poet whom Hölderlin had visited during the Easter vacation of 1790, belonged to the Prussian Foreign Service and was, at that time, attached to the Prussian Legation in Nürnberg. In his letter to Stäudlin and Neuffer, Hölderlin mentioned having visited Schubart while he was in Nürnberg. What is striking about the "Visitors' Book" is that it records Hölderlin presence in Nürnberg on the 26th — forty-eight hours after he was supposed to have left the town!

It is highly unlikely that two independent sources would have made coincidental errors in dates, particularly since the two days in question were Christmas Day and the day after Christmas. The seemingly inescapable conclusion is that Hölderlin returned to Nürnberg on Christmas day from Erlangen and then, beginning on the afternoon of the 26th, made the long trip all the way from Nürnberg *over* Erlangen to Bamberg, which would explain why he arrived "long after midnight." Since this would have put him in Waltershausen one day later than he reported, it would explain why he said "tomorrow" instead of "today" in the letter to his mother on 3 January.

All these hints and bits of evidence fit together so neatly that we are compelled to assume that the above reconstruction of the trip, at which Beck arrived, is substantially correct. This, however, raises much knottier questions than were raised by the discrepancy in dates that started Beck's search in the first place. First, why did Hölderlin suddenly interrupt his trip on Christmas Day, backtrack to Nürnberg, when he was already traveling behind schedule (Charlotte von Kalb had stipulated that he should arrive in Waltershausen at Christmas), and then continue his trip the next day at a hurried pace over bad roads in an obvious attempt to make up for the lost time? Secondly, why did he conceal these irregularities from both his mother *and* his friends? His dishonesty toward his friends makes the circumstances appear even more suspicious. He might normally have wanted to conceal from Mother the fact that he had acted in a way that she would have considered irresponsible; but that will not explain why he practiced the same subterfuge on his friends. Beck admits that his own theory — that Hölderlin decided to return to Nürnberg impulsively because he wanted to spend as much time as possible with his friends and enjoy the active intellectual life of the city before going on to isolated Waltershausen — does not explain why he did not say as much to Neuffer and Stäudlin, who surely would have understood his feelings.[32]

There exists no positive evidence to help us unravel the mystery. But there is one item of negative evidence that allows us to speculate: We do not know when Hölderlin first discovered that he was headed for an "out-of-the-way" village[33] far from Jena and Schiller. We recall that two weeks before he left home he had

32   VI, 2, p. 648.
33   Beck refers to Waltershausen as "sein abgelegener Bestimmungsort" *(Ibid.).*

been unable to remember the name of the town. The general designation "near [*bei*] Jena" would indicate that he still thought that he would be on the outskirts of the university town. That had been one of the main attractions of the job.

When did this enthusiasm suddenly evaporate? When did he discover that he would actually be more than 100 kilometers away?

It may well be that he did not discover the truth about Waltershausen's location before he left home on 20 December. Since he knew that he would be traveling by public coach, he may well have set out on a prescribed route that meant nothing more to him than a list of towns through which he was supposed to pass. This conclusion may not be as far-fetched as it sounds at first. Even today, when one drives one's own car and plots one's course with the help of precisely scaled maps, few people who move to Greencastle, Indiana have any true conception of relative distances, and thus most are quite disappointed to learn that they have not really moved to a suburb of Indianapolis after all, but rather have condemned themselves to the same type of village life that Hölderlin discovered in Waltershausen.

It may be that he first discovered the truth along the way — in Erlangen or on the coach from Nürnberg. What would have been his reaction? Certainly dismay and disappointment, and probably an immediate evaporation of all his former enthusiasm for the job in which he had no real interest anyway. He may have returned to Nürnberg impetuously and then, having had some time to consider his action, he would surely have seen that he could not simply fail to appear and had no choice other than to go on to Waltershausen and make the best of a disappointing situation. To fail to show up and report for duty would have meant a Church appointment back in Württemberg. Even more frightening, such an irresponsible act would have been fatal to any budding relationship which he hoped to be springing up between himself and Schiller. In Waltershausen he might never lay eyes on Schiller; but he would at least be living with people who knew the great man and who visited Jena regularly. Such connections might prove useful in the future. All these considerations might have moved him to reconsider during the two wasted days. Then he would certainly have tried to make up for lost time and make the normal two-day run from Nürnberg to Bamberg in one day.

All this is speculation. But it would explain why Hölderlin would have concealed his actions from his friends — particularly from Stäudlin, who knew Schiller. Hölderlin would certainly not have wanted Schiller to learn that he had almost run away and not lived up to his end of the bargain. Most of all, such vacilation would have been a typical reaction to bad news.

This much, at least, can be said about Hölderlin's reaction to Waltershausen: He tried to make the best of an unpleasant situation. Although Frau von Kalb had asked him to arrive before Christmas, she had neglected to inform her husband; and so Hölderlin arrived unexpected. Münch, the former *Hofmeister* whom Charlotte von Kalb had come to dislike, probably because he was too severe in his punishment of her son, had not yet left. But Hölderlin pulled himself together and tried to look on the bright side. Things must not have appeared quite as bleak as they may have seemed on the road. At least the job still allowed him to escape from Mother and Church. He could, after all, go back to the plan he had outlined in his letter to Mother back in August and work hard until he had enough money to move to Jena with her blessing.

He was already looking beyond Waltershausen and had little real interest in educating his nine-year-old pupil. Of course, the same could be said of any *Hofmeister* in that day. But Hölderlin, because his dedication to his ambitions was so single-minded and because he had never developed the capacity to deal with problems involving other people and necessitating compromise, was faced with a singularly difficult task in reconciling his dreams, his demand for a good deal of time for his own pursuits, and his need for isolation and solitude with his duties as *Hofmeister* to Fritz von Kalb.

The year he spent as Fritz von Kalb's tutor in Waltershausen and Jena, roughly the year 1794, was Hölderlin's first experience in the adult world of social responsibilities. That experience, together with his stay of six months in Jena in 1795, is the first of four cycles in his life in which he would leave home full of hopes and ambitions, experience initial elation at his good fortune in having found a "stiuation" [*Lage*] so well suited to his needs, and then suffer a severe psychic shock as a result of a series of direct conflicts with those people with whom he came into contact every day. The second cycle ran from December 1795 until the late spring of 1800. That was his longest period of struggle and involved both his stay at the Gontard house in Frankfurt, where he fell in love with the wife of his employer, and his abortive attempt to establish a literary journal while he was living with Sinclair in Homburg. Each of those first two periods involved a job as *Hofmeister,* which ended in his having to leave under something of a cloud, followed by an attempt to establish a literary reputation against great odds and under great financial burdens. Later the cycles became much shorter. Twice more he tried to establish his financial independence, once in Hauptwyl in Switzerland and then in Bordeaux in southern France, as a *Hofmeister.* But neither of these last attempts to earn his living as a tutor was followed by a period of complete withdrawal into his work, during which he tried to establish himself as a free-lance writer. By then he was too sensitive for that. By then his failure as a *Hofmeister* alone was enough to drive him back to Mother, broken, timid, fearing contact with the world, and finally, in 1802, quite mad.

We are concerned with the young Hölderlin and will, therefore, pursue the story only up to June 1795, when he fled from Jena, thus bringing the first cycle

to an end. By that time the pattern for his life had already been established.
From then on he would repeat the process of venturing out into the world,
succumbing to a severe psychic shock, fleeing from the scene of his anguish,
devoting himself entirely to his work, and then, under great financial burden and
personal hardship, giving up and returning home. By then we shall have
demonstrated that the story of the adult Hölderlin is, in essence, the tale of how
the same defense mechanisms of withdrawal and forced poetization of the world
about him that he had developed as a student proved inadequate for adult life,
which demanded compromise and a realistic perception of the social world. In
1795 the story of the young Hölderlin properly comes to an end. His behavior at
Waltershausen was the first indication that there would never be, properly
speaking, an adult Hölderlin, but only a stereotyped re-enactment of the youth's
vain attempt to make his way in a man's world.

Up until now Hölderlin's life at Waltershausen has been judged according to
the fluctuations in his relationship to Fritz von Kalb alone. Looking at things
from that point of view, the following outlines emerge. From January until July
his letters were uniformly cheerful about how he was faring in his new job; from
July until October he maintained a strict silence about his pupil and devoted his
letters largely to discussions of philosophical themes, his novel, and his concern
for the progress of his own education. Then in October the first hint of discord
arose. He now found his *Hofmeister* duties burdensome. The discord between
student and teacher increased when they were sent to Jena, where Hölderlin,
surrounded by a throbbing intellectual life, began to resent Fritz' demands on
his time and energies and began to beat the boy. Finally, in January 1795, after
Charlotte had come and tried to lend a hand, Hölderlin wrote his mother,
soundly denouncing the boy, admitting that he had given up his job, and
declaring his intention of staying in Jena, where he hoped to study at the
university and support himself by contributing to Schiller's journals and
completing *Hyperion* as quickly as possible.

Externally it would seem that Hölderlin's changing attitude toward the boy
and his job was an understandable reaction to the boy's behavior. As long as
Fritz loved him, respected him, and seemed to be progressing in his studies,
Hölderlin professed deep love for him. Later, when the boy's father made
Hölderlin aware of the fact that Fritz was masturbating, Hölderlin, always
horrified by the unpleasant side of life, reacted immoderately. He was, no doubt,
unable to hide his disgust from the boy, and their relationship could only
deteriorate. Hölderlin's action would, of course, have been aggravated by the
fact that he resented having to spend his precious time, which he needed for his
own studies, in supervising the boy's sexual habits.

I once suggested such an interpretation.[34] The persistent feeling that

---

[34] Roy Shelton, *Friedrich Hölderlin's Letters: A Biographical Study* (Nashville,
Tennessee: Vanderbilt University, 1966), pp. 113ff.

something more could be discovered and that Hölderlin's attitude and behavior in Waltershausen must surely be of a more complex origin than a mere overreaction to Fritz von Kalb's sexual aberrations and his own inability to deal with the problem have led me to spend several months in reappraising this most important year in the life of the young Hölderlin. During that time it became clear to me that Fritz von Kalb's behavior played a relatively minor role in determining Hölderlin's attitudes toward his job and that other events, which are only hinted at in the available documents, were of much greater importance. If the following appraisal is, at best, speculative and anything but complete, it must be remembered that we are dealing with the life of a poet whose life was considered unimportant for many years. Much of the evidence has been lost during decades of a lack of interest. Perhaps what really motivated Hölderlin in 1794 could never have been discovered in any event. The following account will not satisfy the reader who demands answers to all the questions. It is also unsatisfying to me. Much rests on speculation, and another person might treat the material differently. I think, however, that it is better to raise those questions about traditional readings of history and point out possible explanations (as long as one does not attempt to paper-over the still unanswered questions) than to perpetuate simplistic presentations that obviously do not do justice simply because they appear to give complete knowledge. If I cannot provide a satisfactory explanation for Hölderlin's failure at Waltershausen and its destructive effect on his development after that, I can at least point out the shortcomings of the traditional view, to which I too once subscribed, and suggest possibilities that have not been raised before.

In seeking to understand the influences which led Hölderlin to completely reverse his attitude toward his pupil and particularly in order to understand just how unimportant the actual behavior of Fritz von Kalb was in determining Hölderlin's own attitudes, it is helpful to examine two letters in which Hölderlin described his experience at Waltershausen to his mother. The first was written in April 1794, four months after he had assumed his teaching duties.

"At last, dear Mother! I can once again satisfy my desire to communicate with you. I am happy if you and my whole family are doing as well as I. I am healthier than ever, do what there is for me to do with zest, and find for the little that I can do a thankfulness that I would never have expected. My situation is, in fact, very favorable; in friendly association with good, clever people, in undisturbed activities and beneficial joys of mind and heart, with the obliging kindness with which the smallest comfort that I might want is provided, with the prospect of a situation even more beneficial to my education — I would really have to take great pleasure in complaining if I did not assure you that I am very satisfied."

"My time is divided between my teaching, the social life of the house, and my own work. My teaching is having the greatest success. There is no thought of my having to resort to the violent method even once; an expression of dissatisfaction tells my Fritz enough, and only seldom does he need to be punished with a stern word. When we are all together socially, we mostly read aloud, first Herr Major, then Frau von Kalb, then I, alternating; and then we often discuss [what was read] at mealtime or on walks, seriously or jokingly, each to his own taste. Whenever I am, however, somewhat distracted by my own work, they know how I mean it, and I do not have to be entertaining if I am not in the mood. That this suits me perfectly, you can well imagine. The time that I have left over for my own pursuits is now more precious to me than ever; I will probably spend the next winter in Weimar, in the circle of great men that that city contains. Then I will instruct, in addition to my pupil, a son of the *Konsistorialpräsident* Herder and live in his house. Frau von Kalb, who is a trusted friend of Goethe and Wieland, also wants to introduce me to them. Next summer I will go there and bring the young Herder back here, and then, with him and my Fritz, will go without the parents to Weimar for the fall, perhaps for a long time."[35]

In a continuation of the letter he went on to say: "I find everywhere that a prophet counts for little in his own country, and, away from home, too much!"[36]

The thoroughly optimistic, self-assured tone of the letter is complemented by other evidence as well. From the beginning he spoke of Fritz in the most laudatory terms. In January he wrote his sister: "I can adjust well to my situation . . . . Had I no joy in the world, my dear little boy would make up for that . . . . He is perfectly suited to be educated in accordance with more humane principles."[37] When Fritz fell ill that spring, he wrote his mother: "Sometimes I was very worried about him. The beautiful young soul has all my love."[38] As late as the middle of July Hölderlin wrote Neuffer that Fritz was "of a right good type, honest, cheerful, tractable, with harmonious, in no way eccentric, intellectual talents, and pretty as a picture from head to foot."[39]

For six months whenever Hölderlin spoke of the boy he added a few more brushstrokes to a flattering portrait of a bright, responsive, good-natured boy, who loved his *Hofmeister* and would have done anything to please him. Discipline, he emphasized, was no problem whatsoever. One can summarize all his remarks about Fritz during these first six months of 1794 in Hölderlin's own words: "My teaching is having the greatest success."

Charlotte von Kalb also believed that he was making progress with her son. In June she replied to Frau Gok's complaints about how hard life had been for her: "You possess, however, in your knowledge of the good character and rearing of

35   No. 78.
36   78.50f.
37   72.15ff.
38   79.23f.
39   83.74ff.

your children a very secure fortune — I am judging the others by our dear friend Hölderlin, who, through his extraordinary concern for my son, is bringing me the good fortune of being able to call myself a happy mother also. My husband and everyone who knows him appreciate him very much. If we might just convince him of how grateful we are and how we would do anything that might contribute to his contentment."[40] She wrote to Herder: "He [Hölderlin] seeks to keep his pupil's mind active and alert, and he will surely exclude from his instruction anything that amounts merely to dead or verbal knowledge. Otherwise he allows him the most complete freedom and seeks to deprive him (through the boy's own renunciation) only of that which might harm him morally or physically, determined, of course, by the situation and his own insight."[41] Even as late as August she was writing Schiller's wife: "The only person who is sometimes dissatisfied with Hldn. — is he himself."[42] And in an undated letter to Frau Schiller she wrote: "If Fritz is becoming a promising little boy, it is through him [Hölderlin] alone."[43]

In sharp contrast to his own and Frau von Kalb's optimistic estimates of his progress with Fritz stands the letter to Mother in January 1795, in which he explained why he had been forced to give up his post.

"Do not be surprised, dearest Mother, that now, when you, judging from your last letter, supposed me already to be in Nürnberg, I am writing you again from here.

"I think that this surprise should not be very unpleasant for you when I have explained in more detail.

"I am here at my own expense, without finding it necessary to be a burden to you in any way. I was, for good reasons, not quite frank to you about my affairs up until now. I thought that I could overcome the difficulties and real sorrows that I encountered to an uncommon degree on my path through continued and purposeful endeavor, and did not suppose that the step would finally become necessary which makes it impossible for me to avoid telling you some things about which I was silent until now, because I must render you an account of the change that I have made. That my pupil, as well as having mediocre natural talents, was still ignorant in the highest degree when I began his education was, of course, not pleasant, and yet [was] no reason not to undertake his education with all earnestness, and I did that, as God is my witness and as his parents also recognize, with all conscientiousness in accordance with my best judgment.

"That, however, a complete insensitivity to all reasonable teaching with which I wanted to affect his unruly nature was in him; that here neither a firm

40 VI, 2, p. 691.
41 Hellingrath Edition, VI, p. 246.
42 *Ibid.,* p. 697.
43 Hans Heinrich Borcherdt, *Schiller und die Romantiker. Briefe und Dokumente* (Stuttgart, 1948), p. 666.

word would bring forth respect nor a friendly word devotion was, of course, a bitter discovery for me. I sought the reason for this almost continued callousness in the whippings, which, judging from everything, had been administered to him to excess before my arrival. Often it seemed that I had awakened him from his sleep; he was frank, reasonable; in the meantime, no sign of his rudeness seemed to manifest itself in him, and on such days he made incredibly fast progress in his studies. I was idolized as if I had worked miracles with the child; my honest preacher in Waltershausen pressed my hand so warmly and admitted to me that he, after all the attempts that he had made with the boy, had despaired and had been put to shame by me; and even the uneducated people in the village and in the house felt the happy metamorphosis that had taken place with the child. That made me happy and brave. But, just as quickly and unexpectedly, he fell back once more into the greatest apathy and slothfulness. His father — with too great forebearance toward me, of course — had made me aware of a vice, traces of which had been noticed on the child from time to time. The condition of his disposition and spirit finally made me even more attentive, and I discovered, unfortunately, partly through his own admission, more than I feared. I cannot possibly explain myself more clearly to you. I almost never left his side for one moment, watched him nervously day and night; his body as well as his soul seemed to recover, and I hoped once more. But in the end he knew how to get around my watchfulness, and his callousness, the result of that vice, increased, particularly toward the end of the summer, to such a degree that it almost robbed me of my health and cheerfulness, and thus my mental powers of their fitting activity. I exerted all means in an attempt to help — in vain! I frankly declared my sorrow that all means had failed several times, asked for advice, for support; they consoled me and asked me to endure for as long as it would be possible for me. To recompense me, to some extent, for many lost bitter hours and also to divert the boy and to give him more exercise through dancing lessons etc., they sent us to Jena. Through unspeakable effort, almost continuously staying awake at night, and through a just strictness, I succeeded in decreasing the frequency of the malady for a while, and so [his] progress in his moral and scientific education was once more quite good. But it did not last long; the complete impossibility of really affecting the child and helping him attacked my health and my disposition most violently. The fearful night-watches disturbed my mind and made me almost incapable of any work in the daytime. Meanwhile, Frau von Kalb came; the noble woman suffered very much over her child, and also over me. She and Schiller asked me to make just one more attempt. Even the Major sought to console me and wrote in person that I should just try to hold out as long as I could. We left for Jena, and since there, despite the efforts of the doctors and my continued exertion, the vice increased in the child every day, while my health, my courage, [and] my good spirits decreased with each day, Frau Major declared to me that she could no longer watch me suffer any longer; she did not want me to perish for no reason, advised me to come here and maintain myself here as long as I could, promised me that she would exert all her influence for my future happiness, and provided me with money for a quarter year."[44]

Nine months, it is true, separated the two letters. Much had happened in the meantime. But the traditional explanation, which contents itself with the observation that relations between teacher and pupil deteriorated rapidly after Hölderlin learned that Fritz was masturbating, does not suffice to explain the glaring discrepancies between the remarks Hölderlin made about Fritz during the early months of 1794 and those he made after he had given up his job. His revelations to his mother in January 1795 indicate downright subterfuge on his part, for he had continually talked about the intelligence and sunny disposition of his pupil. Now he asserted that he knew from the very beginning that Fritz was "ignorant in the highest degree" and that he possessed only mediocre talents. The tone of the letter is, of course, dictated by repugnance toward the boy's sensuality. But that is not all. Now Hölderlin was being honest. He had always disliked the boy, which, as we shall see, contradicts his letter to Schiller, in which he outlined his plans for the boy's education. His repulsion was emphasized by certain stylistic devices that contrast sharply with the style of his earlier letters. He never mentioned Fritz by name now. All the terms of endearment with which he had embellished his earlier letters had fallen away. Earlier he had been fond of using the personal pronoun "my" in connection with Fritz; the pronoun "my" has now vanished and is replaced with "her son" or "their boy." All the pleasant characteristics he had observed in his pupil a few months before have given way to a completely negative appraisal: "sloth," "depravity," "stubbornness."

Most important of all, he now admitted that he had *always* known that Fritz was a brat and had recognized from the very beginning that his education would be an exceedingly difficult undertaking. Furthermore, he indicated that he had held out as long as he did only because Frau von Kalb, her husband, and Schiller had asked him to be patient and endure a little longer. Even if due allowance is made for exaggeration due to Hölderlin's obvious agitation, one fact remains indisputable: He had remained silent about his real feelings for many months. His letter makes it quite clear that he had known that Fritz was masturbating for some months, for he said that the situation had worsened considerably near the end of the summer. And yet as late as July he had still been writing laudatory accounts of the boy's character.[45]

Up until now no one seems to have read carefully Hölderlin's account to his mother and compared his story with the optimistic letters that he had written

[44] No. 92.
[45] 83.74ff.

from January until July. If anyone had done so, he would have concluded, as we must conclude, that the earlier optimistic accounts were, at least, very greatly exaggerated. Why would Hölderlin have insisted on representing his job as just the position for him? Partially, of course, he exaggerated the limited success he was having as *Hofmeister* in letters to his mother because he rightly feared that it was only a matter of time until she tried to convince him that he should come home and accept a Church appointment.

But that was only part of the reason. More important was his belief that, in coming into contact with the von Kalbs, he was getting close to being introduced to the intellectuals with whom Charlotte was acquainted. As always, Hölderlin's optimism was the result of self-deception. Fear of Mother's interference and the belief that he would be able to earn enough money as *Hofmeister* to make possible a life as an independent author combined to force him to try to make the best of life at Waltershausen, although he found life in the "out-of-the-way" village and his duties as tutor quite distasteful.

Enthusiasm for Fritz was never central to his early optimism. In the first of the two letters to his mother, Fritz and the great success he was having with the boy were mentioned only in passing. The greater part of the passage was devoted to a description of the idyllic, basically irresponsible life he was leading in Waltershausen. He spoke mostly of how he, the Major, and Frau von Kalb read to each other aloud and then discussed what they had read; he wrote of how he was able to be himself at all times, to give free expression to his moods even if they made him unsociable, and to allow his ruminations about his "work" to determine his moods. In brief, he concentrated on just those aspects of life at Waltershausen that corresponded to his ideas of what a perfect *Lage* for writing and self-education should be. The little vignette about the *Hofmeister* socializing with the members of the family like a trusted and cherished friend reads curiously like something from a novel.

Life at Waltershausen was actually quite different from the idyllic scenes that Hölderlin painted in his letters. Through the entire year he spent among the von Kalbs he gave no indication in any of his letters that he was aware of the tragedy that haunted the family. Charlotte was eleven years younger than the Major, whom she had married in 1783 thanks to the match-making of her brother-in-law, the Major's unscrupulous brother, who had been relieved of his post in the Weimar government because of misconduct, and who had married Charlotte's sister Elenore in order to get his hands on her inheritance.[46] He was probably interested in finding an equally lucrative match for his brother, who was, at that time, returning from the United States, where he had fought in the Revolutionary War. The Major was, no doubt, a better husband to Charlotte than his brother was to Elenore. At least he did not follow his brother's example and run

---

46　VI, 2, p. 644.

through her inheritance, bankrupting the family. Charlotte's marriage was, however, unhappy from the beginning. The young, imaginative, romantic Charlotte found no fulfillment in her union with the older man and, consequently, spent months at a time away from home. By 1793 they were little more than strangers living under the same roof for several months out of the year.[47]

Hölderlin perceived none of this. His remarks about his employers show that same propensity for judging positively, uncritically, unperceptively, all those who were kind to him. Those early letters from Waltershausen contain only one type of reference to the von Kalbs: They were always filled with praise, and somehow they seem to have earned the praise through being nice to him. The Major was "the most educated, most pleasant man in the world," because "he received me as a friend and has not changed since."[48] The Major let the young *Hofmeister* ride his horses and took time to talk with him.[49] To Hegel he wrote of Charlotte: "You will hardly find a Frau von Kalb in your Bern. It would surely do you good to bask in her sunlight."[50] By then, however, he was far beyond the point at which he might have been able to form an unbiased opinion, because he was convinced that Charlotte would use her influence with established authors on his behalf.

All this sounds familiar. We have seen how, during his student years, he had developed the capacity to withdraw into himself, shut out everything around him, and devote himself almost exclusively to his own studies and poems. We have seen, moreover, how, at an early age, he had come to prefer his dream-world to real life and how he had developed the capacity to select from among his acquaintances those people whose personalities he could remold in his imagination so that they could fill the role of "beloved" or "friend." Something similar seems to have happened at Waltershausen. Hardly interested in Fritz von Kalb, unable to forget his own concerns long enough to formulate a realistic appreciation of others and respond to their needs, he solved the problem of adjusting to his environment by proclaiming that the situation in which he found himself corresponded perfectly to the *Lage* that he had created in his imagination. In Maulbronn the Nast cousins had become the poet's "friend" and "sweetheart." Similarly, at Waltershausen Fritz von Kalb became, in Hölderlin's mind, the responsive little boy who loved his tutor — that portrait of Fritz that appears in letter after letter during the first six months of 1794. But it was a portrait of a mental image. There was no more an original for Hölderlin's verbal painting of teacher and student living together in perfect harmony and close friendship than there had been for the equally idealized picture of the young

47 VI, 2, p. 645.
48 71.7ff.
49 71.29ff.
50 84.28ff.

poet finding consolation for his sorrows in the waiting arms of Luise Nast. Nor was the wish-dream of the idyllic life among loving family members in Waltershausen any nearer to the truth than his dream of himself as the "philosophic mind" had been during his last years in Tübingen. It was all a dream. It would have to end just as surely as the *Bund* had come to an end in the normal course of things.

It was in the midst of this mixture of reality and dream that he lived from January until he learned from the Major that Fritz was masturbating and that he was expected to cope with the problem himself. But even before then there is considerable evidence that Hölderlin was already under great strain. He knew that, eventually, he would find himself at the crossroads once more. Sooner or later he would be leaving Waltershausen, either to go to Jena or some other intellectual center or — back to the Duchy, to the mother-dominated world of Church and family life. This particular course of strain influenced him from the very first. During his first weeks at Waltershausen, he warned his mother that his letters would probably be irregular and brief because the mail-coach ran irregularly and he often did not know that mail was about to be collected until about an hour before the coach was to leave.[51] A truly loving son, who had nothing to conceal from his mother, would not have waited until the mail-coach was about to leave before he started his letters.

"I love the great and beautiful potential even in depraved men," he had written Karl. In that same letter he had defined his dream for the future: "that I might awaken seeds in our age that will bring forth fruit in a future one." But he had no time for "individuals." His resolve to pursue the education of Fritz von Kalb in earnest was doomed from the start, because he refused to admit to himself that the boy was one of those "individuals," that he was quite untalented, and that he might even be "depraved." His mind closed, his dreams fixed on the life that, under the influence of his reading, he conceived as the only one possible for him — he admitted no discrepancies between the dream and surrounding reality. Success as an intellectual, as an author, was imperative. He succeeded in striking an acceptable balance between his duties as *Hofmeister* during the first three months of his stay because his teaching duties were not really very demanding. The letter to his mother in April represents the culmination of the first of three periods into which his stay in Waltershausen naturally falls. That careful balance was doomed from the beginning because it rested on the fallacious assumption that Fritz von Kalb was a bright, cooperative little boy who would treat his *Hofmeister* as tenderly and courteously as did his parents — and whose education would not take much time.

---

51   73.29ff.

Then something happened. In March 1794 Hölderlin wrote Schiller. It was the first letter of a rather one-sided correspondence which would extend over many years. In that inconstant exchange of letters Hölderlin all too often humbled himself shamelessly before the older man, who had been his hero and model for years.[52] Even after he had come to resent Schiller and had learned to assert himself against his hero's overpowering influence, he was never quite able to rid himself of a stifling sense of awe of the man. That probably contributed a good deal to his inability to gain Schiller's respect as an equal. As month after month went by after his flight from Jena, Hölderlin felt compelled to humble himself and beg for Schiller's respect again and again.[53] Most of all he wanted the great man to confirm his own conviction that he was indeed talented and had something to offer to the world. It seems that the more he felt compelled to reject Schiller's influence on his poetry, the more he needed the man's personal approval. Finally he was reduced to begging for one kind word from Schiller and wrote Schiller repeatedly without any excuse for doing so except to send Schiller another poem, even though Schiller had long since stopped answering his letters.[54]

The first letter of this unhappy and, for Hölderlin, humiliating correspondence was ostensibly an explanation of how he was proceeding to teach Fritz von Kalb. What he produced may well be one of the most bizarre letters ever written concerning the proper way to educate a young man.

"In an hour in which the nearness of a great man made me very serious, I promised to do honor to mankind in my present sphere of activity, which is so extensive in terms of its results. I promised it to you. I give you an accounting.

"Educating my pupil to be a human being was and is my purpose. Convinced that all humanity whose other name is not Reason or which is not directly related to the same is not worthy of the name, I thought that I would not be able to develop early enough in my pupil his most noble self. Now he could never be in the innocent state of nature and was never in it. The child could not be so sheltered that all social influences on his awakening talents might be excluded. If, therefore, it was possible to bring him to a consciousness of his

---

52 As late as 2 June 1801, when he wrote Schiller of his plan to lecture in Jena, he added: "Should you advise against it, then I will be more content on another course and will see how I shall support myself.

"You will not disdain to lend some light to the course of my life through your interest, because I don't really seek in a vain way to attach an importance to it which it does not possess.

"You are the joy of a whole people and seldom see that. So it may not seem entirely unworthy to you, when you see a new joy of life, which came from you, light up in one who honors you completely" (232.66ff.).

53 See Böhm's remarks about Hölderlin's ambivalent attitude toward both Frau Gok and Schiller (Böhm, II, p. 678).

54 When Schiller finally responded, Hölderlin wrote: "Your letter will be unforgettable for me, Noble Man. It has given me new life" (144.1f.).

moral freedom, to make of him an accountable person, then that had to take place. Now, as it seems to me, he hardly has any receptivity for the larger moral relationships, but he was receptive to the more limited ones, of which the relationship of the friend to a friend was, in my case, the only useful one.

"I did not seek his favor. I also tried to guard against his trying to gain mine, and here nature needed no great resistance. Rather I followed the dictates of my heart, which, in good moments let me become a trusted brother of the cheerful, quick, adaptable nature of the boy. He understood me, and we became friends. I sought to relate all my instruction concerning what should and should not be done to the authority of this friendship – the most innocent that I know. But, since every authority to which the action and thought of man is related sooner or later causes inconveniences, I gradually ventured to add whatever he should or should not do was not to be done or not to be done merely for his sake or my sake; and I am sure that, if he has understood me in this, he has understood the most important thing.

"The means to my end are based, to some extent or other, on this. I will not burden you with a detailed explanation. The deep respect for you with which I grew up, through which I have often been strengthened or humbled, and which even now does not let me become lax in my own or my pupil's education – this respect prevents me from becoming too verbose."[55]

The purpose of this letter could only have been to attract Schiller's attention in the hope that, with Charlotte's help, Hölderlin could count on Schiller's help in the future. Interesting is the way in which he approached Schiller. He did not say simply that he was being bold enough to enclose a poem, which he hoped Schiller would consider good enough to appear in his *Thalia*. He did not get around to that until the end of the letter, after he had tried to impress Schiller with the conscienciousness with which he was proceeding to instruct Fritz. Even more, he concocted the entire educational plan so that he might appear learned, so that he could demonstrate to Schiller that he too was a "philosophic mind." This was not simply subterfuge (although Schiller would surely have been justified in considering it such), for Hölderlin probably believed everything he said. Through the torturous thread of reasoning, in which he tried to display his knowledge of Kant ("humanity whose other name is not reason . . . is not worthy of the name") and Rousseau ("the innocent state of nature"), he may well have been reproducing exactly the twisted type of thinking that led to his complete failure with Fritz von Kalb. The train of his thoughts was carefully, if subconsciously, calculated to justify falling back on the old "friend" stereotype. He probably seriously believed that all the high-flown philosophizing and amateurish psychology would serve his pupil's interests. We can see, however, that Hölderlin was actually busy deceiving himself into the belief that Fritz

---

[55]   76.1ff.

could be made into the "friend" — the only male figure to whom Hölderlin had ever been able to relate. When faced with the necessity of relating to other men as real human beings, he was puzzled, or repelled, or did not quite know how to behave. Hence his resentment when Neuffer did not live up to his ideas about him and entered into the social life of Stuttgart; hence his repeated attempts to interest Karl in those things that moved him; hence his desire to transform Fritz von Kalb into the stereotyped "friend."

There may be even greater significance to that letter. The letter may indeed mark March 1794 as a crucial turning point in his development. He had recovered from the disappointment of learning that he would, in fact, not be near Jena, but had condemned himself to a quiet, undisturbed, but also unpromising, country life by convincing himself that he had found just the right place in which to pursue his studies and write his novel, that he had found a pupil who was not only an intelligent boy, but also a worthy "friend," and that, while at Waltershausen, he would be able to make the contacts necessary for him to begin a career as an author. Although it is true that all these notions would have never occurred to him if he had not had that peculiar ability to ignore reality and transform his surroundings into a dream-life more in keeping with his idea of the poet's paradise, it is also true that his letters during those first three months in Waltershausen show him far more relaxed than he had been in years.

Then, beginning with the letter to Schiller, his letters changed. They were no longer scribbled off in the last few minutes before the mail-coach left town; they gradually assumed all the characteristics of well-reasoned essays. From that point on he was not simply reporting that he was happy — he was now trying to prove it to himself. The letter to Mother in which he described the beautiful, relaxed life at Waltershausen was the first of many carefully worded letters to members of his family. At the same time, he limited his remarks more and more to his own feelings, his own studies, his own "work" — and spoke less and less of people and events. Already in the letter to his mother in April, he was writing that "the time that I have left over for my own pursuits is now more precious to me than ever." Soon he would be writing of little else.

Why did all this suddenly change in the spring? Why did his letters begin to show signs of tension and of his preoccupation with his work? We cannot say with much certainty. But near the end of that letter he wrote to Schiller in March, shortly before he mentioned the fact that he was enclosing a poem, a curious passage occurs.

"She [Charlotte von Kalb] informed me that I might have had the good fortune of being near you for a few months. I am deeply aware of what I have thrown away. Never before have I lost so much due to my own guilt. Let me believe, great and noble man, that your nearness would have worked wonders in me. Why must I be so poor and yet be so interested in the realm of the spirit? I shall never be happy. And yet I must exert my will, and I *will*. I will become a man. Grant me, now and then, an attentive glance! The good will of man is, after all, never completely wasted."[56]

It is impossible to say what opportunity he had allowed to slip through his fingers. We do know, however, that it would have meant being close to Schiller for several months. It is no wonder that he was plunged into deepest despair. Already one senses the end of the relaxed frame of mind in which he had written all his letters since his arrival in Waltershausen. Whatever the event that so disappointed him may have been, he began to write more and more exclusively about his studies and his work on *Hyperion*. It was as if the sudden disappointment, whatever its nature, caused him to throw himself with redoubled effort into the business of "preparing" himself for the next winter in Weimar, as if he was afraid that his chance of establishing his independence was slipping away once and for all.

As early as 20 April he began his letter to Mother: "I hasten to assure you that I am healthy in body and happy in spirits and am at present still settled in Waltershausen."[57] Near the end of that same letter, he wrote: "I cannot and do not want to think of changing my situation now."[58] Obviously Frau Gok was concerned that she might well lose her son for the Church and had made reference to her hope that he would soon be ready to come home and settle down.

His answer to this new pressure from home was a number of letters to family members, which he was sure his mother would read. He continued to emphasize his happiness and his intention to stay in Waltershausen. On 21 May he wrote Karl: "I doubt that I will leave my present situation so quickly. I am in the right state of mind for self-education; [I have] also motivation from without, and on good days my other activities serve as hours of convalescence. It is uncertain as yet whether I will not spend next winter in Jena as well as in Weimar. Both [prospects] are, as you can imagine, most pleasant to me. Here I live very quietly. I recall only a few periods in my life that I might have spent with equal composure and peace.

"You know, Brother! how valuable it is not to be distracted by anything. You enjoy this good fortune also. Rejoice in it! When one has even a single hour of the day left over for the free activity of the spirit, in which one can see to one's most important, noblest needs, then that is a lot — at least enough to strengthen one and cheer one up for the rest of the time.

"Brother! sustain your better self, and let nothing suppress it, nothing! I am very interested in knowing what direction your spirit is taking. Be so good, Dear, as to inform me of such things as often as you can."[59]

---

56 76.47ff.
57 79.3f.
58 79.29f.
59 80.11ff.

Here one can already sense how difficult it had become for him to give up part of his precious time for Fritz, when he knew (but would not yet admit even to himself) that the boy was really not worth the effort. Already he let it be known that those few hours each day that he could devote to his own work served to strengthen him for "the rest of the time," which is as much as admitting that his *Hofmeister* duties had now become a burden to him. And yet, something else emerged in that letter to his brother. His customary antisocial attitude, which he had expressed to Karl in his letter in August 1793, had not changed. He had suppressed it for a number of reasons. He had wanted to do everything he could to convince his mother that he was happy and that it would be a mistake to insist that he come back to the Duchy; similarly he sought to convince Schiller that he was doing his best to educate Fritz von Kalb. To his brother, however, he still wrote in the same old tone; he still emphasized the theme of remaining true to oneself and letting one's "better self" be distracted by nothing. The old polarity of life and dreams still haunted him. He still felt that he had to shut all other people out in order to accomplish anything.

The continuation of the same old attitudes was a sure sign that his talk about how happy he was, how much he loved Fritz, and how much he enjoyed the company of the von Kalbs was a valiant, but vain, effort at self-deception. This impression is supported by the letter that he wrote his brother-in-law in June 1794. He did not quite feel at ease writing the man who had married his sister.

"You will allow me, dearest Brother-in-law," he wrote, "to give you news about me once in a while. I would have done it sooner if I had not always hoped to find the opportunity of entertaining you with something more interesting than I am myself.

"But in my lonely situation, which I find favorable in a number of ways, I must limit my news to my own existence."[60]

Later he went on to say: "I find more with each day that fate did not deal with me badly when it put me in the limited circle in which I live. One is more likely to straighten out one's thoughts and feelings when the objects round about are not too many.

"And yet my life is by no means hermit-like."[61]

These two letters are quite significant because they show that he was trying to communicate indirectly to his mother once again and reenforce through letters to others, who would then communicate with her, the notion that he was well and happy. His fear that an eventual confrontation with her was inevitable was, however, fully justified. Sometime in June, before he wrote his brother-in-law, his mother suggested that he accept a Church appointment near her, which seems to have involved the definite stipulation that the applicant marry.

[60] 81.2ff.
[61] 81.10ff.

Beck believes that the crisis may have been instigated by Elise Lebret, who had not yet given up all hopes of becoming Frau Hölderlin.[62] This may well have been the case, for, more than a year later, Hölderlin wrote Hegel that he was hesitant to accept a teaching position in Tübingen because of Elise.[63]

Now, however, faced with more direct demands from Mother, Hölderlin simply avoided answering her letter as long as possible. He concluded his letter to Brother-in-law Breunlin with the request: "Be good enough, dearest Herr Brother-in-law, to inform my dear mother of my continued well-being, because I will not be able to write this week, perhaps next week also."[64] Had he been taken to task for his failure to write, he could have appealed to the fact that he had been with the von Kalbs in Völkershausen all the time. Nevertheless, when he finally did get around to responding to her suggestions, he made no secret of the fact that he had found it very difficult to reply. On 1 July he wrote: "I almost fear that my long silence may have been particularly out of place at this time. You probably saw, however, from the letter I wrote my brother-in-law what was partially the reason for it. Beyond that, I confess to you that one part of your letter made it almost impossible for me to answer it as soon as I received it, even though I had already made up my mind in principle, as far as this case is concerned. I have seen for a long time that I would just about have to give up my education if I should choose a settled home-life. You will perhaps, as you have in so many other cases, throw up to me the example of others who would consider themselves fortunate to find so early a good post, as people say. But I believe it is neither immodesty nor day-dreaming when I consider necessary for my nature, as far as I know its needs, for now a situation in which I might foresee the possibility of nourishing my spirit through a multiplicity of objects, without the limitations of a settled burgher existence. Dear Mother! It is one's duty to know one's individual character, whether it be good or bad, and, as far as possible, to stay in circumstances or to try to get into such as are beneficial to just this type of character. Beyond that, it is completely against my principles to enter a position in *bourgeois* society in this way. If it only looked bad in my case, still I want to and should, particularly in such an affair, avoid even this."[65]

No one would deny that his decision not to take the position in question was a normal reaction, since, as it seems, accepting the position, which Hölderlin did not really want anyway, would have made it necessary for him to marry someone whom he either did not know at all or, at least, did not love. But he did not limit his remarks to a rejection of the specific offer. He rejected family life and the prospect of a settled position in society in general. He underlined, it is

62 VI, 2, p. 680.
63 107.10ff.
64 81.47.
65 82.4ff.

true, that phrase "just now," as if he could not yet bring himself to initiate his mother into the secrets of his grand scheme to "exert a general influence" on humanity through withdrawing from all contact with people. This was indeed the case. Not until 1798, while he was living with Sinclair in Homburg, did he try to make his mother understand his feelings and convince her that he could never accept the life that she had in mind for him.[66] But even now he leaves no doubt that marriage and family are not for him. There is no hint that his adolescent attitude toward marriage, that Neuffer had so swiftly outgrown after he left Tübingen, was changing. This is seen clearly in his letter to Neuffer in April 1794, which shows almost no understanding for Neuffer's more mature attitude toward life. There was only forgiveness for his friend's betrayal of the ideals of the *Bund*.

And yet there is some indication that Hölderlin knew that he was inferior to Neuffer in this regard. He wrote: "You are on the right path, Brother! You leave others with their heads muddled and go *your* way. It is a great art not to give one's whole heart to interesting objects if they would crowd out others that are already in one's heart. This is your art. You close your heart to nothing that is good and great but make only the appropriate room for it so that it might exist side by side with other things. Good for you! I wish I were able to do the same. A peaceful inner life is the highest thing that man can possess."[67]

In his remarks to Neuffer one sees a progressive, an obsessive exclusiveness in his opinions. This becomes particularly apparent when one compares the above letter, written before he "threw away" whatever opportunity there was to locate near Schiller, with the letter Hölderlin wrote his friend within two weeks after he had rejected his mother's suggestion that he accept a Church appointment. In that second letter to Neuffer, Hölderlin showed that he still dreamed of settling down with the girl of his dreams from time to time but then made it clear that he had now reached the conclusion that his nature would not let him even consider marriage as a real possibility. "When I dream that one day such a woman might become mine and that my hearth and home might be near you and Rosine, then I am sometimes able to set limits to the eternal yearning for another place, for another activity, or rather understand it better. All the more so since I see so clearly from my present situation how a restricted,

---

[66] Even then, when he was trying to make her understand, he was not completely able to assert himself. On 28 November 1798, he wrote: "My present work is to be my last attempt, Dearest Mother, as you say, to become somebody on my own *|auf eignem Wege ... einen Werth zu geben|*; if I fail in this, then I shall quietly and modestly seek to be useful to men in the most unpretentious post that I can find; I will take the striving of my youth to be that which it so often is — pride that arose by chance, an exaggerated inclination to leave the sphere prescribed to me by my natural talents and the circumstances in which I grew up" (168.28ff.). Two weeks later he admitted: "On every occasion I feel wonderfully how you rule me. . . ." (170.17f.).

[67] 75.34ff.

peaceful sphere of activity, simply because no multiplicity of objects tire us out, keeps all our faculties active and us all the stronger and purer, and how many a beautiful joy is concealed there, which one would not be able to see in passing. Well, as fate wills it! We cannot make valleys out of mountains and mountains out of valleys. But on the mountain we can enjoy the broad heavens and the open air and the proud height, and in the valley the peace and quiet and become all the better acquainted with the lovely and magnificent things that we have overlooked from above. Even better! If there is something to do on the mountain, then we clamber up; if we can plant and build in the valley, then we stay there."[68]

These characteristics that we have pointed out in those few letters of his correspondence from March to the middle of July that have survived — the reappearance of reticence toward his mother, his firm reiteration of his earlier rejection of family life because, as he believed, he was different from others and belonged on the mountain top, and the marked narrowing of his letters' range of content so that he now limited his remarks to his own interests or his hermit-like life — are traits that we have seen before. We have learned to recognize them as sure indications that his surroundings oppressed him, that he was unable to relate to those around him, and that he was once more withdrawing into that make-believe world of poetry and ideas from which, judging from his letters from January, February, and March, he had almost emerged until the disappointment at not being allowed to locate near Schiller. Even in those early months in Waltershausen he had ventured out timidly, falteringly, and had related, as we can see in retrospect, more to fantasms than to real people. Now, when he felt oppressed once more, he knew only one place to turn for solace. Automatically he scurried back to his books and his poetry.

Developing concomitantly with the disappearance of the von Kalbs from his consciousness, there began a period of renewed interest in philosophy. He now began writing of his study of Kantian aesthetics. Again, these references began to appear in his letters shortly after he wrote Schiller in March. In early April, for example, he wrote Neuffer: "Otherwise [aside from writing the poems, which are to appear in the summer number of Schiller's *Thalia*] I have been concentrating on my novel alone. I am determined to take my farewell of art if, in the end, I have to laugh at myself about this also. Incidentally, I am now kind of returning from the realm of the abstract, in which I had lost myself with my whole being. I now read only when I am out of sorts [*nur bei dürftiger Laune*]. I have been reading only Schiller's treatise *Über Anmut und Würde*. I do not recall having read anything in which the best from the intellectual realm and from the realm of feeling and fantasy has been so perfectly harmonized. If only this illustrious spirit stays among us a few more decades!"[69]

[68] 83.7ff.
[69] 77.10ff.

It was just after this letter that he wrote his mother that the time he had for his own work was more precious to him than ever. In May he wrote Karl: "Kant is almost the only thing that I am reading. More and more the magnificent spirit is revealed to me."[70] In June he wrote his brother-in-law: "As far as scientific [studies] are concerned, I am now dividing my time exclusively between Kant and the Greeks, am also seeking to produce something myself from time to time."[71] And on 10 June he wrote Hegel: "My activity is now fairly concentrated. Kant and the Greeks are my only reading. I am seeking to become well-versed in the aesthetic part of Critical Philosophy."[72]

Now we can summarize those influences that caused him to withdraw into himself and his books once more and devote himself exclusively to the world of ideas to the exclusion of social contacts. First, there was still the unrelenting fear of his mother's demands on behalf of the Church. This was and would remain a never ending source of tension. This made it imperative for him to succeed as a tutor in Waltershausen and, at the same time, prepare himself for life in Jena. Success as a tutor and establishing himself as an author were his short- and long-range goals. There was always the possibility that these goals would conflict with each other. That was a particularly perilous possibility for Hölderlin, who needed absolutely harmonious surroundings in order to produce.

Naturally his growing disenchantment with Fritz would have been a source of tension. But, while it alone has been singled out up until now, it was only one of a number of aggravating factors that constantly kept him on edge. Probably far more important than his feelings for Fritz was his fear that he would not accomplish his long-range goal. He may have half-suspected that he had not made a particularly striking impression on Schiller at the interview in September. If so, then there is little wonder that the knowledge that he had "thrown away" an opportunity to correct Schiller's opinion of him agitated him so greatly. But then he still felt that he could count on Charlotte to put in a good word for him with Schiller. Soon after the disappointment he was writing Neuffer that some of his poems were to appear in Schiller's journal during the summer. This must have elevated his spirits and yet deflated him at the same time; for he knew that Schiller's kindness was mostly a result of Charlotte von Kalb's influence.

Finally, unspoken at this time but always present, there was the constant inability to accomplish the mutually inimical goals of becoming a great poet and philosopher at the same time. Years later, when he finally opened his heart to his mother, he would conclude that he had erred tragically in dispersing his energies and devoting so much of his time and energy to the study of philosophy simply because he did not think it enough to be a mere poet.[73] In the late spring of

---

70 80.36f.
71 81.27ff.
72 84.46ff.
73 173.106ff.

1794, just when he felt time to be of the greatest importance, this state of being at odds with himself and not yet quite knowing why, probably kept him on edge as much as anything, because it made it difficult for him to make progress on *Hyperion*. He was doing double duty. His novel dragged on month after month with no end in sight. And yet he felt that, in order to attract Schiller's attention and solicit his help, he had to become a philosopher as well as a novelist.

Why did he feel it necessary, at just that time, to master Kantian aesthetics? Of course, it is true that the novel was becoming more philosophical in nature, but that is no answer. The gradual development of the philosophic aspects of *Hyperion* was a result of its author's conviction that he must prove himself as a philosopher. One might ask: Why did he feel it necessary to write a novel that would be not only a story of a young Greek's love for Melite, but also a philosophical treatment of *Bildung*, when, as the final version of *Hyperion* shows, the task was something like trying to mix oil and water? For *Hyperion* is really not very clear philosophy and not very compelling fiction. There is good reason to suspect that *Hyperion's* development illustrates better than anything else Schiller's stifling influence on Hölderlin. As early as 1790 Hölderlin had discovered "the philosophic mind," which he had made a model for his life. The living model was, of course, Schiller himself. And, during the 1790s, Schiller had turned more and more to philosophy. Hölderlin followed suit and hurled himself into a study of Kantian aesthetics, starting at the *end* of Critical Philosophy in order to treat the very question with which Schiller had struggled unsuccessfully in *Über Anmut und Würde*. Now, Hölderlin, however superior he was to Schiller as a poet (or would be when he finally broke through to formal originality), could not deep step with Schiller, who had a truly amazing gift for juggling categories and terms — probably because Hölderlin took the clichés much more seriously than Schiller did and demanded that the answers *feel* right as well as sound impressive. The result was, therefore, increasing tension and, inevitably, a growing resentment toward Schiller, which appeared first in October 1794 when he wrote Neuffer that he was sure he would be able to provide a more satisfactory answer to Kant's aesthetic dilemma than Schiller had managed in *Über Anmut und Würde*.[74]

From these complex and interrelated influences arose the impulses that drove Hölderlin into a new period of withdrawal. The external world was shut out. His novel and philosophic studies strained his capacities to the utmost. Here, as in his school days, he preferred the world of the intellectual formulation and the poetic dream to the real world. The solutions he had reached behind the sheltering walls of the *Stift* had not adjusted to reality. He had not allowed reality to correct his theories. None of those adolescent ideas that he had brought with him from Tübingen had changed at all. This is dramatically

[74]   88.92ff.

illustrated in his letter to his brother in August 1794. It could easily have been written a year earlier, so similar it was to the letter we cited at the beginning of this chapter in which he had first revealed to Karl his intention of continuing his studied avoidance of real people and real life.

"I have been in your debt for a long time now, dear Brother! But in the compact that our hearts concluded there is no provision stating that we are to make a lot of words with each other and write long letters, but that we are to become men and recognize each other as brothers under that condition. In ceaseless activity one develops into a man; through constantly striving to act out of duty, even if it does not bring joy, even if it seems to be only a little duty, as long as it is duty, does one develop into a man; through renouncing desires, through renouncing and overcoming the self-seeking part of our being that always wants to be comfortable and well, through waiting quietly until a greater sphere of activity opens up and through convincing oneself to limit oneself to a narrow sphere of activity if good results from that and if no greater sphere of activity opens up; through a peacefulness that is not offended by men's weakness, is not disturbed by their vain displays, false greatness, or feigned humility, and is only interrupted by pain and joy over the well-being or misery of humanity, only by the feeling of one's own imperfection – does one develop into a man; through unrelenting efforts to correct and expand one's concepts under the unshakeable maxim to recognize no authority at all in judging their legitimacy of reasonableness, but rather to test for oneself; under the holy, unshakeable maxim not to let one's conscience be swayed by one's own or someone else's false philosophizing, by the dismal Enlightenment, by the high-and-mighty nonsense that smears so many a holy duty with the name prejudice, but to avoid, just as much, letting oneself be confused by fools or villains who would like to condemn or make foolish a thinking spirit, a person who feels his worth and his rights in the person of humanity, in the name of free-thinking and the nonsense about freedom – through all this and much more does one develop into a man. We must make great demands on each other, Brother of my heart! Do we want to be like those poor people who are so satisfied in their knowledge of their limited value? Believe me, I feel rather strange when I consider the hopes people have for the coming centuries and then compare with that the crippled, small-minded, crude, presumptuous, ignorant, slothful youths of whom there are so many everywhere, and who are to play their role then. The few who are exceptions have to cheer up and support each other. One other thing! It is now necessarry that one say to oneself: Be clever; say nothing, however true it may be, if you are sure that it will serve no purpose. Never sacrifice your conscience to your cleverness. But be clever. These are golden words: Cast not your pearls before swine! And, whatever you do, don't do it in the heat of passion! Calculate shrewdly, and then execute with zeal! – I am certain that you agree with me that brothers should speak to each other in this way. Enclosed is a letter from Frau Major to our dear Mother. It is evidence of how seldom one does one's duty as a teacher when a teacher who acts generally out of conviction and conscience is regarded as something special in spite of the thousand mistakes that he makes."[75]

Rather than merely paraphrasing the letter, we have produced an admittedly inadequate translation above in order to show how amateurish Hölderlin's philosophizing still was two months before he would claim that he was surpassing Schiller in his treatment of aesthetics within the framework of Kant's system and how Hölderlin's real surroundings were being absorbed into the dream-world that he was constructing in his loneliness. The theme of "becoming a man" was both the goal of his life and the subject of his novel. It was worth spending some time in working out his thoughts on the theme in detail, as he would write Neuffer in October in an attempt to explain why he still had not finished the long-promised *Hyperion.*[76] If we assume that he was working hard on the novel and studying diligently Kant's *Critique of Judgement* and Plato's dialogues, then it is not surprising that he would write of his studies to Karl, whom he wanted to interest in those same themes. What is somewhat odd about the letter is the fact that Hölderlin was not talking about his studies at all but rather about his relationships with real people. His friendship for Karl was in no way realistically circumscribed in the letter or, for that matter, in any of the letters that followed. Little can be discovered about Karl from Hölderlin's letters, because he never wrote about Karl's problems, interests, or concerns. All his remarks, all his advice, all his admonitions were goal-directed. The goal was two-fold: first, to make of Karl a carbon copy of himself, therefore into the "friend" with whom he might share all his thoughts; secondly, he wanted to warn Karl concerning the evil people in the world and to prevent him from becoming one of those wordly young men whom he so despised. Little had changed during the past year. The "depraved," "slothful" "individuals" about whom he had written in August 1793 were still in his mind in August 1794. The only answer was further withdrawal into his studies, an intensified effort to move carefully through the world of men and avoid being touched by those around him. To accomplish this task it was necessary to "be clever."

We do not know the details of how Hölderlin tried to cope with the problem of disciplining Fritz von Kalb after he learned that the boy was masturbating. But the letter he wrote Neuffer just after he received the news that Rosine was probably dying of consumption shows that he was less capable than ever to deal with real problems realistically.

"Could I but help you, Friend of my soul! God knows, I would gladly give my life for that. My joy has deserted me, and, in the midst of that which

75   86.2ff.
76   88.68ff.

surrounds me, I am admonished by your sorrow, and I know not how I could endure it if you did not at least save yourself.

"Dear One! You will, you must sustain your spirit, whatever may come. You belong to mankind. You have no right to desert them. Through great joy and great pain one develops into a man. A future such as a hero in battle might expect awaits you. You will not go through life without feeling; the royal consciousness of having overcome an unspeakable torment will accompany you; you will struggle upward into the region of the imperishable. You will stay with me and be a man, but a godlike man.

"Dear, Unforgettable One! You also belong to me. Of all the things to which my heart was devoted with hopes of an enduring commitment, only the *Bund* with you has endured. I was never as rich as you. I was never as happy in love, know not whether I ever will be, but I was often inexpressibly happy through you and hoped to become even happier in that way. Do you no longer know me, am I nothing to you anymore, my Brother? Let us endure together in this gloomy zone, work together, and nourish our hearts from victory alone. I vow to you that, except for humanity, nothing on earth shall have such a claim on me as you; I will be yours, like your soul; and if I bow down before no mortal man, I will bow down to you eternally. Conquering worlds, destroying and rebuilding states will never seem as great to me as overcoming such torment.

"Grant me the consolation of my life and yourself the triumph of all triumphs! I shall not leave you. I shall shout that to you without end, and I would say it if I were returning from your corpse and hers: Pain can cast me to the ground, but it can never overcome me as long as I *will*.

"Let her go on, if it is to be so, along the endless path to perfection! You will hurry after her, even if you tarry here for years yet. Pain will give wings to your spirit; you will keep step with her; you two will remain united, as you are now, and whatever is united will surely be reunited."[77]

Others have seen in Hölderlin's response one of the loftiest expressions of grief in all literature.[78] To this extent we can agree: The letter belongs to literature, not to life. It is hardly a realistic attempt to console a friend who was suffering from such a blow. Seen as a real letter to a grief-stricken friend, the intended loftiness becomes unfeeling cruelty. The letter is eloquent testimony to the sad fact that one year in the real world had not brought about social maturation in Hölderlin but rather had caused an even more profound withdrawal reaction, a further intensification of all those studied feelings and sentiments that, from now on, would serve Hölderlin as lame substitutes for real feelings for others. Only because we have been schooled to appreciate the

[77] 87.2ff.
[78] Beck sees Hölderlin's response to Neuffer's grief differently and points out that he seems to forget his own problems, "adapts perfectly to the suffering [friend], and places himself at his disposal" (VI, 2, p. 744).

artist-centered conception of that age have we been unable to see until now just how out of place the letter was. For Hölderlin was not a real friend trying to give consolation. Automatically his artist's soul, which had been bent to the task of *self*-expression in the composition of *Hyperion* for many months, exploited the tragedy as he would have exploited any other opportunity for self-expression. Hence his concentration on his own sorrow, his plea that Neuffer console *him,* and his reversion to the theme of "becoming a man," the importance of overcoming great sorrow for the sake of one's future greatness, and the call to duty in which he admonished the sufferer to "let her go on," because Neuffer, after all, had an obligation to abstract "mankind." Unable to attain that moment of self-obliteration which is the prerequisite of true *com*-passion and which would have moved him to offer a quiet, less shrill type of consolation, he again pushed into the center of the stage all those themes that shielded his ego from the external world. Neuffer's beloved was dying; Hölderlin's response was simply to push into the bereaved young man's arms a lover who was never to die and leave him mourning — "mankind."

"I will never leave you," he wrote. But the cruel image of the corpses, which he, in his inability to differentiate between what was permissible in a novel and what would have been appropriate in a letter of consolation, was compelled to include, shows quite clearly that he had already left those who might have been his real friends and had decided that his place was forever on the mountain, far away from the valley where real men plant and reap and go about the business of living.

But now he was to be ripped cruelly from his dream-world and propelled into the dirty business of living; now he had to try to cope with the task of disciplining Fritz von Kalb.

From 25 August until 10 October 1794 Hölderlin seems to have fallen silent about his pupil. We do not know what happened during that time, but from his letter to Neuffer on 10 October we can see that he was near the breaking point.

"My present, external profession has often been difficult for me. Surely I can tell you about it. I have been silent up until now even to you, because to you in particular I have given only too much justification for assuming that I am displeased with everything that is not silver or gold and that I complain constantly that the world is no Arcadia. But I have just about outgrown that childish cowardice. But I *am* a man. I cannot help but wish for success for consciencious, often very strenuous efforts. It has to be painful for me when this success is almost completely lacking because of the very mediocre talents of my student, because of the very erroneous way in which he was handled in his younger years, and other things, which I will spare you. That it hurts me would not, in itself, be significant, but that I have thus been disturbed in my other projects does not seem so insignificant to me. It would probably not be very pleasant to you either if half your day were spent in instruction, from which you got nothing but a little patience, and the other half ruined for you by the knowledge that the other party did not profit from it. — Well, I seek to keep my spirits up as well as possible, and, if the sun shines in my window, I get up happy and use to the best possible advantage a few morning hours — the only time at which I actually have peace."[79]

This was the first time that Hölderlin gave any indication that his opinions about Fritz had changed. But a number of hints in Charlotte von Kalb's letters indicate that something was wrong before that. In late August or early September she had written Schiller: "Things will get better — if resignation and tenacity, attentiveness and activity — motivate the teacher more and more, as well as the pupil — the only person who is sometimes dissatisfied with *Hldn* — is — is he himself."[80] By 25 October, about two weeks after Hölderlin had written the above-mentioned letter to Neuffer, Charlotte was writing Schiller: ". . . it seems to me, Hölderlin is neglecting his physical well-being — And then it is exceedingly important not to destroy his courage, his hopes, his self-confidence. I may be wrong and hope that I am. —— Teaching this boy is a difficult task — He really has very limited talents. If he could just become useful; no one expects him to become learned as well [*gelehrt soll er auch nicht werden*]! — Hölderlin is very sensitive so do not let him know that I have written *you* anything about this subject, — I suppose H. is — under considerable stress — and so perhaps are his demands on the child."[81]

By then it was definite that Fritz and his tutor were to be sent to Jena. Charlotte, who hoped that the change of scene would relax both of them, recognized, significantly, that Fritz was not to blame completely for the difficulties that had arisen between teacher and pupil. Much of the reason for that difficulty lay with the teacher. She recognized that Hölderlin had become extremely agitated in recent months and that the child was suffering for it. Moreover, she showed a good deal of insight when she said that Hölderlin should under no circumstances find out that Schiller knew that he was failing as a teacher, because he was "very sensitive."

But she did not really understand *why* Hölderlin was so sensitive, why he found it so difficult to cope with the boy, and why he was degenerating physically as a result of his battle with Fritz. Had she been able to read his letter to Neuffer, in which he had made no secret of the fact that he was not as concerned about Fritz as with the progress of his novel, then she might have realized even then that, in the first place, Hölderlin was simply ill-equipped to fulfil his duties and that there was hope for the *Hofmeister's* recovery only if he had time to study without having to discipline his pupil. Finally, she might have

[79] 88.43ff.
[80] VI, 2, p. 697.
[81] *Ibid.*

understood that sending Hölderlin to Jena with Fritz would only make matters worse.

Once in Jena, Hölderlin suddenly found himself amidst the swirling intellectual life for which he had longed since 1790. But he was already physically and mentally exhausted from months of trying to pursue his study of philosophy, write his novel, and, at the same time, cope with Fritz von Kalb. Soon after they arrived in Jena Hölderlin wrote Neuffer: "I now have my heart and head full of things that I should like to do as far as thinking and writing are concerned, and also with what I am duty-bound to do through actions. The nearness of truly great minds and also the nearness of truly great, spontaneous hearts depresses and exhilarates me alternately. I must work my way out of the twilight and slumber, awaken and shape half-developed, half-extinguished talents, tenderly and firmly, if I am not finally to take my flight into a tragic resignation, in which one consoles oneself with other immature and powerless people who let the world go its way, where one observes the rising and the setting of truth and right, the blossoming and the withering of art, the life and death of everything that interests the human being as a human being, quietly, from one's quiet corner, and, at most, answers mankind's demand with one's negative virtue. Better the grave than that condition! And yet I have almost no other prospect."[82]

But what is this? Not one word about Fritz von Kalb! On the other hand, Hölderlin's arrival in Jena had not quite revived his spirits. Further on in the letter the most revealing passage appears: "A passage which I happened to see in the announcement of Wieland's complete works still burns my heart. It said: Wieland's Muse arose at the beginning of German poetic art and will end with its *decline!* Oh dear! Call me a child! But something like that can ruin my week. So be it! If it must be so, then let us break our lyres and do what the artists *dreamed!* That is my consolation!"[83]

Hölderlin's arrival in Jena marked a new and fateful beginning in his development — not because he would still be unable to deal with Fritz von Kalb effectively, but because his dreams, those precious dreams that had supported him throughout his school years, to which he had again taken flight during the late spring and summer, were now becoming a source of torment themselves. This is one of the most foreboding developments in the case of mental disturbance. For, at a certain stage of development, when one's isolation from reality is so complete that only the dreams are left, then those dreams become a source of danger — simply because they cannot be fulfilled. Anyone can dream of himself as a great poet, a great statesman, an illustrious intellectual — and these dreams are usually helpful. But at a certain point they become hazardous.

---

[82] 89.11ff.
[83] 89.32ff.

When one lives in dreams for years, when the pursuit of imagined and thoroughly unrealistic goals have been used as an excuse to cling to the dream and avoid real life, then the dreams become a threat. They demand fulfillment. Hölderlin, faced with the need to earn a living, had run out of time. The dreams of the greatness that he would attain if he but had the opportunity could no longer serve as excuses for not meeting challenges. He was now in Jena. As he wrote his mother, he lived with a bookdealer, had access to professors, had the friendship and good will of Schiller, and had the opportunity to hear Fichte's lectures. He now had everything that he needed to prove to Mother and to himself that his way had been right, that he was really intended to pursue the life of the intellectual, that he was really the equal of Schiller, and that he really had within himself the potential to accomplish his goal.

"If only" had now become "now that." Already mentally exhausted, he now had to fulfil his dreams or — abandon them forever, slip back into that "tragic resignation" into which he would, in fact, retreat in just a few months.

His failure to finish *Hyperion* and take advantage of the opportunities that presented themselves to him in Jena is the subject of our next chapter. But when he arrived in Jena he already felt the strain of that challenge. In the next few months he would find that, even among intellectuals, one had to face real problems and that the life of a writer was nothing like the existence of inner peace that he had always imagined. Now he had the extra burden of Fritz von Kalb added to the hard task of proving himself in Jena. The young man who was thrown into deepest depression by the fantastic claims of a book advertisement could only be overwhelmed.

Fritz von Kalb was now a hindrance to him — nothing more. "The half-day that I have to sacrifice to my little one," he wrote his mother on 17 November, "I am even more loathe to give away here, since so much moves me to be about my own business."[84] Word of Hölderlin's rapid decline had already reached Charlotte, who wrote Schiller on 9 December: "Much that I hear tells me of the extremely severe treatment that my Fritz is having to suffer at the hands of his teacher. — (Do not, I beg you, let *Hölderlin* suspect in the slightest that I have been informed about it. His sensitivity knows no limits, and people are actually saying that a confusion of his mind [*Verstand*] underlies this behavior; I believe that this — just like all the stories — that people have told me, is very exaggerated. Once more I beg you [to see to it] that *he learns nothing*. Others do not want him to harbor any suspicion against you either — that is, those people who have written me."[85]

Charlotte arrived in Jena shortly before Christmas and immediately took Fritz and Hölderlin to Weimar. Hölderlin was particularly sad that he had to leave Jena. On 26 December he wrote his mother: "I confess that I was

---

84   90.4ff.
85   VI, 2, p. 697.

determined, for a number of sound reasons, to quit my job and see if I could not maintain myself here; I explained to Frau Major, who could only find my reasons valid, and the thing would just about have been decided if Schiller had not found a happy solution and convinced me to stipulate that the arrangement would be terminated if, by Easter, my reservations, which he also found valid, had not been satisfied. Since these reservations primarily concern my pupil, you will find it proper that I do not go into them needlessly."[86]

Charlotte soon realized that Hölderlin had become useless as far as her son's education was concerned and allowed him to resign. On 14 January 1795 she wrote Schiller that Hölderlin had indeed resigned and urged Schiller to help him by giving him "easy tasks."[87] "He is a racing wheel!" she concluded.[88] To Frau Gok she wrote: "Hölderlin must develop in such a way that he can one day join in the common cause of the Good and Beautiful! — It would have been the grossest robbery if I had been inclined to tie him to the child and the child to him in this situation any longer .... I would also like *H.* never again to be placed by circumstances in a position where he has to take a teaching assignment. His spirit cannot stoop to such a trivial task — Or rather his spirit is too affected by it .... Jena and a position at the university is [he says] the goal of his hopes now. And I do not think that it will be too hard for him. — *You* make his present sojourn and this important epoch in his life as easy as you can! ... keep all trivial cares from him so that no unnecessary worry takes up his time and delays his education! The pound that you give him from his property will be compounded a thousand times. — And I know that your motherly heart will do that without hesitating!"[89]

Now the question of insanity has arisen and thrusts itself into the biographer's subject-matter. It cannot be avoided any longer because it was raised by those who lived with him and knew him well. We are not limited by the terminology of psychology. Whether Hölderlin had already passed over the theoretical line that divides sanity from insanity is not really so very important. What is important to us is the fact that the system of defense mechanisms that had served him during his school days proved to be no defense against the problems of adulthood and that these mechanisms were fast becoming threats themselves. He was failing, even though all the prerequisites that he had himself laid down for success had been met. And everyone, including Schiller and his mother, would soon know it. This could only have had a decisive and destructive effect on his development from then on.

86   91.39ff.
87   II, 2, p. 714.
88   *Ibid.*
89   II, 2, p. 715.

At some time before April 1794, before he had again started to withdraw into himself, he had written the optimistic poem: "Das Schiksaal," which ends with the lines:

> Im heiligsten der Stürme falle
> Zusammen meine Kerkerwand,
> Und herrlicher und freier walle
> Mein Geist in's unbekannte Land!
> Hier blutet oft der Adler Schwinge;
> Auch drüben warte Kampf und Schmerz!
> Bis an der Sonnen lezte ringe,
> Genährt vom Siege, dieses Herz.[90]

In September 1795, after the first series of failures had driven him back to Nürtingen, he sent the poem "An die Natur" to Schiller. The contrast between the optimism of the above stanza and the concluding stanzas of "An die Natur" gives some indication of how the experiences of Waltershausen and Jena had affected him.

> Todt ist nun, die mich erzog und stillte,
> Todt ist nun die jugendliche Welt,
> Diese Brust, die einst ein Himmel füllte,
> Todt und dürftig, wie ein Stoppelfeld;
> Ach! es singt der Frühling meinen Sorgen
> Noch, wie einst, ein freundlich tröstend Lied,
> Aber hin ist meines Lebens Morgen,
> Meines Herzens Frühling ist verblüht.
>
> Ewig muß die liebste Liebe darben,
> Was wir lieben, ist ein Schatten nur,
> Da der Jugend goldne Träume starben,
> Starb für mich die freundliche Natur;
> Das erfuhrst du nicht in frohen Tagen,
> Daß so ferne dir die Heimath liegt,
> Armes Herz, du wirst sie nie erfragen,
> Wenn dir nicht ein Traum von ihr genügt.[91]

We are forced to remark, by way of conclusion, that his failures were not the work of a cruel fate which happened to thrust Fritz von Kalb into his path. The encounter with the boy was only the external event through which reality finally broke through Hölderlin's defenses and threatened to destroy him. The events at Waltershausen were merely the actual manifestation of the sterility of

[90] I, 1, p. 186 (lines 81–88).
[91] I, 1, pp. 192f. (lines 49–64).

Hölderlin's dedication of self to a "mankind" without "individuals." For all his poetic concern for mankind, he still had not learned to show real compassion for real people.

In this sense, his life stands in marked contrast to men like Goethe and Schiller, although they also took their poetry and intellectual activities seriously. Goethe adopted orphaned boys and educated them, found a professorship for the young, struggling Schiller, convinced Cotta to publish Sachse's autobiography, and took time to write an introduction to the work. However much Schiller has been taken to task by Hölderlin enthusiasts for not understanding his young friend, he, nevertheless, showed far more patience with Hölderlin than Hölderlin showed for Fritz von Kalb. Kant, who has been stereotyped as the man who lived alone and existed only for his work, found time to get a publisher for the penniless Fichte and to persuade the publisher to advance Fichte a sum of money.

Hölderlin never did anything like that. He was always the recipient of others' kindness. It is true that he was never in a position to help much. It is also true that the impulse to help out was not lacking. But he had no real feeling for others; so great was his concentration on his own problems that he never realized that others' problems were no less serious than his own — and might demand solutions other than reading books or enjoying the beauties of nature, which he advised his mother to do when she had to sell her house in 1797.

We should add, of course, that this was not Hölderlin's fault. But it was the case, and it was symptomatic of a mind which never matured beyond its adolescent turmoil. The good intentions were there, and the words came to his lips. But actions and genuine consolation were beyond him.

The old Goethe wrote of life:

> Als Knabe verschlossen und trutzig,
> Als Junge anmaßlich und stutzig,
> Als Mann zu Taten willig,
> Als Greis leichtsinnig und grillig!
> Auf deinem Grabstein wird man lesen:
> Das ist fürwahr ein Mensch gewesen![92]

Hölderlin was never "zu Taten willig." Perhaps that is why, near the end of his life, when he was already hopelessly insane, he wrote:

> Nicht alle Tage nennet die schönsten der,
>   Der sich zurüksehnt unter die Freuden wo
>   Ihn Freunde liebten wo die Menschen
>   Über dem Jüngling mit Gunst verweilten.[93]

---

[92] *Goethes Werke. Historische-Kritische Gesamtausgabe* (143 vols.; Weimar: Hermann Böhlau, 1887—1920), II, p. 289.

[93] II, 1, p. 280.

As an old man he still looked back to those days when he had not been expected to act and when he could rely on the protection of others. The year at Waltershausen was the first indication that it would always be so. For, although he suffered from his experiences there, he learned nothing from them. As Charlotte wrote Schiller shortly after Hölderlin had resigned: "Hölderlin considers this year as lost — I consider it of the greatest importance to all of us."[94]

94 VI, 2, p. 714.

12.

HYPERION IN JENA

We conclude our study of the development of the young Hölderlin's mind and character with an investigation of the three *Hyperion* fragments that originated before the end of 1795. Our primary aim in this chapter is not to provide a critique of *Hyperion*, or even of its early variants. We shall treat the fragments just as we have treated Hölderlin's poems throughout this study – as documents helpful to us in our attempt to understand Hölderlin's growth. Nevertheless, we shall devote more attention to *Hyperion* than we have paid to any other single work. Not because Hölderlin's early work on *Hyperion* was more important than his other undertakings. These fragments are certainly not superior to many of the poems that he had written by that time. Particularly the Tübingen Hymns are far more polished and succinct statements of Hölderlin's *Weltanschauung,* if for no other reason than simply because they are completed works in a genre in which their author was most competent, while the early *Hyperion* fragments – and, we are tempted to say, the final version as well – are abortive attempts at expression in a genre that Hölderlin never really mastered. We shall now discuss the origins of *Hyperion,* first, because it was the work that obsessed its author to such a degree that he frittered away the opportunities that presented themselves to him in Jena, and, second, because Hölderlin's half success at combining the craft of the novelist with the thought-forms of the Idealistic philosopher provides an exhaustive inventory of Hölderlin's mind at a time in which his views and ideas were themselves fragmentary and as yet incohesive. The subject matter of the novel is thus, in many ways, identical with the mind of its author, while Hölderlin's unrealistic attitude toward the relationship between the author's poetic mission and the successful pursuit of his career provides a striking example of that uncompromising hostility toward reality that would plague him for the rest of his life.

We shall now undertake a summary of what little we know about Hölderlin's earliest work on *Hyperion,* a discussion of the three fragments dating from 1794 and 1795, and an account of how Hölderlin, driven by an obsessive desire to finish the novel at all costs, failed to take advantage of his opportunities in Jena.

Hölderlin began working on a novel set in modern-day Greece while he was still a student in Tübingen. We know little about his early work. Hölderlin mentioned the novel very seldom in his own letters of that time, and the letters of his friends and acquaintances yield only very general information and are quite unreliable because, as we shall see, they often seem to reflect very faulty knowledge about what Hölderlin had written and indicate almost complete ignorance about what he wanted to make of *Hyperion* in the future. Magenau encouraged Hölderlin in his work on *Hyperion* in June 1792; that is the first written reference to the work.[1] In the following autumn Magenau wrote Neuffer that Holz was working on "a second Donamar, Hyperion."[2] He knew little in detail except that Hyperion was supposed to be "a freedom-loving hero and genuine Greek, full of strong principles."[3]

Others, including Neuffer and Stäudlin, soon knew about *Hyperion*, but their letters yield largely unreliable or misleading information. Stäudlin, who read fragments of Hölderlin's manuscript, wrote his young friend in September 1793 that he was particularly impressed by "the beautiful language" and the "liveliness of presentation." But then he went on to suggest that Hölderlin "not fail to include in this work veiled passages about the spirit of the time."[4] This advice is somewhat puzzling, to say the least. One can hardly imagine that the same Hölderlin who had been so vehemently repudiating the modern age and yearning so soulfully for the lost age of Plato's Greece would have failed to imbue his "freedom-loving hero" with similar sentiments. One would have to wonder, in that case, why Hölderlin had decided to write a novel about modern Greece at all! Most certainly, Stäudlin's remarks reflect ignorance of Hölderlin's work — a conclusion supported by Hölderlin's confession to Neuffer that he had sent Stäudlin only "the most uninteresting parts."[5]

The only substantive information about *Hyperion* that we possess from that early date is found in Hölderlin's letter to Neuffer in the summer of 1793, a few months before he graduated. That the recipient should have been Neuffer is significant. Throughout the seven years of work on *Hyperion*, Hölderlin seems never to have written anyone about his work in specific terms other than Neuffer and Susette Gontard. As we have seen, the relationship between the two young men had grown somewhat cool since Neuffer's graduation. Although Hölderlin spent a good deal of time with Hegel and Schelling, he was more alone spiritually than he had been at any time since he had come from Maulbronn. And he had suffered from his loneliness. In May 1793 he made one of several somewhat petulant attempts to renew the old friendship and recapture the spirit of the *Bund*. He wrote Neuffer: "You had to become once again the person you used to be during the time of our common joys and undertakings; otherwise our friendship was done for. But, praise God! I know you once more."[6]

---

1 VII, 1, pp. 28f.
2 III, p. 296.
3 *Ibid.* Beck thinks this may indicate that Hölderlin had read to him from the manuscript toward the end of the fall vacation.
4 VII, 1, pp. 37f.
5 Stäudlin had said in his letter to Hölderlin: "Concerning the plan, you will receive my judgment when I have received more than this fragment" *(Ibid.)*
6 57.14ff.

Neuffer's response was so warm, so reminiscent of the *Bund,* that Hölderlin was quite overwhelmed. His rhapsodic reply contains the first extant testimony about *Hyperion* from Hölderlin's pen and provides us with a veritable gold-mine of information about his work on the novel up until then and about his hopes for *Hyperion's* future. Just how much *Hyperion* already occupied him can be seen in the way in which he jumped from how happy he was at having found his friend once again to the high hopes he had for *Hyperion.*

"You are right, Brother of my heart! Your genius was very close to me during these past days. In fact, I have seldom felt with such certainty and quiet joy the interminability of your love for me. I believe that for some time now your genius has been communicating even your attributes to me [*Sogar Dein Wesen hat mir Dein Genius seit einiger Zeit mitgeteilt*]. I wrote Stäudlin of the many happy hours I have had. Understand! That was because your spirit lived in me. Your peace, your beautiful contentment with which you view present and future, nature and men — these I felt. Even the bold hopes with which you look forward to our goals are alive in me. In fact, I wrote Stäudlin: Neuffer's quiet flame will burn ever more splendidly when my straw-fire has perhaps long since burnt itself out; but this 'perhaps' holds no fear for me anymore, least of all in those divine hours when I return from the lap of blissful nature or from the grove of plane-trees by Illisus, where, stretched at length among Plato's pupils, I have watched the flight of the magnificent man as he roams into the dark expanses of the primeval world or, with my head spinning, follow him into the depth of depths, the farthest end of the spirit land, where the soul of the world sends out its life in the thousand pulsations of nature, or the forces that have been sent out return after their immeasurable orbits, or when I, drunk from the Socratic goblet or Socratic Friendship at the banquet, have hearkened to the enthusiastic youths as they pay homage to holy love with sweet, fiery orations, as the scamp Aristophanes drops in his witticisms, and as, finally, the master, Socrates himself, teaches them all with his heavenly wisdom what love is — then, Friend of my heart, I am, of course, not so despondent, and I think sometimes that I will have to be able to communicate a small spark of that sweet flame that warms and illuminates me in such moments to my work, which now completely absorbs me [*in dem ich wirklich lebe und webe*], my Hyperion, and must also produce, from time to time, something else for the pleasure of men."[7]

He needed no encouragement from Stäudlin to emphasize the "spirit of the times." Like Hegel, Schelling, and Conz, he was already an ardent admirer of Plato. The Greece whose *Untergang* he lamented in "Griechenland" was the land of Platonic Friendship, of companionship with the true friends who were always ready to plunge into philosophic discussion. To Hölderlin Greece meant the *Bund.* He had learned to grieve so sincerely for Plato's Greece that it is no

7   60.1ff.

wonder that he hoped to "communicate a small spark of that sweet flame" to *Hyperion*. His remarks to Neuffer show how little he now communicated to Stäudlin — the man who had been his model a few short years before. By 1793 he had grown reticent even to his publisher. One must understand how deep his spiritual isolation was in order to grasp how powerfully the vision of Plato's Greece moved him and how Plato's thought was already influencing the development of the Hyperion theme.

Two of Plato's dialogues seem to have captured Hölderlin's imagination by then. The *Symposium* is treated unequivocally. He identified Socrates' speech as the passage that particularly impressed him. It is, of course, in that speech that Socrates defines love as the key to all true knowledge and the only proper state of mind for the philosopher — a truth that Socrates had learned from Diotima! Beyond the *Symposium*, however, another dialogue, in which love is treated in much the same way, seems to have been in Hölderlin's mind. Such turns of speech as "roaming into the dark expanses of the primeval world" and the "immeasurable orbits" suggest the mythology of the *Phaedrus*, with which Hölderlin would later hope to reconcile Kant's treatment of aesthetics and which would exert a great influence on the *Hyperion* fragments in question, particularly the *Metrical Version* and *Hyperion's Youth*.

It is striking how the little that we are able to glean from Hölderlin's letters and the few, very general remarks made by his friends give us such a shadowy outline of his as yet inchoate conception of *Hyperion,* and yet how much that vague outline anticipates the final version of the novel. He was, for example, already planning to publish the work in two volumes, or "books."[8] He recognized, moreover, that what he had written up until then was unimpressive in comparison with his somewhat grandiose plans for the work. And yet his rudimentary grasp of the task that he had set for himself should not mislead us into concluding that the philosophic aspects of *Hyperion* were not even then uppermost in his mind. Even at that early date he knew quite well that he intended to use the novel as a vehicle for philosophic expression. Of the samples he was sending Neuffer, he wrote: "This fragment seems to me to be more of a hodge-podge of whims than the carefully planned development of a clearly conceived character, because I am leaving obscure the themes behind the ideas and sentiments — and [I am doing] that because I want to occupy [the reader's] faculty of taste through a portrait of ideas and sentiment (for aesthetic enjoyment) rather than his intellect through an orderly psychological development. Naturally, in the end, one will have to be able to trace everything back to the character and the circumstances acting upon it."[9]

8 "... the whole second book ..." (60.59).
9 60.47ff.

These are the ideas of the student of philosophy, the friend of Hegel and Schelling, the enthusiastic student who had incompletely digested *The Critique of Judgment;* they are not the ideas of the practicing novelist. He outlined a method of composition of which (he thought) Kant would have approved. From *The Critique of Judgment* he learned that the purpose of the aesthetic faculty was to mediate between *Verstand* and *Vernunft,* thus making supersensual knowledge possible, even if that knowledge was tentative and consisted only of regulative ideas.[10] He seems, at that point, to have accepted Kant's doctrine of the Primacy of Practical Reason. He had not yet studied Kant's aesthetics in detail, and thus he was not yet aware of the fact that the Primacy of Practical Reason excluded the very type of metaphysical knowledge that Plato seemed to promise. At that time he saw no problem in adapting Kant's means to Plato's end.

He did not begin to perceive the very deep gulf that separated Plato's promise from Kant's method until he studied Kant's and Plato's treatments of aesthetics in the spring of 1794. When he did come to understand the complexity of the task, he did not try to avoid it. On the contrary, solving the problem became an obsession. In order to understand why this happened it is necessary to recall that Hölderlin seems to have made little if any progress on *Hyperion* from the autumn of 1793, when the pressure of school-life was removed, until April 1794, when he realized that he was failing in his job of civilizing — let alone educating — Fritz von Kalb and became agitated at having missed a chance to locate in Jena. It was at just that time that he began mentioning renewed work on *Hyperion* — references in his letters that were inevitably followed by remarks about his study of Kant and "the Greeks," by which he meant Plato.[11] We have already seen that Hölderlin was most productive during periods of stress and that he fastened on philosophical themes, such as Schiller's construction, "the

10 The weakness of Kant's treatment and the precarious position of aesthetics that resulted from his treatment is most evident in § 8 of *Kritik der Urtheilskraft,* in which Kant tried to provide some basis for the universal validity of aesthetic judgments, which tended to contradict his position that such judgments did not rest on objective concepts of the *Verstand,* but rather sprang from the subjective forms of the *Vernunft.* "Here one should note above all that a generality which does not rest on concepts of the object (even on mere empirical concepts) is not at all logical, but aesthetic, i.e. contains not an objective but a subjective quantity of judgment, for which I also use the term *common validity* [*Gemeingültigkeit*], which denotes the validity of the relationship of a concept [*Vorstellung*] not to the cognitive faculty, but to the subject's feeling of pain and pleasure" (1793 Edition, p. 23). Kant had already indicated in § 6, however, that this "common validity" rested upon the subject's habit of speaking of beauty *as if* it were an attribute of the object, which is, in fact, not the case: "He will speak of the beautiful as if beauty were an attribute of the object and the judgment logical (constituting knowledge of an object from concepts [*Begriffe*] of it) although it [the judgment] is only aesthetic and contains merely a relationship of the concept [*Vorstellung*] of an object to the subject — because it is similar to the logical [judgment] in that one can assert its validity for everyone" (pp. 17f.).

11 II, 2, p. 678.

philosophic mind," as answers to problems that were not really philosophic in nature at all, but strictly personal. Thus it was that the intended reconciliation of Kant and Plato became an intense, *personal* problem when Hölderlin once again found himself at odds with life and reverted to the old habit of seeking purely intellectual solutions to real problems, which, because they were, in fact, personal in nature, did not lend themselves to conceptual solutions. Eventually, when those problems multiplied to the point that even Hölderlin had to admit that they were insoluble, first at Waltershausen and then at Jena, the philosophic problem became an obsession. The conflict between the disappointing thought-forms of Critical Philosophy and Platonic metaphysics became for him the old, life-long conflict between the soulless, godless, meaningless modern world and the god-filled world of antiquity – a conflict which was really between undeniable reality and the dream-world that he had been creating since the Tübingen Hymns. In that way the intellectual task of reducing tension and cancelling out the contradictions between Kantian epistemology and Platonic metaphysics substituted symbolically for the much more difficult task of reducing tension between himself and the world in which he lived.

In his last letter from Waltershausen in October 1794, Hölderlin wrote Neuffer: "This summer most [of my morning hours] I spent on my novel, the first five letters of which you will find this winter in Thalia. I am almost through with the first part. From my old papers almost not a single line remains. The great transition from youth to manhood, from Affect to Reason, from the realm of fantasy into the realm of truth seems to me to be worthy of such a slow treatment. And yet I am looking forward to the day when I will be through with the whole thing, because I will then try to develop in accordance with the ideals of the Greek drama a plan that is almost even dearer to my heart – the death of Socrates."[12] A few lines later he wrote: "Perhaps I can send you an essay concerning the aesthetic ideas; since it can be considered a commentary to Plato's *Phaedrus* and since a passage of that work is my express text, perhaps it would be useful to Conz. Chiefly it is to contain an analysis of the Beautiful and the Sublime in which the Kantian [analysis] is simplified and expanded in the other direction [*von der anderen Seite vielseitiger wird*], as Schiller has already done to a degree in his essay *Über Anmut und Würde,* although he dared to take one less step beyond the Kantian boundary than he, in my opinion, should have. Do not smile! I can be wrong; but I have tested, and tested rigorously."[13]

The essay was never written. *Hyperion* took its place. Hölderlin's hopes of finishing *Hyperion* in a short time were not realized. The fragment that appeared in November 1794, which he then looked upon as "the first five letters" of the first part, had by January 1795 become "one of those rough masses" that he

[12] 88.64ff.
[13] 88.89ff.

hoped to revise by Easter.[14] The more he worked on the novel, the more he became hopelessly embroiled in philosophic problems. The *Thalia-Fragment,* which was at least still a prose narrative, gave way to the *Metrical Version,* which is largely an exposition of Hölderlin's philosophic ruminations. During the spring of 1795, while he was slowly running out of money and rather quickly destroying his health, he tried to combine the two fragments. The result was *Hyperion's Youth.* It too remained a fragment.

Hyperion was no longer merely a novel. It was now Hölderlin's *magnum opus* in which he was determined to solve all the outstanding dilemmas of Critical Philosophy — an undertaking that could only bring him into spiritual conflict with Schiller and thus make it difficult for him to follow the older man's advice and collaborate on his journals.

But, before we tell what happened at Jena, it is time to look into the *Hyperion* fragments themselves.

Hyperion is autobiographical in the most profound sense of the word. In all its versions the novel's central theme is the growth of a young Greek, who cannot be satisfied with the spiritual poverty of modern life, into the rejected prophet of his people. We should actually say that such a development was *supposed* to be the theme. The novel is pervaded with a deep pessimism that Hölderlin never managed to overcome. That pessimism finally caused Hölderlin to make of his hero a hermit who never fulfils the mission for which he was destined. His education, "the transition from the realm of fantasy into the realm of truth," never bears fruit. Hyperion never emerges from his wanderings in the wilderness to address his people in the thundering tones of an Old Testament prophet. He is never quite ready to deliver his Sermon on the Mount. The two versions that come to any sort of resolution at all are the *Thalia-Fragment* and the final version of the novel. In both cases Hyperion has returned to his homeland after much suffering and tells his story to his friend Bellarmin through letters. In the *Thalia-Fragment* he ends the last letter as follows:

"Then recently I saw a little boy lying at the side of the road; with great care his mother, who was watching over him, had spread a cover over him, that he might sleep softly in the shade. But the boy would not stay and tore the cover away; and I saw how he tried to gaze at the friendly light, and tried and tried again until his eyes ached and, weeping, he turned his face to the earth.

"Poor Boy! I thought. Others fare no better; and I had almost decided to leave off this restless curiosity. But I cannot! I shall not!

---

[14] On 26 January he wrote Hegel: "My productive activity is now directed almost completely toward the restructuring *(Umbildung)* of the materials of my novel. The fragment in *Thalia* is one of these rough masses. I think I shall be through with it by Easter; let me, in the meantime, keep quiet about it" (94.18ff.).

"It must be known, the great secret that gives me life or death."[15]

The completed novel ends:

"Like the lovers' quarrel are the dissonances of the world. Reconciliation is in the midst of strife, and all that is put asunder finds itself once more.

"The veins separate and come back together in the heart, and everything is a single, eternal, glowing life.

"So I thought. More to follow."[16]

Why did Hölderlin not end his novel? Why did he not answer the question that lay at the bottom of all the versions: How does modern man, imprisoned in the temporally determined spiritual limitations of modern life, become the poet-prophet of the Tübingen Hymns?

These questions can be answered in two ways. First, Hölderlin never found the answers himself. He continued to regard all that happened to him, all that he had done, and the business in which he was engaged at a given time as a prelude to real life, as preparation for the eventual fulfillment of his poetic mission. He thought that real life, a fulfilling life, was to be found in the very thing that he was not doing but had decided to do as soon as he escaped from his present situation. If he could only get away from school, he had thought while he was a student; if he could only get to Jena, he thought while at Waltershausen. But, of course, when he actually found himself in Jena he discovered that that was not really what he wanted either. And so he dreamed on: If he could only finish *Hyperion;* if only Schiller would not insist that he do those silly translations; if only he could support himself through writing what he wanted to write and not be bothered by other things. And then finally: If only he could find another teaching job in quiet surroundings so that he might not have to live in the constant state of agitation that he found unavoidable while he was in Jena.

Hyperion, like his creator, was always *becoming* the poet-prophet, was always "educating" himself — and always suffering because he could never give up his dreams and settle down with Melite (Diotima) or become the prophet that he felt he should be.

The above interpretation of *Hyperion* would have been rejected by its author. Although Hyperion does suffer from the same dreamy ambivalence that plagued his creator, Hölderlin did not consciously set out to commemorate his own failures in his novel. In *Hyperion* he justified his procrastination, glorified the poet who devoted himself to an endless self-education in order to fulfil a mission that, in reality, could not be fulfilled in the modern world. In the Tübingen Hymns Hölderlin had created the type of message that the poet-prophet would have brought to mankind. Such poetry presupposed that metaphysical insight into the Platonic Ideals was possible. The poems had been their own

15 III, p. 219.
16 III, p. 160.

justification. The poet had spoken with the voice of the heavenly inspired prophet who had already succeeded in transcending the temporal. When he set about writing *Hyperion* and depicting the development of the sensitive young man into the poet-prophet of the Tübingen Hymns, however, he found himself faced with an essentially epistemological question: How is metaphysical knowledge possible? Of course, that had also been Kant's question. But it actually underlies the problem that Hölderlin had set out to resolve: How can the poet restore alienated man to nature?

There was never any question in his mind but that aesthetic knowledge of nature was the key issue. On that point Kant, Schiller, Herder, and, by virtue of his very nature, Hölderlin himself were in full agreement. Plato had said the same thing. But the more Hölderlin studied Plato in the spring of 1794, the more he came to realize that the agreement between Critical and Platonic Philosophy was strictly verbal. For Kant had proposed an absolute dichotomy between *Verstand* (the organ that provides knowledge of nature) and *Vernunft* (the faculty of moral legislation) and then proclaimed that these two diverse faculties were to be reconciled by the *Urtheilskraft* (the faculty that posits aesthetic and teleological judgments), *but in such a way as to maintain the Primacy of Practical Reason.* Such an understanding of the role of *Urtheilskraft* made metaphysical knowledge as absolute knowledge in the Platonic sense and poetry as the communication of such knowledge impossible.

Just as he was beginning his study of Kantian aesthetics, he found support in Schiller's *Über Anmut und Würde.* Schiller wrote: "In Kantian Moral Philosophy the idea of *duty* is presented with a certain rigor which frightens away all the graces and which could easily tempt a weak intellect to seek moral perfection in a dismal and monkish asceticism. However much the great philosopher sought to guard against that misinterpretation, which must be the most offensive of all to his joyful and free spirit, he has, nevertheless, or so it seems to me, given impetus to [such a misinterpretation] through the rigorous and harsh polarization of the principles affecting the will of man."[17] This remark went to one of the weakest points in Kant's entire system: How are the *Verstand* and the *Vernunft* actually reconciled through the *Urtheilskraft?* How can man be a citizen of the moral world and a citizen of nature at the same time? Most important of all: Does not the doctrine of the Primacy of Practical Reason condemn man as a part of nature to deny his natural origin whenever his natural instincts run counter to the demands of *Vernunft* and the duty it imposes? Is man not, therefore, *condemned to freedom,* since his Reason exiles him from nature?

Schiller then posited a solution under the term "the beautiful soul." "Man ... is not intended to perform moral actions, but to be a moral being. Not virtues but *virtue* is his purpose, and duty is nothing but an inclination to do

17   Schiller, *Nationalausgabe,* XX, p. 284.

one's duty."[18] And then he continued: "One speaks of the beautiful soul when the moral feeling of all sentiments has been secured to such an extent that it can leave the direction of the will to the affect without fear and without running the risk of conflicting with the decisions of the will. For that reason, in the case of the beautiful soul, the individual actions are not actually moral, but rather the whole character is. One cannot consider any individual action meritorious because the satisfaction of an instinct can never be called meritorious. The beautiful soul has no merit other than that it is."[19]

Now Schiller was no great original thinker. Authors of histories of German literature have made a great deal of "the beautiful soul" and have enthroned Schiller as the aesthetician of "German Classicism." Since "die deutsche Klassik" is a fiction anyway, one might just as well make Schiller the aesthetician of a phantom movement and act as if Schiller were actually a great thinker who wrote essays that had substance. But when one has stripped away all the Kantian verbiage, one discovers that Schiller wrote in a very complicated way *about* the dilemma but provided no real solution for it. He says merely that the person who "naturally" acts in accordance with moral obligation should be called "the beautiful soul." But providing a name for a solution without providing the solution itself is no great accomplishment. Such verbal postulates are mere clichés. One could, with just as much justification, insist that the person who is moral by nature be called "the aesthetic soul," "the complete man," or even "Übermensch." Schiller never quite understood that there is something meritorious about calling things by simple names and thus saying what one means. There would have been nothing wrong with calling a person who is moral by nature "a person who is moral by nature" – except that such a straightforward designation much too obviously refers to a problem and cannot, therefore, masquerade as a solution.

Schiller should perhaps not be taken too severely to task. He lived in an age in which an obscure style was considered a sign of great profundity. Kant was, unfortunately, one of those individuals who think clearly but cannot write clearly. During his lifetime his influence was all too often limited to passing on his terminology and stylistic complexities to men of inferior intellect who were ready to cover up their shortcomings by affecting a tortured style and confounding their readers. Hegel's sudden deterioration of style in *The Phenomenology of the Spirit* may be, as Walther Kaufmann has suggested, an example of how one man, who could, as he had demonstrated in his early essay on religion, write clearly, intentionally adopted a poor style because philosophers were supposed to write poorly.[20] Schiller may not have been that

18 *Ibid.,* p. 283.
19 *Ibid.,* p. 287.
20 Walter Kaufmann, Hegel. Reinterpretation, Texts, and Commentary (New York, 1965), p. 117f.

cold-blooded; he may really have been unable to distinguish between clichés and terms that meant something. In any case, he never succeeded in getting beyond the clichés. When he did try to think he became confused and produced glaring contradictions, such as the irreconcilable assertions that, on the one hand, "grace" was the mark of the person who was *instinctively* moral,[21] and, on the other hand, that this instinctive grace was to be found in "arbitrary actions."[22] Such inconsistencies were to be expected, because Schiller was not really offering a tenable solution to the problem but rather restating the contradiction that was inherent in Kantian thought. He had to say that grace was instinctive in order to involve man as a natural being; but he also had to assert that grace was to be found in "arbitrary actions" in order to preserve the Primacy of Practical Reason. *How* grace could be both instinctive and arbitrary at the same time he never tells us, which is too bad because that was the whole point. When he tried in the second part of the essay, he had "the beautiful soul" suddenly becoming "the sublime soul," which, as Schiller defined it, no longer had anything to do with instinct but is once again determined by the moral law.[23]

Now, as Hölderlin saw, Schiller had been running in a large circle. During his course he had invented new terms, but he had also ended up right back where he had started with the Primacy of Practical Reason still intact. That limitation had been inherent in Critical Philosophy from the very beginning of Schiller's study of Kant. He had never progressed beyond the Kantian promise of the apparent reconciliation because he never seriously defended the autonomy of aesthetics against the onslaught of Practical Reason. From beginning to end he did not get beyond the safely Critical formulation that appears in his letter to Körner in February 1783. "The beautiful product," he had written, "may, and indeed must, conform to rules; but it must appear to be free of all rules."[24]

Hölderlin, despite his initial enthusiasm, soon realized that he demanded more of art than Schiller would allow it to give. In order for art to provide the kind of metaphysical insight that Hölderlin claimed for his poetry it had to be liberated from the tyranny of Practical Reason and its absolute moral law, which rests on the assumption that absolute knowledge of nature is not to be had and that such knowledge is an illusion created by the *Urtheilskraft*, which treats nature *as if* it meant something — meaning being determined, of course, by *Vernunft*. While Hölderlin was attracted to Critical Philosophy because it offered

---

[21] *Schillers Werke* (Nationalausgabe), XX, p. 287. Even here Schiller seems aware that he has solved nothing, for he says that the beautiful soul acts "as if" only instinct were at work.

[22] *Ibid.*, p. 254.

[23] "In the affect the *beautiful* soul must be transformed into a sublime soul (*Ibid.*, p. 294); "Controlling the instincts through moral strength is *spiritual freedom,* and dignity [*Würde*] is its expression in the phenomenon" *(Ibid.).*

[24] *Schillers Briefe mit geschichtlichen Erläuterungen* (3 vols; Berlin: Hempel Verlag, n.d.), I, p. 838.

the alluring prospect of moral freedom which allowed the individual to determine his own destiny, he was repelled by the historical corollary, which set as the price of moral freedom the progressive and irreversible alienation of man from nature. Kantian thought was seductive because it liberated man from dogmatic restrictions. But to Hölderlin it all seemed terribly one-sided in its emphasis on the moral law. Natural man was merely trading one prison cell for another. Formerly he had been imprisoned by society's restrictions; now he was being denied access to nature by the very doctrine that had brought about his moral emancipation. Hölderlin's reading of Plato as well as his natural desire to elevate the poet to a position of prominence led him to conclude that progress could only be made through redefining the function of aesthetics within the epistemological process. That explains his original, positive reaction to Schiller's *Über Anmut und Würde*.[25] But a more detailed study of the essay, which seems to have extended over a period of several months, led him to reject Schiller's solution. His rejection of Schiller was incomplete. He shrank from the conclusion that Schiller was really running in verbose circles and said only that his hero was taking one less step beyond the Kantian boundary than he should have. His hesitation was inevitable because he was still infatuated with Schiller as a man. But he saw, correctly I think, that Schiller's method of dressing up his very modern, very conceptual, very cerebral thought in Classical garb by dragging in the myth of Venus and her belt, which was supposed to impart grace to the wearer, was merely a trick, an exercise in combinatorics, which served only to obfuscate the fact that Schiller's second-hand Kantianism and the art and thought of Plato's Greece were actually worlds apart.

Hölderlin thought that he could solve the problem in an essay concerning the beautiful and the sublime. He planned to use Plato's *Phaedrus* as a text — perhaps following Schiller's lead in using a Classical allusion so as to demonstrate that modern thought could be brought into agreement with ancient art and thought. He did not finish the essay because he soon came to realize that the reconciliation of Reason and Nature could not be achieved through conceptual argument alone. Hölderlin had to express himself through poetry. He had to show the reconciliation rather than merely delineate it conceptually. To Hölderlin the problem was not merely a conceptual incongruity but a problem in life itself. Moreover it was an historical problem that could, as he soon came to see, not be solved in finite time.[26] It was for these reasons that *Hyperion* became the vehicle of philosophic expression.

25 77.16ff.

26 Hölderlin defined this problem rather clearly in his second letter to Schiller after his departure from Jena, dated 4 September 1795, in which he spoke quite plainly about how the reconciliation was aesthetically possible, but theoretically insoluble within finite time: "Displeasure with myself and with my surroundings has driven me into abstraction; I am seeking to develop the idea of an infinite progression in philosophy; I am seeking to show that the relentless demand which must be made of every system: the union of the subject

Gradually Hölderlin had come to believe that the problem of man's alienation could not be solved within the framework of modern life. Modern life was, after all, the product of that alienation. Here he drew from the Rousseau-Herder tradition that the thought of any given age (including the present) had absolute validity only within the context of that age. Within the framework of all history, however, it possessed only relative validity. Thus he altered the historical aspect of Schiller's thought so that man's self-determination in freedom, which Schiller had seen as the absolute law of historical progression,[27] had validity only within the really rather narrow context of modern thought. Above that, however, Hölderlin saw an absolute law of history which transcended the limitations of time.

This line of thought appeared already in the *Vorrede* of the *Thalia-Fragment*.

"There are two ideals of our existence: a condition of the greatest simplicity in which our needs coincide with each other and with our strengths and with everything with which we are connected *through the simple organization of nature,* without our doing anything; and a condition of the highest refinement in which the same would take place with infinitely strengthened and multiplied needs and strengths *through the organization that we are in a position to give to ourselves.* The eccentric course, through which man progresses as a species and as an individual [*im allgemeinen und einzelnen*] from the one point (of more or less pure simplicity) to the other (of more or less perfected refinement) seems always to be the same *as far as their essential directions are concerned.*

"Several of these [essential directions] along with their rectification were to be illustrated in the letters of which the following are a fragment."[28]

and the object in an absolute (*Ich* or whatever one wants to call it) is indeed possible aesthetically, in intellectual intuition, but is possible theoretically only through an infinite approach, like the approach of the quadrant to the circle, and that a type of immortality is just as necessary to the realisation of a system of thought as it is for an ethical system" (104.9ff.).

27 Perhaps the most succinct statement of Schiller's view of history is found in his essay: "Etwas über die erste Menschengesellschaft nach dem Leitfaden der mosaischen Urkunde (1790): "But man was destined for something different; and the forces that were within him beckoned him to a quite different kind of happiness [than that of the primitive, innocent state]. What nature had done for him during the time of his infancy, he should now do for himself, as soon as he attained his majority. He was to become the creator of his own happiness, and only the interest that he showed in that was to determine the measure of his happiness. He was to learn to seek out once more the state of innocence, which he now was losing, through his *reason* and come back as a free, reasonable spirit to the point from which he had begun as a plant; from a paradise of ignorance and slavery he was to work his way up, even if it were to take thousands of years, to a paradise of knowledge and freedom, that is, to the point where he would obey the moral law in his breast just as steadfastly as he had served instinct in the beginning, as plants and animals still serve it" (*Schillers Werke* [Trenke Edition], V, p. 19). A few lines later it becomes clear how far Schiller's reaction to man's expulsion from nature differed from that of Hölderlin, when Schiller writes: "This falling away of man from instinct . . . is without doubt the most fortunate and the greatest event in the history of man; from that moment he dates his freedom . . .." (pp. 19f.).

28 III, p. 163.

There is nothing original in the first sentence, which is merely a restatement of the old nature-reason dualism. But in the second sentence something quite new appears. For he now speaks of progress from harmony with nature in "simplicity" to an analogous harmony in freedom, which he still held to be the goal of all human life, as the "eccentric course." Man's progress was no longer to be thought of as development in one direction, from nature to freedom, but rather an "eccentric" development in a number of different directions.

What did Hölderlin mean by the "eccentric course?" In 1961, after a careful study of all the evidence relating to *Hyperion's Entstehungsgeschichte*, Professor Lawrence Ryan succeeded in defining more precisely than anyone before him what Hölderlin meant by the term "eccentric course." In doing so, he demonstrated how that symbol lies at the bottom of the entire novel. Professor Ryan's interpretation corresponds so closely to what we have been able to learn about Hölderlin's thought-processes as to anticipate our task of unravelling the connections between Hölderlin's thought-processes and his poetic symbols.

According to Professor Ryan the "eccentric course" represents man's eternal fluctuation between a condition of simplicity to one of refinement. There is, therefore, not one line of development, as Schiller had supposed, but two. There is progress from the state of natural simplicity *and back again*. Moreover, the two conditions of which Hölderlin speaks differ according to whether man is self-determined or nature-oriented. Professor Ryan speaks of the conditions as "Selbstbezogenheit" (being determined by one's relationship to oneself) and "Seinsgehörigkeit" (being determined by one's relationship to all being). The former condition is attained in the individual's self-determination in freedom. This was the only type of growth that either the Enlightenment or Critical Philosophy would admit. The "eccentric course," however, designated a cyclical growth pattern in which man defines himself as an individual, thus alienating himself from nature, and then returns to the womb of nature.[29]

It is this two-fold growth process that distinguishes Hölderlin from both Kant and Schiller, whose views Hölderlin did not consider incorrect but rather one-sided. He continued in the *Vorrede:* "Man would like to be *in* everything and *above* everything, and the maxim in Loyola's epitaph

non coerceri maximo, contineri tamen a minimo

can designate the all-craving, all-subjecting, hazardous side of man as much as the highest and most beautiful condition attainable to him."[30]

This sentence seems to be nothing less than a rejection of the Primacy of Practical Reason, which had led Schiller to conclude that "the beautiful soul" must become "the sublime soul" whenever there is a conflict between reason and nature. And yet Hölderlin in no way rejects reason but only the Primacy of

---

[29] Lawrence Ryan, *Hölderlins Hyperion. Exzentrische Bahn und Dichterberuf* (Stuttgart, 1965) pp. 8ff.
[30] III, p. 163.

Practical Reason. It was Hölderlin's task to redefine the relationship between man's reason and his nature so that nature might regain its position of equality, if not its own primacy. That does not mean that Hölderlin sought to deny man's right to self-assertion, to self-definition, to "Selbstbezogenheit." To have done so would have been to betray an essential part of his own nature, just as he would have been betraying himself if he had accepted without reservation the Primacy of Practical Reason. His hope was to demonstrate that alienation from nature, self-determination, man's apparent repudiation of nature, was itself a part of the natural order of things, and that each of these "essential directions" in which one might strike out in the assertion of freedom would eventually be "rectified." Man's natural instincts, his determined existence as a dumb brute, driven by animal instinct alone, could be overcome through his assertion of reason. But nature could not be escaped, "subjugated," or thwarted, because man's denial of his nature would make his freedom meaningless.

Hyperion is, in all its versions, the story of a modern Greek and the torment he endures because, as a modern man, he has lost contact with nature and has allowed himself to believe in the illusion of Critical Philosophy that man can "subjugate" nature to his own will. His task is to find his way back to the lap of nature — in order to venture out once more! He accomplishes that task by allowing himself to be "rectified," drawn back into the womb of nature, to become a hermit who, for a short time at least, does not try to liberate himself as an individual. The warrior who had gone forth to do battle in the early poems had now become the philosopher, the warrior of reason, who could make sense of his suffering only when he returned to "Stille" and allowed his self-determined individuality to be extinguished. Only then, after his return to Greece, could Hyperion "play with the spirits of those past hours."[31] Through the telling of his story, which is not so much a telling to Bellarmin as a telling to himself, Hyperion sorts out his experiences in the profane modern world of reason and comes to understand how they fit into the scheme of the "eccentric course" of his life, which will, we can be sure, be the familiar scheme of venturing forth into life and withdrawing in order to extract "the spirits" of his experiences.

In all the versions he reaches the conclusion at the very outset that reason is not enough. Hyperion opens the first letter of the *Thalia-Fragment:*

"I will return once more to my native Ionia; in vain did I leave my fatherland and *seek truth.*

"How could words satisfy my thirsting soul?

"Words I found everywhere; clouds, but no Juno.

"I hate them like death — all the miserable half-way houses between

---

[31] III, p. 166.

Something and Nothing. My whole soul strives against that which has no substance.

"Whatever is not everything is nothing to me."[32]

Here again he does not assert that modern thought is completely devoid of truth but merely that it is a half-way house [*Mittelding*] between something and nothing. In the prose draft of the *Metrical Version* of *Hyperion,* the young man to whom the old Hyperion tells his story (and who is surely supposed to follow Hyperion's example from then on) characterizes his mental state before he met Hyperion more specifically, but in much the same way:

"Through no fault of my own the school of fate and wise men had made me tyrannical against nature. This complete disbelief that I harbored against everything that I received from her hands allowed no love to flourish within me. The pure, free spirit, so I believed, could never be reconciled with the senses and their world and [I believed] there were no joys other than those of victory; I often demanded of fate the original freedom of our being. I often rejoiced in the struggle that reason waged against the unreasonable, because I was secretly more interested in gaining the feeling of superiority than in communicating the beauty of the lawless forces which stir the human heart. I heeded not the aid that nature offers in the great business of education, for I wanted to work alone, and I did not accept the willingness with which nature offered her hands to reason, for I wanted to master nature."[33]

The *Metrical Version* begins:

> Gestählt vom Schiksaal und den Weisen war
> Durch meine Schuld mein jugendlicher Sinn
> Tyrannisch gegen die Natur geworden.
> Unglaubig nahm ich auf, was ich wie sonst
> Aus ihrer mütterlichen Hand empfieng,
> So konnte keine Lieb in mir gedeihen.
> Ich freute mich des harten Kampfes, in dem
> Das Licht die alte Finsternis bekämpft,
> Doch kämpft ich mer, damit ich das Gefühl
> Der Überlegenheit erbeutete,
> Als um die Einigkeit und hohe Stille
> Den Kräften mit zu teilen, die gesezlos
> Der Menschen Herz bewegen, achtet' auch
> Der Hülfe nicht, womit uns die Natur
> Entgegenkömmt, in jeglichem Geschäfte
> Des Bildens, nahm die Willigkeit nicht an,

---

32 III, p. 164.
33 III, p. 186.

Womit der Stoff dem Geiste sich erbietet,
Ich wollte zähmen, herrschen wollt ich, richtete
Mit Argwohn und mit Strenge mich and andere.[34]

Hyperion's Youth begins:

"In the first years of maturity [*Mündigkeit*], when man has torn himself away
from happy instinct and the mind [*Geist*] begins to reign, it is usually not much
inclined to sacrifice to the graces."[35] He then continued with a slightly altered
version of the prose concept of the *Metrical Version*.

In all the fragments either Hyperion or the young man who is about to
become his student is characterized in this way. The details and the images that
Hölderlin used to throw the former into relief are important. It is, as we shall
soon see, the young Hyperion or his pupil who serves as a representative of
modern man who has liberated himself through reason but who has inad-
vertently gone too far in proclaiming his spiritual freedom. The sin of youth is
hybris — an element that Hölderlin emphasized more and more in each
succeeding version. Critical Philosophy, as Hölderlin understood it, showed all
the immoderate, self-assertive qualities of immaturity. To be able to act
independently of natural instincts was not enough. The protagonist was
determined to "subjugate" nature and thus establish the domination of his
reason over the sensual world through his moral law once and for all.

Now the development of Hyperion is a two-fold symbol. It represents, first of
all, the growth of a young poet from the point at which reason has established
its most repressive reign on through a life of unfulfilled dreams — the "eccentric
course" — until he learns to strike a balance between freedom and instinct. But
the story has another — an historical — dimension. For the story of Hyperion's
growth is also a symbolic recounting of man's growth in history from the
original state of harmony with nature, the age of myth and poetical symbol, to
the age of reason and the philosophic concept, and on to a future age in which
the two would be reconciled. Thus man would eventually come to enjoy both
moral freedom and oneness with all being at the same time. When Hölderlin
speaks of "the blessed days of childhood"[36] he is speaking of both his own
childhood and the historical childhood of mankind. "The lost paradise"[37] refers
to both a biographical and an historic past. Hyperion yearns for his own
childhood — "what I once dreamed as a child."[38] Modern man, the creature of
reason, yearns for the same thing. Because the biography of Hyperion and the
history of man coincide (and because Hyperion is a poet and is, therefore, able
to anticipate the coming age), it is possible for him to attain insight into the

[34] III, p. 187.
[35] III, p. 199.
[36] III, p. 164.
[37] III, p. 165.
[38] III, p. 234.

destiny of historical man through objectifying his own life and "playing with the spirit" of his past experiences.

Here Hölderlin was truly a child of his time. Kant, Schiller, Herder, and Lessing had always written as if the history of mankind was analogous to the life of man. Kant had spoken of the Enlightenment as the coming of age of mankind.[39] Schiller had treated primitive societies as groups of essentially childish men whose reason had not yet been awakened.[40] Lessing had spoken of "the education of the human race"[41] as an educational program designed by God, who changed textbooks from the Old Testament to the New Testament (and presumably to a more rationalistic text) as men progressed toward maturity. Herder had represented the development of language as a gradual loss of the pictorial, mythological quality of primitive peoples' language and the growth of an abstraction-laden idiom in which logic and reason prevail.[42] All of these representations had equated the growth of mankind with the growth of the individual; both were seen as a progression from an original childish state of imagination and poetic image to a final stage of rational thought.

The enthronement of reason was central to all of these interpretations of history. Kant had applauded the Enlightenment as the liberation of man from dogma. Lessing had applauded the entire course of history as the gradual unfolding of God's plan for the education of the human race. Schiller stood more or less with Kant and Lessing, although he was vaguely aware that in the course of his history man had lost something precious. Herder, in this sense anyway, stood much closer to Hölderlin than did the others. For he concluded as a result of his study of literature that the growing preponderance of reason had taken place not only at the expense of ignorance but also at the expense of much of the poetic, imaginative dimension of experience, without which human life was more reasonable, but poorer in spirit.[43]

The coincidence of the poet's development in his life and mankind's development in history makes it possible for Hyperion to be more than merely a maker of verses. He is able to transcend the limitations of time and become the poet-philosopher who perceives truth in mythological symbols and yet is able, as a child of the modern age, to explain that vision, to a limited degree at least, in the philosophic language of the present. He perceives a far broader vision than

---

[39] Immanuel Kant, "Beantwortung der Frage: Was ist Aufklärung? " *Berliner Monatsschrift,* December, 1784, pp. 481—494.

[40] See "Etwas über die erste Menschengesellschaft" in *Schillers Werke* (Trenke Edition), V, pp. 18ff.

[41] This parallel between the education of the individual and the history of man is seen most clearly in "Erziehung des Menschengeschlechts," §§ 1—3 (Gotthold Ephraim Lessing, *Gesammelte Werke* (2 vols.; Munich: Carl Hanser Verlag, n.d.), I, p. 1010.

[42] "Even when the language became more regular . . . it remained a type of song. . . ." (Suphan Edition), V, p. 58.

[43] The emotional basis of Herder's rejection of the culture of his time can be seen most clearly in "Journal meiner Reise im Jahre 1769" (Suphan Edition), IV, pp. 343—461.

others because he is not merely a philosopher but also a poet and thus has been able to perceive that human history does not run in a straight line away from "Seinsgehörigkeit" but must eventually return to that original state — this time in full consciousness of the joy's of "the lost paradise." But when he professes his beliefs to his contemporaries he speaks in abstractions and expresses himself in a curious mixture of philosophic concept and poetic image. In this way the old Hyperion tries to teach the young man in the *Metrical Version* and in *Hyperion's Youth*.

In order to understand the symbolic meaning of the events in Hyperion's life, it is helpful to consider how the old Hyperion, after he had already run his "eccentric course," conceptualized the eventual reconciliation between nature and reason. When the young man first approached Hyperion he was asked how he had found men during his wanderings, to which he replied: "More bestial than godly." Without a moment's hesitation Hyperion retorted: "That is because so few are human."[44] In response to the young man's request that he develop more fully that remark, the old Hyperion replied:

"We should not deny our nobility. We should keep the archetype [*Urbild*] of all existence within us pure and holy. The measure against which we judge nature is without limit, and the instinct to structure the formless in accordance with the archetype that we bear within us and subjugate resistant nature to the holy spirit is insuppressible. But even more bitter is the pain [that we suffer] in battle with her, even greater the risk that we will throw down our heavenly weapons in disgust, surrender to fate and our senses, deny reason, and become animals — or even that we, embittered by nature's resistance, will fight against her, not in order to establish peace and unity in her and thus between her and the divine part of us but rather in order to destroy her, so that we destroy violently every natural yearning, deny every sensitivity, and thus destroy the bond of union that connects us to the other spirits, make the world round about us into a desert and take the past as a model for a future devoid of hope."[45]

Hyperion, characteristically, began his teaching by cautioning against the sin of Critical Philosophy, which would result in a complete alienation from nature and thus in "a future devoid of hope." He went on to warn specifically that it was not enough to treat nature *as if* it were meaningful.

"Often phenomena present themselves to our senses so that it seems to us as if the divine had become visual within us — symbols of the holy and eternal within us. Often the greatest reveals itself in the smallest. The archetype of all unity, which we preserve in our spirit — it is reflected in the peaceful motions of our heart, presents itself in the face of this child."[46]

44 III, p. 188.
45 III, p. 188 and p. 190.
46 III, p. 190 and p. 192.

"I know that instinct alone causes us to see in nature an affinity to the immortal and to believe that there is a spirit in matter, but I know that this instinct justifies us in doing so. I know that we ourselves enliven the world with *our* soul when the beautiful forms of nature announce to us the presence of the divinity, but what is there that we would not make just as it is? "[47]

Here Hyperion admits the insistence of Critical Philosophy that nature means something only because we project into the natural world that meaning that we find in ourselves. But he denies that proposition on another level. ". . . what is there that we would not make just as it is?" This is the crucial turn in Höderlin's thought: Even if we admit that the form of meaning must originate, as far as we are concerned, in reason, there is still no more perfect representation of reason's meaning than nature's phenomena. If we had the power to create a world that would most perfectly symbolize the truth that originates within us, we would merely re-create the natural world with its beauty. Thus Hölderlin thought to establish the identity of truth and beauty that had been fundamental to Platonic thought. Hyperion advises the young man: "When you encounter in the guise of beauty what you bear within you as truth, then accept it and give thanks, for you have need of nature's aid.

"But keep your spirit free! Never lose yourself!"[48]

Hyperion's teaching thus consists of a dialectical progression. Thesis: Man must remain receptive to natural beauty (animal). Antithesis: Man must maintain his freedom from the sensual world (godly). This leads him to the proposition that man must synthesize these divergent tendencies through love. And it is in this attempt to synthesize reason and nature through love that Hölderlin hearkens back to Plato and thus differs markedly from his contemporaries.

In the prose draft of the *Metrical Version* Hyperion says: "When our original infinite being became passive, for the first time the full and free force perceived the first limitations; when poverty was paired with abundance, then arose love. Are you asking when that was? Plato says: On the day that Aphrodite was born. Hence at the time when the beautiful world began for us, when we came into consciousness — we became finite. Now we feel deeply the limitations of our being, and the inhibited force strives impatiently against its fetters; and yet there is something in us that keeps these fetters gladly — for if the divine within us were not limited by some resistance, then we would know nothing other than ourselves and thus nothing of ourselves; and not to know anything of ourselves, not to feel and being destroyed are for us one and the same thing.

"We cannot deny our instinct to liberate, ennoble ourselves and to progress eternally — that would be bestial; we cannot, however, deny the instinct to be

[47] III, p. 192.
[48] III, p. 203.

determined, to receive, either — that would not be human. We could but perish in the struggle of these conflicting instincts. But love unites. She strives incessantly for the highest and the best, for her father is abundance; she does not, however, deny her mother, poverty; she hopes for aid. To love so is human. That highest need of our being, which compels us to ascribe to nature an affinity to the immortal within us and to believe in a spirit in matter — is love."[49]

When he reworked this passage into iambic verse, he wrote:

> — Wie sollten wir den Trieb
> Unendlich fortzuschreiten, uns zu läuten,
> Uns zu veredlen, zu befrein, verläugnen?
> Das wäre thierisch. Doch wir sollten auch
> Des Triebs, beschränkt zu werden, zu empfangen,
> Nicht stolz uns überheben. Denn es wäre
> Nicht menschlich, und wir tödteten uns selbst.
> Den Wiederstreit der Triebe, deren keiner
> Entbehrlich ist, vereiniget die Liebe.
>
> Wenn deine Pflicht ein feurig Herz begleitet,
> Verschmähe nicht den rüstigen Gefährten.
> Und wenn dem Göttlich in dir ein Zeichen
> Der gute Sinn erschafft, und goldne Wolken
> Den Äther des Gedankenreichs umziehn,
> Bestürme nicht die freudigen Gestalten!
> Denn du bedarfst der Stärkung der Natur.
>
> Dem Höchsten und dem Besten ringt unendlich
> die Liebe nach, und wandelt kühn und frei
> Durch Flammen und durch Fluthen ihre Bahn,
> Sie wartet aber auch in fröhlichem
> Vertraun der Hülfe, die von außen kömmt,
> Und überhebt sich ihrer Armuth nicht.[50]

Love then bears within itself the elements of reconciliation. As the Greeks perceived, love shares in both abundance and poverty. Love is godly, for her father was a god; thus she is, to a degree, independent of the sensual world. Hölderlin, as we have seen from frequent passages from the *Hyperion* fragments, equated the divine with reason, for both existed independent of the senses. But love is also the daughter of poverty — the offspring of unspirited nature to which she is bound. Her natural limitation makes for inexpressible yearning for the flight of the unfettered spirit. But limitations also make consciousness possible.

---

[49] III, p. 192 and p. 194.
[50] III, pp. 195 (lines 146—167).

With consciousness it is possible to bring the beautiful objects of the natural world into agreement with the postulates of reason.

Here again Hölderlin was trying to bring Critical Philosophy into agreement with Platonic metaphysics. Where Kant and Schiller had never succeeded in demonstrating *how* the *Urtheilskraft* reconciled *Verstand* and *Vernunft* through aesthetic judgments, Hölderlin appealed to the mythology of the *Phaedrus*. There Plato says: "Thus far I have been speaking of the fourth and last kind of madness, which is imputed to him who, when he sees the beauty of the earth, is transported with the recollection of true beauty; he would like to fly away, but he cannot; he is like a bird fluttering and looking upward and careless of the world below; and he is therefore esteemed mad."[51] Beauty is then not merely the way of looking at nature *as if* it meant something but is rather the occasion for the recollection of true beauty, the beauty of the eternal Ideals, the beauty that is at the same time absolute truth. Plato goes on to say: "But, as he forgets earthly interests and is wrapped in the divine, the vulgar deem him mad, and rebuke him; they do not see that he is inspired."[52]

The deity that lies dormant in the philosophic spirit and is awakened by the perception of beauty so that it desires a reunion with the true world of Ideals must, of course, suffer in the modern world in which man is alienated from the true forms. "Alas!" Hölderlin writes in the *Thalia-Fragment*, "the god within us is lonely and impoverished. When will he find all his kinsmen? Who were once there and will be there? When will come the great reunion of the spirits? For, as I believe, we were once all together."[53]

This is the striking symbol that Hölderlin found to designate the loneliness of the individual and of modern man in general. It was the image of the wanderer who yearned for the reconciliation of all men and for the time in which all men would once more be joined together. That was the final goal of man. But there are indications that Hölderlin believed that the goal would never be attained in the real world. Indeed, it could not, because everyday reality presupposes an individuated subject apart from the object. Certainly the goal would never be attained through the type of love as it is known on earth. The learning of love would lead man astray. The "eccentric course" would consist of many "essential directions" and their "rectifications." The old Hyperion cries in *Hyperion's Youth:* "The history of my youth is a succession of contradicting extremes."[54] The honing of love, the constant, never ending redefinition of love through a series of encounters with beautiful objects, and disappointments in love — all these comprise the process of "education" of which Hyperion is symbolic.

---

51 *The Works of Plato,* translated and edited by B. Jowett (4 vols.; Tudor Publishing Company, n.d.), III, p. 408.
52 *Ibid.*
53 III, p. 167.
54 III, p. 205.

In the fragments, however, only one of these essential directions is developed: Hyperion's unhappy love for the beautiful woman, who is named Melite in the *Thalia-Fragment* and Diotima in *Hyperion's Youth*. The adoption of the name Diotima is significant because it shows that at some point during the winter in Jena Hölderlin became aware of his intellectual kinship to Plato and of how much closer he stood to Plato than he did to Kant, Schiller, or Fichte. Not only is the Platonic concept of love implicit in the *Thalia-Fragment;* before that, in his letter to Neuffer in the summer of 1793, Hölderlin had referred specifically to Socrates' speech at the banquet and had expressed the hope of communicating the spirit of Plato's *Symposium* to *Hyperion*. In that speech Socrates tells how, as a young man, he had learned the secret of love as the key to all wisdom through the wise Diotima. The quintescence of her teaching is found in her closing remarks about the relationship between love, truth, and beauty.

"For he who has been instructed thus far in the things of love, and who has learned to see the beautiful in due order and succession, when he comes toward the end will suddenly perceive a nature of wondrous beauty — and this, Socrates, is that final cause of all our former toils, which in the first place is everlasting — not growing and decaying, or waxing and waning; in the next place not fair in one point of view and foul in another, or at one time or in one relation or in one place fair, at another time or in another relation or in another place foul, as if fair to some and foul to other, or in the likeness of a face or hands or any other part of the bodily frame, or in any form of speech or knowledge, nor existing in any other being; as for example, an animal, whether in earth or heaven, but beauty only, absolute, separate, simple and everlasting, which without dimunition and without increase, or any change is imparted to the ever-growing and perishing beauties of all other things. He who under the influence of true love rising upward from these begins to see that beauty, is not far from the end. And the true order of going or being led by another to the things of love, is to use the beauties of the earth as steps along which he mounts upward for the sake of that other beauty, going from one to two, and from two to all fair forms, and from fair forms to fair actions, and from fair actions to fair notions, until from fair notions he arrives at the notion of absolute beauty, and at last knows what the essence of beauty is. This, my dear Socrates, . . . is that life above all others which man should live, in the contemplation of beauty absolute. . . ."[55]

Hyperion was meant to depict that gradual progress up the scale of beauties to the final, absolute, everlasting beauty — which implies that it was supposed to demonstrate mankind's progress to absolute truth as well. There are strong indications that Hölderlin meant it that way from the very beginning; for he indicates that "becoming a brother to men" had not satisfied him. In the final version the incident with Alabanda at the end of the first book demonstrates

---

55 *The Works of Plato,* III, pp. 341ff.

how Hyperion was beginning his upward path with friendship, but could not be satisfied with that alone.[56]

But Hyperion was, of course, a modern youth, and for him absolute love could only be for the perfect woman. Diotima then becomes both teacher and object of love. His love for her and the stormy course of their romance comprise the heart of the narrative segments of the early fragments. That story is divided into three parts: the encounter, the disappointment, and the farewell. In each of these parts Hölderlin gives ample evidence that Diotima (or Melite, since we shall concentrate more on the *Thalia-Fragment* in order to show that the ideal significance of the beloved was actually there from the beginning) was the Platonic symbol for the perfect realization of love. In the *Thalia-Fragment*, which we shall take as our model, Hyperion encounters Melite after he has already despaired of finding fulfillment among men. He had tried to "buy pearls from beggars who were poorer than I."[57] He speaks of how he had often thought that he had found the true friend, only to be disappointed. "How often I believed that I had made the holy exchange and then demanded and demanded, and then the poor person stood there, embarrassed, perplexed, and even spiteful — he wanted only a pastime, nothing so serious."[58]

This disappointment in friendship is alluded to in the *Metrical Version* also:

> Einst hatte wohl der fromme Mäonide
> Mein junges Herz gewonnen, auch von ihm
> Und seinen Göttern war ich abgefallen. —[59]

In *Hyperion's Youth,* after Hyperion had found that his teacher had left him to find his own way, he "sought consolation among men." "I idolized many a man at first glance . . . . I think with regret of how I strove with all my love to buy a sincere laugh, how I often gave away my whole soul in a word, to receive a wise crack in return . . . ."[60] This inability to find fulfillment in friendship was now symbolized in Hyperion's relationship to Gondara Notara, who shared

---

[56] It is strikingly autobiographical that Hölderlin had Hyperion's friendship to Alabanda go sour because the political conspirators with whom Alabanda was collaborating were cynical men whom Hyperion regarded as evil because they expressed sentiments which repelled him (and which anticipate the low opinion of man that characterizes modern totaletarians): "We do not beg for man's hearts. For we do not need his heart or his will. For he is in no case against us, for everything is [working] for us; and the fools and the clever ones and the simple-minded and the wise, and all vices and all virtues of coarseness and refinement stand . . . in our service, and blindly aid us along toward our goal" (III, p. 34). This leads Hyperion to reject them — and Alabanda, who has, through associating with such men, betrayed Hyperion's friendship: "He is evil, I cried, he is evil. He pretends to be boundlessly trusting and lives with such [men] — and conceals it from you" (III, p. 35).

[57] III, p. 164.
[58] *Ibid.*
[59] III, p. 187.
[60] III, p. 211.

many of Hyperion's opinions but was far more realistic than the hero. "[Notara said that] I had as yet never seen a human being in my life . . . I had always moved among intellectual phenomena, and it was [he said] a shame that these vanished as soon as I approached them, but one had to like such a queer fellow given to fantasy."[61]

When Notara left Hyperion said: "I got used to expecting joy from strange hands and had now become even poorer than before. I was like a beggar whom the rich man has kicked away from his door and who now returns to his cabin to console himself there and who now feels his misery even more bitterly between his poor walls. The more I brooded in my loneliness, the more desolate it became within me. It is truly a hurt without equal, an interminable sensation of obliteration when being has lost its meaning so completely. An indescribable despondency oppressed me. Often I dared not open my eyes to men. I had hours in which I feared a child's laughter. At that time I was very still and patient [and] often had a strange, superstitious belief in the healing powers of many things; often I secretly expected consolation from a little possession that I had bought, from a boat ride, from a valley that a mountain hid from me. Along with my courage, my strength also vanished. I really believed that I was perishing."[62]

It was while he was suffering from this deep depression over his disappointment with friendship that Hyperion, who seemed to have despaired of ever trying again, encountered his Melite. He was, of course, aware that he suffered from a complete isolation from all nature, and he felt the stirring of his yearning once more.

"My old friend Spring surprised me in my gloominess. At another time I would have felt him from afar when the torpid branches stirred and a soft breeze brushed my cheek. At another time I would have hoped that he was bringing a softening of every pain. But hoping and anticipation had gradually vanished from my soul.

"Now he was there in all the glory of youth.

"It seemed to me that I should also become happy again. I opened my window and got dressed, as if for a festival. The heavenly stranger was to visit me also.

"I saw how everything poured forth into the out-of-doors, onto the friendly sea of Smyrna and its beach. Strange sensations were aroused in me. I went out also."[63]

Here we see the narrative description of that state of spirit that Hölderlin had expressed conceptually through the phrase "tyrannical toward nature." In the

---

61 III, p. 212.
62 III, p. 213.
63 III, p. 166.

Metrical Version and in *Hyperion's Youth* the young man who was to learn from Hyperion reflects upon his past and expresses his former attitude in philosophic concepts. In the *Thalia-Fragment* and in Hyperion's own story in *Hyperion's Youth,* the same spiritual condition is represented with greater artistic skill. For Hyperion now reproduces those feelings in such a way that both he and the reader actually experience his former feelings rather than merely contemplating a number of philosophic concepts. But the frame of mind represented in both the philosophic discussion and in the artistic representation is the same. In both cases it is a question of the man of reason who has gone to extremes, who has isolated himself from nature in his zeal to experience the victory of reason over unreason, and who thus suffers a terrible emptiness. Hölderlin, the philosopher-poet, gives the reader both a philosophic and a poetic representation of the state of spirit in question. Naturally it is the younger man who provides the discussion in rationalistic concepts, while Hyperion, who has outgrown that stage long ago, speaks as a poet.

It is now time for the "essential direction" to be "rectified." And it is at just the moment at which reason's assertion of its own autonomy reaches its extreme that the crucial encounter takes place. It is at that moment that the young man encounters Hyperion. It was at that moment in Hyperion's life that he had encountered Melite. The young man's encounter with Hyperion represents the first stage in the progression toward perfection — the awakening of friendship. Hyperion is already at a higher stage when he encounters Melite. Since Hyperion has already gone through the stage of friendship, he is now ready for the more clear representation of the love-beauty synthesis in the person on the beautiful woman.

"Ah! *she* appeared to me in this painful feeling of my loneliness, with this bleeding heart devoid of all joys; lovely and holy, like a priestess of love, she stood there before me; as if woven of light and fragrance, so spiritual and tender; above her smile filled with peace and heavenly goodness reigned with the majesty of a god her large, enraptured eye, and, like little clouds in the morning light, her golden locks fluttered about her forehead in the spring wind."[64]

Hyperion's description of how he felt at that moment of encounter recalls once more Plato's description of the moment of madness when the philosopher first glimpses the beautiful object.

"Years have passed! Springs have come and gone; many a magnificent image of nature, many a remembrance of your Italy produced of a heavenly fantasy, enthralled my eye; but most have been swept away by time; only *her* image has remained with me, along with everything connected with her. Still she stands there before me as in the holy drunken moment in which I found her; I press it to my heart, the sweet phantom; her voice, the lisping of her harp; like a friendly

[64] *Ibid.*

arcadia where blossoms and tall corn are lulled in the eternally still air, where the harvest ripens without the noon sultriness, and the sweet grape thrives, where no fear encircles the secure land, where one knows nothing save the eternal springtime of the earth and the cloudless sky, and its sun, and its friendly stars — thus it stands there open before me, the shrine of her heart and spirit."[65]

Again in the *Thalia-Fragment:* "That evening of the day of [all] my days is unforgettable to me, along with everything of which I became aware in my drunkenness."[66]

In the opening scenes of the *Thalia-Fragment,* Melite is described as the Platonic ideal that lends its coloring, its aura, its magic to everything that comes in contact with it. "Everything was compelled toward her. A part of her being seemed to communicate itself to everything. A new tender sense, a new intimacy had come among all [people], and they knew not what was happening to them."[67]

In *Hyperion's Youth* Diotima is called "the triumph of the youthful spirit, the quiet uniting of our thought and poetry."[68] Notara's mother tells Hyperion: "The olden poets and wise men were, however, her element; in this sense she was a special being; she was always very secretive, but people had already noticed that she celebrated in her heart the memory of great men of ancient Greece, just as pious souls celebrate the feast of Panagia and other blessed ones; also, in other ways, there was something . . . superhuman about her."[69]

In *Hyperion's Youth* the old Hyperion, who has not seen Diotima for many years, says of her: "Now I honor as truth what was revealed to me obscurely in her image. I foresaw the Ideal of my eternal existence as she stood before me in her grace and majesty, and, for that reason, I like to return to this blessed hour, to you, Diotima, Heavenly Being."[70]

This appreciation of Diotima came only after many years, long after the part of his life in which she had played an active role. Only through the telling of the story, only through the objectifying of himself and his past life did Hyperion become aware of why his love for her was important in his development. Through the telling of the story Hyperion was at last able to discern the structure of his life and thus to distinguish the significant from the meaningless. That knowledge was the reward for the long struggle. It was the reward that the original Diotima had promised Socrates — the fulfillment of love's purpose, the final recognition of the unity, the identity of beauty and truth, which Diotima symbolized in the life of Hyperion.

---

65 III, p. 167.
66 III, p. 168.
67 *Ibid.*
68 III, p. 221.
69 III, p. 218.
70 III, p. 217.

But all that came many years afterwards. Socrates' Diotima had spoken of hardships. As one proceeds from one love to another, from one level of awareness to a higher one, one inevitably errs. The old Hyperion said that his youth had been a never-ending alternation between extremes. One sees that tendency of youth to think only in the most extreme terms in the vocabulary of the young man who comes to hear Hyperion's teaching. For him there were only "godly" and "bestial," reason or unreason. It was the old Hyperion who suggested "human" as a compromise. The "eccentric course," the progression from one level to the next highest is then also a progression from one sin to another. The young Hyperion's love for Melite is the story of youth's sin against the beauty. His transgression is typical in that it resulted from his ignorance. As a modern man, dedicated to reason, he was unable to perceive the symbolic quality of Melite's beauty and thus unable to love in the right way. But only when he did learn to love in the right way would he be able to attain beauty and truth.

Overwhelmed by Melite's physical beauty, Hyperion was unable to see that she symbolized something beyond the senses. The *sight* of her awakened him from his spiritual lethargy; his *reflection* on her beauty, which took place many years after the experience, when he had attained that "disinterested" vantage point of which Kant had spoken,[71] allowed him to see in her that enduring beauty that existed apart from all bodies. As a child of the modern world, whose characteristic spiritual condition was one of intense yearning, Hyperion wanted to possess her immediately.

Through the interplay of Hyperion's and Melite's personalities Hölderlin demonstrated the deep abyss that separated modern man from classical art, in which was embodied the pure synthesis of truth and beauty. Hyperion and Faust are two of the earliest representatives of that figure which has haunted European literature for the last two centuries: the anguished searcher after truth who, despite the sincerity of his yearning, is so frantic that he cannot perceive that beauty and truth exist in all life and thus experiences life in such a fragmentary way that he doubts the validity of his visions of beauty.

Hyperion feels instinctively that Melite is somehow divine: "Melite spoke many a heavenly word, naively, without any intent, in pure, holy simplicity. Often when I heard her speak I thought of the picture of Dadalus, of which Parnasius said that their appearance, with all their simplicity, had something godly."[72] But it was just that godliness that was too much for Hyperion. Much as Faust was overwhelmed by the spirit of virginal purity and serenity in Gretchen's room, Hyperion discovers that the very idea that there might exist a perfection beyond his grasp is quite unbearable. That reaction manifests itself

71 *Kritik der Urteilskraft* (1793 Edition), p. 17.
72 III, p. 168.

first a few hours after Hyperion had first met Melite. He sat with his friends in Notara's garden. Melite was with them. Still enthralled with her beauty, Hyperion had sat silently through much of the conversation. Then, when he heard the others begin to speak of friendship among the ancient Greeks, he arose from his torpor.

"We should not speak of that . . . .

"Such magnificence would destroy us poor things. Of course, those were golden days when men exchanged weapons and loved each other until death, when men produced immortal children in the rapture of love and beauty, deeds for the Fatherland and heavenly songs and eternal words of wisdom, and, yes! when the Egyptian priest chided Solon, 'You Greeks are always youths!' We have now become old men, more clever than all the magnificent ones who have gone on; it is just a shame that so much vigor has to languish in this alien element!"[73]

It was thus inevitable that his love for Melite would be torment for him. "Forgive me, Holy One!" he wrote. "I have often cursed the moment I found her and raved in my soul against the heavenly creature that she had awakened me to life only to crush me with her majesty."[74]

Unable to partake of the godliness that he could no longer deny, Hyperion was continually reminded of his own spiritual poverty. His very sanity depended on her presence. "But what I was, I was through her. The good woman rejoiced at the light that shone in me and did not think that it was only a reflection of her own. I soon felt that I was poorer than a shadow if she did not live in and around and for me, if she did not become mine; and that I became nothing when she withdrew from me. It could not have been otherwise; I could but question her every look and sound with this deadly fear, follow her glance as if my love was about to flee from me, either to fly to heaven or to return to the earth."[75]

Also in the *Thalia-Fragment* he wrote: "As long as I was near her and her enrapturing spirit lifted me above all of men's poverty, I often forgot even the cares and desires of my heart. When I was away I concealed it from myself in vain and there arose in me the noisy lament: She does not love you! I raved and struggled. But my grief persisted in torturing me. My restlessness increased from day to day. The higher and the mightier her spirit shone above me, the more dismal and unruly became my soul."[76]

Now his infatuation was becoming an obsession. "In my life there was no sleep and no waking any more. There was only *one* dream of her, a blessed, painful dream, a struggle between despair and hope."[77]

[73] III, p. 169.
[74] III, p. 170.
[75] *Ibid.*
[76] III, p. 172.
[77] III, p. 171.

Melite's inner peace was not communicated to Hyperion. He became, on the contrary, more miserable than he had ever been before. Her presence, which served as a constant reminder of his own spiritual poverty, robbed him of even the comfort of that spiritual lethargy, that spiritual death, into which he had descended before he met her. She had aroused him from that state of lethargy, but she had not been able to satisfy that renewed yearning that she had caused to be kindled in his breast. Seeing her became torment. The very sight of her was a reminder of his own worthlessness. And so, because he was unable to partake of her inner peace and because she was unable to help him, she, the very symbol of that inner peace and freedom from yearning that comes from perfect knowledge and its incorporation in perfect beauty, became a source of increasing agitation for him.

"Finally," he wrote, "she seemed to avoid me. I had even decided never to see her again and had, with nameless anguish, succeeded in defying my heart and staying away for a few days."[78] It was, of course, impossible for him to stay away for long. A few days later he heard that Notara and his family had left town and that Melite was at home alone. Unable to control himself and his yearning for her, he rushed to her, justifying his inability to restrain himself with a remark that expresses what he hoped to get from her with the utmost simplicity: "I wanted to change. Oh, I wanted to become like her."[79]

What follows that is the first of two scenes in the *Thalia-Fragment* in which Melite becomes Hyperion's teacher and directs him to learn renunciation of the beautiful bodies for the sake of true, ideal beauty. In this, the first of those scenes, he apologized for treating her coldly during the previous days, to which Melite replied: "I have been grieving over you. I would gladly have granted peace to you. I often wanted to beg you to be quieter. You are such a completely different person in your good hours. I confess, I fear for you when I see you so gloomy and irritable."[80] Then she continued with an allusion to that past time of childhood happiness and innocent oneness with all nature. "It is such a painful riddle that a spirit such as yours should be burdened with such cares. There was surely a time when it was free of this restlessness. Can you no longer recall it? Could I but bring it back to you! This quiet festival, this holy peace within you, in which even the softest sound coming from the depths of the soul is perceptible, and the softest motion from without, from heaven, from the branches and the flowers — I cannot express how I have often felt when I stood there before divine nature and everything earthly fell silent within me — he is so near then, the Invisible One."[81]

---

78 III, p. 172.
79 III, p. 174.
80 *Ibid.*
81 III, pp. 174ff.

The goal that Melite set for Hyperion was that condition of inner peace and harmony with all being in which the poet hears the voice of the divinity speaking through all nature. In that state nature would no longer be a collection of individual beings, each doomed to die, but an aggregate of interrelated symbols through which the Absolute would be able to speak to man. Crucial to the attainment of that state is the attitude of the subject. The original Diotima's words to Socrates when she told him that the beautiful body is meaningful only to him who transcends the physical dimension are echoed in a way that shows to how great an extent Kant had influenced Hölderlin's understanding of Plato. ". . . you have control over yourself; I know it. Tell your heart that one searches for peace in oneself in vain if one does not give it to oneself. I have always cherished these words so much. They are my father's words, a fruit of sorrow, as he said. Grant this peace to yourself and be joyful! You will do it. It is my first request."[82]

But Hyperion's reaction shows how far he was from understanding what she was trying to teach him. " 'As you will, as you will, Angel of Heaven!' I cried as I, without realizing what was happening to me, seized her hand and pulled her violently to my grieving heart.

"As if awakened from a dream, she twisted loose, as kindly as possible, with a majesty in her eye that crushed me to the earth.

" 'You must change,' she cried more violently than before!"[83]

Melite's father, whose wisdom she had hoped to impart to Hyperion, was "a peculiar man [who], in disgust over the present situation of the Greeks, had gone away to Smyrna long before. . . ."[84] In *Hyperion's Youth* Diotima's father had been Hyperion's old teacher and friend. Hyperion, filled with despair over the disappearance of Diotima, is writing to him when the fragment breaks off. The teaching which Melite repeats in the *Thalia-Fragment* is, for a man of Hyperion's fiery temperament, an admonition to learn renunciation. Now that she has awakened Hyperion to a renewed yearning for beauty, she had to teach him that the peace he sought could only be found in himself and that the mere physical possession of her, or of any beautiful object, was not the same as the possession of true beauty. Only in renouncing physical beauty could one ascend the ladder to the next step and thus hope to gain true knowledge.

That knowledge comes to Hyperion when, along with Notara, Melite, and other friends, he visits Homer's cave. Once more the memory of Greece's past greatness is more than he can endure. He leaves the others and goes down to the sea. Even now he can only mutter the name Melite, but he knows now that he yearns for her in vain. "Alas, there was no peace anywhere in the world that I

[82] III, p. 175.
[83] *Ibid.*
[84] III, p. 168.

might find. To be near her or far from her, whom I loved so namelessly and whom I had so namelessly and inexpressibly tormented, was all the same."[85] Now he was ready to learn how to renounce the individual. There on the shore Melite found him. "With heavenly tears she beseeched me to come to know at least the nobler, stronger part of my being, as she knew it, [and] to direct my glance to the independent, indominable, godly that was in me as it was in everyone — whatever did not spring from this source, [she said], would lead to death; whatever came from it and returned to it would be eternal — whatever need and deficiency united would cease to be *one,* just as need would cease; whatever was united in that and for that which was alone great, alone holy, alone unshakeable, its unity must exist like the eternal through and for which it existed; and so — here she had to stop. The others were coming after her. In that moment I would have dared a thousand lives to hear her out! I never heard her out. Perhaps I shall hear the rest beyond the stars."[86]

Melite's teaching remained, therefore, a lesson half-taught and half-learned. Already Hyperion felt something stirring within himself. His attitudes began to change. No longer did he insist that his companions not mention the glorious past of their homeland. He said rather: " 'Let that which perishes perish,' I cried in the midst of the enthralled company, 'it perishes in order to be reborn; it grows old in order to regain its youth; it is separated in order to be more perfectly united; it dies in order to live more fully.' "[87]

Hyperion did not as yet fully understand the implication of his own words. Only when the long years of wandering on foreign soil were behind him; only when he returned to his native land and began writing his serialized account of those events of his youth to Bellarmin in the *Thalia-Fragment* or told his story to his young friend in *Hyperion's Youth* — did he begin to understand Melite's (Diotima's) importance to him. But the words he spoke to his friends on the way back from Homer's cave indicate quite clearly that he was now beginning to understand why it was necessary to renounce the physical and dare to search for that spiritual fulfillment in which, before he had met Melite, he had not even believed. He accepted the death of Greece's past age of greatness and the entire natural process of physical aging and death — the very process that would eventually destroy Melite's beauty. Now he had at least some vague presentiment of the eternal recurrence of things, of the cycle of growth, aging, death, and rebirth, which he had represented as the "eccentric course" in the *Vorrede* of the *Thalia-Fragment.* Now he had overcome the feeling of anxiety and hopelessness from which he had suffered in the beginning of the fragment.

But not the need to suffer! All life is suffering. The mere intellectual acceptance of Melite's teaching was not enough. Intellectual acceptance of the

85 III, p. 179.
86 *Ibid.*
87 III, p. 180.

fact that beauty symbolized truth demanded that he act on that belief, that he live his life from that point on according to that teaching. Melite had served her purpose, and so she forced him to keep his word and go with his friends to Asia Minor, as he had promised. When he returned he found Melite gone. He never saw her again.

As can be concluded from the above discussion, Hölderlin was struggling to reconcile two different and, in reality, antagonistic elements in *Hyperion*. On the one hand there is the story of the young Hyperion, which revolved around the figure of Melite and thus seems to hold out the promise of a true reconciliation of nature and reason, and thus the promise of attaining absolute knowledge in life. That story and the promise it symbolized was dear to Hölderlin's heart. There can be little doubt, I think, that the love story was the germ of the novel which Hölderlin brought with him from Tübingen. But, on the other hand, there is also the teaching of the old Hyperion, which is more in the spirit of Critical Philosophy and which thus gives little hope that Melite's bright promise would ever be fulfilled in Hyperion's life on earth.

It is not very important how we designate these conflicting elements. Throughout this discussion we have spoken of Platonic and Critical thought, ancient and modern views of life, poetic vision and philosophic concept. Whether we use one designation or the other is of no particular significance. We are dealing with two ways in which the subject relates to the object of knowledge. First, there is the object-centered thought, which Hölderlin found in Plato's *eros* theory. According to that view it is the business of man to experience oneness with the objective world, which implied a certain loss of autonomy as an individual — that is to say, the individual is limited in his freedom by reality. That did not imply a dogmatically empirical function of the mind; in Plato's view the mind was to penetrate the outer appearance and, through the power of love, arrive at the essence, or the "Idea," or "Form" of the object of knowledge. That element of love made the mind active in its attempt to find knowledge, not merely a passive organ registering sense impressions. But cognition through reason was only the prelude to the subject's identification with the objective world, which was always understood as maintaining its independence of the human mind. Put succinctly and in an admittedly simplified form, the final goal of the subject was to find his place in the objective world. All the "spirits," as Melite said, would eventually "find each other." It was the business of the subject to find his way to the others, not to invent them.

Modern philosophy is subject-oriented. This is particularly true of German philosophy from Kant on. However much Kant insisted that it was not his *intention* to deny the existence of the objective world, he eventually came to the realization that his original denial that knowledge of the "Ding an sich" was possible amounted to the same thing. Kant's famed Copernican Revolution shifted the search for absolutes, for the firm basis of all knowledge, from the objective world *into the subject.* This is particularly obvious when one considers that the so-called Golden Age of German philosophy ended with the monstrosity of Hegelianism, with *all* reality being viewed as *Geist,* an all-pervading subject in search of *self*-knowledge. Since Kant, metaphysics was no longer possible. Everything objective was derivative and could thus have no absolute validity. The absolute must be sought in the subject and, therefore, in the only area in which the subject possessed complete autonomy from natural law — in the realm of morality. Fichte's enthronement of duty was an exaggeration and disturbed the precarious balance of Kant's system. But, as Hölderlin may have suspected, that balance rested on the assumption that the objective world possessed some sort of reality independent of the subject — the one assumption which, according to Kant's own rules, he could not legitimately make.

When Hölderlin set for himself the task of reconciling the object-centered view, to which he as a poet was naturally inclined, and the subject-oriented view, which he felt compelled to reckon with because he was attracted to the morally liberating quality of Critical Philosophy, he found himself facing a problem which simply could not be solved. For in trying to attain Plato's ends through Kant's means he was, in fact, using epistemological tools forged in the belief that there could be no direct knowledge of the objective world in order to attain just that kind of knowledge. Thus the poetic representation found in the *Thalia-Fragment* is contradicted by the conceptual argument advanced in the *Metrical Version,* in which the old Hyperion admits the subjective ground of all knowledge and then tries to pass off that admission as meaningless on the grounds that everything would be just as it is now if knowledge rested on an objective ground.

That contradiction was not solved in *Hyperion's Youth,* which is little more than an unsuccessful attempt to reconcile the *Thalia-Fragment* and the *Metrical Version.* There are some variations in the story of Hyperion's youth. Additional information is given about Hyperion's teacher, who is revealed to be Diotima's father; the theme of disappointment in friendship before Hyperion encountered his beloved is also developed. But the most significant change is found in the progression of the heroine's name from Melite to Diotima. In Hyperion's account of his youth, the Platonic element had become more important than before. But for just that reason there is striking lack of unity between the early chapters, in which Hyperion still talks like the student of Fichte, and the later chapters, in which he recounts his youth always with an eye toward Plato. And, also for that reason, he proved unable to salvage reality for the objective world — or a task for the poet.

Late in 1795 Hölderlin wrote Hegel about the "airy spirits of metaphysics" that he had brought with him from Jena.[88] Years later he wrote his mother that

---

[88]   128.36.

he had suffered unspeakable agony because he had felt compelled to play the philosopher and had feared being regarded as "merely a poet."[89] When he finished *Hyperion,* however, the influence of Critical Philosophy had been greatly reduced. He was able to finish the novel only when he learned that he would be able to write it as "merely a poet." But until that time he suffered. And he suffered most of all during the six months that he spent at Schiller's side and in Fichte's lecture hall in Jena.

In January 1795 Hölderlin gave up his teaching position and returned to Jena from Weimar on the advice of Charlotte von Kalb. As can be seen from his letter to Mother explaining why he had given up his position so abruptly, he was in a state of extreme nervous agitation. He was afraid that he would not be able to convince his mother to let him stay in Jena, and so he took pains to impress upon her how important the opportunity to work with Schiller would be for his career and how well he understood the importance of frugality. "With my limited way of living, I think I can get by quite well until Easter on seven Carolines," he wrote. "Schiller is showing a right warm interest in me. If I can finish a work that I have been working on for years by Easter, then I will not be a burden to you even then. I am now in a period that is probably decisive for my future life. Even Herder, whom I visited in Weimar, is very interested in me, as Frau von Kalb has just written me, and has sent word to me that I might visit him as often as I am in Weimar."[90] And then: "Over there [in Weimar] I even spoke with the great Goethe. Association with such men sets all one's faculties in motion."[91] Then he told her that his plan was to attend lectures in Jena until the fall, at which time he would either lecture himself, find a new position as *Hofmeister* in Switzerland (probably to be near Hegel), or become some young man's companion.[92] He concluded: "Support my courage through your kind interest in my destiny. Do not, dearest Mother, let unfounded worries shake those hopes that you surely harbor for me, because a mother will never cease having hopes for her son! Grant me the undisturbed use of my powers, which I am now enjoying almost for the first time since my early youth. Believe me [when I say that] I have not preferred my paltry meal (which I enjoy *once* a day) to a rich table and, for now anyway, to my home hearth out of childish motives."[93]

This letter set the frenzied tone for his entire stay in Jena. During that time he seems to have gone to seed rather badly. Already extremely nervous because of his recent experiences with Fritz von Kalb, excited by the nearness of such men as Schiller and Fichte, aware that it was of crucial importance that he finish

89   173.116ff.
90   92.81ff.
91   92.94f.
92   92.95ff.
93   92.104ff.

Hyperion before his money ran out — Hölderlin proceeded to punish himself physically through adopting a spartan regimen which, as fragile as he was, he could not endure. On 19 January he wrote Neuffer: "I work alone all day. Go in the evening to Fichte's lectures and, as often as I can, to Schiller. He is taking a right faithful interest in me. How things will be in the future, I do not know myself. Here I am in need of nothing other than you, my Brother."[94]

But those assurances were somewhat exaggerated — probably because he wanted Neuffer to reassure Mother so that she would agree to his plan.[95] In reality he was living on one meal a day, spending his daylight hours working on *Hyperion* in a room that stayed unheated all winter because he refused to spend money for wood.[96] Worst of all, the dream of finishing *Hyperion* quickly eluded him. When he wrote his mother in January, he was sure that he would be able to finish the novel by Easter. When he wrote next on 22 February, he tried to put up a brave front, but he was obviously not nearly so optimistic as he had been a month earlier. "The work that has occupied me until now is going well. It would, of course, be too much good fortune if he [Schiller] were to accept this for *Die Horen*. I must doubt that, because it is becoming two volumes in size, and he will not want to take a fragment and can probably not take the whole thing, because a fragment of it was printed in his previous journal, in which he was less particular, and, therefore, a part of the work would have to be served up for a second time. Anyway, I will, as he desires, present him with the work, of which the first volume will be ready by Easter."[97]

This was not really quite honest. *Hyperion* was not just then "becoming" two volumes long; Hölderlin had been planning on two volumes since 1793 and had written Neuffer in October 1794 — four months before this letter to Mother — that he had almost finished the first part. Once again he was revealing the bleaker side of things to Mother only by degrees, perhaps because he only admitted his troubles to himself when he could not deny their existence any longer.

He now realized that Schiller would probably not publish *Hyperion* in his *Horen*. Once more, however, Schiller came to rescue, contacted his own publisher, Cotta, and convinced him to publish *Hyperion*.[98] In April Hölderlin

---

[94] 93.74ff.

[95] In a postscript he wrote: "One more request! Couldn't you visit my mother and soothe her if you should find that she is not completely satisfied with the change in my situation[?]" (93.113ff.).

[96] On 22 February he wrote her: "I wrapped myself up during the cold spell in order not to use so much wood. It is fairly expensive here, and mostly fur" (95.71ff.).

[97] 95.34ff.

[98] Schiller assured Cotta: ". . . I hope to exert my influence on it [the first volume]. I am counting on Hölderlin for *Die Horen* in the future, for he is industrious, and by no means lacking in the talent [needed] to become somebody in the literary world someday" (III, p. 304).

and Cotta agreed on the terms of the venture. Hölderlin would receive 100 *Gulden* upon completion of the novel – not when he finished the first volume, as Hölderlin wrote Neuffer on 28 April.[99]

By the end of April then a set of circumstances had arisen with which Hölderlin simply could not cope. He had received eleven *Gulden* as an advance from Cotta; already he had been forced to borrow from his mother again;[100] through Schiller's aid he now had a publisher for a novel that he could not finish. *Hyperion* was growing in size and had become far more complex than he had originally envisaged. He was now having trouble deciding even what narrative technique he should employ. Should he write it in verse? Should he try to make it into a straight prose narrative? Should he return to the epistolary form? Moreover, Schiller was saving space in *Die Horen* for Hölderlin's translations of Greek poems.

Publication in Schiller's journal was, as Hölderlin seems to have understood, his best prospect for immediate financial remuneration. He needed cash – not only because he was undermining his health by limiting himself to one meal a day and by refusing to buy wood to heat his room, but also because he simply could not bear the shame of borrowing from Mother again. Common sense dictated that the first order of business was finishing the translations for *Die Horen*. But from his letters it becomes clear that *Hyperion* absorbed all his creative energies and that what little time he had left over was spent with Schiller or in the lecture hall.

In order to understand why Hölderlin's stay in Jena – an opportunity for which he had yearned since before he left Tübingen – came to nothing, one must understand the many pressures to which he was subjected. He had emerged from his trials with Fritz von Kalb in a pitiable state. We can say without running the danger of exaggerating that he was on the verge of mental collapse. He had failed in his first job, and his mother knew it. That would have been bad enough. But, even worse, the opportunity for which he had so longed suddenly presented itself to him at just that time in his life when he was in no condition to take advantage of it. Here it is important that we distinguish carefully between the historical significance of his stay in Jena and its biographical implications. However much hearing Fichte's lectures may have contributed to Hölderlin's intellectual development, the aid he received from Frau von Kalb and Schiller which made it possible for him to stay in Jena inevitably contributed to a psychological shock that was far more destructive than had been his experience with Fritz von Kalb. His stay in Jena raised his hopes; those hopes were crushed.

The lot of a young writer who has not yet succeeded in making a name for himself is at best very trying. The young aspiring author needs, most of all,

---

[99] 99.45f.
[100] Frau Gok's accounts show 100 florines sent to Jena on 30 March (VII, 1, p. 290).

self-confidence. In addition he needs a good deal of shrewdness. Whatever his ideals, whatever message he fells called upon to impart to mankind, he also must eat. He must not be above hacking out something in order to fill his stomach. Great works are seldom written on an empty stomach or with fingers stiff from the cold.

These two qualities — self-confidence and simple business sense — Hölderlin lacked inherently. Under the best of circumstances he would have had a difficult time of it. The circumstances under which he tried to work in Jena made it impossible for him to survive. He had, in one sense, the two things that an aspiring author must have for success. He had, first of all, the idea for a great novel. There was no reason why *Hyperion* should have been any less a success than *Wilhelm Meister* or *Ardinghello;* and so the work that he had conceived as a student in Tübingen might have made his name, or at least won him a patron. It might have made him successful *in the long run.* But it could not put bread in his mouth in the here and now. And yet he also had the second thing that every young author needs to survive. He had connections and thus the opportunity to support himself through hack-work. Hölderlin knew Greek well enough, far better than most educated men of his day and certainly better than Schiller — the only person he had to please. With his knowledge of Greek and his poetic talent, the translations should have been almost mechanical, almost like a pianist's finger-exercises. But it would appear that he never seriously tried to finish the translations. And then, when he saw that he was about to disappoint Schiller, he fled without so much as a word.[101]

Given Hölderlin's nervous condition, a great number of things contributed to his failure in Jena. First, following the traumatic experience with Fritz von Kalb, Hölderlin came back to Jena very nearly in a state of collapse. He was in no condition to face the hardships that awaited him there. The frightful conditions in which he lived weakened him even further. But perhaps most important of all, he pinned his hopes on *Hyperion,* which made it necessary to solve a philosophical problem that was insoluble — at least as long as he set about the task armed with the weapons supplied by Fichte and Schiller.

The end of the story of the young Hölderlin is the tragic tale of *Hyperion* in Jena. The character of Hyperion, which was nothing less than Hölderlin's understanding of his own personality, was diametrically opposed to both the spirit and the basic tenets of Critical Philosophy, let alone Fichtean Idealism. Between Hyperion's dreams and Fichte's philosophy there could only be outright antagonism. But as late as April Hölderlin was writing his brother in simulated Fichtean prose,[102] and although Hölderlin's letters to Schelling and Hegel are lost, we know from their correspondence with each other that

---

[101] Hans Heinrich Borcherdt, *Schiller und die Romantiker* (Stuttgart, 1948), pp. 111ff.
[102] See No. 97.

Hölderlin was full of praise for the man who would have rejected the dream-world of Hyperion out of hand.[103]

Gradually the signs of despair began to appear. The letter to Karl in which Hölderlin mouthed Fichte's lectures contains another example of that shame-faced communication to Mother, whom he wanted to thank for the money she had lent him. "I will never forget that I was supported in my present situation with such goodness."[104] One week later, on 20 April, he wrote Rike: "I believe that my stay here is in no sense useless. It would be my fault if it were useless for me."[105] And then he continued: "A thousand greetings to our dear Mother! Could I but become worthy of all the goodness that I constantly receive from her."[106]

Now began the old habit of withdrawing from those around him — even though he was right where he had wanted to be since he had left school in the fall of 1793! On 28 April he wrote Neuffer: "I go out among men almost not at all."[107] And then he continued reflectively: "It is strange — I shall never live except in dreams. Was that not always my situation? And since I have eyes I have not loved any more."[108] He knew that *Hyperion* could not save him and even regarded it as a failure. "Don't be scandalized by the little work [*Werkchen*]," he wrote. "I am going on and writing it off because it's been started, and it's better than nothing at all, and I console myself with the hope that I will soon be able to salvage my credit with something else."[109]

In early May Hölderlin received word that Rosine Stäudlin had died of tuberculosis. "I am a poor consoler," he wrote the bereaved Neuffer. "I stumble around in the world like a blind man and am supposed to show my suffering brother a light that might bring him joy in his sorrow."[110] Near the end of the letter, he said: "Were you here, then I might well stay. But, as things are, I will hardly hold out. Now we both go impoverished through the world; we both have nothing but what we are to each other, except for that which is a beautiful world in and above us, my Neuffer! And should we kind of half live for each other? I am coming soon. . . ."[111]

He came soon. Back to Württemberg. Without a word to Schiller, he slipped away in the late spring. It had been almost eighteen months since he had left home. He had left with high hopes. The hopes had been dashed. He had left determined to live the life of the "philosophic spirit." He had learned that the

---

103   97.104f.
104   98.9ff.
105   98.71ff.
106   99.29.
107   99.54ff.
108   99.47ff.
109   100.16ff.
110   100.62ff.
111   VI, 1, p. 757.

philosophy of his time was contrary to his very nature. He had left as a young man filled with idealistic dreams. And if he did not return an old man at twenty-five, he was no longer young either. For he had learned that there was more to escape from in life than Mother and Church. And he had learned that for him life would be a hard, an excruciatingly hard struggle, wherever he might be.

He was now ready to meet his Diotima. It was still several months before he laid eyes on Susette Gontard, but his life, as life is normally understood, was as good as over. For he would love Susette much as he had loved Luise Nast. It would be her task to reconcile him with the world so that he might "become a poet" at her feet. He would become a great poet. Nothing could stop that. But he would never become a man.

Magenau saw that clearly when he saw Hölderlin in 1795, and it must have preyed on his mind. For, a year later, in November 1796, he wrote Neuffer about the encounter.

He called their former *Bundesbruder* "a living dead man."[111]

SELECTED BIBLIOGRAPHY

The following selected bibliography is not intended as a complete bibliography of all the materials consulted during the course of my research. It is rather a mere listing of the works which I either cite directly in the notes or which I found to be particularly useful in the writing of this book.

Beck, Adolf (ed.). "Aus der Umwelt des jungen Hölderlin, Stamm- und Tagebucheinträge," *Hölderlin-Jahrbuch* (1947), pp. 18–46.

— "Die Gesellschaftlerin Charlottens von Kalb. Eine Episode im Leben Hölderlins. Versuch der Sammlung und Erklärung archivalischer Dokumente," *Hölderlin-Jahrbuch* X (1957), pp. 46–66.

Beissner, Friedrich. *Hölderlin: Reden und Aufsätze.* Weimar, 1961.

Betzendörfer, Walter. *Hölderlins Studienjahre im Tübinger Stift.* Heilbronn, 1922.

Böckmann, Paul. *Hölderlin und seine Götter,* Munich, 1935.

Böhm, Wilhelm. *Hölderlin.* 2 vols.: Halle, 1928–1930.

— "Hölderlin als Verfasser des 'Ältesten Systemprogramms des deutschen Idealismus,'" *Deutsche Vierteljahrsschrift für Literaturwissenschaft und Geistesgeschichte.* IV (1926), pp. 339–426.

— "Zum 'Systemprogramm.' Eine Erwiderung," *Deutsche Vierteljahrsschrift für Literaturwissenschaft und Geistesgeschichte.* V (1927), pp. 734–743.

Borcherdt, Hans Heinrich (ed.). *Schiller und die Romantik: Briefe und Dokumente.* Stuttgart, 1948.

Hartmann, R. Julius. *Das Tübinger Stift: Ein Beitrag zur Geschichte des Deutschen Geisteslebens.* Stuttgart, 1918.

Haym, Rudolf. *Die Romantische Schule: Ein Beitrag zur Geschichte des deutschen Geistes.* Edited by Oskar Walzel. 5th ed.; Berlin, 1928.

Hellingrath, Norbert von. *Hölderlin-Vermächtnis.* Edited with an introduction by Ludwig Pigenot. 2d ed. revised; Minchen, 1944.

Hook, Erich. "Wilhelm Heinses Urteil über Hölderlins 'Hyperion,'" *Hölderlin-Jahrbuch* (1950), pp. 109–119.

Hoffmeister, Johonnes (ed.). *Briefe an und von Hegel.* Vol. I; *1785–1812.* Hamburg, 1952.

— "Zum Geistesbegriff des deutschen Idealismus bei Hölderlin und Hegel," *Deutsche Vierteljahrsschrift für Literaturwissenschaft und Geistesgeschichte.* X (1932), pp. 1–44.

Huch, Ricarda. *Die Romantik.* Vol. II: *Ausbreitung und Verfall.* 12th ed.: Leipzig, 1924.

Korff, Hermann August. *Geist der Goethezeit: Versuch einer ideelen Entwicklung der klassisch-romantischen Literaturgeschichte.* Vol. III: *Frühromantik.* 3rd ed.: Leipzig, 1959.

Kretschmer, Ernst. *The Psychology of Men of Genius.* Translated with an introduction by R.B. Cattel. New York, 1931.

— *Physique and Character: An Investigation of the Nature of Constitution and the Theory of Tempernment.* New York, 1936.

Lange, Heinrich. *Hölderlin. Eine Pathographie.* Munich, 1942.

— *Genie, Irrsinn und Ruhm.* Munich, 1942.

Leube, Martin. *Das Tübinger Stift 1770–1950: Geschichte des Tübinger Stifts.* Stuttgart, 1954.

Litzmann, Carl C.T. *Friedrich Hölderlins Leben. In Briefen von und an Hölderlin.* Berlin, 1890.

Michel, Wilhelm. *Das Leben Friedrich Hölderlins.* Bremen, 1949.

Mommsen, Momme. "Hölderlins Lösung von Schiller. Zu Hölderlins Gedichten 'An Herkules' und 'Die Eichbäume' und zu den Übersetzungen zu Ovid, Vergil und Euripedes," *Hölderlin-Jahrbuch,* IX (1965), 203–244.

Pellegrini, Alessandro. *Friedrich Hölderlin: Sein Bild in der Forschung.* Berlin, 1965.

Petersen, Julius (ed.). "Die Briefe Charlottens von Kalb an Schiller," *Jahrbuch der Goethegesellschaft,* XII (1926), 104–168.

Ryan, Lawrence. *Hölderlins Hyperion. Exzentrische Bahn und Dichterberuf.* Stuttgart, 1965.

Strauss, Ludwig. *Das Problem der Gemeinschaft in Hölderlins 'Hyperion.'* Leipzig, 1933.

— "Hölderlins Anteil an Schellings frühem Systemprogramm," *Deutsche Vierteljahrsschrift für Literaturwissenschaft und Geistesgeschichte,* V (1927), 679—734.

— "Zu Böhms Erwiderung," *Deutsche Vierteljahrsschrift für Literaturwissenschaft und Geistesgeschichte,* V (1927), 743—747.

Zeller, Eduard. *Die Philosophie der Griechen in ihrer geschichtlichen Entwicklung.* 6 vols.: Hildesheim, 1963 (reprint).